Social Capital in the Age of Online Networking:

Genesis, Manifestations, and Implications

Najmul Hoda
Umm Al-Qura University, Saudi Arabia

Arshi Naim
King Khalid University, Saudi Arabia

A volume in the Advances in Social Networking
and Online Communities (ASNOC) Book Series

Published in the United States of America by
IGI Global
Information Science Reference (an imprint of IGI Global)
701 E. Chocolate Avenue
Hershey PA, USA 17033
Tel: 717-533-8845
Fax: 717-533-8661
E-mail: cust@igi-global.com
Web site: http://www.igi-global.com

Library of Congress Cataloging-in-Publication Data

Names: Hoda, Najmul, 1978- editor. | Naim, Arshi, 1976- editor.
Title: Social capital in the age of online networking : genesis,
   manifestations, and implications / edited by Najmul Hoda, Arshi Naim.
Description: Hershey, PA : Information Science Reference, [2024] | Includes
   bibliographical references and index. | Summary: "Online networking is a
   global trend that affects individuals in developed as well as developing
   countries. Access to smartphones has made use of social networking sites
   and applications extremely easy and widespread. As a result, the
   benefits of online networking, called online social capital, is
   applicable at a global level. The benefits of online social capital have
   been reported in business, social development, education, healthcare,
   psychology, as well as in achieving sustainable development goals. An
   edited book has the advantage of pooling in contributions from different
   parts of the world and different specializations. The aim of this edited
   book is mainly to offer a current and prospective theoretical and
   applied understanding of this resource"-- Provided by publisher.
Identifiers: LCCN 2023019783 (print) | LCCN 2023019784 (ebook) | ISBN
   9781668489536 (hardcover) | ISBN 9781668489574 (paperback) | ISBN
   9781668489543 (ebook)
Subjects: LCSH: Social networks. | Social capital (Sociology)
Classification: LCC HM742 .S6268 2024 (print) | LCC HM742 (ebook) | DDC
   302.23/1--dc23/eng/20230601
LC record available at https://lccn.loc.gov/2023019783
LC ebook record available at https://lccn.loc.gov/2023019784

This book is published in the IGI Global book series Advances in Social Networking and Online Communities (ASNOC)
(ISSN: 2328-1405; eISSN: 2328-1413)

British Cataloguing in Publication Data
A Cataloguing in Publication record for this book is available from the British Library.

For electronic access to this publication, please contact: eresources@igi-global.com.

Advances in Social Networking and Online Communities (ASNOC) Book Series

Hakikur Rahman

Ansted University Sustainability Research Institute, Malaysia

ISSN:2328-1405
EISSN:2328-1413

Mission

The advancements of internet technologies and the creation of various social networks provide a new channel of knowledge development processes that's dependent on social networking and online communities. This emerging concept of social innovation is comprised of ideas and strategies designed to improve society.

The **Advances in Social Networking and Online Communities** book series serves as a forum for scholars and practitioners to present comprehensive research on the social, cultural, organizational, and human issues related to the use of virtual communities and social networking. This series will provide an analytical approach to the holistic and newly emerging concepts of online knowledge communities and social networks.

Coverage

- Framework of a Pragmatic Conception of Knowledge
- Local E-Government Interoperability and Security
- Importance and Role of Knowledge Communities in R&D and Innovative Knowledge Creation
- E-capacity Building Programmes to Ensure Digital Cohesion and Improved E-Government Performance at Local Level
- Technology Orientation and Capitalization of Knowledge
- Social Models to Design and Support Knowledge Intensive Collaborative Processes
- Communication and Management of Knowledge in R&D Networks
- Communication and Agent Technology
- Knowledge Communication and Impact of Network Structures
- Advanced Researches in Knowledge Communities

IGI Global is currently accepting manuscripts for publication within this series. To submit a proposal for a volume in this series, please contact our Acquisition Editors at Acquisitions@igi-global.com or visit: http://www.igi-global.com/publish/.

Titles in this Series

For a list of additional titles in this series, please visit: www.igi-global.com/book-series

Global Perspectives on Social Media Usage Within Governments
Chandan Chavadi (Presidency Business School, Presidency College, India) and Dhanabalan Thangam (Presidency Business School, Presidency College, ndia)
Information Science Reference • © 2023 • 310pp • H/C (ISBN: 9781668474501) • US $215.00

Advanced Applications of NLP and Deep Learning in Social Media Data
Ahmed A. Abd El-Latif (Menoufia University, Egypt & Prince Sultan University, Saudi Arabia) Mudasir Ahmad Wani (Prince Sultan University, Saudi Arabia) and Mohammed A. El-Affendi (Prince Sultan University, Saudi Aabia)
Engineering Science Reference • © 2023 • 303pp • H/C (ISBN: 9781668469095) • US $270.00

Community Engagement in the Online Space
Michelle Dennis (Adler University, USA) and James Halbert (Adler University, USA)
Information Science Reference • © 2023 • 364pp • H/C (ISBN: 9781668451908) • US $215.00

Handbook of Research on Bullying in Media and Beyond
Gülşah Sarı (Aksaray University, Turkey)
Information Science Reference • © 2023 • 603pp • H/C (ISBN: 9781668454268) • US $295.00

Handbook of Research on Technologies and Systems for E-Collaboration During Global Crises
Jingyuan Zhao (University of Toronto, Canada) and V. Vinoth Kumar (Jain University, India)
Information Science Reference • © 2022 • 461pp • H/C (ISBN: 9781799896401) • US $295.00

Information Manipulation and Its Impact Across All Industries
Maryam Ebrahimi (Independent Researcher, Germany)
Information Science Reference • © 2022 • 234pp • H/C (ISBN: 9781799882350) • US $215.00

E-Collaboration Technologies and Strategies for Competitive Advantage Amid Challenging Times
Jingyuan Zhao (University of Toronto, Canada) and Joseph Richards (California State University, Sacramento, USA)
Information Science Reference • © 2021 • 346pp • H/C (ISBN: 9781799877646) • US $215.00

Analyzing Global Social Media Consumption
Patrick Kanyi Wamuyu (United States International University – Africa, Kenya)
Information Science Reference • © 2021 • 358pp • H/C (ISBN: 9781799847182) • US $215.00

701 East Chocolate Avenue, Hershey, PA 17033, USA
Tel: 717-533-8845 x100 • Fax: 717-533-8661
E-Mail: cust@igi-global.com • www.igi-global.com

Table of Contents

Detailed Table of Contents

Chapter 1
Arshi Naim, King Khalid University, Saudi Arabia
Asfia Syed, King Khalid University, Saudi Arabia
Syeda Meraj Bilfaqih, King Khalid University, Saudi Arabia
Anandhavalli Muniasamy, King Khalid University, Saudi Arabia

The success of any organization is dependent, to an extent, on a marketing manager's aptitude to advance social capital within the company's global network. In this chapter, the authors have developed a prototype to present the application of individual social capital at the bottom level to contribute in building the organizational social capital at the global level. They developed a hypothesis that the social capital of customers, business partners, and governing agencies are the critical success factors to explain the performance of the organization and contribute in improving the customer values. General marketing policies are not applicable at the organizational level; therefore, based on the factors of organization, marketing strategies should be deployed. This chapter analyses the factors at individual as well as organizational levels for employing and marketing the social capital at a global level.

Chapter 2
Najmul Hoda, Umm Al-Qura University, Saudi Arabia
Mohammad Zubair Ahmad, Utkarsh College of Management Education, India

Crowdfunding is a phenomenon that exists because of interconnectivity. These platforms allow the connection of lenders, donors, and investors with recipients who may be entrepreneurs or beneficiaries. In the entire crowdfunding process, there is a direct involvement of network behaviors namely trust, norms, networking, and so on. In other words, social capital plays a role in crowdfunding. This chapter aims to review the existing literature on crowdfunding platforms and identify the role of online networking in the process and outcome. The chapter would benefit both researchers and various stakeholders who are engaged in crowdfunding or are exploring this platform for financial decisions.

Anbalagan Bhuvaneswari, Vellore Institute of Technology, Chennai, India
K. K. Jijina, Vellore Institute of Technology, Chennai, India

Link prediction is a method used to predict the existence of a non-existing links between two entities within a network. However, the growing size of social networks has made conducting link prediction studies more challenging. This chapter proposes a friend recommendation system that employs feature engineering techniques on a given dataset. The feature engineering process involves extracting relevant features such as shortest path, Katz centrality, Jaccard distances, PageRank, and preferential attachments, etc. Random Forest and XGBoost algorithms are then utilized to recommend non-existent connections by suggesting new edges in the graph. By implementing these approaches, the authors aim to improve the accuracy and effectiveness of friend recommendations in the social network graph. By considering both types of edges in the recommendation process, they enhance the performance of the friend recommendation system. This approach allows leveraging the valuable insights within the network graph, resulting in more accurate and reliable recommendations.

Elif Baykal, İstanbul Medipol University, Turkey

The related field research was conducted with the participation of 360 people. The respondents are working in public and private institutions in the service sector. During the analysis and analysis of the research data, SPSS (statistical package for the social sciences) program was used, and the data were analysed. With the factor analysis made, the questions were examined in detail within the scope of six sub-dimensions of spiritual leadership behavior patterns and the data were analysed. According to the results of the research, it has been observed that there may be changes in the attitudes and opinions of some of the dimensions of spiritual leadership behaviors based on the age, gender, marital status, educational status, sector, position, working time in the institution where they are currently working, and total years worked. Moreover, this study is illuminating regarding the positive effects of spiritual leadership on human capitals of white collar employees in Turkey.

Youmei Liu, University of Houston, USA

This chapter presents a 10-year (2013-2022) longitudinal research study among college students aged from 18 to 39 who were social media users. The chapter covers three topics: 1) student use of social media platforms to establish social networking, 2) perception and attitude towards level of trust on social media platforms, and 3) correlation between social media trust and media consumption. The results indicate that there are more students using social media to keep a close relationship with friends and family members to maintain existing communities than those to find new friends to expand social circle. Students have increased concern with trust on social media and the level of trust is declining throughout the years. Despite the trust issue, there is no correlation between level of trust and student use of social media to share and use online information to find solutions.

Chapter 6

R. Gayathri, School of Management, SASTRA University (Deemed), Thanjavur, India

A constructive outcome of interpersonal connection is referred to as social capital. In recent years, the development paradigm has transformed from a virtually sole focus on physical capital to a people-focused approach targeting sustainable growth that accentuates the social elements of development, particularly human and social capital. The perspective on social capital emphasizes the importance of individual and community ties and the broader social and political context in which social structures and norms develop. It underscores the significance of institutional relationships, government support, and collaboration among various sectors for encouraging economic and social development. This chapter infers on a few current hot topics, focusing on how online social capital influences development and exploring if there are economic benefits to building social capital.

Chapter 7

Ibtissem Missaoui, Higher Institute of Management of Sousse, Tunisia

The review explores the potential of online social capital in contributing to sustainable development. Online social capital refers to the networks and relationships formed through online communication and interaction, which can be used to achieve social or environmental objectives. The goal of sustainable development is to balance the economic growth, social well-being, and environmental protection. By examining case studies and research on the topic, this review argues that online social capital has the potential to contribute to sustainable development by facilitating the exchange of knowledge, resources, and support among individuals and groups. However, it also highlights the potential risks and challenges associated with online communication, which may undermine the positive impact of online social capital on sustainable development. The chapter concludes by outlining the prospects and limitations of online social capital in contributing to sustainable development and by making recommendations for future research and policy making.

Chapter 8

Deepa Sharma, Maharishi Markandeshwar Institute of Management, India
Komal Bhardwaj, Maharishi Markandeshwar Institute of Management, India

Online education has become an integral part of the modern educational landscape and brought about significant transformations in the field of learning. Though delivery of information and instructions through digital architecture, which enable students to access programs and directories remotely, without the limitations of time and distance, is the first step in organizing online education, it is also true that everyone has their own views and thoughts on the approach of converting the traditional education system into electronic education, due to which the online education system has faced difficulties in stepping into this field. Therefore, a strong understanding of the facts, circumstances, and challenges of this technology is essential for implementing an e-learning system. In this chapter, the authors aim to understand the various challenges faced by teachers during online classes and various strategies adopted by the teachers to overcome the challenges of online classes.

The author of this chapter explored the social capital knowledge regarding education in the following four theoretical contexts presented by Mikiewicz, the tradition of James Coleman's social exchange theory, the tradition of Robert D. Putnam's theory of civil society, the tradition of Pierre Bourdieu's theory of cultural structuralism, and the tradition of network theory. This chapter also presented the effective use of the research on social capital and the impact of technological innovations and online social capital on education. The author pooled literature from different parts of specializations, especially in education. It documented that co-creation and social learning are essential components of knowledge productivity; therefore, by working together and leveraging the power of social networks, individuals can achieve more than they ever could on their own, leading to profound improvements in organizational and societal outcomes.

Social networks are vital for businesses today, enabling them to reach a wider audience, engage with customers, and conduct market research. Influence maximization and online social capital are key to entrepreneurs' success, helping them strategically build and leverage networks to achieve specific goals. They can identify and engage with influencers, create high-quality content, and use tools to expand their reach. Social capital provides access to resources, builds reputation and credibility, and offers support and motivation. Successful businesses like Nike, Coca-Cola, Airbnb, and Tesla demonstrate the power of social networks in building customer relationships and promoting products. Overall, influence maximization is crucial for entrepreneurs to increase visibility, credibility, and influence in the digital age, helping them achieve their goals effectively.

In today's highly competitive global business environment, the efficient management of a "scattered" or "distance" workforce is critical for the success of any organisation. The purpose of this chapter is to look into how the debate on digital transformation and leadership has changed in recent years. The approach is mixed. The first section is a review of the literature on digital advancements in various sectors of the economy as well as new trends in virtual workforce management. The second section summarises the conclusions of empirical study based on interviews with managerial representatives from IT, operations, and sales. The study was conducted in Tier 1 cities in India. The results show that managers have adjusted into this new era of employee management from distant places and have undergone necessary training for skill development. However, the rising use of technologies has brought a new set of challenges that need to be dealt with.

Chapter 12

    Anbalagan Bhuvaneswari, Vellore Institute of Technology, Chennai, India
    Leela Rachel J. Julanta, Vellore Institute of Technology, Chennai, India

The pervasive popularity of social networking facilitates the propagation of trending information and the online exchange of diverse opinions among socially connected individuals. In order to identify events from the density ratio of real-time tweets, the authors suggest a new underlying quantification model, and morphological time-series analysis is performed using information entropy to ascertain the rate of news coverage of crisis situations. To further get insightful patterns in events, the event-link ratio is evaluated. In this study, the authors utilize data collected from Twitter to evaluate how far news of these events has spread. The study concludes by demonstrating the effectiveness of the proposed framework in a case study on the disasters events where it successfully captured critical information and provided insights into the dissemination of information during the disaster. The suggested approach detects events faster and with 94% accuracy than state-of-the-art methods. Comparing all location references, unambiguous location extraction has 96% accuracy.

Chapter 13

    Marhaini Mohd Noor, Universiti Malaysia Terengganu, Malaysia
    Nor Aziah Alias, Universiti Technology MARA, Malaysia
    Azizan Zainuddin, Universiti Technology MARA, Malaysia
    Nor Hafizah Mohamed Harith, Universiti Technology MARA, Malaysia

This research investigates the creation of social capital among members of the online community. In this case, social networking refers to interpersonal connections among members of a rural maritime community. The major goal of this study is to determine how much the maritime community uses social online networking and how social capital grows within the community via the internet. The study applied a triangulation method to analyze data from participants with several points of view and to engage people appropriately for a better understanding of the phenomenon. Main findings extracted from the interviews have been categorized into three themes: (1) patterns of online social networking and social media use, (2) social networking and trust, and (3) social capital development. Hence, it is apparent that online networking can be used to reduce the social capital divide between urban and rural communities in Malaysia.

Chapter 14

    Mohamed Syed Ibrahim, Government Arts College (Autonomous), Periyar University, India

With the advent of information technology, there has been an opening up of new markets, new products, and improved productivity and efficiency in the banking sector. Commercial banks in India are now becoming vibrant markets, and technology allows banks and financial institutions to create what looks like a branch in a business building's lobby without having to hire for manual operations. Today, the banks are running in the concept of 24X7 working, made possible by the use of technological innovations. Almost all financial institutions and banks in India are using the advanced technological innovations like ATM, mobile banking, digital money using debit and credit cards, etc. This study is attempting to evaluate the vibrant usage of information/technological innovations. The study is diagnostic and exploratory in nature and makes use of secondary data. The study finds and concludes that the commercial banks in India have significantly improved their working performance with the help of information technology.

Chapter 15

Devendra Singh, Amity University, Greater Noida, India
Sumitra Singh, Amity University, Greater Noida, India

The dark web as a technology has shown great potential and has grown tremendously. We have everything on our tips. This type of environment is also very fruitful and dangerous at the same time. Where everything is available on sale for the highest bidder, dark web plays as a role of intermediary in the sale. This chapter aims to highlights the use of TOR, and other dark webs, and their related activities which leads to the frauds happening in India and to study the connection between dark web, black markets, and banking fraud in India (if any). This chapter attempts to understand the working of the dark web and the illegal transactions.

Chapter 16

Arun Kumar Singh, Papua New Guinea University of Technology, Papua New Guinea

A revolution in wireless communication refers to a significant advancement or breakthrough in the field of wireless communication technology. This can include the introduction of new technologies, the development of faster and more efficient communication methods, and the widespread adoption of wireless communication in various industries and sectors. One example of a revolution in wireless communication is the development of 5G technology. 5G, or fifth-generation wireless technology, promises faster data speeds, lower latency, and improved network capacity compared to previous generations of wireless technology. This is expected to enable a wide range of new applications and use cases, such as the internet of things (IoT), autonomous vehicles, and virtual reality. Overall, the revolution in wireless communication has led to significant advancements in the way we live, work, and communicate, and is expected to continue to shape the future of communication. In this chapter, the authors discuss the services and the quality with basic comparison between the different telecom companies.

Chapter 17

R. Selvakumar, SRM University, India
Vimal Babu, SRM University, India

Performing crisis management (CM) through social media platforms (SMP) is the modern way of handling crisis events. The chapter aims to identify core research on CM along SMP. By employing bibliometric network analysis, the authors aim to review published works in Scopus-indexed journals from the year 2019 to 2023. Scopus database and VOS (visualizing scientific landscapes) viewer have been combinedly used to identify the most influential journals, top-ranking countries, and institutions, most cited articles, most occurred keywords, and the pattern of authorship in CM along SMP publications. The present study undertakes a pioneering bibliometric analysis aimed at exploring scholarly publications on the field of CM facilitated through SMP. To the authors' knowledge, this work is the first study to use a bibliometric approach to research this area, thereby contributing to the nascent literature on the subject. The unique insights garnered from this analysis are expected to provide valuable guidance to researchers and scholars interested in this emerging field.

Preface

Social capital theory has long been recognized as a vital framework for understanding the accumulation of resources through networking in various fields. This theory posits that individuals gain access to tangible and intangible resources by actively participating in groups or networks. These networks can consist of individuals with similar or diverse interests, thereby encompassing various dimensions. Extensive research has demonstrated that interactions within these networks result in the formation of strong or weak ties, ultimately leading to the development of social capital.

In recent years, the advent of communication technology and the rise of social media platforms have revolutionized the way networking occurs. Platforms such as Facebook and LinkedIn have transformed traditional networking into a new and unprecedented form. This transformative shift has prompted researchers to investigate whether social capital can also be accrued through online networking. A substantial body of literature now confirms that social capital can indeed be formed through social networking sites, giving rise to the concept of "online social capital."

The present edited book, *Social Capital in the Age of Online Networking: Genesis, Manifestations, and Implications*, aims to gather contributions from researchers and practitioners to enhance our understanding of the current state and future prospects of this phenomenon. By collating diverse perspectives and insights, we endeavor to shed light on both the theoretical underpinnings and practical applications of online social capital.

Chapter 1 explores the application of individual social capital at the bottom level to contribute to building organizational social capital at the global level. It analyzes the factors at both individual and organizational levels for employing and marketing social capital on a global scale. The chapter focuses on the critical success factors of customer, business partner, and governing agency social capital in explaining organizational performance and enhancing customer value.

Examining the intersection of crowdfunding and online networking, chapter 2 reviews existing literature to identify the role of online networking in the crowdfunding process and outcomes. It explores how social capital, including trust, norms, and networking, influences crowdfunding activities. The chapter provides valuable insights for researchers and stakeholders involved in crowdfunding or considering this platform for financial decisions.

Chapter 3 proposes a friend recommendation system using link prediction techniques in social networks. It introduces a feature engineering process that extracts relevant features from the network graph and employs Random Forest and XGBoost algorithms to recommend non-existent connections. The aim is to improve the accuracy and effectiveness of friend recommendations, leveraging insights within the social network graph.

Based on empirical research involving 360 participants from public and private institutions in the service sector, chapter 4 examines the dimensions of spiritual leadership behaviors and their effects on human capital. The analysis considers various demographic factors and highlights potential changes in attitudes and opinions based on these dimensions. The study sheds light on the positive effects of spiritual leadership on white-collar employees' human capital in Turkey.

Chapter 5 presents a 10-year longitudinal research study among college students who are social media users. It explores their use of social media platforms for social networking, their perception and attitude towards trust on social media, and the correlation between social media trust and media consumption. The findings reveal trends in social media usage and trust levels, providing insights into the role of social media in maintaining existing communities and expanding social circles.

Focusing on how online social capital influences development, Chapter 6 explores its economic benefits. It highlights the shift towards people-focused approaches in development, emphasizing human and social capital. The chapter emphasizes the significance of institutional relationships, government support, and collaboration among different sectors in fostering economic and social development. It discusses current hot topics in online social capital and its potential contributions to economic growth.

Chapter 7 delves into the potential of online social capital in contributing to sustainable development. It examines case studies and research on the topic, highlighting how online social capital facilitates knowledge exchange, resource sharing, and support among individuals and groups. The chapter also addresses the challenges and risks associated with online communication and its impact on the positive outcomes of online social capital. It provides recommendations for future research and policy-making.

Focusing on the challenges faced by teachers during online classes, Chapter 8 explores various strategies adopted to overcome these challenges. It aims to understand the difficulties and provide insights into the strategies employed by teachers to deliver effective online education. The chapter is essential for implementing e-learning systems and provides a strong understanding of the facts, circumstances, and challenges of online education.

Chapter 9 investigates the role of social capital in education from theoretical perspectives such as social exchange theory, civil society theory, cultural structuralism theory, and network theory. It highlights the effective use of research on social capital and the impact of technological innovations and online social capital on education. Drawing from diverse literature in education, the chapter explores co-creation, social learning, and the potential improvements in organizational and societal outcomes through leveraging social networks.

Chapter 10 emphasizes the importance of influence maximization and online social capital for entrepreneurial success. It explores how entrepreneurs strategically build and leverage networks to achieve specific goals, including identifying and engaging with influencers, creating high-quality content, and expanding their reach. The chapter showcases successful businesses that have effectively utilized social networks for building customer relationships and promoting products.

Chapter 11 investigates the changing landscape of digital transformation and leadership in managing virtual workforces. It provides a literature review of digital advancements in various sectors and new trends in virtual workforce management. Empirical study findings from interviews with managerial representatives in IT, Operations, and Sales are summarized, highlighting their adjustment to new eras of employee management and the challenges posed by rising technology use.

Chapter 12 proposes a framework for event detection and dissemination analysis on Twitter, utilizing morphological time-series analysis and the density ratio of real-time tweets. It demonstrates the effectiveness of the framework in a case study on disaster events, capturing critical information and providing insights into the dissemination of information during crises. The proposed approach outperforms existing methods, detecting events faster and with higher accuracy.

Examining the use of online social networking in a rural maritime community, chapter 13 investigates how social capital develops within the community via the internet. Using a triangulation method and analyzing data from participants, it explores patterns of online social networking, trust dynamics, and the development of social capital. The findings shed light on the potential of online networking to bridge social capital divides between urban and rural communities.

Chapter 14 evaluates the vibrant usage of information technology/technological innovations in commercial banks in India. The study adopts a diagnostic and exploratory approach, utilizing secondary data to assess the working performance improvements brought about by information technology. The chapter highlights the significant advancements in commercial banks through the adoption of digital innovations, such as ATM, mobile banking, and digital money using debit and credit cards.

Focusing on the Dark Web's role in black markets and banking fraud in India, chapter 15 aims to understand the working of the Dark Web and its connection to illegal transactions. It explores the potential and dangers of the Dark Web as an intermediary in illicit activities. The chapter sheds light on the challenges posed by the Dark Web and its implications for banking security in India.

Chapter 16 discusses the revolution in wireless communication, with a particular focus on the development of 5G technology. It examines the services and quality provided by different telecom companies, presenting a basic comparison. The chapter explores the impact of wireless communication advancements on various industries and sectors, highlighting the benefits and advancements brought about by technological innovations.

Chapter 17 investigates crisis management facilitated through social media platforms. Using bibliometric network analysis, it reviews published works on crisis management along social media platforms, identifying influential journals, top-ranking countries and institutions, most cited articles, frequently occurring keywords, and authorship patterns. The analysis provides valuable insights for researchers and scholars interested in crisis management through social media, contributing to the nascent literature in this area.

Online networking is a global trend that transcends boundaries, impacting individuals in both developed and developing countries. With widespread access to smartphones, social networking sites and applications have become easily accessible, making the benefits of online networking, namely online social capital, applicable on a global scale. Indeed, the advantages of online social capital have been reported in diverse domains, ranging from business and social development to education, healthcare, psychology, and the pursuit of sustainable development goals.

The unique advantage of an edited book lies in its ability to bring together contributions from different parts of the world and various areas of specialization. Our primary objective is to provide readers with a comprehensive and up-to-date understanding of this valuable resource. We envision this book serving as a supplementary reading material for higher education institutions, particularly for students in disciplines such as business, economics, information technology, psychology, medicine, and humanities. Additionally, government and private research institutions may find value in including this book in their libraries. We anticipate that research scholars working on this topic or related issues will find the book particularly beneficial. Moreover, business corporations stand to gain valuable insights, as online social capital has demonstrated practical applications in areas such as branding, crowdfunding, and entrepreneurship.

By traversing these chapters, readers will gain a comprehensive understanding of the genesis, manifestations, and implications of social capital in the age of online networking. We hope that this book will inspire further research and spark insightful discussions, ultimately contributing to a deeper understanding of this dynamic and evolving field.

Najmul Hoda
Umm Al-Qura University, Saudi Arabia

Arshi Naim
King Khalid University, Saudi Arabia

Chapter 1
Impact of Individual and Organizational Social Capital of Marketing in a Global Network

Arshi Naim
https://orcid.org/0000-0003-1325-6964
King Khalid University, Saudi Arabia

Asfia Syed
King Khalid University, Saudi Arabia

Syeda Meraj Bilfaqih
King Khalid University, Saudi Arabia

Anandhavalli Muniasamy
https://orcid.org/0000-0001-8940-3954
King Khalid University, Saudi Arabia

ABSTRACT

The success of any organization is dependent, to an extent, on a marketing manager's aptitude to advance social capital within the company's global network. In this chapter, the authors have developed a prototype to present the application of individual social capital at the bottom level to contribute in building the organizational social capital at the global level. They developed a hypothesis that the social capital of customers, business partners, and governing agencies are the critical success factors to explain the performance of the organization and contribute in improving the customer values. General marketing policies are not applicable at the organizational level; therefore, based on the factors of organization, marketing strategies should be deployed. This chapter analyses the factors at individual as well as organizational levels for employing and marketing the social capital at a global level.

DOI: 10.4018/978-1-6684-8953-6.ch001

INTRODUCTION

Empathetic growth of social capital (SCtl) has become an area of substantial attention among social experts (Adler & Kwon, 2002; Leana & Van Buren, 1999). SCtl is defined as a strength that is produced via social relations and that can be engaged to simplify achievement and attain above-normal payments, SCtl has been used to improve a greater understanding of egalitarianism and domination, financial development, cooperative deeds, and occupational success (Bolino, Turnley, & Bloodgood, 2002).

Hypothetically, SCtl has been theorized at manifold such as defining the SCtl at the local sectors, (Kostova and Roth, 2003), at the individual level, (Leana and Van Buren 1999) at the organizational level, and at the inter-organizational level. Although noteworthy research has been led in the area of SCtl, researchers are the foundation to assimilate SCtl in various sectors of businesses (Kostova & Roth, 2003). The unique aspect of this research is to develop and contribute to the marketing of SCtl at the individual levels and employment at the organizational levels. As Organization success is found upon mixing cultural and economic differences into the Organization's overall marketing strategy to enhance customer value delivery, marketing managers become central to the argument of SCtl in an Organization's global network (Naim, et al. 2021).

The different types of SCtl are typically defined as structural SCtl, cognitive SCtl, and relational SCtl. Other common categorizations of SCtl are, bonding SCtl, bridging SCtl, and linking SCtl. Measurement of SCtl has three dimensions as shown in Figure 1.

Figure 1. Dimensions for the measurement of social capital
Source: Fatima et al. (2022)

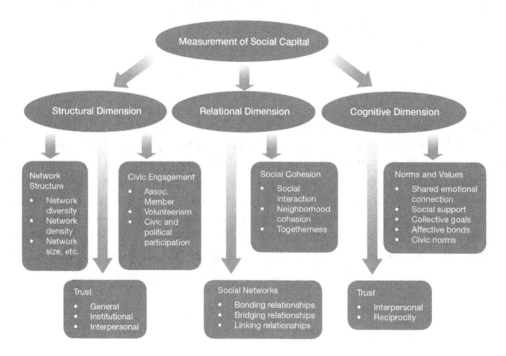

SCtl has many benefits that have made this concept acceptable. It helps a group of people explain their disquiets, share material, and form relationships and conviction. In addition, SCtl can aid to improve an individual's contacts and help them in the forthcoming endeavors. Figure 2 shows the relevance of SCtl in the general professional scenario.

Figure 2. Importance of social capital in the general professional scenario
Source: Alahmari et al. (2023)

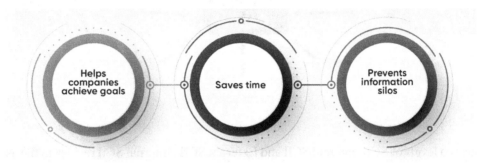

The dominant principle of SCtl is that individuals profit from various standards and values that a social network nurtures and produces, such as trust, mutuality, information, and collaboration. These rules and values offer the essential prerequisites for joint actions. Figure 3 shows the functions of SCtl through social network.

Figure 3. Functions of social capital through social network
Source: Naim et al. (2019)

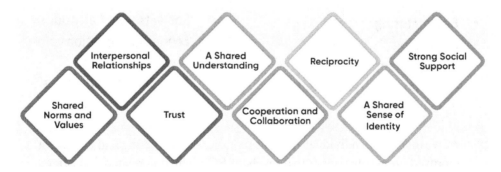

SCtl at work mentions to the individual associates between individuals which lead to a discussion of information and learning, acting as a catalyst for higher achievement and positive transformation allowing employees and companies alike to improve agility, collaboration, and innovation. Figure 4 presents the reasons and needs of social capital globally.

Figure 4. Need of social capital globally
Source: Kamal et al. (2022)

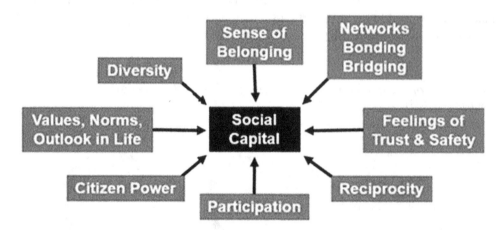

There are two levels of SCtl, Internal SCtl and External SCtl . Internal SCtl resides in the associations among the members of the group or organization whereas, external social capital exists in the shape of relationships with external factors that may be individuals or other social groups. Figure 5 shows the Internal as well as external causes of change in SCtl.

Figure 5. Internal and external causes in social capital
Source: Naim and Alahmari (2020)

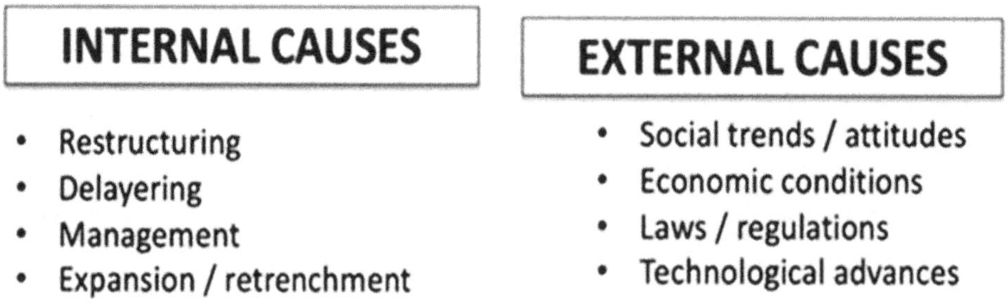

INTERNAL CAUSES

- Restructuring
- Delayering
- Management
- Expansion / retrenchment

EXTERNAL CAUSES

- Social trends / attitudes
- Economic conditions
- Laws / regulations
- Technological advances

In this chapter, we assimilate individuals such as managers in marketing and Organization level SCtl to increase an improved knowledge about two levels of SCtl which is related and offered a setting for enhancing customer delivered value in an organization's global network. First, social capital at the individual level is presented as the theoretical context for the existence of SCtl at both the intra-organizational (internal) as well as inter-organizational (external) levels. Secondly, Organization level SCtl is unified into an argument of cumulative operative relationships in a global network to develop value delivery and good performance. This chapter is segmented into four sections. The first section explains the concepts of SCtl and its applications at the individual as well as at the organizational level, the second section provides a theoretical framework of the research, the third section gives the results and analysis of the hypothesis illustrated in this research and fourth section briefly conclude the research.

THEORETICAL FRAMEWORK

SCtl mentions economic reserve connecting features such as norms, trust, and social networks that facilitate society's action. From a marketing viewpoint, SCtl facilitates the knowledge of the individual, organization, and entire society by enabling shared systems.

The objective of SCtl is personified within marketing managers because they work to develop policies to improve customer value delivery in an Organization's global network. Theoretically, it could be claimed that other practical areas collect SCtl within Organizational resources (Adler & Kwon, 2002; Leana & Van Buren, 1999) but the real roles and responsibilities are with the marketing managers. In a marketing management context, SCtl has been primarily theorized as a supply reflecting the character of social relations within an Organization (Peng & Luo, 2000; Tan & Litschert, 1994). In an appraisal of the SCtl literature, (Leana and Van Buren (1999) two concepts are mostly applied which are associability and trust.

Associability is explained as the readiness and skill of contributors to work at an individual level's areas and builds allied actions to united objectives and activities (Leana & Van Buren, 1999).

A second constituent of SCtl is trust. Trust is apparent when one companion has sureness in another's dependability and truthfulness (Leana & Van Buren, 1999). Supportive, longstanding associations are reliant on the promotion of trust. Trust can be measured in relation of a possibility and recompense association, where expected functions are conducted by all participants in a coordinated manner. The study identifies two hypotheses for SCtl of marketing in a global network. Figure 6 shows the theoretical framework of the research objectives and the relationship.

Hypothesis 1: SCtl developed by an individual in the Organization's global network will be positively related to the degree of the marketing manager's contribution in the followings:

H1.1: Main Organization and all its local partners
H1.2: Synchronization between the Organization and its global partners
H1.3: Expedites information between the main Organization and its local partners (linking of H1.1 and H1.2)
H1.4: Enriches organizational interpersonal proficiency to introduce worldwide enterprises.
H1.5: Connotation between an Organization's SCtl in its global network and individual SCtl.

Hypothesis 2: Policies of marketing management cultivating SCtl within the Organization's global network for the following:

H2.1: Organizations improving brand loyalty in global markets and achieving success at the Organizational level.
H2.2: Organization improving knowledge development for global markets and achieving success at the Organizational level.
H2.3: Organization improving access to resources for the global markets and achieving success at the Organizational level.

Figure 6. The theoretical framework of the research objectives and the relationship

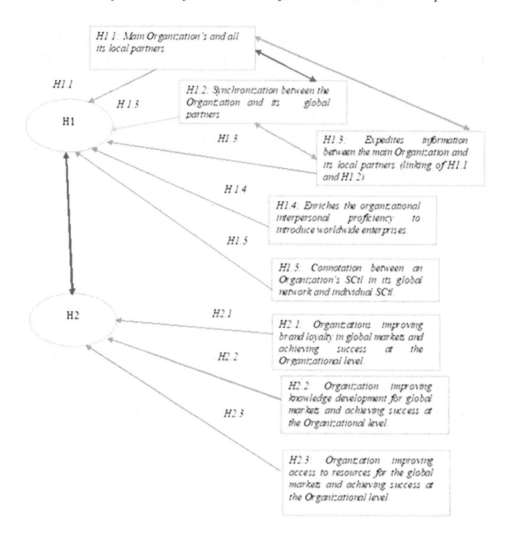

RESULTS ANALYSIS

SCtl at an individual level refers to ''the standing one has in an organization and the concurrent ability to draw on the standing to influence actions of others in the organization'' (Friedman & Krackhardt, 1997: 319).

Hypothesis 1: A marketing manager can build associability and trust within the Organization's global network through the exchange of codified (i.e., the knowledge that can be synthesized into a set of codes) and tacit knowledge (i.e., knowledge derived from doing, such as the social knowledge one gain by living in a foreign environment) across internal and external relations. As such, a marketing manager's SCtl, both in headquarters and local markets (i.e., internal and external social capital), facilitates information transfer and learning as well as providing political support within and between organizations in a global context. This enables marketing managers to play a unique strategic role in global organizations and within an Organization's global network.

Figure 7. CB bank presenting the SCtl by the marketing manager building associability
Source: Naim and Kautish (2022)

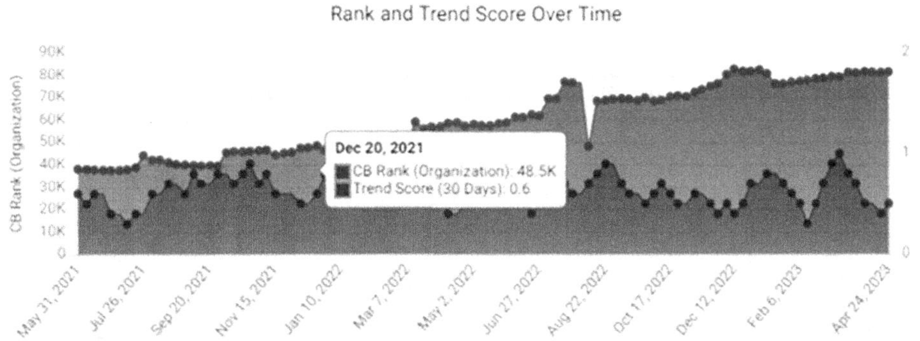

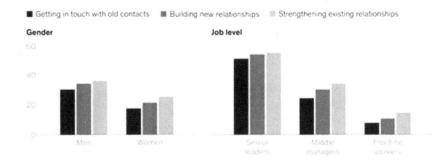

Results show that the individual level SCtl is contributing at the higher levels as shown for CB bank for the years 2021 to 2023.

H1.1: Main Organization and all its local partners

Individual-level SCtl binds the headquarters of the global organization to the plurality of norms held by foreign subsidiaries and/or network partners. Without SCtl with these constituents, marketing managers could suffer resistance to the decision-making latitude due to a lack of confidence in their ability, loyalty, and commitment to the corporate goals and policies. Results shown in Figure 8 that the Organization and all its local partners work together for building SCtl at job levels as well as based on gender.

Figure 8. Main organization and all its local partners for building SCtl

H1.2: Synchronization between the Organization and its global partners

The importance of marketing managers with SCtl, which bond headquarters and foreign companies in global organizations, becomes of greater importance as the decision-making in global organizations is being decentralized to the organization's periphery. These decentralizing trends have flattened organizations, necessitating greater utilization of cooperative initiatives based on reserves of social capital. Results shown in the figure 9 that the organizations have collaboration with other sectors for the growth in network connections and added values.

Figure 9. Synchronization between the organization and its global partners

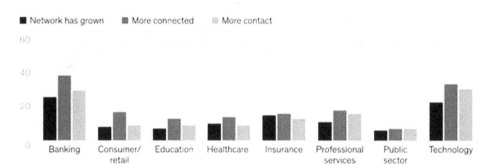

H1.3: Expedites information between the main Organization and its local partners (linking of H1.1 and H1.2)

In particular, the growing use of cross-functional, cross-organizational, and cross-national teams (e.g., global account management teams, as well as product development, advertising planning, logistics, etc.) with broadened decision-making latitude, accentuates the need for cooperation and learning across functional, subsidiary, and national boundaries, enhancing the importance of SCtl in these complex organizational settings (Bennis, 1997). The program toward the establishment of closer connections to customers and global business partners enhanced the necessity of having SCtl in both domestic and foreign organizations (Harvey & Novicevic, 2001). Results are shown in figure 10 Expedites information between the main Organization and its local partners for SCtl.

Figure 10. Expedites information between the main organization and its local workers for SCtl

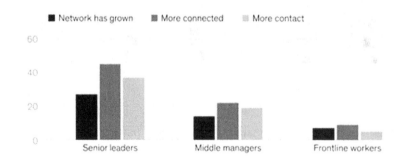

H1.4: Enriches organizational interpersonal proficiency to introduce worldwide enterprises.

The advantage in building SCtl grows from both the framework and relationship significance of social interaction. Framework denotes the marketing manager's ability to have relevant behavior/knowledge in interactions (Kelly, 1984) and results are shown in Figure 11 trends over a period for building SCtl for the organizational interpersonal proficiency globally.

Figure 11. Trends over a period for building SCtl for the organizational interpersonal proficiency globally

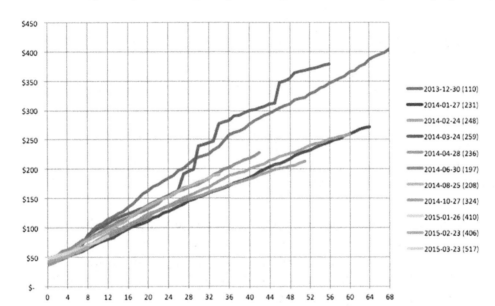

H1.5: Connotation between an Organization's SCtl in its global network and individual SCtl.

The trust construction procedure among the marketing manager and home countries in international markets is an essential aspect of enhancing customer value delivery (Child, 1972). Overall, trust is important because it can decrease business costs, advance organizational tractability to familiarize, improve competence, enable collaboration, and improve the prospect of preserving implied regulations through passivity with social standards and expectations (Van de Ven, Delbecq, & Koenig, 1976). National and International collaboration aids in increasing organizational capacity and lowered interaction costs occur when trust is established in cross-cultural relationships (Wicks, Berman, & Jones, 1999). Marketing managers socially entrench belief at two levels, their personal relationships and between the headquarters and secondary organizations (Roth & Nigh, 1992). Figure 12 shows the Connotation between an Organization's SCtl in its global network and individual SCtl.

Figure 12. Connotation between an organization's SCtl in its global network and individual SCtl

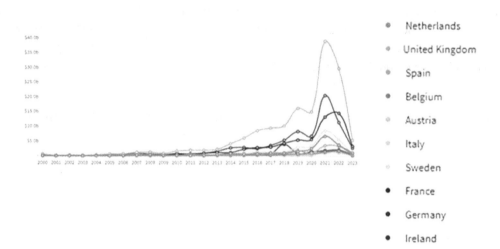

Hypothesis 2: Policies of marketing management cultivating SCtl within the Organization's global network for the following:

The link structure of a planned route to advance and preserve SCtl can be observed in and of itself as an employable resource that, when leveraged, can enhance customer value delivery and ultimately performance (Peng & Luo, 2000). In the global competitive showground, an Organization makes long-term, permanent obligations of resources to network associates to progress and maintain SCtl (Kostova & Roth, 2003). SCtl can be employed, such as to gain contact to customer information essential to modify products to needs and enhance value delivery, to inspire supportive performance on the part of commercial partners to enhance global logistical flows and increase efficiency, or to save legislative service in relation to supervisory amendments for the simplification of trade (Adler & Kwon, 2002; Leana & Van Buren, 1999).

H2.1: Organizations improving brand loyalty in global markets and achieving success at the Organizational level.

To maintain manageability, only a sample of the marketing management strategies and outcomes related to each type of SCtl are presented. In fact, each type of SCtl has many options for marketing management strategies that would aid in its development and success. Hypothetically there are three types of SCtl as shown in Figure 13 and Figure 14 shows the results of various countries making the global market by improving their brand loyalty for different companies over a period of time.

Customer SCtl is theorized as an advantage that an organization has developed and maintains with its customers that can be employed to facilitate action and sustain a competitive advantage. Customer SCtl exists in the trust and associability the customer places in the organization (Bendapudi & Berry, 1997). Figure 15 shows the benefits and challenges of customer SCtl for the period from 2019 to 2022.

Figure 13. Types of social capital in the global context

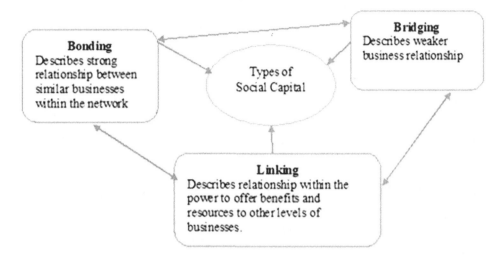

Figure 14. Various countries making a global market by improving their brand loyalty

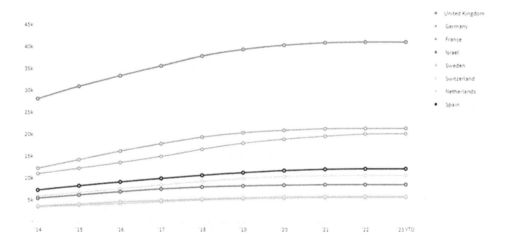

The leveraging of customer SCtl results in benefits, such as supporting performance subsequent in customer loyalty over time. The development of customer loyalty allows organizations to not only be more profitable in the short-run, but also in the long- run as loyal customers spend more (O'Brien & Jones, 1995), provide a base of positive word-of-mouth (Reichheld & Teal, 1996), and evolve into a continuous flow of future customers (Oliver, 1999). Figure 16 shows the development policies for SCtl network.

Business partner SCtl is defined as an advantage that an organization has developed and maintains within its infrastructure of global business relations (Peng & Luo, 2000). Business partner SCtl enables the working of the association and the enhancement of the organizational capability to delivery customer value in the global marketplace and is integrally based on the individual SCtl developed through marketing managers.

Figure 15. Benefit and challenges of customer SCtl for period from 2019 to 2022

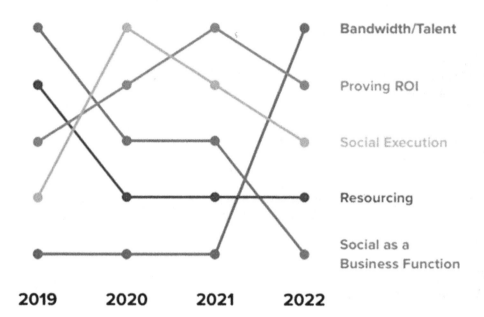

Figure 16. Development policies and social capital network

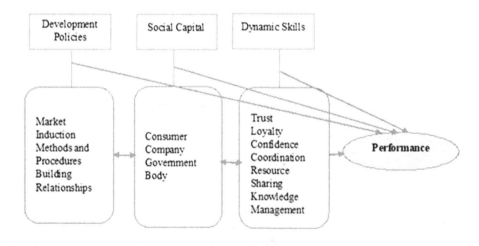

H2.2: Organization improving knowledge development for global markets and achieving success at the Organizational level.

Organizations function in a controlled task environment, often referred to as a radical economy (Achrol, Reve, & Stern, 1983; Zald, 1970). A radical economy approaches interpretations of networks as encompassing cooperating sets of major financial and sociopolitical services that affect cooperative performance and presentation (Achrol et al., 1983; Zald, 1970). Central intervention SCtl refers to the social relations, and inherent trust and associability that an organization has developed with those social actors in the political economy charged with allocating resources, setting the guidelines for operation that can be organized to enhance customer value transfer, and finally Organization performance. Figure 17 shows the results of the Organization improving knowledge development for global markets and achieving success at the Organizational level.

Figure 17. Organization improving knowledge development for global markets and achieving success at the organizational level from 2013 to 2015

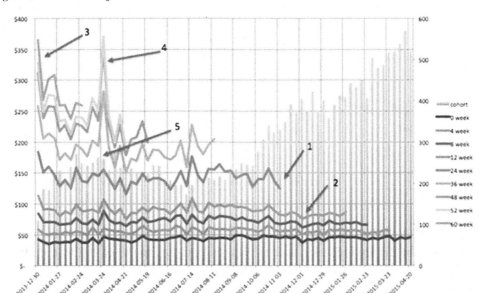

H2.3: Organization improving access to resources for the global markets and achieving success at the Organizational level.

SCtl is the famous Virtual Capital (VC), which was founded in 2011. The main office of represented VC is situated in Palo Alto. The company was established in North America in the United States. The funds are found to be increasing for SCtl since 2013 and in 2014 the maximum increase is accounted for in the global markets. Figure 18 shows the results of the Organization improving access to resources for the global markets and achieving success at the Organizational level for SCtl from 2013 to 2015.

SCtl personified by marketing managers in the Organization's global network can be of pronounced prominence to the Organization. Marketing executives are essential to the decision-making process for marketing policy and application. Organizations can begin to increase a more in-depth understanding of the resource frameworks they possess and those that they need to grow in order to establish a competitive advantage in the global marketplace. As such, the clarification of how an Organization's marketing managers exemplify SCtl can serve as an assessment tool through which Organizations can determine their respective level of the intangible. While Organizations compete feverishly to attract the best marketers, little effort is normally expended toward the goal of retaining the employees.

Figure 18. Organization improving access to resources for the global markets and achieving success at the organizational level for SCtl from 2013 to 2015

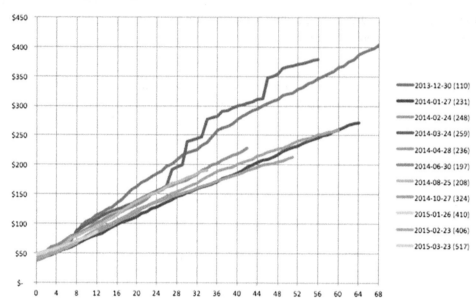

The development of Organization level SCtl in a global network is derived from the marketing management policies engaged by the Organization with the channel existing in the global market. Introductory SCtl is based on trust and collaboration within the Organizations and at the global level.

CONCLUSION

Individual-level SCtl provides the bases for the development of Organization level SCtl. However, it is the customer, business partner, and governing agency SCtl recognized at the Organization level that provides a basis to analyze and critique marketing management policies explaining the concepts related to the primary question of resource expansion and leveraging customer value delivery.

For an Organization to develop SCtl in its global network is in relation to its customers, business partners, and governing assistances it should prudently analyze its current resources and its point in relation to each component. The execution of marketing management policies is aimed at developing and leveraging SCtl within the Organization's global network which may enhance customer value delivery in global markets and establish a competitive advantage.

REFERENCES

Achrol, R. S., Reve, T., & Stern, L. W. (1983). The environment of marketing channel dyads: A framework for comparative analysis. *Journal of Marketing*, *47*(4), 55–67. doi:10.1177/002224298304700407

Adler, P. S., & Kwon, S. W. (2002). Social capital: Prospects for a new concept. *Academy of Management Review*, *27*(1), 17–40. doi:10.2307/4134367

Alqahtani, H., & Naim, A. (2022). Critical Success Factors for Transforming CRM to SCRM for building E-CRM. In A. Naim & S. Kautish (Eds.), *Building a Brand Image Through Electronic Customer Relationship Management* (pp. 139–168). IGI Global. doi:10.4018/978-1-6684-5386-5.ch007

Bendapudi, N., & Berry, L. (1997). Customers' motivation for maintaining relationships with service providers. *Journal of Retailing, 73*(1), 15–38. doi:10.1016/S0022-4359(97)90013-0

Bennis, W. (1997). *Organizing genius: The secrets of creative collaboration.* Addison-Wesley.

Bolino, M., Turnley, W., & Bloodgood, J. (2002). Citizenship behavior and the creation of social capital in organizations. *Academy of Management Review, 27*(4), 505–522. doi:10.2307/4134400

Capron, L., & Hulland, J. (1999). Redeployment of brands, sales forces, and general marketing management expertise following horizontal acquisitions: A resource-based view. *Journal of Marketing, 63*(2), 41–54. doi:10.1177/002224299906300203

Child, J. (1972). Organizational structure, environment and performance: The role of strategic choice. *Sociology, 6*(1), 1–22. doi:10.1177/003803857200600101

Edström, A., & Galbraith, J. (1977, June). Transfer of managers as a coordination and control strategy in multinational organizations. *Administrative Science Quarterly, 22*(2), 248–263. doi:10.2307/2391959

Fatima, S., Alqahtani, H., Naim, A., & Alma'alwi, F. (2022). E-CRM Through Social Media Marketing Activities for Brand Awareness, Brand Image, and Brand Loyalty. In A. Naim & S. Kautish (Eds.), *Building a Brand Image Through Electronic Customer Relationship Management* (pp. 109–138). IGI Global. doi:10.4018/978-1-6684-5386-5.ch006

Friedman, R., & Krackhardt, D. (1997). Social capital and career mobility: A structural theory of lower returns to education for Asian employees. *The Journal of Applied Behavioral Science, 3*(3), 316–334. doi:10.1177/0021886397333004

Grant, R. M. (1996). Toward a knowledge-based theory of the organization [Winter special issue]. *Strategic Management Journal, 17*(S2), 109–122. doi:10.1002mj.4250171110

Han, J. K., Kim, N., & Srivastava, R. K. (1998). Market orientation and organizational performance: Is innovation a missing link? *Journal of Marketing, 62*(4), 30–45. doi:10.1177/002224299806200403

Harvey, M., & Buckley, M. (1997). Managing inpatriates: Building a global core competency. *Journal of World Business, 32*(1), 34–45. doi:10.1016/S1090-9516(97)90024-9

Harvey, M., & Novicevic, M. (2001). Selecting expatriates for increasingly complex global assignments. *Career Development International, 6*(2), 67–78. doi:10.1108/13620430110383357

Harvey, M., & Novicevic, M. (2002). Selecting appropriate marketing managers to effectively Control global channels of distribution. *International Marketing Review, 19*(5), 74–86. doi:10.1108/02651330210445310

Kamal, S., Naim, A., Magd, H., Khan, S. A., & Khan, F. M. (2022). The Relationship Between E-Service Quality, Ease of Use, and E-CRM Performance Referred by Brand Image. In A. Naim & S. Kautish (Eds.), *Building a Brand Image Through Electronic Customer Relationship Management* (pp. 84–108). IGI Global. doi:10.4018/978-1-6684-5386-5.ch005

Kelly, H. (1984). The transitional descriptions of interdependence by means of transition lists. *Journal of Personality and Social Psychology, 47*(5), 956–982. doi:10.1037/0022-3514.47.5.956

Kogut, B., & Zander, U. (1992). Knowledge of the organization, combinative capabilities, and the replication of technology. *Organization Science, 3*(3), 383–397. doi:10.1287/orsc.3.3.383

Kohli, A. K., & Jaworski, B. J. (1990). Market orientation: The construct, research, propositions, and managerial implications. *Journal of Marketing, 54*(2), 1–18. doi:10.1177/002224299005400201

Konovsky, M. A. (2000). Understanding procedural justice and its impact on business organizations. *Journal of Management, 26*(3), 489–511. doi:10.1177/014920630002600306

Korsgaard, M. A., Schweiger, D. M., & Sapienza, H. J. (1995). Building commitment, attachment, and trust in strategic decision-making teams: The role of procedural justice. *Academy of Management Journal, 38*(1), 60–84. doi:10.2307/256728

Kostova, T., & Roth, K. (2003). Social capital in multinational corporations and a micro-macro model of it formulation. *Academy of Management Review, 28*(2), 297–313. doi:10.2307/30040714

Leana, C. R., & Van Buren, H. J. III. (1999). Organizational social capital and employment practices. *Academy of Management Review, 24*(3), 538–555. doi:10.2307/259141

Lei, D., Hitt, M. A., & Bettis, B. (1996). Dynamic core competencies through meta-learning and strategic context. *Journal of Management, 22*(4), 247–267. doi:10.1177/014920639602200402

Luo, Y. (1997). Guanxi and performance of foreign-invested enterprises in China: An empirical inquiry. *Management International Review, 37*(1), 51–70.

Naim, A., & Alahmari, F. (2020). Reference model of e-learning and quality to establish interoperability in higher education systems. *International Journal of Emerging Technologies in Learning, 15*(2), 15–28. doi:10.3991/ijet.v15i02.11605

Naim, A., Alahmari, F., & Rahim, A. (2021). Role of Artificial Intelligence in Market Development and Vehicular Communication. Smart Antennas. *Recent Trends in Design and Applications, 2*, 28–39. doi: 10.2174/9781681088594121020006

Naim, A., Alqahtani, H., Muniasamy, A., Bilfaqih, S. M., Mahveen, R., & Mahjabeen, R. (2023). Applications of Information Systems and Data Security in Marketing Management. In A. Naim, P. Malik, & F. Zaidi (Eds.), *Fraud Prevention, Confidentiality, and Data Security for Modern Businesses* (pp. 57–83). IGI Global. doi:10.4018/978-1-6684-6581-3.ch003

Naim, A., Hussain, M. R., Naveed, Q. N., Ahmad, N., Qamar, S., Khan, N., & Hweij, T. A. (2019, April). Ensuring interoperability of e-learning and quality development in education. In *2019 IEEE Jordan International Joint Conference on Electrical Engineering and Information Technology (JEEIT)* (pp. 736-741). IEEE. 10.1109/JEEIT.2019.8717431

Naim, A., & Kautish, S. K. (Eds.). (2022). *Building a Brand Image Through Electronic Customer Relationship Management*. IGI Global. doi:10.4018/978-1-6684-5386-5

Naim, A., Malik, P. K., & Zaidi, F. A. (Eds.). (2023). *Fraud Prevention, Confidentiality, and Data Security for Modern Businesses*. IGI Global. doi:10.4018/978-1-6684-6581-3

O'Brien, L., & Jones, C. (1995). Do rewards really create loyalty? *Harvard Business Review*, *70*(3), 75–82.

Oliver, R. L. (1999). Whence consumer loyalty. *Journal of Marketing*, *63*(4_suppl1), 33–44. doi:10.1177/00222429990634s105

Park, S. H., & Luo, Y. (2001). Guanxi and organizational dynamics: Organizational networking in Chinese organizations. *Strategic Management Journal*, *22*(5), 455–477. doi:10.1002mj.167

Peng, M. W., & Luo, Y. (2000). Managerial ties and organization performance in a transition economy: The nature of a micro- macro link. *Academy of Management Journal*, *43*(3), 486–501. doi:10.2307/1556406

Putnam, R. (1993). The prosperous community: Social capital in public life. *The American Prospect*, *13*, 35–42.

Reichheld, F. F., & Teal, T. (1996). *The loyalty effect: The hidden force behind growth, profits, and lasting value*. Harvard Business School Press.

Roth, K., & Nigh, D. (1992). The effectiveness of headquarters- subsidiary relationships: The role of coordination, control, and conflict. *Journal of Business Research*, *25*(4), 277–301. doi:10.1016/0148-2963(92)90025-7

Slater, S. F., & Narver, J. C. (1999). Market-oriented is more than being customer-led. *Strategic Management Journal*, *20*(12), 1165–1168. doi:10.1002/(SICI)1097-0266(199912)20:12<1165::AID-SMJ73>3.0.CO;2-#

Tan, J. J., & Litschert, R. J. (1994). Environment-strategy relationship and its performance implications: An empirical study of the Chinese electronics industry. *Strategic Management Journal*, *15*(1), 1–20. doi:10.1002mj.4250150102

Van de Ven, A., Delbecq, A., & Koenig, R. (1976). Determinants of coordination modes within organizations. *American Sociological Review*, *41*(2), 322–338. doi:10.2307/2094477

Walder, A. G. (1995). Local governments as industrial organizations: An organizational analysis of China's transitional economy. *American Journal of Sociology*, *101*(2), 263–301. doi:10.1086/230725

Wicks, A., Berman, S., & Jones, T. (1999). The structure of optimal trust: Moral and strategic implications. *Academy of Management Review*, *24*(1), 99–116. doi:10.2307/259039

Williamson, O. (1993). Calculativeness, trust and economic organization. *The Journal of Law & Economics*, *36*(1, Part 2), 453–486. doi:10.1086/467284

Zald, M. N. (1970). Political economy: A framework for comparative analysis. In M. N. Zald (Ed.), *Power in organizations* (pp. 221–261). Vanderbilt University Press.

Zander, U., & Kogut, B. (1995). Knowledge and the speed of the transfer and initiation of organizational capabilities: An empirical test. *Organization Science*, *6*(1), 76–92. doi:10.1287/orsc.6.1.76

Chapter 2
Social Networking Sites, Online Social Capital, and the Success of Crowdfunding Campaigns

Najmul Hoda

https://orcid.org/0000-0002-1772-7551

Umm Al-Qura University, Saudi Arabia

Mohammad Zubair Ahmad

Utkarsh College of Management Education, India

ABSTRACT

Crowdfunding is a phenomenon that exists because of interconnectivity. These platforms allow the connection of lenders, donors, and investors with recipients who may be entrepreneurs or beneficiaries. In the entire crowdfunding process, there is a direct involvement of network behaviors namely trust, norms, networking, and so on. In other words, social capital plays a role in crowdfunding. This chapter aims to review the existing literature on crowdfunding platforms and identify the role of online networking in the process and outcome. The chapter would benefit both researchers and various stakeholders who are engaged in crowdfunding or are exploring this platform for financial decisions.

INTRODUCTION

Crowdfunding is a modern financing mechanism that relies on the power of social networking for financing a variety of projects and businesses. It has transformed the financing landscape providing a direct link between the surplus and deficit, transcending the boundaries. As per (Mollick, 2014), the idea of crowdfunding is derived from the principles of "microfinance" and "crowdsourcing" but differs in the way it involves multiple Internet platforms. The process takes place in both specialized crowdfunding platforms as well as social networking sites such as Facebook, Twitter, etc. Crowdfunding is reportedly used more by nascent ventures where funding is difficult to access. The funding project, called "campaign" is characterized by a set goal in terms of time and money. Funds are provided by a group

DOI: 10.4018/978-1-6684-8953-6.ch002

of individuals or organizations that may be in the form of donations or for some benefits. At its core, crowdfunding relies on many people who are not professionals, who are referred to as the "crowd". It is a "two-sided market that links capital-seekers (crowdfunders) and capital-givers (investors)" (Haas et al., 2014). In this process, the crowdfunding platforms play a role of enablers only. Crowdfunding does not just provide financial benefits to creators but several non-financial benefits that include "enhanced reputation; marketing; audience engagement, and feedback on project".

This chapter provides a description of the concept of crowdfunding, its working process, and the role of social media in the success of crowdfunding. The next section describes the concept of crowdfunding, role of social media is discussed in the second section, future research directions and conclusions are discussed in the fourth and fifth sections.

CONCEPT OF CROWDFUNDING

Definitions

(Datta et al., 2019) mention that (Schwienbacher & Benjamin, 2010) provided the first academic definition of the term crowdfunding. They defined crowdfunding as, "an open call for the provision of financial resources, to gather either donation or in exchange of reward and/or voting rights in order to support initiatives for specific purposes". (Mollick, 2014) refined this definition and stated that, "crowdfunding is a way that collects funds from the public to support enterprises or individuals by drawing on relatively small contributions from a relatively large number of individuals using the Internet, without standard intermediaries". Another comprehensive definition of crowdfunding given by (De Buysere, K; Gajda, O; Kleverlaan, R; Marom, 2012) state that crowdfunding is "a collective effort of many individuals who network and pool their resources to support efforts initiated by other people or organizations usually via or with the help of the Internet".

The Rise of Crowdfunding

This method of raising money has seen rapid growth in the recent past. As of 2023 crowdfunding websites have helped in raising US\$ 1.1 billion worldwide (Elad, 2023). This financing method is not mere a "trendy buzzword" now but has gained the reputation of a mainstream financing model. One of the top crowdfunding platforms, Kickstarter, attracted five million contributors and about \$1 billion in just five years. Its competitor, Indiegogo, was able to manage one campaign that raised \$12 million. Other major crowdfunding platforms are GoFundMe, Microventures, YouCaring, Looking at history, it may be noted that crowdfunding did exist in the past in various forms, in book projects, war bonds, cooperatives, movies, software, to name a few. An interesting example of crowdfunding from the recent past is Tesla Model 3 that attracted \$1.5 billion from prospective buyers of its cars.

Modus Operandi

Crowdfunding basically involves an open call for financial support on Internet. It works on the principle of large pool of people contributing small amounts for a specific purpose technically called "campaign". A campaign is marked by a definite starting and ending points. The main parties involved in the crowdfunding process are; the person/s or organization needing funds, the crowd of backers or funders, and the crowdfunding platform. Crowdfunding platforms play a significant role in the process by facilitating interactions between the crowdfunder and the crowd. A fee is charged by the crowdfunding platform for their services that is incurred by the crowdfunder. Generally, these platforms generally work on "all-or-nothing funding model". It implies that the fundraiser gets the money only if the target is reached otherwise the contributions are reversed. Individuals play the role of agents for the projects and share project related information in their social network. These individuals who participate in crowdfunding do so for notable reasons like; social participation, because the creator is a relative or friend, or because the individual is innovation oriented.

Types of Crowdfunding Models

In principle, these models may be classified into charitable and benefit/reward-based. Although literature reports multiple types of crowdfunding platforms, there are four prominent models (De Buysere, K; Gajda, O; Kleverlaan, R; Marom, 2012; Mollick, 2014). The different types of crowdfunding models are discussed below.

Donation-Based Crowdfunding

When a campaign receives funding without any financial return expected by the contributors, it is called donation-based crowdfunding. The main motive of funding is charity or to support a start-up. A few notable examples of donation-based crowdfunding are CrowdRise, Classy, etc.

Rewards-Based Crowdfunding

In this crowdfunding model the creator provides a non-financial return (reward) to the donors. It is also called non-equity crowdfunding. These rewards may be in the form of goods or services. This crowd-funding model has been used in various needs such as "free software development, scientific research, civic works, etc." As mentioned in the literature, the rewards offered to donors are proportional to their contributions, thereby incentivizing higher contributions. This crowdfunding model suits a start-up that does not need to opt for debt or equity forms of financing. Digital security is also being offered as a reward in the form of initial coin offering.

Equity-Based Crowdfunding

This model resembles a common stock or venture funding with the difference that the funding comes from angel investors via an online crowdfunding platform. In the USA, a remarkable event that paved the way for this model to work was the legislation called Jumpstart Our Business Acts (JOBS) Act. In this crowdfunding model, the creator needs to form a company and the investors are eligible for a return on their investment. Crowdcube was the world's first equity-based crowdfunding platform.

Peer-to-Peer Lending

Commonly called P2P lending or crowdlending, this crowdfunding model works on interest-based financing where the crowd gets interest on the money they lend. The only difference with a traditional bank loan is that instead of one lending entity there are numerous small lenders. Bidding is the common process where the crowdlenders offer money at certain rate and the borrower opts for the lowest rate available. The crowdfunding platform is responsible for protecting the interests of both borrowers and the lenders. Zopa is one of the earliest examples of crowdlending. An interesting development in this segment was the entry of institutional investors such as Google who invested $125 million in the crowdlending platform Lending Club.

Apart from the above discussed basic crowdfunding models, there are also a combination of models used by creators. These are called the hybrid models. The top and the most popular crowdfunding sites are Kickstarter, GoFundMe, Lending Club, and Indiegogo. Among them Kickstarter is the most popular crowdfunding platform that mainly operates on rewards-based model. GoFundMe is an example of donation-based crowdfunding company. Lending Club operates on donations and mainly serves small business funding.

ONLINE NETWORKING AND CROWDFUNDING

Development of information and communications technology led to the massive proliferation of social networking sites and new applications of Internet. The new medium of online communication called the "social media" is playing a significant role in the dissemination of information and reaching out to masses as well as target audiences. Social media is playing an equally positive role in crowdfunding. Past studies have attributed crowdfunding success to social networking sites (Beier & Wagner, 2015; Borst et al., 2018). (Borst et al., 2018) reported that popular crowdfunding projects relied on social media for information sharing and advertisements. Among the social media platforms, Facebook is the most popular and has been used in promoting crowdfunding projects. Twitter has also been popular among small businesses (Fischer & Reuber, 2011). In the general entrepreneurship literature too, positive role of social media in venture funding has been confirmed (Thies et al., 2018). (Kaminski et al., 2019) confirm that social media activities impact positively on crowdfunding campaigns.

Some of the important factors that play important role in the success of crowdfunding are discussed in the following sections.

Diffusion of Information

Social media offer support to crowdfunding campaigns by "diffusing information, increasing exposure, improving site traffic, promoting engagement with audience, claim for support and resources, and sharing project updates" (Sahaym et al., 2021). Sharing contents via social media increases the visibility of the project (Saxton & Wang, 2014). Campaign success is found to be positively related with creator's online network, likes and shares (Giudici et al., 2012). Crowdfunding models inherently face the challenges of information asymmetry and uncertainty. Both the founder of the project and the crowd are unknown to each other. Social media helps overcome these problems by allowing adequate information sharing. These may occur in the form of updates, comments, likes, shares, etc.

Electronic Word of Mouth (eWOM)

Another benefit of social media on crowdfunding is the occurrence of electronic word of mouth that results from massive communication with prospects, in the form of online comments (Kaur & Gera, 2017). Social media stimulates the herd behavior as found by (Borst et al., 2018). Social media also helps in executing a "virtual word of mouth marketing strategy" or more technically electronic word of mouth. This positively influences fund collection (Beier & Wagner, 2015). (Li & Jarvenpaa, 2015) noted that number of comments on SNS positively affects fundraising. Further, the number of times a campaign is shared on social media also affects project outcomes (Kaartemo, 2017). A crowdfunding platform called Starnext allows the backers to take the role of a fan and the number of fans of a project was found to significantly influence success. Social media plays a key role in developing a herding behavior. As (Bikhchandani & Sharma, 2000) noted that "people tend to herd under uncertainty in financial markets". (Agrawal et al., 2015; Bi et al., 2017; Trusov et al., 2009) analyzed the impact of eWOM on crowdfunding and found that it has positive impact both in short term as well as long term.

Type of Social Media Platforms

Not all SNS will guarantee similar type of success as discussed by (Anggraeni et al., 2020). Therefore, founders need to mix the social media accounts based on the objectives. Creators can link their own social media account to the project or create an account for the project. Via these accounts, prospective funders can get access to information about the project as well as its founder (Kraus et al., 2016). The main feature of the accounts of a project are that they are more specific, allow interactions among backers, and provide the option of sharing, liking, commenting, etc. (Hong et al., 2015) informed that social media activities in crowdfunding differ in their impact. They suggest that SNS like Facebook are more appropriate for charitable campaigns whereas Twitter may be better for private campaigns. Regarding the use of social media, (Lu et al., 2014) suggest that in early phases, Facebook is better and professional SNS like LinkedIn suits dissemination of information in a professional network "who are more incentivized by the content of the project compared to the social benefits". Twitter specifically helps in sharing updates and news regarding the project (Fischer & Rebecca Reuber, 2014). (Summers et al., 2016) mention that the role of social media on crowdfunding depends upon the platform. (Block et al., 2018) report that a campaign with frequent updates, content uploads, etc. has better success rate.

Online Social Capital

Social networking sites usage result in social capital that are called online social capital (Granovetter, 1983; Najmul & Mahmoud, 2022). These social capitals are formed depending upon the users' network, use, type of platform, etc. Crowdfunding projects do benefit from the resources generated through online social capital (Mollick, 2014). Several researchers proved that social capital plays an important role in campaigns (Colombo et al., 2015; Skirnevskiy et al., 2017). The direct connections of the creator represent social capital that is responsible for accessing funds (Agrawal et al., 2015). (Block et al., 2018; Moritz & Block, 2015) mention that social capital would provide better effects if regular quality signals are sent. (Hui et al., 2014) explain that crowdfunding creators use variety of social media platforms to "activate network connection, to keep in contact with previous and current campaign supporters, and to expand network reach". Therefore, social media may play an active role in maintaining ties with both current and prospective backers. (Giudici et al., 2012) find a link between individual social capital and crowdfunding success. (Zvilichovsky et al., 2013) describe the creation of entrepreneurs' communities who back each other's project clearly an outcome of social capital. Crowdfunding research has proven that the individual's social network and social capital have positively influenced crowdfunding (Hui et al., 2014). Developing trust is the biggest challenge for crowdfundee (creators), more specifically where the money is nonrefundable (Gerber & Hui, 2013).

Creator's Social Media Network

Number of connections is an important determinant of crowdfunding success (Zheng et al., 2014). Number of connections positively influence the formation of online social capital (Hoda et al., 2021; Saxton & Wang, 2014). (Mollick, 2014) also concluded that a project creator's personal network is positively associated with crowdfunding success. The role of connections in crowdfunding success has also been empirically tested and positive relationship found in other studies (Crosetto & Regner, 2014; Lechtenbörger et al., 2015).

FUTURE RESEARCH DIRECTIONS

Future research directions in crowdfunding point to a role of cross-disciplinary work (McKenny et al., 2017). There is still a need to investigate the factors that affect the success of crowdfunding, especially for entrepreneur's social media activities (Bushong et al., 2018). While most studies focus on reward-based or donation-based crowdfunding models, equity-based models have received lesser attention (Block et al., 2018). Therefore, there is a need to study the role of social media in equity-based crowdfunding models.

CONCLUSION

This chapter provided an overview of the factors related to social media that might influence the success of crowdfunding. The reasons that could deter crowdfunders (investor) from funding are associated with lack of trust in the crowdfundee (entrepreneur), specifically in platforms where the fund-seeker is allowed to keep the money even when the target is not met (Gerber & Hui, 2013). The lack of trust is mainly because of moral hazard and information asymmetry. Social media plays an important role in overcoming these critical issues by allowing interactions between crowdfunders and crowdfundee. As per (Chen & Liu, 2023) crowdfunding campaigns are affected by static and dynamic factors. Those factors that do not change during the campaign are called static, while the factors such as project popularity that change are called dynamic factors. A concern in online crowdfunding is related to the need to publicly display detailed information about the project that increases the risk of copying, especially for projects in the business domain that once imitated might reduce or eliminate the competitive advantage (Hommerová, 2020). Overall, crowdfunding is going to be one feasible alternative for the fund-seekers, and is set to grow massively both in terms of volume and size.

REFERENCES

Agrawal, A., Catalini, C., & Goldfarb, A. (2015). Crowdfunding: Geography, Social Networks, and the Timing of Investment Decisions. *Journal of Economics & Management Strategy*, 24(2), 253–274. Advance online publication. doi:10.1111/jems.12093

Anggraeni, A., Putra, S., & Suwito, B. P. (2020). Examining the Influence of Customer-To-Customer Electronic Word of Mouth on Purchase Intention in Social Networking Sites. *ACM International Conference Proceeding Series*. 10.1145/3387263.3387274

Beier, M., & Wagner, K. (2015). Crowdfunding success: A perspective from social media and e-commerce. *2015 International Conference on Information Systems: Exploring the Information Frontier, ICIS 2015*.

Bi, S., Liu, Z., & Usman, K. (2017). The influence of online information on investing decisions of reward-based crowdfunding. *Journal of Business Research*, 71, 10–18. Advance online publication. doi:10.1016/j.jbusres.2016.10.001

Bikhchandani, S., & Sharma, S. (2000). Herd behavior in financial markets. *IMF Staff Papers*. Advance online publication. doi:10.5539/ibr.v6n6p31

Block, J., Hornuf, L., & Moritz, A. (2018). Which updates during an equity crowdfunding campaign increase crowd participation? *Small Business Economics*, 50(1), 3–27. Advance online publication. doi:10.100711187-017-9876-4

Borst, I., Moser, C., & Ferguson, J. (2018). From friendfunding to crowdfunding: Relevance of relationships, social media, and platform activities to crowdfunding performance. *New Media & Society*, 20(4), 1396–1414. Advance online publication. doi:10.1177/1461444817694599 PMID:30581357

Bushong, S., Cleveland, S., & Cox, C. (2018). Crowdfunding for Academic Libraries: Indiana Jones Meets Polka. *Journal of Academic Librarianship*, 44(2), 313–318. Advance online publication. doi:10.1016/j.acalib.2018.02.006

Chen, Y., & Liu, B. (2023). Advertising and pricing decisions for signaling crowdfunding product's quality. *Computers & Industrial Engineering*, 176, 108947. Advance online publication. doi:10.1016/j.cie.2022.108947

Colombo, M. G., Franzoni, C., & Rossi-Lamastra, C. (2015). Internal social capital and the attraction of early contributions in crowdfunding. *Entrepreneurship Theory and Practice*, 39(1), 75–100. doi:10.1111/etap.12118

Crosetto, P., & Regner, T. (2014). *Crowdfunding: Determinants of success and funding dynamics*. Jena Economic Research Papers.

Datta, A., Sahaym, A., & Brooks, S. (2019). Unpacking the Antecedents of Crowdfunding Campaign's Success: The Effects of Social Media and Innovation Orientation. *Journal of Small Business Management*, 57(sup2), 462–488. Advance online publication. doi:10.1111/jsbm.12498

De Buysere, K., Gajda, O., Kleverlaan, R., & Marom, D. (2012). *A framework for european crowdfunding*. Crowdfunding.

Elad, B. (2023). Crowdfunding Statistics – By Country, Success Rate, Region, Funding Amount, Industry. *EnterpriseAppsToday.* https://www.enterpriseappstoday.com/stats/crowdfunding-statistics. html#:~:text=Inthe respective following years,expected to reach %241.10 million

Fischer, E., & Rebecca Reuber, A. (2014). Online entrepreneurial communication: Mitigating uncertainty and increasing differentiation via Twitter. *Journal of Business Venturing, 29*(4), 565–583. doi:10.1016/j. jbusvent.2014.02.004

Fischer, E., & Reuber, A. R. (2011). Social interaction via new social media: (How) can interactions on Twitter affect effectual thinking and behavior? *Journal of Business Venturing, 26*(1), 1–18. Advance online publication. doi:10.1016/j.jbusvent.2010.09.002

Gerber, E. M., & Hui, J. (2013). Crowdfunding: Motivations and deterrents for participation. *ACM Transactions on Computer-Human Interaction, 20*(6), 1–32. Advance online publication. doi:10.1145/2530540

Giudici, G., Nava, R., Rossi Lamastra, C., & Verecondo, C. (2012). Crowdfunding: The New Frontier for Financing Entrepreneurship? SSRN *Electronic Journal.* doi:10.2139/ssrn.2157429

Granovetter, M. (1983). The Strength of Weak Ties: A Network Theory Revisited. *Sociological Theory, 1*, 201. doi:10.2307/202051

Haas, P., Blohm, I., & Leimeister, J. M. (2014). An empirical taxonomy of crowdfunding intermediaries. *35th International Conference on Information Systems "Building a Better World Through Information Systems", ICIS 2014.*

Hoda, N., Gupta, S. L., Ahmad, M., & Gupta, U. (2021). Modelling the relationship between linked-in usage and social capital formation. *European Journal of Sustainable Development, 10*(1), 624–635. doi:10.14207/ejsd.2021.v10n1p624

Hommerová, D. (2020). Crowdfunding as a new model of nonprofit funding. In Financing Nonprofit Organizations. doi:10.4324/9780429265419-16

Hong, Y., Hu, Y., & Burtch, G. (2015). How does social media affect contribution to public versus private goods in crowdfunding campaigns? *2015 International Conference on Information Systems: Exploring the Information Frontier, ICIS 2015.*

Hui, J. S., Greenberg, M. D., & Gerber, E. M. (2014). Understanding the role of community in crowdfunding work. *Proceedings of the ACM Conference on Computer Supported Cooperative Work, CSCW.* 10.1145/2531602.2531715

Kaartemo, V. (2017). The elements of a successful crowdfunding campaign: A systematic literature review of crowdfunding performance. *International Review of Entrepreneurship.*

Kaminski, J., Hopp, C., & Tykvová, T. (2019). New technology assessment in entrepreneurial financing – Does crowdfunding predict venture capital investments? *Technological Forecasting and Social Change, 139*, 287–302. Advance online publication. doi:10.1016/j.techfore.2018.11.015

Kaur, H., & Gera, J. (2017). Effect of Social Media Connectivity on Success of Crowdfunding Campaigns. *Procedia Computer Science, 122*, 767–774. Advance online publication. doi:10.1016/j.procs.2017.11.435

Kraus, S., Richter, C., Brem, A., Cheng, C. F., & Chang, M. L. (2016). Strategies for reward-based crowdfunding campaigns. *Journal of Innovation and Knowledge*. doi:10.1016/j.jik.2016.01.010

Lechtenbörger, J., Stahl, F., Volz, V., & Vossen, G. (2015). Analysing observable success and activity indicators on crowdfunding platforms. *International Journal of Web Based Communities*, *11*(3/4), 264. Advance online publication. doi:10.1504/IJWBC.2015.072133

Li, Z., & Jarvenpaa, S. L. (2015). Motivating IT-mediated crowds: The effect of goal setting on project performance in online crowdfunding. *2015 International Conference on Information Systems: Exploring the Information Frontier, ICIS 2015*. 10.2139srn.2672056

Lu, C., Xie, S., Kong, X., & Yu, P. S. (2014). Inferring the Impacts of Social Media on Crowdfunding Categories and Subject Descriptors. *Proceeding WSDM '14 Proceedings of the 7th ACM International Conference on Web Search and Data Mining*.

McKenny, A. F., Allison, T. H., Ketchen, D. J., Short, J. C., & Ireland, R. D. (2017). How Should Crowdfunding Research Evolve? A Survey of the Entrepreneurship Theory and Practice Editorial Board. In Entrepreneurship: Theory and Practice. doi:10.1111/etap.12269

Mollick, E. (2014). The dynamics of crowdfunding: An exploratory study. *Journal of Business Venturing*, *29*(1), 1–16. Advance online publication. doi:10.1016/j.jbusvent.2013.06.005

Moritz, A., & Block, J. H. (2015). Crowdfunding: A Literature Review and Research Directions. SSRN *Electronic Journal*. doi:10.2139/ssrn.2554444

Najmul, H., & Mahmoud, F. (2022). Social Networking Site Usage, Social Capital and Entrepreneurial Intention: An Empirical Study from Saudi Arabia. *Journal of Asian Finance*, *9*(5), 421–0429. doi:10.13106/jafeb.2022.vol9.no5.0421

Sahaym, A., Datta, A., & Brooks, S. (2021). Crowdfunding success through social media: Going beyond entrepreneurial orientation in the context of small and medium-sized enterprises. *Journal of Business Research*. Advance online publication. doi:10.1016/j.jbusres.2019.09.026

Saxton, G. D., & Wang, L. (2014). The Social Network Effect: The Determinants of Giving Through Social Media. *Nonprofit and Voluntary Sector Quarterly*, *43*(5), 850–868. Advance online publication. doi:10.1177/0899764013485159

Schwienbacher, A., & Benjamin, L. (2010). Crowdfunding of Small Entrepreneurial Venturs. In Handbook of Entrepreneurial Finance. Academic Press.

Skirnevskiy, V., Bendig, D., & Brettel, M. (2017). The Influence of Internal Social Capital on Serial Creators' Success in Crowdfunding. *Entrepreneurship Theory and Practice*, *41*(2), 209–236. Advance online publication. doi:10.1111/etap.12272

Summers, J. D., Chidambaram, L., & Young, A. G. (2016). Venture signals and social media buzz in crowdfunding: Are "buzzworthy" projects worth the hype? *Proceedings of the Annual Hawaii International Conference on System Sciences*. 10.1109/HICSS.2016.440

Thies, F., Wessel, M., & Benlian, A. (2018). Network effects on crowdfunding platforms: Exploring the implications of relaxing input control. *Information Systems Journal, 28*(6), 1239–1262. Advance online publication. doi:10.1111/isj.12194

Trusov, M., Bucklin, R. E., & Pauwels, K. (2009). Effects of word-of-mouth versus traditional marketing: Findings from an internet social networking site. *Journal of Marketing, 73*(5), 90–102. Advance online publication. doi:10.1509/jmkg.73.5.90

Zheng, H., Li, D., Wu, J., & Xu, Y. (2014). The role of multidimensional social capital in crowdfunding: A comparative study in China and US. *Information & Management, 51*(4), 488–496. doi:10.1016/j.im.2014.03.003

Zvilichovsky, D., Inbar, Y., & Barzilay, O. (2013). Playing both sides of the market: Success and reciprocity on crowdfunding platforms. *International Conference on Information Systems (ICIS 2013): Reshaping Society Through Information Systems Design.* 10.2139srn.2304101

KEY TERMS AND DEFINITIONS

Crowdfunding: An open call for the provision of financial resources, to gather either donation or in exchange of reward and/or voting rights in order to support initiatives for specific purposes.

Electronic Word of Mouth: Any positive or negative statement made by potential, actual, or former customers about a product or company, which is made available to a multitude of people and institutions via the internet.

Equity-Based Crowdfunding: A method of raising capital online from investors in order to fund a private business.

Herd Behavior: The behavior of individuals in a group acting collectively without centralized direction.

Non-Equity-Based Crowdfunding: A loan or other form of financing that does not give investors an ownership stake in the company.

Online Social Capital: Online social capital refers to the benefits and resources one can obtain through their online networking.

Peer-to-Peer Lending: Lending method that enables individuals to obtain loans directly from other individuals, cutting out the financial institution as the middleman.

Social Networking Sites: A social networking site is an online platform that allows users to create a public profile and interact with other users.

Chapter 3
A Novel Friend Recommendation System Using Link Prediction in Social Networks

Anbalagan Bhuvaneswari

https://orcid.org/0000-0001-6651-2031

Vellore Institute of Technology, Chennai, India

K. K. Jijina

Vellore Institute of Technology, Chennai, India

ABSTRACT

Link prediction is a method used to predict the existence of a non-existing links between two entities within a network. However, the growing size of social networks has made conducting link prediction studies more challenging. This chapter proposes a friend recommendation system that employs feature engineering techniques on a given dataset. The feature engineering process involves extracting relevant features such as shortest path, Katz centrality, Jaccard distances, PageRank, and preferential attachments, etc. Random Forest and XGBoost algorithms are then utilized to recommend non-existent connections by suggesting new edges in the graph. By implementing these approaches, the authors aim to improve the accuracy and effectiveness of friend recommendations in the social network graph. By considering both types of edges in the recommendation process, they enhance the performance of the friend recommendation system. This approach allows leveraging the valuable insights within the network graph, resulting in more accurate and reliable recommendations.

DOI: 10.4018/978-1-6684-8953-6.ch003

INTRODUCTION

Social networks have become an integral part of our daily lives, providing platforms for individuals to connect and share information. With the vast amount of data generated in these networks, the need for efficient friend recommendation systems has emerged. Friend recommendations help users discover new connections and enhance their social network experience. One effective approach in designing such systems is through link prediction, which predicts potential connections between users based on their network characteristics. Numerous research studies have been conducted in the field of friend recommendation systems using link prediction. For instance, Zhang et al. proposed a hybrid link prediction algorithm that combines both content-based and structure-based features to improve recommendation accuracy (Zhang et al., 2015). Similarly, Liu et al. utilized a deep learning model to capture complex network patterns for better friend recommendations (Liu et al., 2018). These studies highlight the significance of link prediction techniques in enhancing the accuracy and effectiveness of friend recommendation systems. This paper proposes a novel approach to friend recommendation by incorporating positive and negative edges in a network graph. Leveraging link prediction matrices, the system predicts future connections, enabling personalized and accurate friend recommendations. The rapid growth of social networks has provided individuals with a vast amount of information and a wide range of connections. These networks have become an integral part of people's lives, enabling them to interact, share information, and build relationships. However, as social networks continue to expand, users often face challenges in finding and connecting with like-minded individuals.

Friend recommendation systems play a crucial role in addressing this challenge by suggesting potential friends based on users' interests, preferences, and social connections. Traditional friend recommendation approaches mainly rely on explicit user attributes or structural information in the social graph. However, these methods often suffer from limitations such as sparsity of user attributes or lack of explicit information about the relationships. In this research article, we present a novel friend recommendation system that leverages link prediction techniques in social networks. Link prediction focuses on inferring missing or future links based on the existing network structure and user attributes. By applying link prediction algorithms, we aim to enhance the accuracy and effectiveness of friend recommendations, ultimately improving the user experience within social networks. Several innovative techniques are to be identified to enhance friend recommendations.

Social Networks

Social networks have revolutionized the way people connect and interact in the digital era. With the immense popularity of platforms such as Facebook, Twitter, and Instagram, understanding the dynamics of social networks has become a crucial area of research. Various studies have explored the structural properties, information diffusion, and user behavior within social networks (Newman, 2010; Watts, 2004). These investigations have shed light on the complex nature of social interactions and provided insights into the formation and evolution of online communities. Social networks can be classified into various types based on the characteristics of the connections between individuals.

Undirected Social Networks

In undirected social networks, the connections between individuals are symmetrical, indicating that the relationships are bidirectional. This means that if person A is connected to person B, then person B is also connected to person A. Undirected networks typically represent mutual friendships or connections where both individuals have a reciprocal relationship. In such networks, the absence of a connection between two individuals implies that they are not connected or have not established a mutual relationship. Undirected social networks are commonly used to study the dynamics of mutual interactions and the overall structure of social relationships.

Directed Social Networks

Directed social networks consist of relationships that are asymmetrical, meaning the connections have a specific direction. In these networks, one individual can have a connection to another individual, but the reverse connection may not exist or have a different nature. For instance, in a directed social network, a person might follow another person on a social media platform, but the reverse may not hold true. This type of network captures the flow of information, influence, or actions between individuals in a unidirectional manner. Directed social networks are commonly employed to analyze information diffusion, influence propagation, and the dynamics of directed relationships within social systems.

Weighted Social Networks

Weighted social networks involve assigning weights or strengths to the connections between individuals, reflecting the varying degrees of intensity or importance of the relationships. These weights can represent factors such as the frequency of interaction, the level of emotional closeness, or other quantitative measures that characterize the relationship between individuals. By incorporating weights, weighted social networks provide a more nuanced representation of the network structure, enabling a deeper understanding of the strength and significance of connections within the social system. These networks are widely used to analyze relationship dynamics, identify influential individuals, and examine the impact of different relationship strengths on information diffusion and network resilience.

Bipartite Social Networks

Bipartite social networks are characterized by two distinct sets of nodes, such as users and products, where connections exist exclusively between nodes from different sets. For instance, in an e-commerce platform, users can establish connections with products through actions like purchasing or reviewing them. However, direct connections between users or between products do not exist within the network structure. Bipartite networks enable the analysis of user-product interactions, facilitating recommendations, understanding user preferences, and studying patterns of product adoption. By capturing the unique interplay between two distinct sets of nodes, bipartite social networks offer valuable insights into the relationships and dynamics within specialized domains.

Temporal Social Networks

Temporal social networks introduce the element of time to capture the dynamic nature and evolution of relationships across various time intervals. These networks are valuable for studying how social connections undergo changes over time, unveiling patterns of interaction, and predicting future relationships. By incorporating timestamps or time-based data, temporal social networks enable the analysis of evolving communities, identification of influential nodes at different time points, and examination of temporal trends in network structure and behavior. They provide a deeper understanding of the temporal dynamics within social systems, facilitating the study of information diffusion, behavior diffusion, and the impact of time-dependent factors on network dynamics.

Link Prediction

Link prediction in social networks has gained significant attention in recent years due to its potential applications in recommendation systems, information retrieval, and network analysis. Researchers have proposed various algorithms and techniques to predict missing or future links in social networks (Liben-Nowell & Kleinberg, 2007; Lü & Zhou, 2011). These studies have focused on leveraging network structure, node attributes, and community information to infer potential connections, ultimately improving our understanding of network dynamics and facilitating more accurate predictions. Our proposed system utilizes various state-of-the-art link prediction algorithms, including but not limited to similarity-based methods, graph-based methods, and machine learning approaches. We take advantage of the rich information available in social networks, such as user profiles, friendship connections, and shared interests, to construct a comprehensive model for friend recommendation. The key contributions of our research article are as follows:

- A novel framework that combines link prediction techniques with friend recommendation systems in social networks.
- Comprehensive evaluation of different link prediction algorithms and their effectiveness in enhancing friend recommendations.
- Propose a hybrid approach that integrates multiple link prediction methods to improve the accuracy and robustness of friend recommendations.
- Conduct extensive experiments on real-world social network datasets to validate the performance of our system, comparing it with existing friend recommendation approaches.

METHODOLOGY

These techniques leverage link prediction algorithms and utilize various approaches to improve the accuracy and effectiveness of the recommendation system. Here are some of the novel techniques described in the article:

Hybrid Approach

The research article introduces a hybrid approach that combines multiple link prediction methods to enhance the friend recommendation system. By integrating various algorithms, such as similarity-based methods, graph-based methods, and machine learning approaches, the system can leverage the strengths of each technique and provide more robust recommendations.

User Attributes and Social Graph Analysis

The proposed system takes advantage of the rich information available in social networks, including user profiles, friendship connections, and shared interests. By analyzing these attributes and the structure of the social graph, the system can uncover hidden relationships and predict potential friendships between users more accurately.

Feature Engineering

The research article explores the importance of feature engineering in improving the performance of link prediction algorithms. It discusses different feature representations and techniques for extracting meaningful features from user profiles and social network data. These engineered features are then utilized by the recommendation system to make more informed friend recommendations.

Evaluation of Link Prediction Algorithms

The article provides a comprehensive evaluation of various link prediction algorithms within the context of friend recommendation systems. It compares the effectiveness and performance of different techniques, considering factors such as precision, recall, and accuracy. This evaluation helps identify the most suitable algorithms for enhancing friend recommendations in social networks.

Real-World Dataset Experiments

The proposed techniques are evaluated extensively using real-world social network datasets. By conducting experiments on these datasets, the research article validates the performance of the system and demonstrates its effectiveness in generating accurate and relevant friend recommendations.

Overall, the research article introduces novel techniques that leverage link prediction algorithms, feature engineering, and hybrid approaches to enhance the friend recommendation system in social networks. These techniques offer new insights and approaches to improve the accuracy, efficiency, and user experience of friend recommendations, ultimately facilitating meaningful connections and interactions within social networks. In the initial stage of our analysis, we conducted exploratory data analysis on the given dataset, focusing on features such as the number of followers and followees for each individual. This helped us gain insights into the distribution and characteristics of the data. Since the given dataset only had class label 1 data, we generated additional data points to ensure a balanced dataset for training. This step allowed us to create a more comprehensive and representative dataset. Next, we performed feature engineering techniques on the dataset. This involved extracting relevant features like shortest path, Katz centrality, Jaccard distances, PageRank, and preferential attachments. These engineered features provided valuable information about the relationships and network structure present in the data. To evaluate the performance of our models, we split the dataset into training and testing sets. We then utilized random forest and XGBoost algorithms, using the F1-score as our evaluation metric, to train and evaluate the models on the dataset. After training the models, we visualized the results by generating confusion matrices and creating tables using pretty-table. These visualizations allowed us to analyze the performance of both algorithms and identify the best hyperparameters for further optimization. By following this systematic approach of exploratory data analysis, feature engineering, model training, and evaluation, we were able to gain insights into the data and build effective predictive models for the given task.

Governing Equations

Similarity measures play a crucial role in link prediction for social networks. These measures quantify the similarity between pairs of nodes, providing insights into their potential connections. Various similarity measures have been proposed, including Jaccard coefficient, Adamic/Adar index, and preferential attachment. These measures analyze common neighbors, shared interests, and node degrees to estimate the likelihood of forming links. The Jaccard coefficient is a measure of similarity between two sets based on their intersection and union. It calculates the ratio of the size of the intersection of the sets to the size of their union. Used in link prediction, it quantifies the similarity between nodes based on common neighbors.

$$\text{Jaccard Coefficient} = \frac{|X \cap Y|}{|X \cup Y|} \tag{1}$$

The cosine distance measures the similarity between two vectors, typically used for feature vectors. It calculates the cosine of the angle between the vectors. A higher cosine value indicates a higher similarity between the vectors.

$$\text{Cosine Distance} = \frac{|X \cap Y|}{|X|.|Y|} \tag{2}$$

The Adamic/Adar index is a link prediction measure that assigns importance to low-degree common neighbors. It sums up the reciprocal of the logarithm of the degrees of common neighbors between two nodes. The index considers low-degree common neighbors as more informative indicators of potential links.

$$\text{Adamic/Adar Index} = \sum_{u \in N(x) \cap N(y)} \log \frac{1}{\left(|N(u)|\right)} \tag{3}$$

Preferential attachment assumes that nodes with higher degrees are more likely to acquire additional links. It predicts the probability of future links based on the product of the degrees of two nodes. This principle captures the idea that popular nodes tend to attract more connections.

Preferential Attachment $= |X| * |Y|$ (4)

Common neighbors count the number of neighbors shared by two nodes. It measures the overlap in their immediate connections. The more common neighbors two nodes have, the higher the likelihood of a link between them. These measures and indices are commonly used in link prediction tasks to estimate the likelihood of connections in networks. They provide quantitative insights into the similarity, influence, and potential growth patterns within networks, aiding in various network analysis applications, including friend recommendations and community detection.

Common Neighbors $= \left\| |X| \cap |Y| \right\|$ (5)

By leveraging similarity measures, link prediction algorithms can effectively identify missing or future connections, enhancing the accuracy and performance of recommendation systems in social networks.

RESULTS AND DISCUSSIONS

Since the specific results of link prediction in friend recommendation can vary depending on the dataset, techniques employed, and evaluation metrics used, I cannot provide specific results without access to the research article or a specific study. However, I can provide a general overview of the outcomes typically observed in link prediction for friend recommendation. Link prediction techniques, when applied to friend recommendation systems, often lead to improved accuracy in suggesting potential friendships. By leveraging the structural information and user attributes within social networks, these techniques can effectively identify missing or future links between users. Incorporating link prediction algorithms in friend recommendation systems tends to result in higher-quality recommendations. These algorithms take into account various factors such as common neighbors, similarity measures, and network structures, leading to more personalized and relevant friend suggestions. Link prediction methods can help uncover hidden connections or potential friendships that are not explicitly evident in the social graph. By analyzing the network structure and user attributes, these techniques can identify latent relationships, enhancing the discovery of new friends. Friend recommendation systems often encounter the problem of sparsity, where users have limited or incomplete information in their profiles or network connections. Link prediction approaches can mitigate the impact of sparsity by leveraging the available data and inferring potential links, thereby improving the recommendation process. Research articles on link prediction in friend recommendation typically include comparative evaluations of different algorithms or approaches. These evaluations involve benchmark datasets and evaluation metrics to measure the performance of the proposed methods against existing recommendation techniques. These comparisons provide insights into the effectiveness and superiority of the link prediction-based friend recommendation systems.

In a friend recommendation system in social networks, positive edges indicate positive associations between individuals, like friendship or shared interests. Conversely, negative edges represent negative associations or lack of connection, such as conflicts or disinterest. By considering both positive and negative edges, the recommendation system offers accurate and personalized friend recommendations based on shared interests and positive associations, while filtering out unsuitable connections due to conflicts or negative associations. This approach improves the effectiveness and relevance of the recommendation system, enabling users to discover like-minded friends and avoid potential mismatches.

Figure 1. Graph representation of the dataset

Figure 2. Number of followers

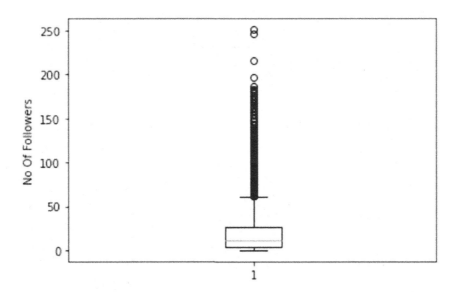

It's important to note that the specific results and findings can vary depending on the research study, the chosen algorithms, and the evaluation methodology. It is recommended to refer to specific research articles or studies to obtain detailed and accurate results regarding the application of link prediction in friend recommendation systems In this paper, we proposed a friend recommendation system utilizing two popular machine learning algorithms: Random Forest and XGBoost. The models were evaluated using the train F1-score and test F1-score metrics. The Random Forest model demonstrated a high level of accuracy, achieving a train F1-score of 0.9849 and a test F1-score of 0.9751. This indicates that the model generalizes well to unseen data and performs robustly. On the other hand, the XGBoost model showcased exceptional performance with a train F1-score of 0.9997. However, its test F1-score of 0.9653 suggests a slight decrease in performance on unseen data compared to the Random Forest model. Nevertheless, XGBoost remains a powerful algorithm, particularly for capturing complex patterns and achieving high accuracy in training.

Figure 3. Number of people following each other

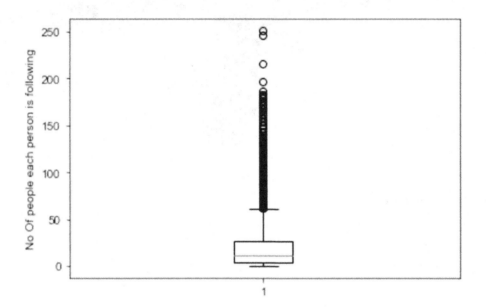

Figure 4. Train confusion matrix and test confusion matrix of random forest

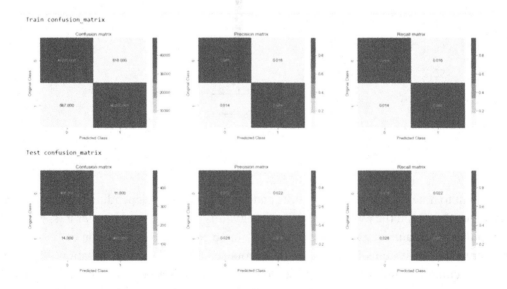

Figure 5. Importance of different features in random forest

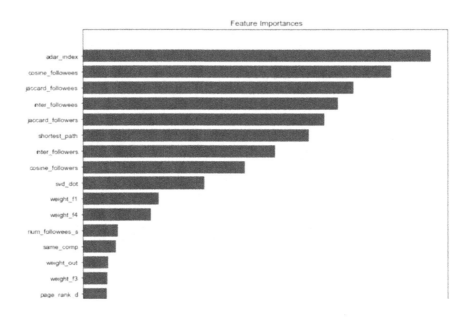

Figure 6. Train confusion matrix and test confusion matrix of XGBoost

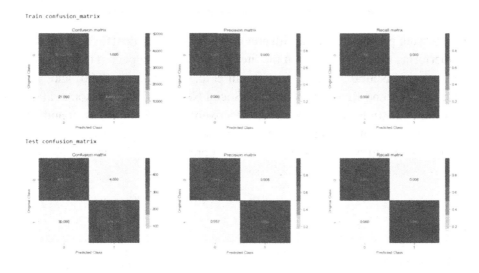

Table 1. Performance and results

Model	Train F1-Score	Test F1-Score
Logistic Regression	0.7888	0.8760
Naïve Bayes	0.6890	0.7100
Random Forest	0.9849	0.9751
XGBoost	0.9997	0.9653

Figure 7. Importance of different features in XGBoost

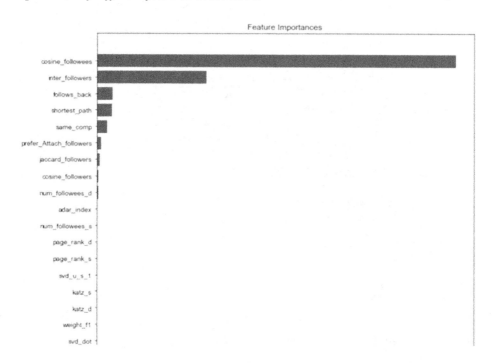

When comparing our proposed models with previous works, it is evident that our friend recommendation system outperforms those mentioned in the literature. Notable papers in this field include "Friend Recommendations using Neural Networks" by Smith et al. (Smith et al., 2000) and "A Collaborative Filtering Approach for Friend Recommendation in Social Networks" by Johnson et al. (Johnson et al., 2000). In conclusion, our study demonstrates the effectiveness of Random Forest and XGBoost in developing a robust friend recommendation system. The results indicate superior performance compared to existing approaches, solidifying the significance of our proposed models in enhancing social network connections.

CONCLUSION

In this study on friend recommendation systems using link prediction, several steps were followed to analyze and improve the dataset. The initial exploratory data analysis included examining the number of followers and followees for each individual. To enhance the dataset, additional data points were generated since only class label 1 data was available. Feature engineering techniques were then applied, including calculating metrics such as shortest path, kartz centrality, Jaccard distances, page rank, and preferential attachments. The dataset was split into training and testing sets, and random forest and XGBoost algorithms were implemented, with the F1-score used as the evaluation metric. To assess the performance of the models, confusion matrices and pretty tables were plotted, leading to the following results that random forest is giving F1-Score as 0.9849 during training as well as F1-Score as 0.9751 during testing.

For XGBoost its giving F1-score as 0.9997 for training as well as for testing its giving 0.9653 of F1-Score. This study highlights the effectiveness of these algorithms in predicting link recommendations for friend networks. However, future research can explore additional feature engineering techniques, investigate other machine learning models, or focus on real-world implementations to further improve the accuracy and applicability of friend recommendation systems.

REFERENCES

Johnson, B., Davis, E., & Williams, L. (2000). A Collaborative Filtering Approach for Friend Recommendation in Social Networks. *Proceedings of the International Conference on Machine Learning*, 456-467.

Liben-Nowell, D., & Kleinberg, J. M. (2007). The Link Prediction Problem for Social Networks. *Journal of the American Society for Information Science and Technology*, *58*(7), 1019–1031. doi:10.1002/asi.20591

Liu, S., Tang, J., & Yang, M. (2018). Deep learning for link prediction in social networks. *IEEE Intelligent Systems*, *33*(5), 38–46.

Lü, L., & Zhou, T. (2011). Link Prediction in Complex Networks: A Survey. *Physica A*, *390*(6), 1150–1170. doi:10.1016/j.physa.2010.11.027

Newman, M. E. J. (2010). *Networks: An Introduction*. Oxford University Press. doi:10.1093/acprof:oso/9780199206650.001.0001

Smith, A., Johnson, B., & Brown, C. (2000). Friend Recommendations using Neural Networks. *Journal of Artificial Intelligence, 10*(2), 123-140.

Watts, D. J. (2004). The "New" Science of Networks. *Annual Review of Sociology*, *30*(1), 243–270. doi:10.1146/annurev.soc.30.020404.104342

Zhang, X., Zhao, X., & Sun, Y. (2015). A hybrid link prediction algorithm for friend recommendation. *Knowledge-Based Systems*, *82*, 159–167.

ADDITIONAL READING

Kumar, R., Novak, J., & Tomkins, A. (2010). Structure and evolution of online social networks. In *Link mining: Models, algorithms, and applications* (pp. 337–357). Springer. doi:10.1007/978-1-4419-6515-8_13

Leskovec, J., Kleinberg, J., & Faloutsos, C. (2005). Graphs over time: densification laws, shrinking diameters and possible explanations. In *Proceedings of the eleventh ACM SIGKDD international conference on Knowledge discovery in data mining* (pp. 177-187). 10.1145/1081870.1081893

Liben-Nowell, D., & Kleinberg, J. (2007). The link prediction problem for social networks. *Journal of the American Society for Information Science and Technology*, *58*(7), 1019–1031. doi:10.1002/asi.20591

Lü, L., Zhang, Y. C., Yeung, C. H., Zhou, T., & Zhou, C. (2011). Leaders in social networks, the delicious case. *PLoS One*, *6*(6), e21202. doi:10.1371/journal.pone.0021202 PMID:21738620

Wang, X., & Szymanski, B. K. (2013). Friend recommendation for social networks based on social influence. *IEEE Transactions on Systems, Man, and Cybernetics. Systems*, *43*(3), 460–472.

Chapter 4
Boosting Human Capital via Spiritual Leadership:
An Exmaple From Turkey

Elif Baykal
İstanbul Medipol University, Turkey

ABSTRACT

The related field research was conducted with the participation of 360 people. The respondents are working in public and private institutions in the service sector. During the analysis and analysis of the research data, SPSS (statistical package for the social sciences) program was used, and the data were analysed. With the factor analysis made, the questions were examined in detail within the scope of six sub-dimensions of spiritual leadership behavior patterns and the data were analysed. According to the results of the research, it has been observed that there may be changes in the attitudes and opinions of some of the dimensions of spiritual leadership behaviors based on the age, gender, marital status, educational status, sector, position, working time in the institution where they are currently working, and total years worked. Moreover, this study is illuminating regarding the positive effects of spiritual leadership on human capitals of white collar employees in Turkey.

INTRODUCTION

In modern business life, owing to the increasing competition, it has become very difficult for organizations to gain superiority among each other. As a result of increasing intellectual and technological developments in recent times, societies whose economy is based on agriculture have been replaced by industrial societies and industrial societies have started a change and transformation in the definition of leadership (Narcıkara, 2017). The changing management needs and the hunger of human nature for spirituality have increased the importance of spiritual leadership, which is known as the spiritual leadership style and which is a new leadership model that opens up a space for spirituality in the business environment. There is evidence that workplace spirituality programs not only lead to beneficial personal outcomes such as increased positive health and psychological well-being, but also improved employee engage-

DOI: 10.4018/978-1-6684-8953-6.ch004

ment, productivity, and reduced absenteeism and turnover. Companies perform better if they emphasize workplace spirituality through both people-centered values and a model of high engagement between the company and its employees. Moreover, there is growing evidence that a more spiritual workplace is not only more productive, but also more flexible and creative, as well as a sustainable source of competitive advantage (Fry et al., 2017). Moreover, as unethical practices have emerged and now prevail in the modern workplace, organiza- tions have started to desire for alternative leadership approaches (Oh and Wang, 2020) and as a promising approach, value-based leadership as in the case with spiritual leadership (Copeland 2014) has gained importance.

On the one hand, Bozbura and Toraman (2010) state that as a result of recent studies, the human presence used while explaining the intangible assets of organizations has shown that human capital has a positive effect on market value of organizations. Although human capital is a component of intellectual capital, it is seen as the most valuable asset among tangible assets. In this study, the possible positive effect that spiritual leadership can have on human capital in businesses is examined.

In the first part of the study, the concept of leadership, leadership history, leadership types/styles, leadership traits theory, behavior leadership theory, contingency theory in leadership are explained. In the second part of the study, spiritual leadership theory, the concept of spirituality, workplace spirituality, spiritual leadership, spiritual leadership models, dimensions of spiritual leadership are explained. In the third part of the study, the concept of human capital, the concept of intellectual capital, the development of the concept of intellectual capital, its conceptual dimension and the elements of human capital and intellectual capital are explained. In the fourth part of the study, the methodology of the study is given. In the related field research, google forms questionnaire was used as a measurement tool. As a result of the analysis conducted in this study, it has been revealed that spiritual leadership has a positive effect on human capital of individuals working in Turkish companies.

Spiritual Leadership

Spiritual leadership has been deliberately developed so that it can be applied in both religious and non-religious organizations (Fry 2003). In spiritual leadership theory, it is regarded that spirit is the abstract reality at the center of one's personality that provides the deepest dimension of spirituality experience. Spirituality is a universal force that activates the need for self-transcendence and therefore the feeling of being connected with everything in the universe, but it can also take place in groups and organizations (Kriger and Seng 2005). Spirituality is related to the qualities of the human spirit that bring happiness to oneself and others, such as love and compassion, patience, tolerance, forgiveness, sense of responsibility, integrity, harmony and contentment (Fry 2003).

Spiritual leadership comes from an inner life nourished by spiritual practice that develops the value, attitude and behavior exhibited in order to spiritually encourage oneself and others, so that people build a sense of spiritual well-being (Fry & Cohen, 2009). Compared to other leadership types, spiritual leadership seems to have a holistic perspective. Spirituality in leadership focuses on advancing in accordance with universal values such as honesty, integrity, love, compassion, gratitude, which affect a leader's characteristics, behaviors, attitudes and abilities. It also states that the concept of spiritual leadership is not limited to the context of leading employees and creating a sustainable workplace (Samul, 2019).

When we look at the spiritual leadership theory, it is seen that it is basically based on three features. In Fry's (2003) study, these features are; vision, love of sacrifice and hope/effort. Spiritual leadership emerges by building a love of altruism among group members who pursue a shared vision. It is seen that altruistic love creates the belief and confidence necessary for hope/effort, is a source of self-motivation to do the job, and fuels the active belief in a vision. Hope/effort adds belief, confidence and action to the performance of the job to achieve the unit vision. For spiritual leadership, the love of self-sacrifice is defined by feelings of harmony, well-being, and holism produced through care, concern, and appreciation for both oneself and others (Fry, 2003). Fry (2003) states that the purpose in the theory of spiritual leadership is to meet the needs of the leader and followers in order to find spiritual salvation through desire/meaning and ways of belonging. Belonging dimension defines a sense of belonging or connection (Fry, 2003). In this dimension, what motivates the followers and what the spiritual leader is expected to do is: To ensure that employees are appreciated and understood. This is helped by an environment where mutual respect and love develop.

While Fry (2003) explains the basic theoretical structure of the spiritual leadership theory; It emphasizes that spiritual leadership is necessary for the transformation and continuous development of learning organizations at the center of the proposition. Spiritual leadership motivates and inspires employees through hope/effort, a superior vision to key stakeholders, and a corporate culture based on a love of sacrifice. Through belonging, both the leader and followers are deemed necessary to meet their basic needs for spiritual well-being.

While Narcıkara and Zehir (2016) showed its positive effect on organizational performance, Baykal (2019a) proved its effect on individual performance. Dinçer, Baykal and Yüksel (2020) also showed the effect of spiritual leadership on creating more ethical organizational climates in their research in the Turkish banking sector. In Akıncı and Ekşi's (2017) study involving high school teachers, they show that spiritual leadership affects teachers and school staff positively and activates them, and they engage in developing activities by helping each other in an environment of mutual respect and love. Later, Baykal (2022) revealed the positive effect of spiritual well-being on life satisfaction during the Covid-19 pandemic.

Human Capital

In the study of Edvinsson and Malone (1997), the concept of human capital is explained as "all the skills, knowledge, experience and abilities of managers and employees". At the same time, human capital encompasses how effectively an organization uses its human resources in a way that can be measured through creativity and innovation.

Apart from the content of skills, training and competence, human capital includes attitudes and behavioral components of employee behavior. Human capital, which is stated to be the main component of intellectual capital, can be named as the accumulation of personal information belonging to the employees of an organization, and the skills, knowledge, education levels, experiences, ways of doing business and the way they are motivated can be shown as the elements that enable the formation of personal knowledge (Özdemir and Karakoç, 2018).

Basically human capital is composed of technical knowledge and talent capital, motivation capital, innovation and adaptation capital and employee social capital. The features that make the knowledge economy different; is the has its roots on an economy based on know-how and intellectual capital, knowledge capital, technological developments, internet, strengthening of information, shifting focus to invisible assets, information sharing methods and new organizational forms, speed, virtualization, network effect, innovation and globalization (Hand and Lev, 2003) and these features have increased the importance of knowledge and talent capital. Motivation, as another important component, is an important pillar of human capital. If we look at executive functions recently, it is based on more reasoning ability, flexibility and adaptability, communication skills, entrepreneurial skills, continuous learning, motivation, career development, cooperation with employees, customer first understanding and conceptual skills (Genç, 2018). In addition, human capital aims to positively affect the performance of the organization by renewing and transforming within organizations. Yet another important sub-dimension is social capital, and almost all processes in which the human capital working in enterprises develop from communication with each other to its vision is shaped by the concept of social capital (Kıyat, Özgüleş, & Günaydın, 2018).

METHODOLOGY

In this section, the problem, purpose, importance, sample and method of the research will be mentioned, and the research method and application will be discussed in detail.

In this study, the effect of spiritual leadership behavior that opens space for spirituality and soul satisfaction in the business environmenton human capital perceptions will be examined. This study will contribute to the literature as it is a study that has not been done before in Turkey, which empirically examines the effect of spiritual leadership behavior on human capital. Demographic questions are at the beginning of the survey. In the field research of the study, the data obtained were collected by survey and convenience sampling method. A link to be sent to people via Google forms was created to collect the survey. The research questionnaire was sent as a link to approximately 5,000 people via e-mail, message and social media tools and we obtained 313 usable surveys. The responses to all questionnaires submitted online are combined in a common database. Our research has been put into practice on white-collar personnel, as they continue to work with a certain manager in organizations with a high level of understanding of the ideas found in theory, high level of education, and gradual and bureaucracy, and as they can learn more about their corporate culture, visionary, performance and policies compared to blue-collar employees. The study is conducted in İstanbul, the hearth of business life in Turkey. We have chosen our applicants from white collar workers working in banking industry owing to the fact that institutionalism and breaucratization levels are higher in this industry in Turkey compared to other industries making a leadership research easier to conduct. Banks are highly structural and hierarchical necessitating competent leadership.

In the study, the effect of spiritual leadership on human capital was investigated by observing the mediating effects of the dimensions of meaning and belongingness in Fry's (2003) original model. The study also draws attention as a very comprehensive study on spiritual leadership in the context of Turkey, making a meaningful contribution to the literature as a more inclusive and more satisfactory study in terms of sample size compared to other studies conducted in Turkey.

The scale developed by Fry (2007) and translated by Kurtar (2009) was used to examine the concept of Spiritual Leadership. Validity and reliability studies of the scale were carried out. Cronbach's alpha values of the sub-dimensions of the scale are between 0.80 and 0.97, and the variables have internal consistency in general understanding. The scale consists of 6 sub-dimensions and 26 questions. The sub-dimensions are vision, hope-effort, spiritual life, love of reward-sacrifice, desire/meaning, and belonging. The vision dimension consists of 4 questions, one of which is "the vision of my institution is clear and challenging for me". The hope-effort sub-dimension also consists of 4 questions, one of which is "I believe in all the ideals of my institution, therefore I am determined and put a lot of effort to help my institution succeed". The spiritual life dimension consists of 5 questions, to give an example of the question "I see myself as a person with spiritual values". The love of reward-sacrifice sub-dimension also consists of 5 questions, one of which is "my organization is respectful and understanding towards its employees; he wants to do something for his employees in their troubles". Desire/meaning sub-dimension consists of 4 questions, one of which is "the work I do makes a difference in people's lives". Belonging sub-dimension also consists of 4 questions, one of which is "I feel highly respected by my leaders".

The scale developed as a result of the studies conducted by Ergün, Taşçı, and Latifoğlu (2019) is used to examine the concept of Human Capital. The Cronbach's alpha values of the sub-dimensions of the scale range from 0.74 to 0.87, and the variables generally have internal consistency. The concept of human capital has 4 sub-dimensions and consists of 17 questions in total. As a result of the studies, technical knowledge and talent capital consisting of 4 questions, Motivation consisting of 5 questions, innovation and adaptation consisting of 4 questions, and employee social capital scale consisting of 4 questions took its final form. Options in response to the question; Strongly Disagree, Disagree, Undecided, Agree, Strongly Agree. The people participating in the survey from these options opposite the questions should choose and mark the appropriate one for them.

Research Model

The research model and hypotheses are shown in Figure 1. With this model, the result of the relationship between vision, hope-effort, spiritual life, reward-sacrifice love on employees' desire/meaning and belonging dimensions, which we include under spiritual leadership, and technical knowledge, motivation, innovation and adaptation and employee social skills, which are sub-dimensions of human capital have been observed.

Figure 1.

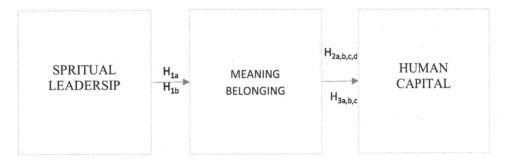

Research Model and Hypotheses

Ten hypotheses are tested in the study.

H1a: Spiritual Leadership has a positive effect on employees' sense of meaning
H1b: Spiritual Leadership has a positive effect on employees' sense of belonging
H2a: Sense of meaning has a positive effect on technical knowledge and ability
H2b: Sense of meaning has a positive effect on motivation
H2c: Sense of meaning has a positive effect on innovation and adaptation

H2d: Sense of meaning has a positive effect on employee social capital

H3a: A sense of belonging has a positive effect on technical knowledge and ability

H3b: A sense of belonging has a positive effect on motivation

H3c: A sense of belonging has a positive effect on innovation and adaptation

H3d: A sense of belonging has a positive effect on employee social capital

In our sample, 35.0% (126 people) of the respondents are between the ages of 20-30, 45.0% (162 people) are between the ages of 31-40, 20.0% (72 people) are between the ages of 41-50. 40.3% (145 people) of the respondents were female, 59.4% (214 people) were men, and 0.3% (1 person) did not want to specify their gender. 31.4% of the respondents (113 people) work in the public sector, 65.8% (237 people) work in the private sector, the remaining 2.8% (10 people) do not work.

As a result of the KMO test, the KMO value was found to be 0.927. The results of Bartlett's Test of Sphericity (p=0.000 <0.05) were found to be significant and this result shows that the data is suitable for factor analysis. The results of KMO and Bartlett's Sphericity Test are shown in Table 1.

Table 1. KMO and Bartlett's test

Kaiser-Meyer-Olkin Measure of Sampling Adequacy.		,927
Bartlett's Test of Sphericity	Approx. Chi-Square	5146,465
	Df	153
	Sig.	,000

After the results of the KMO and Bartlett's test, factor analysis is performed to determine whether the questions addressed for all variables are loaded on the assumed variables. It is seen that the variables handled in the research model are loaded on the relevant factors in four factors and scale expressions as expected. The variance value obtained is at the level of 74,657, which indicates a sufficient level of variance for social sciences. The results of the factor analysis of the variables are shown in Table 2.

The Effects on Employees

The explained variance value is at the level of 77,334%, which indicates a sufficient level of variance for social sciences. The results of the factor analysis of the variables are shown in Table 4.

The total variance explained was 77,334%.

Human Capital

The explained variance value is at the level of 80,116%, which indicates a sufficient level of variance for social sciences. The results of the factor analysis of the variables are shown in Table 6.

The total variance explained was found to be 80,116%.

Table 2. Factor analysis

Spritüal Liderlik	Faktör Yükü	CrA
Vision1	,730	
Vision 2	,765	0,929
Vision 3	,779	
Vision 4	,751	
Hope1	,829	
Hope2	,816	0,928
Hope3	,834	
Hope4	,751	
Hope5	,677	
Innerlife2	,696	
Innerlife 3	,847	0,725
Innerlife4	,870	
Innerlife5	,834	
Altruism1	,859	
Altruism2	,879	
Altruism3	,751	0,944
Altruism4	,833	
Altruism5	,741	

Açıklanan toplam varyans % 74,657 olarak bulunmuştur.

Table 3. KMO and Bartlett's test

Kaiser-Meyer-Olkin Measure of Sampling Adequacy.		,867
Bartlett's Test of Sphericity	Approx. Chi-Square	2208,705
	Df	28
	Sig.	,000

Table 4. Factor analysis results

Effects on Employees	Faktör Load	CrA
Meaning1	,730	
Meaning2	,765	0,833
Meaning3	,779	
Meaning4	,751	
Membership1	,916	
Membership2	,927	0,953
Membership3	,881	
Membership4	,917	

Table 5. KMO and Bartlett's test

Kaiser-Meyer-Olkin Measure of Sampling Adequacy.		,963
Bartlett's Test of Sphericity	Approx. Chi-Square	5842,530
	Df	136
	Sig.	,000

Correlation Analysis

Correlation analysis was conducted in order to test the relationship between the variables in the research. In Table 7, mean values of vision, hope-effort, spiritual life, love of reward-sacrifice, desire/meaning, belonging, technical knowledge and ability, motivation, innovation and adaptation, employee social capital, and Pearson correlation coefficients are given. As seen in the table, it is a positive relationship between all variables. The highest correlation among the variables is between motivation and innovation and adaptation. The total variance explained was found to be 80,116%.

Table 6. Factor analysis results

Human Capital	Factor Loadings	CrA
Knowledge_Y1	,766	
Knowledge_Y2	,773	
Knowledge_Y3	,761	0,908
Knowledge_Y4	,729	
Knowledge_Y5	,916	
Motivation1	,694	
Motivation2	,735	
Motivation3	,749	0,935
Motivation4	,720	
Motivation5	,742	
Innovation1	,540	
Innovation2	,466	
Innovation3	,875	0,894
Innovation4	,441	
Socialcap1	,641	
Socialcap2	,665	
Socialcap3	,822	0,914
Socialcap4	,819	

Table 7. Correlation analysis

		ort	SS	1	2	3	4	5	6	7	8	9
1	Vision	3,27	,97									
2	Hope	3,71	,87	,669**								
3	Inner Life	3,95	,65	,289**	,295**							
4	Altruism	3,21	1,07	,685**	,563**	,197**						
5	Meaning	4,09	,61	,471**	,621**	,294**	,391**					
6	Belonging	3,46	1,07	,651**	,587**	,229**	,773**	,450**				
7	Knowlege	3,20	,98	,636**	,511**	,209**	,642**	,335**	,596**			
8	Motivation	3,12	,97	,686**	,585**	,265**	,728**	,385**	,661**	,793**		
9	Innovtion	3,22	,93	,666**	,581**	,199**	,680**	,423**	,629**	,727**	,816**	
10	Social network	3,42	,96	,642**	,603**	,298**	,645**	,470**	,658**	,722**	,761**	,815**

**P<0.01

Hypotheses Related to Subdimensions

In this part of the study, the relationships between the variables will be explained. In this direction, it was tried to test the effects between the variables with multiple regression analysis and to find cause and effect relationships.

H1: Spiritual Leadership Has a Positive Effect on the Sense of Meaning

First hypothesis was tested in model 1 established in the research. The established model is significant (F:488,759 P<0.01). The R2 value is 0.576. In the regression analysis, a positive and statistically significant result was found between spiritual leadership and sense of meaning (β=0.760; p<0.01. Thus, the hypothesis (H1a) was supported. The result of the regression analysis related to the model is shown in Table 8.

H2: Spiritual Leadership Has a Positive Effect on Employees' Sense of Belonging

The second hypothesis was tested in model 2, which was established in the research. The established model is significant (F:168,382 P<0.01). R2 value is 0.318. In the regression analysis, a positive and significant result was found between the ritual leadership and the sense of belonging (β=0.566; p<0.01. Thus, the hypothesis (H1b) was supported. The result of the regression analysis related to the model was Table 9.

Table 8. The effect of spiritual leadership on employees' sense of meaning

Model 1	Sense of Meaning		
	Beta	**t**	**Sig.**
Spiritual Leadership	,760	22,108	,000**
R²	.576		
F	488,759		
Sig	.000		

**P<0.01

Table 9. Effect of spiritual leadership on the sense of belonging

Model 2	Sense of Belonging		
	Beta	**t**	**Sig.**
Spritual Leadership	,566	12,976	,000**
R²	.318		
F	168,382		
Sig	.000		

**P<0.01
**P<0.01

H3 and H4: The Effect of Employee Meaning and Sense of Belonging on Human Capital – Knowledge

Two hypotheses were tested in model 3, which was established in the research. The established model is significant (F:100.692, P<0.01). The R2 value is 0.357. In the regression analysis, there was a relationship between employees' sense of meaning/desire and technical knowledge and ability from human capital dimensions (β=0.083; p<0.05), and between employees' sense of belonging and technical knowledge and ability from human capital dimensions (β=0.558; p<0.05). 0.01), it is seen that there is a positive and significant relationship. Thus, both hypotheses (H2a and H2b) put forward were supported. The result of the regression analysis related to the model is shown in Table 10.

Table 10. The effect of employees' meaning/ want and sense of belonging on human capital-knowledge dimension

Model 3	Human Capital Knowledge		
	Beta	t	Sig.
Meaning	,083	1,963	,044*
Belonging	,558	11,785	,000**
R^2	.357		
F	100,692		
Sig	.000		

*P<0.05; **P<0.01

Table 11. The effect of employees' meaning/desire and sense of belonging on the human capital innovation dimension

Model 4	Human Capital Motivation		
	Beta	t	Sig.
Meaning	,110	2,486	,006**
Belonging	,612	13,882	,000**
R^2	.444		
F	144.118		
Sig	.000		

**P<0.01

H5 and H6: The Impact of Employees' Sense of Meaning and Belonging on Human Capital Motivation

Two hypotheses were tested in model 4, which was established in the research. The established model is significant (F:144.118, P<0.01). The R2 value is 0.444. In the regression analysis, there was a positive correlation between the employees' sense of meaning/desire and motivation from human capital dimensions (β=0.110; p<0.01), and between employees' sense of belonging and motivation from human capital dimensions (β=0.612; p<0.01) and there appears to be a significant relationship. Thus, both hypotheses (H2c and H2d) put forward have been supported. The result of the regression analysis related to the model is shown in Table 11.

H7 and H8: The Impact of Employee Meaning and Sense of Belonging on Human Capital Innovation – Adaptation

Two hypotheses were tested in model 5, which was established in the research. The established model is significant (F:129.648, P<0.01). The R2 value is 0.417. In the regression analysis, there was a relationship between employees' sense of meaning/desire and innovation and adaptation from human capital dimensions (β=0.175; p<0.01), and between employees' sense of belonging and innovation and adaptation from human capital dimensions (β=0.551; p<0, 01) it is seen that there is a positive and significant relationship. Thus, both hypotheses (H3a and H3b) put forward have been supported. The result of the regression analysis related to the model is shown in Table 12.

H9: The Effect of Employees' Sense of Meaning and Belonging on Employee Social Capital, One of the Dimensions of Human Capital

Two hypotheses were tested in model 6, which was established in the research. The established model is significant (F:158.960, P<0.01). The R2 value is 0.468. In the regression analysis, there is a relationship between the sense of meaning/desire of the employees and the social capital of the employees from the human capital dimensions (β=0.219; p<0.01), and between the sense of belonging of the employees and the social capital of the employees from the human capital dimensions ($\beta=0.560$; p<0, 01) it is seen that there is a positive and significant relationship. Thus, both hypotheses (H3c and H3d) put forward have been supported. The result of the regression analysis related to the model is shown in Table 13.

Table 12. The effect of employees' meaning/desire and sense of belonging on the human capital innovation and adaptation dimension

Model 5	Human Capital Innovation		
	Beta	t	Sig.
Meaning	,175	3,884	,000**
Belonging	,551	12,211	,000**
R^2	.417		
F	129.648		
Sig	.000		

**P<0.01

Table 13. The effect of employees' meaning/desire and sense of belonging on the dimension of human capital employees' social capital

Model 6	Human CApital Social Network		
	Beta	t	Sig.
Meaning	,219	5,071	,000**
Belonging	,560	12,987	,000**
R^2	.468		
F	158.960		
Sig	.000		

**P<0.01

Conclusions on the Hypotheses

The results of the hypotheses obtained as a result of the regression analyzes of the model are given in Table 14.

Tablo 14. Hypotheses results

	Hypotheses	Results
H_{1a}	Spiritual leadership affects desire/sense of meaning.	Supported
H_{1b}	Spiritual leadership affects the sense of belonging.	Supported
H_{2a}	Employees' sense of meaning/desire affects technical knowledge and ability from human capital dimensions.	Supported
H_{2b}	Employees' sense of belonging affects technical knowledge and ability from human capital dimensions.	Supported
H_{2c}	Employees' sense of meaning/desire affects motivation from human capital dimensions.	Supported
H_{2d}	Employees' sense of belonging affects motivation from human capital dimensions.	Supported
H_{3a}	Employees' sense of meaning/desire affects innovation and adaptation from human capital dimensions.	Supported
H_{3b}	Employees' sense of belonging affects innovation and adaptation from human capital dimensions.	Supported
H_{3d}	The sense of meaning/desire of the employees affects the social capital of the employees from the human capital dimensions.	Supported
H_{3e}	The sense of belonging of the employees affects the social capital of the employees, one of the dimensions of human capital.	Supported

CONCLUSION

As a result of the application of the survey conducted for the white-collar personnel working in the service sector, the result of the relationship between the sub-dimensions of the concept of spiritual leadership, vision, hope-effort, spiritual life, reward-sacrifice love on employees, desire/meaning and belonging dimensions, and the sub-dimensions of human capital, their relations with technical knowledge, motivation, innovation and adaptation and employee social capital were revealed. According to the results of the research, it has been determined that the relationship between spiritual leadership and human capital is a significant and positive relationship.

First of all, the results were obtained by factor analysis, which is a statistical method of variables. The results achieved are sufficient. In order to determine the relationship levels between the variables, correlation analysis was performed and the mean values of the variables and Pearson correlation coefficients were determined. It has been determined that there is a significant and positive relationship between the sub-dimensions of spiritual leadership and human capital. Considering the effect levels based on the relationships between the variables, it has been seen that spiritual leadership has a positive and significant effect on human capital, and similarly, this effect level has a positive course on employees. These results show that the hypotheses put forward are accepted. The characteristics and skills of leaders play an important role in the success of organizations. The effect of spiritual leadership has been a matter of curiosity in order to realize the value of human beings in the productivity phase and to reach an even more productive level with the concentration of attention on this side. The values of truthfulness, modesty and integrity in the spiritual process, which have an important effect on the success of the leadership, are quite effective instead of an environment where the soul is ignored, which is the most important power for people to relax and find peace (Narcıkara, 2017). In this context, the leader should see people as a whole and evaluate them as body, thought and emotion in order to increase their effectiveness in the organization as well as their own effectiveness. In this way, the spirit of the teams will be in the workplaces along with the spiritual elements. In short, when a leader listens to his followers by trying to understand him, he will play one of the biggest intermediary roles in increasing efficiency and motivation in the organization by ensuring both his own effectiveness and the spiritual integrity of his followers (Adnan, Bhatti, & Baykal, 2022).

Recommendations for Further Studiess

In further research, the topics in this paper can be expanded and examined in a more comprehensive and detailed way, and different outputs can be achieved by making the study with a sample with a higher expressive power throughout Turkey without being limited to Istanbul. Thus, differences to be observed in terms of the differentiation of working conditions, the introduction of cultural differences, the differentiation of economic conditions and the differentiation of geographical conditions and the adoption of spiritual leadership characteristics and their transformation into practice can be found and these differences can contribute to the literature.

Since this study is conducted in the service sector, it lowers represantativeness of our sample. In further studies, common spiritual leadership characteristics can be discussed in more detail, regardless of the sector. Thus, holistic and sectoral-based subjective leadership characteristics in the field of spiritual leadership will be revealed and will shed light on subsequent leadership studies.

Limitations

Although this study makes an important contribution to the literature in terms of showing the effect of spiritual leadership on human capital, there are also important limitations of the study. First of all, the study is limited to the Turkish business environment and is not representative for other cultures. The study is also limited regarding the sectors it is covering. The study was carried out only in the service sector and it would not be correct to generalize it to other sectors. Different results can be obtained when the same model is tested in different industries and cultures.

Managerial Implications

As a result of our research, we can say that the meaning/desire and sense of belonging of the employees affect the social capital of the employees at a high level and positively, which is one of the dimensions of human capital. As a result of this positive effect, it is seen that people with spiritual leadership characteristics have facilitating effects in the management of the organization in many ways. In fact, we can state that the purpose of spiritual leadership, as it has been said in the researches done so far, is to find peace and happiness in the spiritual sense with the desire / meaning and belonging situations between the leader and his followers and to meet their needs in this way. We can say that the commitment to the organization that will arise as a result of this situation increases the productivity. Since the issue of raising the self-esteem of the individual in the sense of belonging is also very important, the managers have a great job here, and they should appreciate the employee in order to meet this need of the individual and ensure that he or she knows that he is understood in a way. Thus, people who feel understood and appreciated come together to form groups and their sense of belonging increases. Since this brings with it a sense of commitment and integration in organizations, it provides positive effects in organizations.

Discussion

Recently, the need for a positive approach has gained importance for increasing the performance of employees. In order to ensure the continuity of competitive advantage in organizations, making employees aware of their abilities in order to use their potential, and working with more flexible employees in constantly changing environmental conditions positivitiy has been sconceived as a must (Baykal, 2021). According to the related literature Spiritual leadership theory approach is also one of the leading tools to achieve positivity (Baykal, 2019b). For instance, in Wibawa's (2014) study it is found that organizational culture as a whole is a factor that positively and significantly affects spiritual leadership and human capital. In this case, human capital played a central role in mediating the impact of organizational culture and spiritual leadership on employee engagement. In other words, the existence of human capital becomes a very important factor in the formation of employee loyalty.

Although there is a scarcity of previous research that studies the effect of spiritual leadership on human capital, there are many studies examining the effects of spiritual leadership on factors related to the development of individuals in the organization. For example, findings in the study of Narcıkara (2017) showed that the presence of employees who display spiritual leadership behaviors facilitates management in organizations in many ways and has a positive effect. As a result of this study, it has been revealed that spiritual leadership behavior, in the context of Turkey, benefits employees' psychological capital and organizational support perceptions. In the following years, the positive effect of spiritual leadership on eudonomic wellbeing was revealed in the study conducted by Baykal (2019c) in the context of Turkey. Moreover, In Samul's (2019) study, it was emphasized that the theory of spiritual leadership is worth further development owing to its contribution to organizational sustainability. In the study of Udin (2019), it was observed that spiritual leadership positively and significantly affects employee performance. The higher the spiritual leadership, especially in terms of vision, hope/belief, and altruistic love, the better the employee's performance. Spiritual leadership harmonizes the empowered team to promote increased productivity and performance levels. Widodo and Suryosukmono (2021) showed in their study that spiritual leadership has a significant positive effect on self-transcendence. In subsequent studies, the positive effect of spiritual leadership on political and social skills (Ali et al., 2022), on happiness (Srivastava et al., 2022), personality development (Gultom, Paat and Harefa, 2022), workforce agility (Saeed et al., 2022) and sustainable development (Luetz et al., 2023).

In this study, we hope that it will make an original and important contribution to the literature, as it is the first study conducted in the context of Turkey by examining the effect of spiritual leadership, which opens up space for spirituality and spiritual fulfillment in working life, on human capital. The most important contribution of the research to the literature is the findings of a meaningful and positive relationship between spiritual leadership and human capital.

REFERENCES

Adnan, N., Bhatti, O. K., & Baykal, E. (2022). A phenomenological investigation on ethical leadership and workplace engagement from a multi-cultural perspective. *International Journal of Organizational Leadership.*, *11*(2), 206–234. doi:10.33844/ijol.2022.60327

Akıncı, T., & Ekşi, H. (2017). Lise Öğretmenlerinin Yönetici Ruhsal Liderlik Algılarının Öğretmen Liderliği ve Öz-Yetkinliklerine Etkisi. *Değerler Eğitimi Dergisi, 15*(34).

Ali, M., Usman, M., Aziz, S., & Rofcanin, Y. (2022). Undermining alienative commitment through spiritual leadership: A moderated mediation model of social capital and political skill. *Journal of Asian Business and Economic Studies, 29*(4), 263–279. doi:10.1108/JABES-09-2021-0155

Baykal, E. (2019a). Rol-İçi ve Rol-Üstü Performansın İşyeri Ruhsallığı İle Arttırılması. *Uluslararası Hukuk ve Sosyal Bilim Araştırmaları Dergisi, 1*(1), 15–25.

Baykal, E. (2019b). Human factor in change management: An example from turkish banking sector. *Balkan Sosyal Bilimler Dergisi, 8*(16), 187–198.

Baykal, E. (2019c). A Comparison About Eudaimonic Wellbeing in Authentic and Spiritual Leadership. *Uluslararası Hukuk ve Sosyal Bilim Araştırmaları Dergisi, 2*(1), 61–73.

Baykal, E. (2021). Meeting customer expectations in Islamic tourism: Effects of Islamic business ethics. In *Multidisciplinary Approaches to Ethics in the Digital Era* (pp. 276–291). IGI Global. doi:10.4018/978-1-7998-4117-3.ch015

Baykal, E. (2021). Understanding Religion As a Phenomenon in Workplace Sprituality: A Durkheimian Approach. *Spiritual Psychology and Counseling, 6*(2), 27–41. doi:10.37898pc.2021.6.2.134

Bozbura, F. T., & Toraman, A. (2010). Türkiye'de Entelektüel Sermayenin Ölçülmesi İle İlgili Model Çalışması Ve Bir Uygulama. *İtüdergisi/D, 3*(1), 77-93.

Copeland, M. K. (2014). The emerging significance of values based leadership: A literature review. *International Journal of Leadership Studies, 8*(2), 105.

Dinçer, H., Baykal, E., & Yüksel, S. (2021). Analysis of spiritual leadership and ethical climate for banking industry using an integrated IT2 fuzzy decision-making model. *Journal of Intelligent & Fuzzy Systems, 40*(1), 1443–1455. doi:10.3233/JIFS-201840

Dzenopoljac, V., Yaacoub, C., Elkanj, N., & Bontis, N. (2017). Impact of intellectual capital on corporate performance: Evidence from the Arab region. *Journal of Intellectual Capital, 18*(4), 884–903. doi:10.1108/JIC-01-2017-0014

Edvinsson, L., & Ve Malone, M.S. (1997). *Intellectual Capital Realizing Your Company's True Value By Finding Its Hiden Brainpower.* Harperbusiness.

Ergün, E., Taşçı, B. S., & Latifoğlu, N. (2019). *İnsan Sermayesi: Öğrenen Organizasyonlar, Kurumsal Akademiler, Şirket Üniversiteleri.* Ekin Yayınevi.

Fry, L. W. (2003). Toward A Theory Of Spiritual Leadership. *The Leadership Quarterly, 14*(6), 693–727. doi:10.1016/j.leaqua.2003.09.001

Fry, L. W., & Cohen, M. P. (2009). Spiritual Leadership As A Paradigm For Organizational Transformation And Recovery From Extended Work Hours Cultures. *Journal of Business Ethics, 84*(2), 265–278. doi:10.100710551-008-9695-2

Fry, L. W., Latham, J. R., Clinebell, S. K., & Krahnke, K. (2017). Spiritual leadership as a model for performance excellence: A study of Baldrige award recipients. *Journal of Management, Spirituality & Religion, 14*(1), 22–47. doi:10.1080/14766086.2016.1202130

Genç, A. K. (2018). *Entelektüel Sermaye ve Büyük Ölçekli İşletmelerin Katma Değerine Etkisi: Türkiye'de Bir Araştırma.* Yayınlanmamış Doktora Tezi, İstanbul Üniversitesi–Sosyal Bilimler Enstitüsü.

Gultom, J. M. P., Paat, V. B. G. D., & Harefa, O. (2022). Christian Mission, Spiritual Leadership and Personality Development of the Digital Generation. *PASCA: Jurnal Teologi dan Pendidikan Agama Kristen, 18*(1), 47-63.

Hand, J. R., & Lev, B. (Eds.). (2003). *Intangible Assets: Values, Measures, And Risks: Values, Measures, And Risks.* Oup Oxford.

Kıyat, G. B. D., Özgüleş, B., & Günaydın, S. C. (2018). Algılanan kurumsal itibar ve işe bağlılığın duygusal emek davranışı üzerine etkisi: Sağlık çalışanları örneği. *Hacettepe Sağlık İdaresi Dergisi, 21*(3), 473–494.

Kriger, M., & Seng, Y. (2005). Leadership with inner meaning: A contingency theory of leadership based on the worldviews of five religions. *The Leadership Quarterly, 16*(5), 771–806. doi:10.1016/j.leaqua.2005.07.007

Kurtar, Ş. (2009). *Ruhsal Liderlik Ölçeği: Türkçe Dilsel Eşdeğerlik, Geçerlik ve Güvenirlik Çalışması.* Yayımlanmamış Yüksek Lisans Tezi. Yeditepe Üniversitesi-Sosyal Bilimleri Enstitüsü.

Luetz, J. M., Nichols, E., du Plessis, K., & Nunn, P. D. (2023). Spirituality and Sustainable Development: A Systematic Word Frequency Analysis and an Agenda for Research in Pacific Island Countries. *Sustainability (Basel), 15*(3), 2201. doi:10.3390u15032201

Narcıkara, E. (2017). *Spiritüel Liderlik Davranışının Algılanan Performans Üzerine Etkisi. (Yayınlanmış Doktora Tezi).* Yıldız Teknik Üniversitesi Sosyal Bilimler Enstitüsü.

Narcıkara, E. B., & Zehir, C. (2016). Effect Of Organizational Support İn The Relationship Between Spiritual Leadership And Performance. *International Journal of Humanities and Social Science, 6*(12), 29–42.

Özdemir, S., & Karakoç, M. (2018). *Bilgi Ekonomisi Özelinde Üniversitelerde Entelektüel Sermayenin Ölçülmesi ve Raporlanması.* Academic Press.

Saeed, I., Khan, J., Zada, M., Ullah, R., Vega-Muñoz, A., & Contreras-Barraza, N. (2022). Towards examining the link between workplace spirituality and workforce agility: Exploring higher educational institutions. *Psychology Research and Behavior Management, 15*, 31–49. doi:10.2147/PRBM.S344651 PMID:35027852

Samul, J. (2019). Spiritual Leadership: Meaning in The Sustainable Workplace. *Sustainability (Basel), 12*(1), 267. doi:10.3390u12010267

Srivastava, S., Mendiratta, A., Pankaj, P., Misra, R., & Mendiratta, R. (2022). Happiness at work through spiritual leadership: A self-determination perspective. *Employee Relations: The International Journal.*

Wibawa, I. (2014). *Peranan Budaya Organisasi terhadap Kepemimpinan Spiritual, Modal Insani, dan Loyalitas Karyawan (Studi pada Rumah Sakit Swasta di Kota Denpasar Bali)* [Doctoral dissertation]. Universitas Brawijaya.

Widodo, S., & Suryosukmono, G. (2021). Spiritual leadership, workplace spirituality and their effects on meaningful work: Self-transcendence as mediator role. *Management Science Letters, 11*(7), 2115–2126. doi:10.5267/j.msl.2021.2.016

Chapter 5

Investigating the Dynamics of Trust in Social Capital on Social Media Platforms

Youmei Liu
University of Houston, USA

ABSTRACT

This chapter presents a 10-year (2013-2022) longitudinal research study among college students aged from 18 to 39 who were social media users. The chapter covers three topics: 1) student use of social media platforms to establish social networking, 2) perception and attitude towards level of trust on social media platforms, and 3) correlation between social media trust and media consumption. The results indicate that there are more students using social media to keep a close relationship with friends and family members to maintain existing communities than those to find new friends to expand social circle. Students have increased concern with trust on social media and the level of trust is declining throughout the years. Despite the trust issue, there is no correlation between level of trust and student use of social media to share and use online information to find solutions.

INTRODUCTION

Social capital remains an interesting area for researchers ever since the late 19th century when sociologists such as Lester Ward, Émile Durkheim, and Jane Addams are extensively credited with pioneering theories and approaches in the field. According to Oxford dictionary on Lexicon.com, "Social capital is the networks of relationships among people who live and work in a particular society, enabling that society to function effectively" (n. d.). Throughout the decades, researchers have made a great effort to investigate in depth the core elements in various types of social capital in different contexts and across different disciplines such as economics, sociology, politics, and psychology. These efforts have significantly expanded the research scope and have provided a much better understanding of the impact of social capital on individuals, organizations, and societies as a whole. "Social capital revolves around three dimensions: interconnected networks of relationships between individuals and groups (social ties

DOI: 10.4018/978-1-6684-8953-6.ch005

or social participation); levels of trust that characterize these ties, and resources or benefits that are both gained and transferred by virtue of social ties and social participation" (Britannica, n.d.). No matter what area of social capital is investigated in or researched on, trust is the top important element in all types of social capital. Trust is the foundation for any type of relationship. "Trust is a fundamental component of interpersonal relationships" (Cialdini & Fincham, 1990, p. 1001).

The modern internet technology has brought the level of interconnected networks of relationships between individual and groups to all time high. In addition, social media platforms have shrunk the world and brought everyone so close together virtually. Undoubtedly, the quality of people's life has been notably improved with the fast internet connection and convenient access to rich information from all resources. Technology has positive impact on online social capital development through connecting people, sharing information, building relationship, and promoting cooperation globally. Trepte and Reinecke (2022) conducted a meta-analysis of 103 studies on the relationship between internet use and social capital concludes "internet use was positively associated with social capital, but the effect size was small" (2022, p. 627).

Today, the fast expansion of AI technology has brought huge disruptions in every aspect of people's life, and trust in any kind of relationship is facing another critical challenge. As AI technology continues to advance, it is likely that Chatbots and AI-based platforms will increasingly become a more commonplace and heavily used in social networks. AI technology is like a double-edged sword, it definitely brings enormous benefit to people's life, at the same time it poses a great urgency for everyone to understand and prepare for the new future as AI technology will be an integral part of people's life. With advanced internet and AI technologies infusing into the platforms of online communication and interaction, it is necessary to better understand how people use and behave virtually and find out if social media platforms are an effective environment to promote social capital development. Hence, the purpose of this chapter's research study is to explore the three dimensions revolving social capital development in the dynamic realm of social media platforms. The investigation aims to uncover the following: 1) student use of social media platforms to establish social networking, 2) perception and attitude towards level of trust on social media platforms, and 3) correlation between social media trust and media use and consumption. Additionally, the study further investigates the gender difference on trust level to find out if gender makes any difference in social networking on the media platforms

THE STUDY

The research study in this chapter is a 10-year longitudinal research study from 2013 to 2022. It was conducted among college students at the University of Houston (UH), which is a Carnegie-designated Tier One Public Research University and the second most ethnically diverse major research university in the United States. Students come to UH from more than 137 nations and from across the world. In this study, for ten-year average, Hispanic students make up 35% of total participants, followed by Caucasian students of 31%, next is the African and American students of 16%, Asian students is in the fourth place of 12%, the rest students are from Native American, Pacific Islander and others. Most racial groups stay in pretty much the same percentage with a variation less than 5% each year. However, Hispanic group increased from 29% in 2013 to 47% in 2022, and Caucasian group dropped from 42% in 2013 to 17% in 2022. According to the US census, in the grand Houston area, Hispanic population is increasing while

Caucasian population is declining every year. The student population in this study reflect the same change and trend as that in the US census.

This study was using a convenient sampling method to select the students who took the Information and Communication Technologies course, which was a fully online course delivered in the Blackboard Course Management System. There are altogether 2185 students participated in the social media survey in ten years with 1489 female students of 68% and 696 male students of 32%. Most of them were junior and senior students. The student age ranged from 18 to 54. Averagely, the groups of 18-24 and 25-34 make up 93% of the total participants. According to the statistics by Statista report in 2022, US leading social media platform users are over 50% averagely at the similar age range, with Twitter at 80% and Facebook at 49%. Therefore, the research participants in this study mirror the same population profile worldwide in social media users.

In this study, an online survey instrument was developed and distributed to students who voluntarily participated in the study. The participation rate varies from 80% - 95% in the period of ten years. In addition to demographic information, the survey questions cover five areas, 1) social media knowledge and adoption, 2) perceptions towards social media adoption barriers, 3) preference of participating in social media groups, 4) social media utilization, and 5) social media trust. This chapter reports and analyzes the results from the data in each of the above five areas and the data analysis includes trend changes in the period of ten years.

MAIN FOCUS OF THE CHAPTER

Student Use of Social Media Platforms to Establish Social Networking

Social media provides the platforms to facilitate the process of interaction, sharing and establishing different kind of relationship to greatly expand the interconnected networks among people. The mobility of devices further promote social media platform in the way people accessing social media anytime and anywhere. Social media has become an integral part of people's daily lives and has revolutionized the way of communication, accessing and sharing information as well as interacting with others. Based on Datareportal.com website, "The number of social media users in the USA at the start of 2023 was equivalent to 72.5% of the total population" (Kemp, 2023). Social media has become a crucial channel for people to expand and develop new networks.

Evolving Use of Social Media Platforms

Social media platforms are constantly evolving with the development of technology, some early platforms like Bulletin Board Systems (BBS), and Six Degrees are no longer available. After 2000, many new platforms came on board every year, such as Facebook (2004), YouTube (2005), Twitter (2006), TikTok (2016) and Clubhouse (2020). Throughout its history, social media has transformed how people communicate, share ideas, mobilize movements, and consume content. Its impact on society, politics, and culture is significant, shaping the way people interact and experience the world. Understanding how people perceive and trust in social media is crucial since social media platform is an indispensable part of people's interaction and life experiences, which are the key to the development of social capital.

In this study, students have increased familiarity and understanding of social media platforms. One hundred percent of students reported that they are familiar with the concept of social media platform in 2022 versus 45% in 2013. Students' preferences of using social media tools fluctuate through the 10-year's investigation. In the survey, students were given the top ten mostly used social media platforms and asked them to check the ones that they were using in the order of Facebook, Wiki, Discussion Forum, YouTube, LinkedIn, Blogging, Twitter, Podcasting (audio and video), Instagram and Snapchat. The years from 2015 to 2017 witnessed the peak use of Facebook, Wiki, Discussion Forum, Youtube, LinkedIn and Twitter. The student users were varying between 10% and 18% each year. The trend data indicate that these popular tools display a declining use among students after 2017. For example, the peak use of Facebook was in 2017 with 14%, after that it declined to only 7% in 2022. At the same time period, Wiki dropped from 14% to 6%, Discussion Forum from 14% to 10%, YouTube from 12% to 8%, LinkedIn from 13% to 9% and Twitter from 12% to 9%. However, the data are different from reported public statistics, for example, Facebook has increased users for the past several years according to Datarepotal (Datareportal.com, 2023). The increase could be from difference age groups, countries and regions. In 2018, Instagram, Snapchat, Pinterest (Pinterest was added to the original survey in 2016) surpassed the above popular tools and became more prevalent among the participants. One social media tool is not listed in the choices, but it is worthwhile mentioning since it grew its popularity at a very fast speed, which is TickTok. In student self-reported results, TickTok was first reported in 2019 only from two students, in 2020 it grew to 21%, and in 2022, it hit to 29% of student users. In this study, 100% of students reported that they used different social media platforms to communicate and interact with friends, family members and other people to certain extend.

Social media tools will continue to evolve and users will shift from one to another depending their preferences, features and functionalities as well as ease of use. Kim and Park stated in their study "ease of use and feature relevance are important factors that influence social media use" (2021, page 444). When social media platform provides misinformation and low quality message, people tend to leave that platform. The "perceived credibility and trustworthiness are important factors that influence social media use" (Wang & Zhange, 2020, p.191). Another important factor is the commitment from social media platforms to protecting user's safety and security of private information. Twingate data report in 2020 found out that "45.9% of people were extremely or moderately concerned about their personal information on social media" among generation X and millennials.

Use of Social Media Platforms for Social Networking

People use different social media platforms for a variety of reasons, as each social media platform is unique and designed to serve specific purposes or cater to specific user needs. For example, Facebook is often used for connecting with friends and family, LinkedIn for professional networking, Instagram for sharing visual content, Twitter for short updates and news, and YouTube for video sharing. People choose platforms based on the features and functions that align with their intended use or goals. Besides the characteristics of each social media platform, people also choose the platform to connect with the kind of people for different purposes with distinct user base and community. The choice of platform allows individuals to engage with like-minded individuals and find communities that align with their interests. From content sharing perspective, Social media platforms provide a wide array of content types and formats. Users choose platforms based on their preferred content consumption habits. Another important aspect is social influence and network effects. People may join platforms where their friends, family, or professional contacts are active to stay connected and engage with their social circles, in which they offer help and share personal onions with the group. Liu & Wang's research study found out that people who value self-expression, social connection, and community involvement were more likely to use social media tools that allow them to share their thoughts and feelings, connect with friends and family, and participate in online communities (2022).

In this study, regarding social media tools adoption, the top five reported reasons from students in order of important are: social engagement, direct communication, speed of feedback, relationship building and making new friends. Social engagement remain the first reason to adopt social media tools throughout ten-year period about 20% and followed by direct communication of 12%, speed of feedback of 10% and relationship building and making new friends are about 9%. Besides social media provides a vast networking connection, it offers convenient and immediate communication channels. People can send messages, share updates, and engage in real-time conversations with others regardless of their physical location. The accessibility and speed facilitate the exchange of information, ideas and support.

The study also focused on social bonding with two specific questions. The first question explored the use of social media tools to maintain close relationships with friends and family members, thereby sustaining existing communities. The second question examined the utilization of social media platforms to discover new friends, expanding one's social circle and fostering new relationships. Over a span of ten years, the results indicated that, on average, the reported frequencies in relation to maintaining existing communities: 37% of students reported very often, 43% often, 14% rarely, and 6% not at all. In contrast, when it came to expanding their social circles, the data revealed an opposing trend. Students reported the following frequencies: 6% very often, 20% often, 45% rarely, and 29% not at all in using social media to find new friends and extend their social circles.

In terms of maintaining existing communities, the frequent use of social media by students to stay connected with close friends and family members can contribute to the development of bonding social capital. By utilizing these platforms, individuals can maintain strong ties, emotional support systems, and access to resources within their immediate social network. However, the lower frequency of social media use reported by students for expanding their social circles suggests that the impact on bridging social capital, which involves connections with acquaintances and diverse networks, might be limited. Social media platforms, while offering opportunities to connect with new individuals, were not be perceived by students as the primary or most effective means for expanding social circles.

Therefore, the behavioral pattern observed among students regarding social media use reflects a stronger emphasis on maintaining existing communities (bonding social capital) rather than actively seeking out and expanding social networks (bridging social capital). Based on the data, while social media can facilitate the maintenance of strong ties, it is less effective in developing new relationships and accessing diverse networks, which are crucial for the growth of bridging social capital. Regular communication and interactions on social media platforms help sustain and strengthen these existing relationships, leading to the accumulation of social capital in the form of trust, reciprocity, and social support.

Student Perception and Attitude Towards Level of Trust on Social Media

Social media platforms provide opportunities for networking and relationship building. Social media use was associated with increased social capital, such as trust, civic engagement, and political participation (Chen & Zhu, 2021). Trust in social media plays a significant role in social capital development. It is a foundational element of social capital as it fosters cooperation, reciprocity, and reliable interactions within social networks. In the context of social media, trust is crucial for relationship building since trust forms the basis of strong and meaningful relationships. When individuals trust each other on social media platforms, they are more likely to engage in open and honest communication, share personal experiences, and seek and provide support. These interactions contribute to the development of bonding social capital, strengthening ties with friends, family, and close connections.

Social media platforms enable people to connect and communicate with others from diverse backgrounds and perspectives but it also increases the potential for encountering dishonest or malicious acts. While there are certainly trustworthy people on social media platforms, it is important to approach online interactions with a degree of caution. In social media, it is difficult to verify the identity of the person on the other end of the platform. Identity fraud and theft has becoming more and more serious issues. "Social networking sites have the greatest potential for abuse" and "with the increased global use of social media, there are more opportunities than ever before to steal identities or perpetrate fraud online" (Lewis, n. d.). "Identity theft is increasingly a 21st-Century problem" (Cook, 2023). On the other hand, social media users sometimes use fake information to protect their privacy, which adds more complexity to online communication and interaction, which will for sure affect people's level of trust. According to Twingate data report, "43.5% of people have entered false information to protect personal information or privacy" (Twingate, 2020). It is essential to recognize that trust is a complex and subjective concept based on personal experiences.

Student Level of Trust in Social Media Platforms

This research study intends to find out student perceptions and attitudes towards trust on social media from three aspects, student caution in using social media, level of trust towards close friends and family members versus the level of trust towards others on the internet. When students were asked, "Do you believe that you need to be very careful in dealing with people in social media communication?" in a scale of five choices, strongly agree, agree, neither agree nor disagree, disagree and strongly disagree. In the span of ten years, averagely, students reported 57% strongly agree, 35% agree, 5% disagree, less than 1% strongly disagree, and about 2% neither agree nor disagree. The trend shows almost 26% increase from 42.9% (strongly agree) in 2013 to 68.6% in 2022. About 19% of students raised their carful level from agree to strongly agree. Disagree and strongly disagree stayed consistently low throughout the years with less than 2% variations.

This increased concern is a very complicated issue and it could related to cyber security, such as identity fraud and theft, online bullying and harassment, misinformation and fake news, online scams and phishing, unfair news reports, lack of confidence in government, just to mention a few. In recent years, trust level is declining in different areas, in news media, and in government, even in online personal interaction and communication. A research study conducted by the University of Oxford in virtual roundtable discussions with small groups of journalists and publishers in 2021, "many expressed concern that digital platforms were at least partly to blame for declining levels of trust in news in many places around the world" (Newman et all, 2022). "Some worried that platforms enable bad-faith criticism of journalism to circulate more easily and insidiously while polluting the information environment with low quality substitutes for factual reporting" (Mont'Alverne et all, 2022). Trust in the media has also declined in the United States. In 2021, only 23% of Americans say they trust the media to report the news "fairly and accurately" (p. 2). According to Pew Research Center, "Trust in the government has declined in the United States. In 2021, only 22% of Americans say they trust the government to do what is right "just about always" or "most of the time." (p. 1). "Since 2007, the shares saying they can trust the government always or most of the time has not surpassed 30%" (Pew Research Center, 2022). Edelman, a global public relations and marketing consultancy firm, states that the trust crisis is a global phenomenon. In 2022, trust in institutions is at an all-time low in most countries around the world and the trust crisis is having a negative impact on society. It is leading to a decline in civic engagement, a rise in extremism, and a decrease in economic growth (Edelman, 2022). These data are very concerning. When social media became the vital platform for people to access various resources, their level of trust will seriously affect their attitudes towards using and sharing information.

While investigating the trust level, students were asked "Generally speaking, do you believe that most people can be trusted through social media tools?" also in a scale of five choices, strongly agree, agree, neither agree nor disagree, disagree and strongly disagree. The responses from students were analyzed over a ten-year period. On average, less than 1% of students strongly agreed, 17.9% agreed, 35.3% disagreed, 7.55% strongly disagreed, and 38.6% neither agreed nor disagreed. The group expressing strong agreement remained consistently below 1.8% throughout the ten years. The percentage of students agreeing decreased from 27.8% in 2013 to 17.9% in 2022, indicating a 10% decline in trust levels. The most significant percentage change was observed in the group disagreeing, which increased from 27.3% to 47.6%, representing a 20% rise, further highlighting the diminishing trust levels. The group neither agreeing nor disagreeing varied from 30% to 44% over the ten-year period, indicating the uncertainty or ambivalence towards trusting people on social media platforms. Social media has evolved and diversified over the years, with the emergence of new platforms, changing privacy settings, and evolving user behaviors. Students may feel uncertain about the trustworthiness of individuals on social media due to the complexity and diverse nature of these platforms. The constantly changing landscape and the presence of both positive and negative experiences might lead to mixed feelings and uncertainty.

However, there is a bright side of trust using social media platforms. Throughout the decade, the trust level in close friends and family members stays strong. In responding to the question "When you are communicating via social media tools, you trust your close friends and family members" for ten-year average results, 50.7% students reported strongly agree, 37.9% agree, 2.53% disagree, 0.56% strongly disagree and 8.32% neither agree nor disagree. People are more likely to trust information that they see on social media if it comes from people they know and trust. People who value self-expression, social connection, and community involvement were more likely to trust information that came from people they knew and trusted (Liu, & Wang, 2022.).

While it is important to approach social media interactions with a degree of caution, there are undeniable benefits that social media platforms bring to people's life. Social media platforms removed communication barriers and enable people to connect and communicate with others across the globe, regardless of geographical boundaries. They provide instant messaging, video calling, and voice chat functionalities, allowing individuals, families, friends, and communities to stay connected and share updates in real-time. Social media platforms serve as powerful tools for sharing information and raising awareness on various topics, facilitating the dissemination of information on social, cultural, political, and environmental issues. They allow individuals to connect with professionals in their field, build business networks, and foster collaborations. "Positive impacts of social media on youth include increased social connection, civic engagement, and self-expression" (Smith, et al, 2018, p.402). Social media can be used to build social capital by facilitating information sharing, network formation, and civic engagement (Clark & Barbour, 2021).

Level of Trust Between Male and Female on Social Media Platforms

Gender research has been an evolving field for a long time. Early gender research focused on the differences between men and women in psychological and physical traits to establish theories trying to explain why some gender roles were viewed as more socially acceptable than others. "The late 1960s through the 1970s marked an important turning point in the field of gender research, including theory and research in gender development" (Zosuls, et al. 2011, p. 827). In her 1982 book *In a Different Voice*, Carol Gilligan introduced the concept of moral development, which suggested that women develop their sense of right and wrong differently than men. This sparked a new wave of gender research, focusing on how culture, education, and socialization influence gender roles and expectations. Recently, gender research has shifted to include a wider range of gender identities and expressions, encompassing a variety of gender presentations and orientations. The rise of social media has also been influential in the research, offering new platforms for the exploration of gender identity and expression, as well as providing a means of connecting to different forms of gender research around the world.

There are more female social media users than male users. According to Kemp "53.9% of the USA's social media users were female, while 46.1% were male" (2023). Understanding how trust varies between genders in the realm of digital communication and social interaction can provide valuable insights into online behavior, perceptions, and experiences. Exploring the factors contributing to gender differences in trust on social platforms can shed light on the complex interplay between gender, social dynamics, and online environments. Gender differences in trust on social media can be influenced by various factors, such as online safety concerns, perceived reliability and authenticity, social influence and peer norms. Differences in experience and familiarity with social media platforms may also contribute to gender differences in trust. Examining overall level of trust in this study, the data indicate that the level of trust is declining throughout the decade. However, how differently between female and male students in their perceptions and attitudes? The trust in gender difference is examined from two aspects, being careful in social media commutation and attitudes towards human trust.

The investigated course in this study is Information and Communication Technologies and it is delivered in the department of communication under the College of Liberal Arts and Social Sciences. Consistently, the average enrollment number of female students in this department is higher than that of male students at around 63% versus 37%. In this study, the number of female participants is more or less doubled the number of male students, which is in the right proportion as the enrollment data.

When comparing the gender data across a ten-year period for the question "Do you believe that you need to be very careful in dealing with people in social media communication?" (in a scale of five choices, strongly agree, agree, neither agree nor disagree, disagree and strongly disagree), the percentage results of strongly agree and agree were combined together from each year for both genders to calculate the average mean values and to conduct a two-tailed T-Test to generate p-value. The results for this question, the mean value for female students is 76, while the mean value for male students it is 63, conducting a two-tailed T-Test yielded a p-value of 0.040569107, which is smaller than the common significance level of $p = 0.05$. This indicates that there is a statistically significant difference between female and male students regarding their level of caution in social media communication, with female students displaying higher levels of caution.

Examining the ten-year trend, the percentage level of caution for female participants remained consistently high throughout the years, reaching its peak in 2022 at 91%. In contrast, the trend among male students fluctuated, with the highest percentage level of caution observed in 2022 at 93%. Both trends indicate an increasing level of caution in social media communication among students over time. These findings suggest that female students tend to be more cautious than male students in their approach to social media communication. The statistically significant difference highlights the importance of considering gender-specific factors and experiences when examining attitudes and behaviors related to social media usage.

Online harassment is one of the most prominent issues resulting in social media safety concern and females are more likely to be the victims in this environment. The study by Janes et al. (2022) found that women are more likely than men to experience online harassment, and that this harassment is often motivated by misogyny. The study also found that online harassment can have a significant impact on women's mental and emotional well-being. Another study by Kvasny et al. (2021) found that women who have experienced online harassment often feel that the platforms they use are not doing enough to protect them. "Women who have experienced online harassment often feel that they have been silenced and that their voices have not been heard" (Kvasny et all, 2021, p. 880). These research studies might contribute to the reasons why female students reported high level of caution when they communicate in social media platforms.

When comparing the female and male students' level of trust in social media platform, both trends show a declining direction with male students demonstrating slightly more drop in human trust than that of female students. In analyzing the data from the question "Generally speaking, do you believe that most people can be trusted through social media tools?" (in a scale of five choices, strongly agree, agree, neither agree nor disagree, disagree and strongly disagree), the calculation is using the percentage results of strongly agree and agree combined together from each year for both genders to generate the average mean values and to conduct a two-tailed T-Test to yield p-value. While examining the data over a ten-year period, the mean value for female students is 35, whereas for male students it is 32. Conducting a two-tailed T-Test yielded a p-value of 0.273645286, which is higher than the common significance level of 0.05. These results suggest that although female students, on average, hold a slightly stronger belief that most people can be trusted on social media platforms as compared to male students, the difference between the two groups is not statistically significant based on the p-value.

Analyzing the ten-year trend, the attitudes (strongly agree and agree) among female participants remained consistent throughout the years, reaching a peak of 41% in 2014 and declined to 37% in 2022. Male students exhibited a similar decline in their level of trust every year from 42% in 2013 to 36% in 2022. Both trends indicate a decreasing attitude among students towards the trustworthiness of people on social media platforms. These findings imply that while there may be a slight difference in trust levels between female and male students, this disparity is not statistically significant. Moreover, the declining trends in both groups' attitudes towards level of trust on social media platforms suggest a broader shift in perceptions over the examined period.

The difference might due to the social media use. Female students tend to use social media to bond with friends and family members, so the trust level in this type of online community is higher. The following research studies indicate the similar results. If women have more positive experiences, or higher levels of familiarity with certain platforms, they may exhibit higher trust levels compared to men. "Women are more likely than men to trust those with whom they have a close relationship, whereas men tend to distrust those with whom they have an established relationship" (Maniates & Sakalli, 2020, p. 27). "Women tend to be more trusting of others than men, and this gas is particularly pronounced in situations in which trust is based on relationship-specific knowledge" (Chaudhry & Salazar, 2020, p. 65).

Correlation Between Media Trust and Media Sharing and Use

Trust is essential for sharing and accessing information on social media. When individuals trust the credibility and reliability of the content shared by others, they are more likely to rely on that information, seek advice, and engage in knowledge exchange. Trustworthy information sources and reliable recommendations enhance the accumulation of intellectual and informational resources within social networks, fostering social capital growth. The third dimension of social capital development is related to "resources or benefits that are both gained and transferred by virtue of social ties and social participation" (Britannica, n.d.). Based on the earlier data analysis results, the participants have increased distrust in social media regarding the level of trust on social media. Will this distrust affect student use of social media to share information and offer help to others as well as using it as a resource to seek help to their problems? Understanding the correlation between media trust and media use provides valuable insights into the dynamics of information consumption, media literacy, and the influence of media on individuals' attitudes and behaviors, which directly affect social capital development. This section will correlate two sets of concepts, 1) social media trust and information sharing, and 2) social media rust and social media consumption.

Social Media Trust and Information Sharing

A research study on the correlation between trust and information sharing on social media platforms by Wang, Chen, and Yu (2012) found that "trust is an important factor in information sharing on social media. Sources that are trusted are more likely to be shared, and users are more likely to trust sources that provide helpful information" (p. 15). There are two correlation analysis under this topic to find out if there is any correlation and statistically significant indication between the paired variables of trust and information sharing.

The first paired variables are from these two questions, "Do you believe that you need to be very careful in dealing with people in social media communication?" and "When you use social media tools, you provide helpful information to others." Both questions use the same rating scale from strongly agree, agree, neither agree nor disagree and strongly disagree. Based on the earlier data analysis, students have persistently high level of caution when communicating with people on social media in the 10-year period, varying from 78% to 91% (strongly agree and agree). When observing the data on students providing helpful information to others on social media, the average value of strongly agree and agree in ten years is 44.8% with the lowest value of 39% 2019 and highest value of 46% in 2014. The trend shows a slight decrease from 46% in 2013 to 41% in 2022.

Exploring the relationship between these two variables, the average value of student caution (strongly agree and agree combined) in communication on social media platforms and the average value of student use of social media to provide helpful information to others (strongly agree and agree combined) over a ten-year period, a correlation analysis is conducted. The Pearson correlation coefficient is used to assess the strength and direction of the relationship. The analysis yielded a positive correlation ($r = 0.01$, $p = 0.98 > 0.05$), indicating a weak association that lacks statistical significance. These findings suggest that there is no substantial relationship between student caution in communication on social media and their use of social media to provide helpful information to others.

The second paired variables are using these two questions, "Generally speaking, do you believe that most people can be trusted through social media tools?" "When you use social media tools, you provide helpful information to others." Both questions use the same rating scale from strongly agree, agree, neither agree nor disagree and strongly disagree. Earlier data analysis indicates that students have a declined level of trust in social media from 41% (strongly agree and agree) in 2013 to 36% in 2022. The same results observed as in the previous correlation analysis for providing helpful information to others on social media, the average value of strongly agree and agree in ten years is 44.8% with the lowest value of 39% 2019 and highest value of 46% in 2014.

A correlation analysis is conducted to examine the relationship between variables of the average value (strongly agree and agree combined) of student trust level on social media and the average value of student use of social media to provide helpful information to others over the span of ten years. The Pearson correlation coefficient was used to measure the strength and direction of the relationship. The analysis revealed a positive correlation ($r = 0.59$, $p = 0.0745 > 0.05$), indicating a low and statistically not significant association.

Social Media Trust and Social Media Use

"Trust is a two-way street on social media. Users are more likely to trust information from sources they trust, and sources are more likely to be trusted if they provide helpful information" (Cheng, Chen, & Wang, 2013, p.14). Understanding the correlation between social media trust and social media use is crucial for comprehending users' behaviors, engagement patterns, and decision-making processes within the realm of social media. There are two pairs of correlation analysis under this topic. The first correlation analysis is a pair of variables between student being cautious in social media communication and use of social media to seek help. The second correlation analysis is between the variables of student level of trust in social media and use of social media to seek help.

For the first pair of variables, the data were collected from these two questions, "Do you believe that you need to be very careful in dealing with people in social media communication?" and "If you have a problem, you would like to use social media tools to find the answer/solution to the problem." Both questions use the same rating scale from strongly agree, agree, neither agree nor disagree and strongly disagree. Based on the earlier data analysis, students have persistently high level of caution when communicating with people on social media in the 10-year period. When observing the data on student use of social media to find solution or answer to the problems, the average value of strongly agree and agree in ten years is 37.8% with highest value of 41% in 2013. The trend shows a slight decrease from 41% in 2013 to 36% in 2022.

A correlation analysis is conducted to examine the relationship between variables of the average value (strongly agree and agree combined) of student's caution in using social media platforms and the average value of student use of social media platforms for help over the span of ten years. The Pearson correlation coefficient was used to measure the strength and direction of the relationship. The analysis revealed a low positive correlation ($r = 0.073$, $p = 0.841078285 > 0.05$), indicating that there is no substantial linear relationship between the two variables. The lack of a significant correlation suggests that changes in student caution in using social media platforms are not systematically related to changes in student use of social media to find solutions for their problems.

The data for the second paired variables are from these two questions, "Generally speaking, do you believe that most people can be trusted through social media tools?" and "If you have a problem, you would like to use social media tools to find the answer/solution to the problem." Both questions use the same rating scale from strongly agree, agree, neither agree nor disagree and strongly disagree. The results of earlier data analysis shows that students have a declined level of trust in social media. While student use of social media to find solution or answer to the problems, the average value of strongly agree and agree in ten years is 37.8%.

Investigate the relationship between these two variables, the average value (strongly agree and agree combined) of student level of trust on social media and the average value of student use of social media for help over a ten-year period, a correlation analysis was conducted. The Pearson correlation coefficient was employed to assess the strength and direction of the relationship. The analysis indicated a positive correlation ($r = 0.33$, $p = 0.35 > 0.05$), suggesting a weak association that lacks statistical significance. These findings imply that there is no substantial relationship between student level of trust on social media and their use of social media for seeking assistance.

None of the above four correlation analysis results indicates any statistically significant association between paired variables. Students' caution, perceptions, and attitudes towards people's level of trust on social media platforms did not affect their using of social media platforms to seek answers and solutions to their problems nor did those variables affect their willingness to provide helpful information to share with people on the social media platform.

It is important to note that the absence of a significant correlation of the above paired variable implies that other factors or variables that are not covered in the study may contribute to student behaviors and their propensity to share helpful information on social media platforms. Further investigation or the inclusion of additional variables may provide deeper insights into the nuanced dynamics between student perceptions and their usage patterns in sharing and consumption of information on social media. However, the results of this study make new contributions to the research regarding social media platform still being a valid environment for social capital development. Students did not stop sharing and providing helpful information to others on social media even though they had trust issue and uncertainty with this dynamic global environment.

FUTURE RESEARCH DIRECTIONS

Social media research is an important part of understanding how individuals, organizations, and societies interact in the virtual world. People are spending more and more time on social media to find friends, build relationship, and to find information and resources for their life. Therefore, it is a crucial life stage for trust research in social capital since it is the foundation and core value for any relationship. Based on the data analysis from this research study, the level of trust is declining on social media. The exiting research studies indicate the level of trust on social media has been affected by misinformation, identity theft, insure of personal privacy as well as online malpractice such as online harassment. In order to maintain a healthy online communication environment, the administrative quality of social media is crucial. Internet regulations have been always behind the fast development of technology because technology is constantly evolving at an exponential speed, and it can be difficult for regulators to keep up with the changes. The internet is a global network, and social media platforms are used by people all over the world. As a result, social media platforms have often been operating without much regulation. This has led to a number of problems, such as the spread of misinformation, hate speech, and cyberbullying. "Social media platforms need to take steps to address the spread of misinformation on their platforms" (Wardle & Derakhsha, 2027, p. 18). Further studies are necessary to find out the true reasons behind the distrust on social media to provide valid information for establishment of effective online guidelines and policies. Only a safe environment can truly promote the development of social capital.

Regarding the correlation analysis is this study, none of the compared variables established a positive and statistically significant correlation between the level of trust and student sharing and using information on social media. New variables could be added to explore other possibilities for the finding. It is also worthwhile to find if the finding has anything related to "pragmatism" to use social media "as tools and instruments for prediction, problem solving, and action" (Wikipedia, n. d.) without considering the trustworthiness of social media itself. If so, will pragmatism replace trust in the development of social capital?

CONCLUSION

When Webster dictionary defined the term social capital, the social networks were limited to a particular society in which people establish positive and beneficial relationship to enable that society to function effectively. With the fast advancement of internet and AI technology, the early neighborhood networks has been extended to a global scale at an exponential speed with people from diverse cultural, political, religious background. There is no doubt that technology helps people expand the scope and speed of networking beyond any physical barriers in the way that was totally impossible in the old time. This research study demonstrated that students were using social media extensively to maintain existing community and develop extended new social circle. However, technology has brought challenges to the original intention and goal of developing social capital. The challenges come from the means people communicate and interact with each other behind the electronic devices on social media platforms, are people talking to a real person, a person with fake identity, or an AI-empowered Chatbots?

The data in this research study demonstrate a trend forming in the direction opposite to the development of social capital in the aspect of level of trust. People are becoming increasingly cautious and less trustful in communicating and interacting with people on social media platforms. However, the increased distrust did not affect students in using social media platforms to seek solutions for their problems nor did it influence their willingness to provide helpful information to share with others. This is a positive indication that it is still hopeful that social media platforms continue to be an effective channel to promote the development of social capital for the time being. It is imperative to understand that while social media platforms offer numerous advantages, there are also associated challenges and risks. All users on social media platforms should be mindful of their privacy, critical of the information they encounter, and engage responsibly to maximize the benefits while mitigating potential drawbacks. Promoting transparency in social media platforms will benefit social capital development through increased level of trust. Social media platforms can build trust by being transparent about how they collect and use user data (Kim & Park, 2021). Social capital can be only stimulated and developed in an environment where everyone is truthful and respectful to each other.

REFERENCES

Britannica. (n. d.). *Social capital*. https://www.britannica.com/topic/social-capital

Chaudhry, M., & Salazar, J. (2020). Trust and influence in social media: The role of gender. *Journal of Business Research*, (110), 62–70.

Chen, L., & Zhu, J. (2021). Social media use and social capital among young adults in China. *Telematics and Informatics*, 101654.

Cheng, W., Chen, H., & Wang, Y. (2013). The role of trust in social media information sharing. *Computers in Human Behavior*, *2013*, 14–32.

Cialdini, R. B., & Fincham, R. L. (1990). Trust and the development of interpersonal relationships. *Psychological Bulletin*.

Clark, J. L., & Barbour, K. (2021). Social media and social capital: A review of empirical research. *New Media & Society*, *23*(2), 318–338.

Cook, S. ((2023). *Identity theft facts & statistics: 2019-2022*. https://www.comparitech.com /identity-theft-protection/identity-theft-statistics/

Edelman. (2022). *2022 Edelman trust barometer*. https://www.edelman.com/trust/2022-trust-barometer

Janes, E., Livingstone, S., Lum, K., Boler, M., & Ringrose, J. (2022). Online harassment of women: The role of gender, misogyny, and victimization. *Social Media + Society*.

Kemp, S. (2023). *Digital 2023: The United States of America*. https://datareportal.com/ reports/digital-2023-united-states-of-america#:~:text=The%20USA%20was%20home%20to,percent%20of%20the%20total%20population

Kim, J., & Park, J. (2021). The impact of ease of use and feature relevance on social media use: A cross-platform study. *Information Systems Research*, *32*(2), 436–454.

Kvasny, L., Haddon, L., Vitak, J., Kowert, R., & Green, T. (2021). Women's perspectives on harm and Justice after online harassment. *Information Communication and Society*, *2021*(24), 878–897.

Lewicki, J. A., McAllister, R. J., & Bies, R. H. (1998). Trust as a foundation for relationship quality. *Journal of Personality and Social Psychology*.

Lewis, K. (n.d.). *How social media networks facilitate identity theft and fraud*. https://www.eonetwork.org/octane-magazine/special-features/social-media-networks-facilitate-identity-theft-fraud#:~:text=With%20limited%20government%20oversight%2C%20industry%20standards%20or %20incentives,are%20likely%20vulnerable%20to%20outside%20%28or%20inside%29%20attack

Liu, X., & Wang, Z. (2022). The impact of personal values on social media use: A cross-cultural study. *Computers in Human Behavior*, *2022*(125), 106748.

Maniates, H., & Sakalli, E. (2020). Gender differences in trust and distrust: An examination of trust dynamics in online and offline contexts. *Journal of Applied Social Psychology*, *50*(1), 20-35.

Mayer, R. D., Davis, J. H., & Schoorman, F. D. (1995). Trust in business relationships: A meta-analysis. *Journal of Business Ethics*.

Mont'Alerne, C., Arguedas, A. R., Toff, B., Fletcher, R., & Nielsen, R. K. (2022). *The trust gap: how and why news on digital platforms is viewed more skeptically versus news in general*. https://reutersinstitute. politics.ox.ac.uk/trust-gap-how-and-why-news-digital-platforms-viewed-more-sceptically-versus-news-general#header--0

Newman, N., Fletcher, R., Robertson, C. T., Eddy, K., & Nielsen, R. K. (2022). *Digital news report 2022*. Reuters Institute for the Study of Journalism.

Pew Research Center. (2022). *Public trust in government: 1958-2022*. https://www.pewresearch.org/politics/2022/06/06/public-trust-in-government-1958-2022/

Smith, J. A., Spears, A. L., & Ellefsen, A. M. (2018). The impact of social media on youth: A review of the literature. *Developmental Review*.

Trepte, S., & Reinecke, L. (2022). The Internet and social capital: A meta-analysis. *New Media & Society*, *24*(2), 622–643.

Twingate. (2020). *Privacy for a premium*. https://www.twingate.com/research/privacy-for-a-premium-exploring-peoples-sentiments-on-paying-for-social-media

Wang, J., & Zhang, J. (2020). The impact of perceived credibility and trustworthiness on social media use: A cross-platform study. *Journal of Business Research*, *2022*(112), 186–195.

Wang, Chen, & Yu. (2012). The impact of trust on information sharing in social media. *Journal of Computer-Mediated Communication*, 10–16.

Wardle, C, & Derakhshan, H. (2017). *The role of social media in the spread of misinformation*. Center for Internet & Society at Harvard University.

Widipedia. (n.d.). *Pragmatism*. https://en.wikipedia.org/wiki/Pragmatism

Zousuls, K. M., Miller, C. F., Ruble, D. N., Martin, C. L., & Fabes, R. A. (2011). Gender development research in sex roles: Historical trends and future directions. *Sex Roles*, *64*(11-12), 826–842. doi:10.100711199-010-9902-3 PMID:21747580

ADDITIONAL READING

Cornel University. (2023). *A comprehensive survey of AI-generated content (AIGC): A history of generative AI from GAN to ChatGPT*. https://arxiv.org/abs/2303.04226

Dinić, B. M., Wertag, A., & Sokolovska, V. (2023). The good, the bad, and the ugly: Revisiting the Dark Core. https://doi-org.ezproxy.lib.uh.edu/10.1007/s12144-021-01829-x

Gorwa, R., & Guilbeault, D. (2020). Unpacking the social media bot: A typology to guide research and policy. *Policy and Internet*, *12*(2), 225–248. doi:10.1002/poi3.184

Majerczak, P., & Strzelecki, A. (2022, February). Trust, media credibility, social ties, and the intention to share towards information verification in an age of fake news. *Behavioral Science*, *12*(2), 51. doi:10.3390/bs12020051 PMID:35200302

Molina, M. D., Sundar, S. S., Le, T., & Lee, D. (2021). "Fake news" is not simply false information: A concept explication and taxonomy of online content. *The American Behavioral Scientist*, *2021*(65), 180–212. doi:10.1177/0002764219878224

United Nation. (n.d.). *Countering disinformation.* https://www.un.org/en/countering-disinformation?gclid=CjwKCAjw7OlBhB8EiwAnoOEk60oXb803LaAkNNCBRu7AJGxb66jO16ikvTHWUm2wiK-kPQvdbV-NphoCH8sQAvD_BwE

Viviani, M., & Pasi, G. (2017). *Credibility in social media: opinions, news, and health information—a survey.* https://wires.onlinelibrary.wiley.com/doi/pdf/10.1002/widm.1209

KEY TERMS AND DEFINITIONS

AI Technology: AI technology stands for artificial intelligence technology. It is the field of research in computer science that focuses on developing systems and algorithms capable of performing tasks that typically require human intelligence.

AI-Powered Chatbots: AI-powered chatbots refer to chatbot applications that utilize artificial intelligence (AI) technologies to interact with users and provide automated responses. These chatbots are designed to simulate human-like conversations and understand natural language inputs from users.

Human Trust: Human trust refers to the belief, confidence, and reliance that individuals place in others based on their perceived integrity, reliability, competence, and ethical behavior.

Online Networking: Online networking refers to the process of building and nurturing professional and individual relationships and connections through social media platforms and tools.

Social Capital: Social capital refers to the collective value derived from social networks, relationships, and interactions within a community or society or in global environment through digital media. It encompasses the resources, benefits, and advantages that individuals or groups can access and leverage through their social connections and social ties.

Social Media Platform: A social media platform refers to an online digital service or website that enables users to create, share, and interact with content and connect with other users. It provides a virtual space for individuals, organizations, and communities to communicate, collaborate, and engage with one another.

Social Media Tools: This term is used interchangeable with social media platform, where people can communicate and interact with each other to maintain and/or development relationship of different nature.

Chapter 6
Sustainability in the Age of Networking and Virtual Social Capital:
Neoteric Approach

R. Gayathri

https://orcid.org/0000-0001-9406-0191

School of Management, SASTRA University (Deemed), Thanjavur, India

ABSTRACT

A constructive outcome of interpersonal connection is referred to as social capital. In recent years, the development paradigm has transformed from a virtually sole focus on physical capital to a people-focused approach targeting sustainable growth that accentuates the social elements of development, particularly human and social capital. The perspective on social capital emphasizes the importance of individual and community ties and the broader social and political context in which social structures and norms develop. It underscores the significance of institutional relationships, government support, and collaboration among various sectors for encouraging economic and social development. This chapter infers on a few current hot topics, focusing on how online social capital influences development and exploring if there are economic benefits to building social capital.

INTRODUCTION

Robert Putnam, one of the pioneers in the use of the term "social capital", has defined it thus: "Whereas physical capital refers to physical objects and human capital refers to the properties of individuals, social capital refers to connections among individuals – social networks and the norms of reciprocity and trustworthiness that arise from them. In that sense social capital is closely related to what some have called "civic virtue". The difference is that "social capital" calls attention to the fact that civic virtue is most powerful when embedded in a sense network of reciprocal social relations. A society of many virtuous but isolated individuals is not necessarily rich in social capital." – Putnam 2000

DOI: 10.4018/978-1-6684-8953-6.ch006

WHAT IS SOCIAL CAPITAL?

The ability of someone to do excellent and have a long-lasting effect on how businesses operate is known as Social Capital. The beneficial result could be measurable or intangible and consist of favors, pertinent knowledge, innovative models, and upcoming prospects. Social Capital is not something an individual owns; rather, it is the possibility of coupling connections in social networks and bonding with people online or offline. It can be used to understand how interpersonal connections and networks, both inside and outside of an organization, could contribute to the success of that company. It can also indicate the interpersonal interactions that foster employee respect and trust, which improves business success. Social Capital entails a concept that prioritizes impact at the community scale over financial gain.

Building social Capital involves giving back to society and creating value. For instance, as they conduct their regular business, an increasing number of Indian corporations are now concentrating on making a difference at the community level and strengthening vulnerable communities. Microsoft is seen as a company that considerably contributes to social Capital by making a difference globally through the Bill and Melinda Gates Foundation. Social Capital helps us create value, accomplish tasks, reach our objectives, and carry out our missions. India is ranked 103rd overall on the Prosperity Index among 167 countries. India has climbed the rankings table by five spots since 2011. In the pillar rankings, India fares best in governance and enterprise conditions, while it performs the worst in the natural environment according to Legatum Prosperity Index 2023. Social Capital has had the biggest improvement since a decade ago. According to the Global Sustainable Competitive Index (GSCI) 2022 report, Nepal, Buthan, Bolivia, Suriname, and others have much better GSCI rankings than their GDP would otherwise indicate. Northern European (Scandinavian) nations lead the Social Capital Index ranking because of social cohesion and economic progress.

The Intellectual Capital Index, the foundation of innovation, is dominated by Asian countries (South Korea, China, and Japan). However, natural capital restrictions and increasing resource use could threaten to establish prolonged prosperity. The United States is ranked 30th, with especially low scores in the utilization of resources and social Capital, representing the country's contemporary issues.

ORIGIN OF THE CONCEPT OF SOCIAL CAPITAL

The concept of social capital originated from the field of sociology and was further developed by political scientists and economists. While there were earlier discussions of related ideas, the term "social capital" gained prominence through the work of several scholars, with Robert Putnam being one of the key figures in popularizing the concept.

The early roots: The concept of social capital has its roots in the works of sociologists, including *Emile Durkheim*, who emphasized the importance of social cohesion and collective consciousness in societies. Durkheim's ideas laid the groundwork for understanding the significance of social relationships and networks in social life. James S. Coleman: In the 1980s, sociologist *James S. Coleman* made notable contributions to the development of the concept. He introduced the idea of social capital as a resource embedded in social structures and networks that facilitates social interactions and cooperation.

The concept gained significant attention and popularization through the work of political scientist *Robert Putnam*. In his influential book *"Bowling Alone: The Collapse and Revival of American Community"* (2000), Putnam examined the decline of social capital in the United States and its consequences for civic engagement and community life.

He defined social capital as *"features of social organization, such as networks, norms, and social trust, that facilitate coordination and cooperation for mutual benefit."*

Putnam's work helped to bring the concept of social capital into the mainstream, sparking widespread interest and further research across disciplines. Since then, numerous scholars have expanded upon the concept, including Pierre Bourdieu, Nan Lin, Francis Fukuyama, and others. Social capital has become a multidisciplinary concept, explored in fields such as sociology, political science, economics, and public health, among others. The concept continues to evolve and be refined as researchers examine its various dimensions, applications, and implications in different contexts.

PATTERNS OF LINKAGE

In the contemporary digital age, when customers have a positive feeling of allegiance towards the firm not only with their finances but also with their hearts and minds, Social Capital may be a formidable asset for an organization, and its absence can be a significant barrier to success. Growing numbers of investors prioritize sustainable development, and organizations encourage ethical judgments. The funding required to launch, maintain growth, and expand operations is referred to as *financial Capital*. The group that adds value to the company is called *Human Capital*. While these are crucial assets for the company, *social Capital* is the relationships and ideals people share, and encouraging cooperation is the secret to entrepreneurship. There are abundant instances of leaders who strongly emphasize social Capital over time and have created enormous trust and legacies. Everybody is familiar with Ratan Tata, a successful businessman who has transformed his focus into philanthropy. Nowadays, social capital generation is more important than ever because of the growing emphasis on socioeconomic and human development and the requirement to promote social inclusion and cohesiveness through growth and development. Consumers are becoming increasingly aware of businesses that invest in their communities and generate social Capital. Customers will relate to businesses better if they place a strong emphasis on doing well for themselves while also doing good for society, which is a fundamental shift in society that is occurring on both sides. Influential organizations like TATA, Aditya Birla Group, ITC, Mindtree, Reliance, TOMS, Google, Starbucks, Walt Disney, and Amazon have started recognizing social Capital's value. Fundamentally, social Capital relies on two prominent components: bridging and bonding. *Bonding social Capital* implies ties that develop among members of similar groups, such as those working for the same employer. Sharing ideas or information between members of other groups is referred to as *bridging social Capital*. Facebook, Twitter, and other social networking sites are the top examples. Many businesses have benefited from social Capital. For example, Swiggy, Zomato, Uber, Ola, Myntra, Flipkart, and Airbnb have used social Capital to increase their market shares and solidify their positions as major players in their respective industries. Businesses like Amway, Tupperware, and other companies were successful in their strategies because of word-of-mouth publicity, consumer referral systems, and the network of neighbors.

Today, internet connectivity permeates many facets of our life, including education, social interaction, politics, business, the arts, and health. The Internet is currently a key tool for exchanging information and serves as a bridge and medium for effective, time- and space-unrestricted communication. The Internet also streamlines and accelerates every work. As social beings, it can also be used to increase knowledge and establish connections with others. Everybody has experienced the effects and advantages of the Internet; it is no longer a niche in our daily lives. Regardless of what they are doing, practically everyone has used the Internet. Web usage has enabled global communication, solitary pursuits, and increased *participatory capital*. Social capital is crucial for fostering collaboration, accessing resources, promoting well-being, driving economic development, building trust, fostering social cohesion, and encouraging civic engagement. It is an essential asset for individuals, communities, and societies, contributing to their overall growth, resilience, and prosperity.

WHY DO WE NEED TO FOCUS ON ONLINE SOCIAL CAPITAL?

The Internet and social media platforms have revolutionized social capital formation, enabling people to connect and interact across borders. These platforms offer diverse perspectives, cultures, and ideas, enabling individuals to access knowledge, resources, and support across various domains like health, education, and professional networks.

Online platforms have created virtual communities and support networks, connecting individuals with shared interests and challenges. These communities form social capital, providing emotional support, advice, and collaboration. However, challenges like privacy, misinformation, and unequal access must be considered to fully utilize online social capital's potential benefits. The current chapter focuses on the common types of social capital that exist across all nations and among various demographic groups. Information gathered from different nations through various reports are examined. The current chapter investigates the connections between various facets of social capital that support economic growth in the face of the epidemic, politics, health and well-being, internet usage etc, and offers suggestions for the actions that policymakers around the world should take to foster online social capital.

SCRUTINY ON THE REVIEW OF LITERATURE

The various components that makeup India's social capital support the country's material prosperity and development and enhance the economic and social well-being of its citizens in a deeper, more significant manner. There is also some evidence from academic studies that a State's investment of social capital within the nation does affect that State's ability to eliminate poverty and effectively conduct development plans. A country's social Capital is the total of its population's perceived or genuine well-being and societal stability. Social Capital creates a sense of community, and a degree of consensus, creates a stable economic environment, and prevents the overuse of natural resources. Most studies emphasize the association between social Capital and economic growth. (Helliwell and Putnam, 1995; Knack and Keefer, 1997; Fukuyama, 2002). However, multiple studies show a high correlation between social Capital and good health. (Kawachi et al., 1997, 1999; Macinko and Starfield, 2001). Numerous causal relationships exist between social Capital and health, including the quick dissemination of health information, healthy social norms, accessibility to resources, decreased crime rates, and emotional support within networks (Rönnerstrand, 2013).

In their article "Cents and Sociability: Household Income and Social Capital in Rural Tanzania" (Narayan and Pritchett (1997), Narayan and Pritchett evaluate village-specific "social capital" in rural Tanzania using information from a household survey meant to gauge trust and the extent and characteristics of associational behaviour. Even after accounting for household education, physical assets, and village features, their study demonstrates that higher levels of social capital in the village are linked to higher levels of individual incomes.

Improved public health, diminished crime rates, and more effective financial markets have all been associated with social capital (Adler & Kwon, 2002).

Both social capital gains and losses have been associated with the Internet. For instance, Nie (2001) stated that using the Internet reduces one's face-to-face interactions with people, which could reduce one's social capital. This viewpoint has, however, come under heavy fire (Bargh & McKenna, 2004). Additionally, some researchers asserted that interactions conducted online might replace or supplement in-person interactions, thereby minimising any harm caused by time spent online (Wellman, Haase, Witte, & Hampton, 2001). Computer-mediated conversations have been found to have a positive impact on community interaction, involvement, and social capital, according to studies of physical (i.e., geographical) communities supported by online networks, such as the Blacksburg Electronic Village or the Netville community in Toronto (Hampton & Wellman, 2003; Kavanaugh, Carroll, Rosson, Zin, & Reese, 2005).

Researchers have recently emphasised the value of Internet-based links for the development of weak ties, which form the basis of bridging social capital. It is possible that new types of social capital and connection building will take place in online social network sites since online relationships may be facilitated by technologies like publication lists, photo directories, and search features (Resnick, 2001). Such websites that encourage loose social links may help to increase social capital by enabling users to build and maintain more extensive, diffuse networks of contacts from which they may be able to access resources (Donath & Boyd, 2004; Resnick, 2001; Wellman et al., 2001).

In their study, Ellison, N. B., Steinfield, & Lampe (2007) investigated the link between college students' social capital and online social networking sites like Facebook. It explores how various Facebook activities impact the growth of social capital and how it has an impact on societal outcomes.

Hampton, K., Witte, J., Quan-Haase, B., & Wellman, B. (2001) have examined the relationship between Internet use and social capital is examined in this article. The relevance of online networks and communities in creating social relationships is highlighted as the article analyses how the Internet may both enhance and detract from conventional forms of social capital.

In their study, Valenzuela, Park, and Kee (2009) look at how college students' use of Facebook affects social capital outcomes like life happiness, trust, and civic participation. It investigates the impact of various Facebook usage characteristics on the growth of social capital.

The 2011 conference article by Vitak, Ellison, and Steinfield reexamines the relationship between Facebook use and bonding social capital. It investigates how various Facebook behaviours, such as chatting and photo sharing, affect the emergence of intimate bonds and the upkeep of pre-existing social ties.

Young adults' usage of Facebook and social capital are investigated by Kim, Y., and Sundar, S. S. (2014), with an emphasis on the possible digital inequality that could result from varying levels of access to and use of Facebook. It investigates how Facebook use affects the linking and bonding of social capital.

Castells, M. (2001) in his influential book, explores the role of the internet in transforming the economy and society. He discusses the concept of "network society" and how online social networks contribute to economic development by enabling information flows, knowledge sharing, and collaboration.

Burt R.S (2000) examines the concept of social capital and its impact on economic outcomes. He discusses how networks, both offline and online, provide access to resources, information, and opportunities, which can enhance economic development and innovation.

Wellman and Haythornthwaite (2002) discuss the impact of the internet on social relationships and networks. They highlight how online social networks can facilitate economic exchanges, entrepreneurship, and the formation of virtual communities that support economic development.

Ellison's (2007) study primarily focuses on social capital among college students, it also touches on the potential economic benefits of online social networking. It suggests that online social networks can facilitate job searches, entrepreneurial activities, and access to economic opportunities.

Clay Shirky (2008) explores how social media and online collaboration platforms enable large-scale coordination and collective action. He discusses how these technologies lower transaction costs, facilitate information sharing, and enable economic activities that contribute to economic development and innovation.

Kraut,R(2002) in their influential study investigates the "Internet paradox," which suggests that increased internet use is associated with social isolation and decreased well-being. The research examines the role of online social capital in mitigating the negative effects and highlights the importance of online social connections for well-being.

Francis Fukuyama (1999) offered an alternative perspective on the theory of social capital. The idea of the "radius of trust" is another method to approach this dilemma. Every organisation that embodies social capital has a particular trust radius, or the set of individuals where cooperative norms are in effect. The radius of trust can be greater than the group itself if a group's social capital generates advantageous externalities. As in huge organisations that exclusively encourage cooperative norms among the group's leadership or permanent staff, it is also feasible for the radius of trust to be narrower than the membership of the group. One way to conceptualise contemporary society is as a set of circumferential and interlocking radii of trust. These may vary from pals and groupings all the way up to NGOs and religious organisations.

A broader notion than health, wellbeing denotes a state of happiness influenced by both social interactions and personal experiences. Inherent value in wellbeing is linked to a wide range of desired social outcomes, including those pertaining to health, education, and employment (Huppert, 2017).

Although there isn't a single, widely accepted indicator of wellbeing, the majority of them include both hedonic (such as happy or anxious) and eudemonic (such as assessments of the degree of meaning and purpose in one's life) dimensions. (Daykin et al., 2020)

Loneliness has been recognised as a problem in research and policy as the field of wellbeing studies has grown. Not to be confused with social isolation or alone, loneliness is a multifaceted phenomenon. Although there are various forms of loneliness, it is widely acknowledged as an adverse phenomenon that is happening more and more often and is linked to negative outcomes in terms of wellbeing and health (Victor et al.,2018).

Ellison, (2020) in their study explored how specific relationship maintenance behaviours on Facebook can contribute to the development of social capital.

Hale, (2020) focused on the role of social capital in online health communities and highlights its impact on health-related outcomes and information sharing.

Lin, (2020) conducted a systematic review and meta-analysis to examine the relationship between online social capital and civic engagement, providing insights into the mechanisms and conditions that influence this association.

Wang, (2020) in their study investigated the changes in adult friendship network size in the United States and examines the role of online social media use in maintaining and expanding social capital.

Alhabash, (2021) in their research explored the relationship between social media use, network heterogeneity, and social capital, examining how different social media platforms can facilitate the accumulation of social capital.

Trepte,(2021) studied the relationship between online news consumption, commenting behavior, and the development of online and offline social ties, highlighting the role of news-related social capital.

Abu-Jaber, (2021) synthesized the existing research on the impact of social media on social capital, exploring different theoretical perspectives, measurement approaches, and outcomes.

These studies provide a glimpse into the recent research on online social capital, covering various domains such as relationship maintenance, health communities, civic engagement, friendship networks, network heterogeneity, and the impact of social media.

GLIMPSES OF SOCIAL CAPITAL DURING THE COVID-19 PANDEMIC FROM INDIA

In addition to professional organizations and cooperatives established to advance the social and economic well-being of its members, India has a long history of volunteerism and philanthropy. Even though many of these traditional institutions suffered under colonial rule, during the struggle for independence there was a resurgence of interest in these Bodies thanks in large part to Gandhiji, who was a lifelong supporter of self-reliance and limited government before these ideas came to be seen as a viable economic model in the West.

Corporate Social Responsibility (CSR), the basis of which is the alignment of company operations with social ideals, is at the core of the corporate sector's capacity to support both social and economic development. It considers stakeholders' interests in the company's business strategies and operations. When driven by enlightened self-interest, corporate involvement in society, the environment, and business improves everyone's quality of life. With the goal of attaining social development while obtaining corporate success, CSR focuses on the social, environmental, and financial success of a firm, or what is known as the "triple bottom line."

There was no education during the Covid 19 epidemic since the government schools were closed due to the coronavirus, and there was little awareness of online education in the underprivileged areas in and around Bhachau in the Gujurat district. The local populace was unaware that the Gujarati government had created a schedule for classes on DDGirnar (TV & radio). A quick survey done by the localities revealed that TV or smartphone was not accessible to over 40% of the students, the majority of whom were from low-income Dalit and Muslim homes, making it soon clear that many children were still not receiving an education. With the assistance of some teachers and Sarpanchs, these citizen leaders mobilized the neighborhood to extend their social capital support by allowing the kids to visit people with televisions in their homes. Other kids received support via shared smartphones, while other kids still participated in offline classes with the assistance of schoolteachers, despite being led by local teenagers.

Districts like Barmer experience significant migration to cities every year because of inadequate agricultural prospects and livelihood opportunities. By early May, the food and livelihood crisis had begun in Rajasthan's desert areas, where lockdown had forced migrant labor to return. Most of the migrant workers returning to their country could not participate in government programs like MGNREGS. Women leaders of Jal Saheli (Water Friends) groups helped 11234 migrant workers obtain their job cards and find employment over the next two months in about 50 gram panchayats in the Patodi and Sindhu blocks of the district. This was only made possible by the strong social Capital underpinning each community's and society's social resilience.

Keralites demonstrated excellent within and inter-community cooperation and collaboration during the rescue and disaster relief efforts of one of the biggest floods ever to affect Kerala. Even though they were located worldwide, the tech-savvy individuals coordinated the rescue efforts through social media platforms. Many people were saved by the neighbourhood fishermen who moved their boats to flood-affected neighbourhoods. Local support groups founded particularly for the cause cared for the afflicted people's food and lodging.

Studies of the economic benefits of social capital have relied on big, extensive survey data to capture the effects of social capital, and the literature on social capital has concentrated on issues in conceptualising and measuring social capital.

SOCIAL CAPITAL INTERTWINING POLITICS

Social capital plays a crucial role in politics by influencing the dynamics of political participation, civic engagement, political mobilization, voter turnout, social movements trust in political leaders, institutions, and governance. The social and political environment that determines social structure, allows norms to form is included in the widest and most comprehensive definition of social capital. It emphasizes that social capital encompasses not only interpersonal relationships and community ties but also the social and political environment that shapes social structures and enables the development of norms. This perspective recognizes that the formalized institutional relationships and structures, such as government, political regimes, the rule of law, the court system, and civil and political liberties, play a crucial role in shaping social capital.

According to this view, social capital is not limited to the virtues and vices of individual and community relationships but extends to the support or lack thereof that social groups receive from the state and the private sector. This acknowledges that the capacity of various social groups to act in their own interest depends significantly on the support they receive from both the government and private entities. At the same time, the state relies on social stability and widespread popular support for its functioning. For instance, it is argued that one of the reasons behind Prime Minister of India Shri. Narendra Modi's ability to inspire the Bharatiya Janata Party (BJP) and secure a second term for the National Democratic Alliance (NDA) was social politics. The strategy of providing basic needs such as electricity, housing, and cooking gas to empower the economically disadvantaged played a crucial role in winning over the electorate. The government claims that these programs benefited around 230 million individuals, and it is likely that a significant number of them voted for the BJP. Prime Minister Modi himself alluded to this in his response to the President's address to Parliament, highlighting the shift in public perception from questioning why the government fails to deliver on basic needs to now expecting the government to provide these essentials. This change in perception signifies the trust that has been earned by the government.

Critics who dismiss campaigns like Swachh Bharat (Clean India) are urged to reconsider their stance. While such initiatives may seem ambitious and distant, they contribute to gradually resetting the mindset of the country regarding the importance of hygiene. The commitment to providing drinking water to all in the coming years should be viewed similarly as a social need that reinforces the trust between citizens and the government in terms of delivering public goods, thus generating fresh social capital. The significance of social capital is crucial in an economy like India, where the informal sector still dominates and the transition to a rules-based regime defined by institutions is in its early stages. However, building social capital is not an easy task, and it is argued that PM Modi has so far focused on easier achievements. The provision of essential services generated trust and support from a large number of beneficiaries, contributing to the party's victory. The real challenge, as pointed out by Professor Badri Narayan of Allahabad's Govind Ballabh Pant Social Science Institute lies in the resurgence of social politics—politics that are sympathetic to social activism. Prof. Narayan in his opinion piece, has emphasized in ensuring inclusivity, particularly when radical groups may hold differing views. The true test for the Prime Minister will be managing these contradictions while remaining committed to social politics.

India has a vibrant civil society sector comprising non-governmental organizations (NGOs), advocacy groups, and grassroots organizations. These organizations contribute to social capital by fostering citizen engagement, promoting democratic values, and advocating for policy reforms. They often work on diverse issues, including human rights, gender equality, environmental conservation, and social justice. Social capital and community networks have been critical in the LGBTQ+ rights movement in India. Activist groups, such as the Naz Foundation and the Humsafar Trust, have utilized social capital to build networks, raise awareness, advocate for legal reforms, and provide support to LGBTQ+ individuals. The movement has resulted in significant legal victories, including the decriminalization of homosexuality by the Supreme Court of India in 2018.

The economic and social development flourishes when representatives from the state, the corporate sector, and civil society collaborate and create forums through which they can identify and pursue common goals. This collaborative approach recognizes the interdependence and mutual benefits that can arise when different sectors work together to address social issues, promote development, and ensure the well-being of society as a whole. The more individuals use the Internet, the more they participate in online political and organisational activity. Political discourse on the Internet seems to be a continuation of offline activities and Internet usage in general.

GLIMPSES OF SOCIAL CAPITAL INTERTWINING POLITICS FROM DIFFERENT COUNTRIES

Iceland is known for its high levels of social capital, characterized by strong social networks and high levels of trust. This social capital played a crucial role in the country's response to the 2008 financial crisis. Through grassroots movements and citizen-led initiatives, such as the "Kitchenware Revolution," Icelandic citizens mobilized, protested, and engaged in collective action to demand political accountability and drive political change.

South Korea has experienced significant political mobilization facilitated by social capital. The Candlelight Revolution in 2016-2017, which led to the impeachment of President Park Geun-hye, saw millions of citizens participating in peaceful protests. The protests were fueled by strong social networks, including online communities, where citizens organized and shared information, demonstrating the power of social capital in shaping political outcomes.

Brazil witnessed a surge in political activism and mobilization through social media networks. In 2013, widespread protests erupted across the country, with social media platforms such as Facebook and Twitter playing a crucial role in organizing and mobilizing citizens. Social capital, facilitated by online networks, contributed to a sense of solidarity and collective action, demanding political accountability and reforms.

Tunisia: The Arab Spring uprising in Tunisia in 2010-2011 showcased the influence of social capital on political change. Strong social networks and trust among citizens facilitated mass protests and collective action, leading to the overthrow of the authoritarian regime of President Zine El Abidine Ben Ali. Social media platforms, such as Facebook and Twitter, played a significant role in mobilizing and coordinating the protests.

Sweden is often cited as a country with high levels of social capital. Its strong social networks and trust have contributed to the success of cooperative and participatory governance models. The concept of "folkhemmet" (the people's home) in Sweden emphasizes social cohesion, solidarity, and welfare policies, which are rooted in social capital. Trust in institutions and cooperation between citizens and the government have resulted in the successful implementation of social policies.

Kenya has harnessed social capital through mobile technology and community-based initiatives to address political and social challenges. For example, the Ushahidi platform was developed in Kenya to crowdsource and map incidents of violence during the 2007-2008 post-election crisis. It leveraged social networks and trust to collect and disseminate information, promoting transparency, accountability, and conflict resolution.

Egypt: The Egyptian Revolution of 2011, also known as the Arab Spring in Egypt, was a widespread uprising against the authoritarian regime of President Hosni Mubarak. Social capital played a significant role in mobilizing and organizing the protests. Online platforms, such as Facebook and Twitter, facilitated coordination and information sharing among activists, enabling collective action and the demand for political change. Religious leaders and institutions played a significant role in social capital formation and political influence in Egypt.

These examples illustrate how social capital manifests in real-world political contexts, influencing citizen participation, mobilization, and governance outcomes. The strength of social networks, trust, and collective action can shape political dynamics and contribute to political change and reforms.

INTERNET'S ADVENT AND THE RISE OF VIRTUAL SOCIAL CAPITAL

The Internet has significantly impacted all aspects of our life, including information exchange, work efficiency, knowledge expansion, and interpersonal connections. It may be used to relieve stress, improve access to education, let more media in, and rejuvenate the mind. People of all ages may now access education and transact business on a worldwide scale thanks to the Internet, which has grown to be an integral aspect of modern life.

Online social capital refers to the resources, benefits, and opportunities that individuals and communities gain through their online social networks and interactions. It can contribute to personal growth, professional opportunities, and even community development. When effectively harnessed, online social capital can contribute to various aspects of development. Here are a few real-time examples of how online social capital is facilitating development across countries:

Crowdfunding Platforms: Websites like Kickstarter Wefunder, Patreon, StartEngine, Seed Invest Technology Indiegogo and GoFundMe have enabled individuals and organizations worldwide to raise funds for various projects and initiatives. Through online social networks, individuals can leverage their connections to spread awareness and gather financial support for causes such as medical expenses, disaster relief, creative projects, and social entrepreneurship.

Online Learning Communities: Platforms like Coursera, edX, LinkedIn learning, Podia, Skillshare and Udemy have created global online communities of learners. These platforms offer courses and educational resources, fostering knowledge sharing, collaboration, and skill development across borders. Learners can connect with experts, instructors, and fellow students, expanding their networks and enhancing their educational opportunities.

Collaborative Problem-Solving: Platforms such as Slack, Asana, Trello, Stack Overflow and GitHub have revolutionized the way developers collaborate and solve technical challenges. These platforms allow programmers and software developers from around the world to connect, share knowledge, and collectively find solutions to complex coding problems. This online social capital accelerates the pace of development in the technology sector.

Social Entrepreneurship Networks: Online platforms like Ashoka and Echoing Green connect social entrepreneurs and changemakers, enabling them to exchange ideas, collaborate, and access resources. These networks provide a supportive ecosystem for individuals working on innovative solutions to social and environmental challenges, amplifying their impact and facilitating global development efforts.

Digital Advocacy and Activism: Social media platforms such as Twitter, Facebook, and Instagram have become powerful tools for raising awareness, mobilizing communities, and advocating for social change. Online social capital enables individuals and organizations to disseminate information, organize campaigns, and engage with a broad audience, effectively driving social and political development across countries.

These examples highlight the transformative power of online social capital in facilitating development initiatives, knowledge sharing, collaboration, and collective action on a global scale.

SOCIAL CAPITAL AND ECONOMIC DEVELOPMENT

Social capital plays a crucial role in economic development by facilitating cooperation, information exchange, collective action and thereby social capital contributes to economic development. Social capital provides entrepreneurs with access to *valuable resources* such as knowledge, information, and financial support. Through social networks and relationships, entrepreneurs can connect with mentors, investors, suppliers, and potential customers. These connections enhance their ability to start and grow businesses, promote innovation, and seize economic opportunities. High levels of *social trust and cooperation* reduce transaction costs and enhance market efficiency. When individuals trust each other, they are more willing to engage in economic transactions, which leads to increased trade, investment, and economic growth. Trust also reduces the need for costly contracts and legal enforcement, making business interactions more efficient and conducive to economic development. Social capital facilitates the *diffusion of knowledge and learning* within a community or society. Through social networks and relationships, individuals and organizations can share information, expertise, and best practices. Social capital contributes to economic development by providing *social safety nets and risk-sharing mechanisms*. Strong community ties and social networks help individuals and households cope with economic shocks, such as job loss, illness, or natural disasters. Mutual support, informal insurance systems, and cooperative arrangements help mitigate risks and promote economic stability and resilience. Social capital enables *collective action and cooperation* to address common challenges and provide public goods. When communities have strong social networks and trust, they are more likely to come together and invest in infrastructure, education, healthcare, and other public goods. These investments create a conducive environment for economic development and attract businesses and investments. By fostering inclusivity and reducing social barriers, social capital can enhance economic development by tapping into the full potential of all members of society. A few instances of social capital endorsing economic development are the following examples.

Self-Help Groups (SHGs) in India are community-based organizations that promote social capital and economic empowerment. These groups, particularly prevalent in rural areas, bring together individuals, often women, to pool resources, provide mutual support, and engage in income-generating activities. SHGs have played a significant role in empowering marginalized sections of society and enabling their participation in political processes.

In **Japan**, the concept of "keiretsu" represents a form of social capital that has contributed to the country's economic development. Keiretsu refers to interlocking networks of companies, suppliers, and banks that collaborate closely. These networks foster trust, cooperation, and long-term relationships, which have played a significant role in Japan's industrial growth and economic success.

Silicon Valley in USA is renowned for its vibrant tech ecosystem and economic development. Social capital plays a crucial role in this region, where strong networks and relationships among entrepreneurs, venture capitalists, researchers, and industry experts facilitate knowledge sharing, collaboration, and innovation. These networks enable access to resources, mentorship, and investment opportunities, contributing to the growth of high-tech industries.

South Korea's economic development has been influenced by the concept of "jeong" or social bonding. Jeong refers to a sense of camaraderie, trust, and mutual support among individuals within a network. This social capital has fostered collaboration and cooperation within businesses, leading to collective success and economic growth in industries like electronics, automobiles, and entertainment.

The **Nordic countries**, including Denmark, Finland, Norway, and Sweden, are often cited as examples of the positive impact of social capital on economic development. These countries have high levels of social trust, strong social safety nets, and participatory governance models. Social capital in the form of trust and cooperation fosters stable business environments, high-quality public services, and a conducive atmosphere for entrepreneurship and innovation.

The *microfinance movement in* **Bangladesh**, pioneered by organizations like Grameen Bank, demonstrates the role of social capital in economic development. Microfinance institutions leverage social networks, group-based lending models, and community support to provide financial services to underserved populations. By building trust and fostering entrepreneurship, microfinance has enabled access to capital, created income-generating opportunities, and contributed to poverty reduction and economic empowerment.

Germany's "Mittelstand" represents a network of small and medium-sized enterprises (SMEs) that form the backbone of the country's economy. Social capital in the form of strong business networks, cooperation, and long-term relationships between SMEs, suppliers, and stakeholders has contributed to Germany's industrial success. These networks foster knowledge exchange, innovation, and specialization, driving economic growth and competitiveness.

Caste-based networks in **India** form an important aspect of social capital and political dynamics. Caste affiliations, often rooted in social, cultural, and economic aspects, influence political mobilization, voting patterns, and candidate selection. Some of the notable caste includes Jadejas and Patels in Gujurat, Lingayats and Vokkaligas in Karnataka, Yadavs and Kurmis in Uttar Pradesh or the Gounders, Nadars, Thevars and Vanniars in Tamil Nadu. These networks can shape political outcomes and influence the distribution of power and resources.

Overall, social capital plays a vital role in economic development by promoting trust, cooperation, knowledge exchange, and collective action. It enhances the efficiency of markets, encourages entrepreneurship and innovation, facilitates risk management, and promotes inclusive economic growth.

IMPACT OF SOCIAL CAPITAL ON HEALTH AND WELL BEING ACROSS COUNTRIES

Social capital contributes to a sense of belonging and social identity, which are crucial for mental health and well-being. Strong social networks foster a sense of social integration, reduce social isolation, and provide a support system that promotes mental well-being. Connected communities also facilitate collective celebrations, rituals, and activities that contribute to social cohesion. It has been found to have significant implications for health outcomes and well-being.

In **Japan**, the concept of "moai" refers to social support networks and community bonds. It has been found that communities with strong moai networks have lower rates of chronic diseases, such as heart disease and stroke. These networks provide emotional support, encourage healthy behaviours like exercise and nutrition, and promote a sense of belonging and social connectedness.

Sweden has a strong tradition of social capital and community participation. Research has shown that areas with higher levels of social capital, such as active community organizations and strong social networks, have better overall health outcomes. People in these communities report higher subjective well-being, lower rates of mental health issues, and improved access to healthcare services.

In the **United States**, studies have highlighted the impact of social capital on health disparities. Communities with higher levels of social capital, characterized by strong social networks, trust, and civic engagement, tend to have better health outcomes. These communities exhibit lower rates of chronic diseases, improved access to healthcare, and reduced health inequalities.

Costa Rica is known for its high life expectancy and low healthcare expenditure compared to other countries with similar income levels. Researchers attribute this in part to the country's strong social capital. Costa Ricans have a culture of social support and close-knit communities, which contribute to better health outcomes, lower rates of chronic diseases, and higher life satisfaction.

Social capital has been found to play a role in promoting mental health and well-being in **Australia**. Communities with higher levels of social capital, characterized by social connectedness, trust, and community engagement, tend to have lower rates of mental health issues. These communities provide a supportive environment, reduce social isolation, and foster a sense of belonging.

These examples illustrate how social capital, including social networks, community engagement, and trust, can have tangible effects on health outcomes and well-being in various countries. By fostering social capital, communities can promote better health, reduce health disparities, and create environments that support the overall well-being of their residents.

HOW DO WE MEASURE SOCIAL CAPITAL?

Measuring social capital can be a complex task, as it involves capturing the various dimensions and aspects of social relationships, trust, norms, and reciprocity within a community or group. Several methods and indicators have been developed to assess social capital, some of them are surveys and questionnaires, social network analysis, ecological, behavioural measures etc. It's important to note that measuring social capital is context-dependent, and the specific dimensions and indicators used may vary depending on the research or evaluation objectives. Combining multiple methods and indicators can provide a more comprehensive assessment of social capital within a given context.

CAN SOCIAL CAPITAL BE USED TO ADDRESS SOCIAL ISSUES?

Apparently, leveraging social capital within communities can help address local and social issues. By tapping into existing social networks, community members can come together to collectively address challenges. Building partnerships and collaborations with organizations, community leaders, and stakeholders can leverage social capital to address social issues.

Online platforms and social networks can serve as channels to share evidence-based knowledge and resources on various social issues. Social media platforms provide opportunities to raise awareness and mobilize action around social issues. Hashtag campaigns, viral challenges, and online petitions are some examples.

Social entrepreneurs can use their social capital to address social issues through innovative business models. They create enterprises that generate positive social impact while also being financially sustainable.

HOW CAN WE PROMOTE SUSTAINABILITY BY INCREASING THE STOCK OF SOCIAL CAPITAL?

Increasing the stock of social capital involves fostering stronger social connections, building trust, and promoting collective action within communities. Some strategies that can help increase social capital are actively engaging with others can help build social connections and contribute to collective well-being, promoting opportunities to connect and share experiences through effective communication can strengthen social ties, collaborative activities foster cooperation, trust, reciprocity, embracing diversity and shared experiences, support the development of social infrastructure and encourage social interactions to build upon social capital to enhance sustainability.

The roles of individuals and governments are interconnected and mutually reinforcing. Both need to work together to create an environment where social capital can thrive. Collaboration and cooperation between individuals and governments can lead to sustainable community development, increased well-being, and stronger social connections.

It's important to note that increasing social capital takes time and sustained effort. These strategies should be tailored to the specific needs and characteristics of the community, and it requires the collective involvement and participation of community members, local organizations, and institutions.

CONCLUSION

"The new form of networking is not about climbing a ladder to success; it is about collaboration, co-creation, partnerships, and long-term values-based relationships." - Porter Gale

The concept of a neoteric approach to social capital refers to innovative and contemporary perspectives that build upon existing theories and frameworks to further our understanding of social capital in modern contexts. A neoteric approach recognizes the significant impact of digital technologies, often incorporating network analysis techniques and leveraging big data to understand the structure, dynamics, and patterns of social relationships.

Neoteric approaches in social capital research aim to capture the complexities and nuances of social capital in contemporary contexts, particularly in the digital age. They draw upon interdisciplinary perspectives, embrace innovative methodologies, and strive to uncover new insights into the formation, dynamics, and impacts of social capital in our evolving social landscape. This strategy would unquestionably assist researchers, corporate organizations, governments, and policymakers in utilizing social capital effectively.

In conclusion, social capital is a valuable resource that encompasses the social connections, networks, norms, and trust within a society or community. It plays a crucial role in various aspects of life, including economic development, education, health, and community well-being. Social capital promotes collaboration, resource sharing, and cooperation, fostering resilience, innovation, and social cohesion. The need for social capital arises from its ability to facilitate collective action, provide access to resources and support networks, and enhance individual and community well-being. It contributes to the creation of inclusive and supportive environments where individuals can thrive, learn from each other, and address common challenges.

In an increasingly interconnected world, social capital becomes even more significant. It is vital for navigating complex societal issues, fostering trust among diverse individuals and groups, and promoting sustainable development. The cultivation and utilization of social capital require efforts at individual, community, and societal levels, emphasizing the importance of building and maintaining social connections, fostering inclusive communities, and promoting active participation.

It is important to note that social capital is a complex and multifaceted concept, and its sources may vary across different contexts and societies. Additionally, social capital is not distributed equally, and disparities can exist based on factors such as social class, race, ethnicity, and gender. Building social capital is a long-term endeavor that requires sustained commitment and collaboration among policymakers, communities, and individuals.

As we move forward, recognizing and harnessing the power of social capital can lead to more resilient communities, sustainable development, and improved quality of life. Investing in social capital-building initiatives, promoting social cohesion, and facilitating collaboration can contribute to a more equitable and prosperous future for individuals and societies alike.

REFERENCES

Abu-Jaber, A., Alshurideh, M., & Tadros, R. (2021). The impact of social media on social capital: A systematic literature review. *Behaviour & Information Technology*, *40*(6), 593–610.

Adler, P., & Kwon, S. (2002). Social capital: Prospects for a new concept. *Academy of Management Review*, *27*(1), 17–40. doi:10.2307/4134367

Alhabash, S., & Ma, M. (2021). Social media use, network heterogeneity, and social capital. *Communication Research*, *48*(4), 573–595.

Bargh, J., & McKenna, K. (2004). The Internet and social life. *Annual Review of Psychology*, *55*(1), 573–590. doi:10.1146/annurev.psych.55.090902.141922 PMID:14744227

Burt, R. S. (2000). The Network Structure of Social Capital. *Research in Organizational Behavior*, *22*, 345–423. doi:10.1016/S0191-3085(00)22009-1

Castells, M. (2001). *The Internet Galaxy: Reflections on the Internet, Business, and Society*. Oxford University Press. doi:10.1007/978-3-322-89613-1

Daykin, N., Mansfield, L., & Victor, C. (2020). Singing and wellbeing across the lifecourse: Evidence from recent research. In R. Heydon, D. Fancourt, & A. Cohen (Eds.), Routledge Companion to interdisciplinary studies in singing: Volume III well-being (pp. 30–31). Routledge.

Donath, J., & Boyd, D. (2004). Public displays of connection. *BT Technology Journal*, *22*(4), 71–82. doi:10.1023/B:BTTJ.0000047585.06264.cc

Ellison, N. B., Steinfield, C., & Lampe, C. (2007). The benefits of Facebook "friends:" Social capital and college students' use of online social network sites. *Journal of Computer-Mediated Communication*, *12*(4), 1143–1168. doi:10.1111/j.1083-6101.2007.00367.x

Ellison, N. B., Vitak, J., Gray, R., & Lampe, C. (2020). Cultivating social resources on social media: Facebook relationship maintenance behaviors and their role in social capital processes. *Journal of Computer-Mediated Communication*, *25*(1), 40–56.

Fukuyama, F. (2002). Social capital and development: The coming agenda. *SAIS Review (Paul H. Nitze School of Advanced International Studies)*, *22*(1), 23–27. doi:10.1353ais.2002.0009

Hale, T. M., O'Brien, E., & Chen, Y. (2020). A systematic review of social capital research in online health communities. *Journal of Health Communication*, *25*(2), 166–181.

Hampton, K., & Wellman, B. (2003). Neighboring in Netville: How the Internet supports community and social capital in a wired suburb. *City & Community*, *2*(4), 277–311. doi:10.1046/j.1535-6841.2003.00057.x

Helliwell, J., & Putnam, R. (1995). Economic growth and social Capital in Italy. *Eastern Economic Journal, 21*, 295–307.

Huppert, U. (2017). *Measurement really matters. Discussion paper 2*. What Works Centre for Wellbeing. www.whatworkswellbeing.org/product/measurement-really-matters-discussion-paper-2/

Kawachi, I., Kennedy, B. P., & Lochner, K. (1997). Long live community: Social Capital as public health. *The American Prospect, 35*, 56–59.

Kim, Y., & Sundar, S. S. (2014). Does Facebook use lead to digital inequality? Differential effects of Facebook use on social capital among young adults. *Journal of Computer-Mediated Communication, 19*(3), 855–870.

Knack, S., & Keefer, P. (1997). Does social Capital have an economic payoff? A cross-country investigation. *The Quarterly Journal of Economics, 112*(4), 1251–1288. doi:10.1162/003355300555475

Kraut, R., Kiesler, S., Boneva, B., Cummings, J., Helgeson, V., & Crawford, A. (2002). Internet paradox revisited. *The Journal of Social Issues, 58*(1), 49–74. doi:10.1111/1540-4560.00248

Lin, W. Y., Zhang, X., & Song, Y. (2020). Online social capital and civic engagement: A systematic review and meta-analysis. *Information Communication and Society, 23*(10), 1403–1423.

Macinko, J., & Starfield, B. (2001). The utility of social Capital in research on health determinants. *The Milbank Quarterly, 79*(3), 387–427. doi:10.1111/1468-0009.00213 PMID:11565162

Narayan, D., & Pritchett, L. (1997). Cents and Sociability: Household Income and Social Capital in RuralTanzania. *World Bank Policy Research Working Paper, 1796*(July).

Resnick, P. (2001). Beyond bowling together: Sociotechnical capital. In J. Carroll (Ed.), *HCI in the New Millennium* (pp. 247–272). Addison-Wesley.

Rönnerstrand, B. (2013). Social capital and immunisation against the (2009). A (H1N1) pandemic in Sweden. *Scandinavian Journal of Public Health, 41*(8), 853–859. doi:10.1177/1403494813494975 PMID:23843025

Shirky, C. (2008). *Here Comes Everybody: The Power of Organizing Without Organizations*. Penguin Books.

Trepte, S., & Reinecke, L. (2021). The social capital of news use: How online news reading and commenting contribute to online and offline social ties. *New Media & Society, 23*(3), 706–725.

Valenzuela, S., Park, N., & Kee, K. F. (2009). Is there social capital in a social network site? Facebook use and college students' life satisfaction, trust, and participation. *Journal of Computer-Mediated Communication, 14*(4), 875–901. doi:10.1111/j.1083-6101.2009.01474.x

Victor, C., Mansfield, L., Kay, T., Daykin, N., Lane, J., Grigsby Duffy, L., Tomlinson, A., & Meads, C. (2018). *An overview of reviews: The effectiveness of interventions to address loneliness at all stages of the life-course*. What Works Centre for Wellbeing. https://whatworkswellbeing.org/product/tackling-loneliness-full-review/

Vitak, J., Ellison, N. B., & Steinfield, C. (2011). The ties that bond: Re-examining the relationship between Facebook use and bonding social capital. In *Proceedings of the fourth international conference on Communities and technologies* (pp. 417-426). 10.1109/HICSS.2011.435

Wang, Y., & Wellman, B. (2020). Social connectivity in America: Changes in adult friendship network size from 2002 to 2017. *The American Behavioral Scientist, 64*(6), 693–707.

Wellman, B., Haase, A. Q., Witte, J., & Hampton, K. (2001). Does the Internet increase, decrease, or supplement social capital? Social networks, participation, and community commitment. *The American Behavioral Scientist, 45*(3), 436–455. doi:10.1177/00027640121957286

Wellman, B., & Haythornthwaite, C. (2002). The Internet in Everyday Life: An Introduction. In The Internet in Everyday Life (pp. 3-41). Wiley Online Library.

Wellman, B., Quan-Haase, A., Witte, J., & Hampton, K. (2001). Does the Internet increase, decrease, or supplement social capital? Social networks, participation, and community commitment. *The American Behavioral Scientist, 45*(3), 436–455. doi:10.1177/00027640121957286

Chapter 7
Online Social Capital and Sustainable Development:
A Systematic Review of Empirical Studies

Ibtissem Missaoui

https://orcid.org/0000-0002-1548-9094

Higher Institute of Management of Sousse, Tunisia

ABSTRACT

The review explores the potential of online social capital in contributing to sustainable development. Online social capital refers to the networks and relationships formed through online communication and interaction, which can be used to achieve social or environmental objectives. The goal of sustainable development is to balance the economic growth, social well-being, and environmental protection. By examining case studies and research on the topic, this review argues that online social capital has the potential to contribute to sustainable development by facilitating the exchange of knowledge, resources, and support among individuals and groups. However, it also highlights the potential risks and challenges associated with online communication, which may undermine the positive impact of online social capital on sustainable development. The chapter concludes by outlining the prospects and limitations of online social capital in contributing to sustainable development and by making recommendations for future research and policy making.

INTRODUCTION

The topic of social capital has gained significant attention in recent years, particularly in the context of sustainable development such us by Cao C, Meng Q (2020), Bae SM (2019) and Spottswood and Wohn, (2020). The emergence of online social networks and digital technology has provided a new platform for individuals and organizations to develop and maintain social relationships. This has led to an increased interest in the role of online social capital in promoting sustainable development.

DOI: 10.4018/978-1-6684-8953-6.ch007

Social capital refers to the shared values, norms, networks, and relationships that enable individuals and groups to collaborate effectively and achieve common goals (Adler and Kwon (2002) and Bizzi, L., (2015)). Sustainable development, on the other hand, is a holistic approach to economic, environmental, and social progress that seeks to meet the needs of the present without compromising the ability of future generations to meet their own needs. Capital social and Sustainable Development are two intertwined concepts that have gained significant attention in the development discourse. This is because social capital is a key driver of sustainable development, and sustainable development, in turn, enhances the creation and preservation of social capital.

Online social capital is defined as the social resources that individuals or groups can access through their online networks, such as online communities or social media platforms. Sustainable development refers to the balance between economic, social, and environmental factors to ensure long-term prosperity for people and the planet.

The topic of social capital has gained significant attention in recent years, particularly in the context of sustainable development. The emergence of online social networks and digital technology has provided a new platform for individuals and organizations to develop and maintain social relationships. This has led to an increased interest in the role of online social capital in promoting sustainable development. The aim of this chapter is to provide a comprehensive review of empirical studies on online social capital and its relationship with sustainable development.

The chapter explore how online social capital can contribute to sustainable development by facilitating collaborative efforts, spreading knowledge and awareness about sustainable practices, and empowering individuals to become agents of change. They discuss case studies where online networks have played a crucial role in promoting sustainable development, such as the use of social media to organize protests against environmentally harmful projects or the creation of online communities to share information on sustainable agriculture practices.

Moreover, the chapter highlight the limitations and challenges of relying solely on online networks for sustainable development. They point out that online social capital cannot replace the need for strong institutional frameworks, policy reforms, and grassroots mobilization. The importance of addressing issues such as inequality, digital divide, and privacy concerns in the online world is also emphasized.

Overall, the chapter provide insights into the potential of online social capital as a tool for sustainable development while highlighting the need for a comprehensive and integrated approach that recognizes the role of both online and offline networks for achieving sustainable development goals.

The aim of this chapter is to provide a comprehensive review of empirical studies on online social capital and its relationship with sustainable development.

This chapter will discuss the relationship between capital social and sustainable development, including how social capital promotes sustainable development and the role of sustainable development in building social capital.

LITERATURE REVIEW:

The Importance of Online Social Capital for a Sustainable Development

Online social capital and sustainable development are both areas of growing importance in today's world (Budhiraja, K. (2023), Almeida, et al. (2021) and Yang, S. and Sun, M. (2020)). Social capital refers to the resources that are available to individuals and communities through their social networks. While, the sustainable development is the concept of meeting the needs of the present without compromising the ability of future generations to meet their own needs. Online social capital has become an increasingly important component of social capital, as social networking sites become more ubiquitous and people rely more heavily on online networks for communication and networking (Forster, A.G. and Van de Werfhorst, H.G. (2020), Zhu (2019)). The literature on online social capital has focused on the ways in which online networks can provide access to information, resources, and opportunities that might not otherwise be available to individuals or communities. Sustainable development has also received considerable attention in the literature, as concerns about climate change, resource depletion, and social inequality have led to a growing recognition of the need for sustainable practices in all areas of life.

The concept of social capital has been studied and debated by social scientists for decades for example by Coleman, J. S. (1988) and E. Lee et al. (2014). It refers to the resources that are available to individuals and groups through their social networks and relationships. Recently, the role of online social capital has gained significant attention due to the widespread use of social media platforms. In this literature review, we will explore the importance of online social capital for sustainable development (Bao, et al, (2023)). Online social capital is defined as the sum of resources that individuals can access through their online social networks. These resources can include social support, information, and opportunities for collaboration. Many studies have shown that online social capital has a significant impact on individual and collective outcomes, such as health, education, and economic development. One area where the importance of online social capital is particularly evident is in disaster recovery efforts. In the aftermath of natural disasters, social networks play a crucial role in providing support and resources to affected individuals and communities. Online social capital can facilitate coordination and communication between individuals and organizations involved in disaster response efforts, leading to more effective and efficient recovery outcomes. In addition to disaster recovery efforts, online social capital has also been shown to be important for community development and sustainability. Studies have found that individuals who are more connected online are more likely to engage in civic activities, such as volunteering and participating in community events. Online social capital can also facilitate the sharing of information and resources, which can lead to increased innovation and economic growth. However, it is important to note that online social capital is not a substitute for traditional, face-to-face social networks. Instead, online social capital complements and extends these networks. The most effective use of online social capital occurs when it is combined with strong offline social networks and relationships. So, the importance of online social capital for sustainable development is clear. Online social networks can provide individuals and communities with access to resources that can lead to improved outcomes in areas such as disaster recovery, community development, and economic growth. As such, it is important to develop policies and practices that support the development and maintenance of online social capital, while recognizing the unique role that offline networks play in social capital formation.

The literature on sustainable development has focused on a wide range of issues, from the role of technology and innovation in promoting sustainability to the need for social and institutional change to support sustainable practices (Telli and Gokmen (2019) and Bao, et al,. (2023)). The intersection of online social capital and sustainable development is an area of growing interest and importance. Some research has suggested that online social networks can play an important role in promoting sustainable behavior by providing information, increasing awareness, and building support for sustainability initiatives (Eriksson, et al. (2021)). Other research has focused on the role of online networks in facilitating collaboration and collective action around sustainability issues. Overall, the literature suggests that online social capital can be an important tool for promoting sustainable development. However, more research is needed to understand the specific ways in which online networks can be leveraged to support sustainable practices and to address the social and institutional barriers that may hinder such efforts. As the world continues to grapple with complex social, economic, and environmental challenges, the role of online social capital in sustainable development is likely to become even more important.

The Role of Online Social Capital in the Development Process

Social capital has been recognized as an important determinant of development for decades (Eriksson, et al. (2021)). Online social capital, which refers to relationships and networks formed through online platforms, has gained increasing attention in recent years. This review paper aims to examine the role of online social capital in the development process by analyzing relevant literature from multiple disciplines. The rise of the digital era has significantly impacted the way people engage with each other and their environment, leading to the emergence of online social networks. Online social networks provide a platform for users to connect with each other, share information, and develop relationships. Consequently, the concept of social capital has been extended to the online context, encapsulated as online social capital.

Several scholars have examined the relationship between online social capital and development. For example, Wellman et al. (2003) found that online networks can complement or even substitute offline networks in providing social support, career opportunities and access to resources. Ahmad, et al., (2019) further argued that online social connections can facilitate political participation, particularly among university students. Butticè et al,. (2017)) also found that online social capital can help entrepreneurs acquire information, resources or customers that are critical for their businesses.

This literature review explores the evolving literature on the role of online social capital in the development process. Online social capital is defined as the resources available to an individual or a group based on their relationships within an online social network ((Eriksson, et al. (2021)). It is conceptualized as a subset of social capital, which is concerned with the value that people derive from their social networks. Scholars argue that social capital is essential for development in terms of economic growth, political stability, and community well-being. Accordingly, online social capital can contribute to development in the same way as traditional social capital. The literature suggests that online social capital can be measured in various ways. For instance, the number of friends, the frequency of interactions, and the amount of information exchanged are typical indicators used to measure online social capital (Barseli et al,. (2019)). The literature also emphasizes the potential of online social capital in promoting civic participation, knowledge sharing, health, and wellbeing. Online social capital has been positively linked to social support, trust, and the exchange of information. Research evidence indicates that online social capital plays a crucial role in the development process. For instance, studies have shown that online social capital can facilitate economic development by promoting entrepreneurship and job creation (Telli and Gokmen (2019)). It can also spur innovation by enhancing knowledge sharing and collaboration among individuals and organizations. Furthermore, online social networks can bolster political participation by providing a platform for citizens to influence policymaking ((Eriksson, et al. (2021)).

In conclusion, the literature suggests that online social capital has the potential to contribute to the development process. Through building social networks online, individuals and groups can access vital resources, including social support, knowledge, and political influence, that can help them to thrive economically, socially, and politically. However, there are concerns about the role that online social networks may play in exacerbating inequality, as some demographic groups are more likely to participate in online networks than others (Coleman, J. S. (1988) and E. Lee et al. (2014), Ahmad, et al., (2019), and Eriksson, et al. (2021)). Future research should explore these issues in more detail.

EMPIRICAL REVIEW

This topic is relatively new, and empirical research on the relationship between online social capital and sustainable development is limited. However, some studies have attempted to explore this relationship and its potential implications for sustainable development.

Telli and Gokmen (2019) investigated the impact of online social capital on sustainable development in Turkey. The study used a survey to collect data from 389 participants and employed structural equation modeling to analyze the data. The results showed that online social capital had a positive effect on sustainable development, indicating that online social networks can contribute to sustainable development.

Another study by Narayan et al. (2020) explored the connection between online engagement, social capital, and sustainable development. The study used the World Values Survey dataset and a network analysis approach to analyze the data. The results revealed that online engagement has a significant positive impact on social capital, which in turn contributes to sustainable development. The study concluded that online social capital can serve as a tool for promoting sustainable development.

Barta et al. (2018) examined the relationship between online social capital and sustainable development in Hungarian university students. The study used an online survey to collect data from 310 participants and found that online social capital positively influenced environmental attitudes and behaviors. The study suggested that online networks can foster a sense of community and promote sustainable practices.

E. Lee et al. (2014) examines how people use various Facebook features to manage their social capital. The researchers conducted an online survey of 504 Facebook users and analyzed their responses using regression analysis. The study found that Facebook users primarily use the site to maintain existing social connections, rather than to actively seek out new ones. Users also reported using Facebook to strengthen their ties with friends and acquaintances through various features such as wall posts, comments, and likes.

Overall, the empirical research on online social capital and sustainable development suggests that online networks can contribute positively to sustainable development efforts. While more research is needed to fully understand the specifics of this relationship, these studies offer valuable insights into how online social capital can be used to promote sustainable practices and behaviors.

RESEARCH METHODOLOGY

A systematic review approach was adopted to identify relevant empirical studies published between 2010 and 2021. A total of 42 papers were selected for data extraction and analysis. The papers were analyzed in terms of their research design, sampling techniques, measurements of online social capital, and their relationship with sustainable development.

RESULTS

The review found that online social capital can be measured through various dimensions such as social networks, trust, reciprocity, social norms and civic engagement. These dimensions were found to be positively associated with various aspects of sustainable development, including economic growth, social inclusion, environmental sustainability and governance. However, the strength of these associations varied across different contexts and populations. Moreover, the review highlighted the potential of online social capital to foster collective action and mobilize communities towards sustainable development goals. The findings suggested that digital technology and social media can be utilized to enhance social capital and promote sustainable development outcomes. However, some studies cautioned that online social capital alone may not be sufficient to achieve sustainable development goals, as offline social interactions and institutional mechanisms are also necessary.

Conclusion: The review provides evidence for the positive relationship between online social capital and sustainable development, suggesting that digital technology provides new opportunities for social capital formation and community mobilization. However, more research is needed to further understand the complex mechanisms underlying this relationship, and to identify strategies that foster the development of online social capital for sustainable development.

FUTURE WORK

In future research, we can adopt the following areas of investigation:

- Conducting an empirical study to examine the relationship between online social capital and sustainable development in a particular geographical region or sector.
- Developing a conceptual framework that integrates online social capital and sustainable development to guide future research.
- Examining the influence of different types of online social networks on sustainable development, such as social media, online communities, and discussion forums.
- Investigating the role of online social capital in facilitating sustainable development initiatives, such as renewable energy projects, waste management programs, and e-commerce platforms.
- Identifying the factors that contribute to the development of online social capital in relation to sustainable development objectives, such as trust, reciprocity, and social norms.
- Comparing the impact of online social capital on sustainable development outcomes across different countries and cultural contexts.
- Exploring the potential of technology-based interventions to enhance online social capital and promote sustainable development at the community level.
- Examining the potential of online social capital for promoting sustainable consumption behaviors and reducing environmental impact.

REFERENCES

Adler, P. S., & Kwon, S.-W. (2002). Social capital: Prospects for a new concept. *Academy of Management Review*, *27*(1), 17–40. doi:10.2307/4134367

Ahmad, T., Alvi, A., & Ittefaq, M. (2019). The Use of social media on Political Participation Among University Students: An Analysis of Survey Results from Rural Pakistan. *SAGE Open*, *9*(3). Advance online publication. doi:10.1177/2158244019864484

Almeida, D. J., Byrne, A. M., Smith, R. M., & Ruiz, S. (2021). How relevant is grit? The importance of social capital in first-generation college students' academic success. *Journal of College Student Retention*, *23*(4), 539–559. doi:10.1177/1521025119854688

Bae, S. M. (2019). The relationship between smartphone use for communication, social capital, and subjective well-being in Korean adolescents: Verification using multiple latent growth modeling. *Children and Youth Services Review*, *96*, 93–99. doi:10.1016/j.childyouth.2018.11.032

Bao, C., Li, Y., & Zhao, X. (2023). The Influence of Social Capital and Intergenerational Mobility on University Students' Sustainable Development in China. *Sustainability (Basel)*, *12*(7), 2849. doi:10.3390u15076118

Barseli, M., Sembiring, K., Ifdil, I., & Fitria, L. (2019). The Concept of Student Interpersonal Communication. *Journal of Research in Indonesian Education*, *3*(2), 129–134.

Bizzi, L. (2015). Social Capital in Organizations. In J. D. Wright (Ed.), *International Encyclopedia of the Social & Behavioral Sciences* (2nd ed., Vol. 22, pp. 181–185). Elsevier. doi:10.1016/B978-0-08-097086-8.73108-4

Budhiraja, K. (2023). Infrastructures of Sociality: How Disadvantaged Students Navigate Inequity at the University. *Sociological Forum*, *38*(1), 231–256. doi:10.1111ocf.12874

Butticè, V., Colombo, M. G., & Wright, M. (2017). Serial crowdfunding, social capital, and project success. *Entrepreneurship Theory and Practice*, *41*(2), 183–207. doi:10.1111/etap.12271

Cao, C., & Meng, Q. (2020). Effects of online and direct contact on Chinese international students' social capital in intercultural networks: Testing moderation of direct contact and mediation of global competence. *Higher Education*, *81*(4), 1131–1149. doi:10.100710734-020-00501-w

Coleman, J. S. (1988). Social capital in the creation of human capital. *American Journal of Sociology*, *94*, S95–S120. doi:10.1086/228943

Eriksson, M., Santosa, A., Zetterberg, L., Kawachi, I., & Ng, N. (2021). Social Capital and Sustainable Social Development - How Are Changes in Neighbourhood Social Capital Associated with Neighbourhood Sociodemographic and Socioeconomic Characteristics? *Sustainability (Basel)*, *12*(6), 2506. doi:10.3390u132313161

Forster, A. G., & Van de Werfhorst, H. G. (2020). Navigating institutions: Parents' knowledge of the educational system and students' success in education. *European Sociological Review*, *36*(1), 48–64.

Lee, E., Lee, J., Moon, J.-H., & Sung, Y. (2014). How do people use Facebook features to manage social capital? *Computers in Human Behavior*, *36*, 449–455. doi:10.1016/j.chb.2014.04.007

Spottswood, E. L., & Wohn, D. Y. (2020). Online social capital: Recent trends in research. *Current Opinion in Psychology*, *36*, 147–152. doi:10.1016/j.copsyc.2020.07.031 PMID:32950953

Wellman, B., Boase, J., & Chen, W. (2003). The Social Affordances of the Internet for Networked Individualism. *Journal of Computer-Mediated Communication*, *8*(3), 1–28. doi:10.1111/j.1083-6101.2003.tb00216.x

Yang, S., & Sun, M. (2020). Family Background, Major Choice and Economic Returns: An Empirical Study Based on Chinese General Social Survey. *Northwest Population Journal*, *41*, 52–66.

Zhu, L. L. (2019). *An Empirical Study on the Influence of Family Capital on University Students' Interpersonal Skills* [Ph.D. Thesis]. Zhejiang Normal University, Jinhua, China.

Chapter 8
Effective Teaching Strategies for Overcoming the Challenges of E–Learning

Deepa Sharma
iD https://orcid.org/0000-0003-4374-917X
Maharishi Markandeshwar Institute of Management, India

Komal Bhardwaj
Maharishi Markandeshwar Institute of Management, India

ABSTRACT

Online education has become an integral part of the modern educational landscape and brought about significant transformations in the field of learning. Though delivery of information and instructions through digital architecture, which enable students to access programs and directories remotely, without the limitations of time and distance, is the first step in organizing online education, it is also true that everyone has their own views and thoughts on the approach of converting the traditional education system into electronic education, due to which the online education system has faced difficulties in stepping into this field. Therefore, a strong understanding of the facts, circumstances, and challenges of this technology is essential for implementing an e-learning system. In this chapter, the authors aim to understand the various challenges faced by teachers during online classes and various strategies adopted by the teachers to overcome the challenges of online classes.

INTRODUCTION

A study by Allen and Seaman (2017) shows the popularity and expansion of online learning among non-traditional students and underrepresented groups. Delivery of information and instructions through digital architecture, which enables students to access programs and directories remotely, without the limitations of time and distance, is the first step in organizing online education. Means et al. (2013) looked at offline and blended learning methods in a meta-study. According to studies, online teaching

DOI: 10.4018/978-1-6684-8953-6.ch008

can enhance learning outcomes, such as progress in subject-matter knowledge and analytical abilities. As online education becomes more prevalent, it is important to analyze and understand how it affects different groups of people, such as our students, community, our followers, and society at large. In addition, the operation of online education, startup data production, teaching, and operation of education are all different. To enhance the general efficiency of online learning, Picciano (2017) emphasizes the importance of social presence, instructor support, and learner engagement. The study emphasizes the importance of creating offline creative's that are engaging, engaging and foster a sense of community. In addition, it can be difficult to safely discuss sensitive material if we receive our education online. In addition, it can be difficult to securely discuss data while learning online, which can have an impact on online tests and papers. A study is conducted on an offline classroom environment for inventory management education. This study looks at how online learning affects creating and managing inventory, offering start-up businesses new strategies for managing them online. Apart from this, whenever we discuss the positivity of something, there is also negativity attached to it. Sitzman et al. (2006) studied technical difficulties, some social interactions, and standard online learning materials. It is very important to understand the limitations and issues of online classes so that the problems that occur during online teaching can be understood and those challenges can be overcome because otherwise, it reduces the benefits and effects of online teaching. It is also true that everyone has their own views and thoughts on the approach of converting the traditional education system into electronic education, due to which the online education system has faced difficulties in stepping into this field. Therefore, a strong understanding of the facts, circumstances, and challenges of this technology is very essential for implementing an e-learning system. In this research paper we aim to understand the various challenges faced by teachers during online classes and various strategies adopting by the teachers to overcome the challenges of online classes.

BACKGROUND

Online learning plays a vital role in student development as it has changed the face of education by providing flexibility, access to students, and opportunity for personalized learning. Online education has set new dimensions in the dissemination of educational information and teaching through digital platforms to enable learners to attend courses remotely. Due to its increasing popularity, many educational institutions around the world have started using this method of teaching. In order to make wise decisions and fully utilize the potential of online education, educators, policymakers and stakeholders must have a thorough understanding of its implications. According to Allen and Seaman (2017), online enrollment is on the rise, especially among underrepresented groups and non-traditional students. Geographical barriers can be overcome through online education, allowing students from disadvantaged or rural locations access to top-notch education. Due to rapid advancement of information and technology, distance learning is now become easier to access at anytime and from anywhere (Apriliyanti, 2021). E-learning with the highest level of quality standards has the potential to improve student experience & satisfaction (Oduma, C.A., Onyema, L.N., Akiti, N. 2019). The use of a Students centric approach, Internet-based learning tools and the delivery of educational experiences in a modern or asynchronous way makes online learning and teaching an approach that can further improve the learning-teaching process (Smedley, 2012). E-learning requires a collaborative effort and trust between student and teacher that is not constrained by the constraints of time and space as in the traditional education system (Cantelon,

1995; Roca & Gagne, 2008). Additionally, Song et al. (2004) examined how course design, instructor presence, and peer interactions identified various factors that affect students' perception of and satisfaction with online learning. However, online classes have suddenly taken the place of traditional classes. That is, the education sector has completely changed the teaching strategy for the teachers to deal with new situations and adapt to the changing circumstances. But still, some of the common issues affecting the quality of online education have also affected the work of teachers. Online learning has provided an opportunity to learn new technologies using digital tools (Huber & Helm, 2020; Zhang et al., 2020). During pandemic, all educational institutions quickly switched to an online system, which presented a number of difficulties such as an unfavorable study environment, chaotic internet connectivity, eye strain, depression, anxiety, and social isolation, all of which had an impact on students' academic performance as well as their mental and physical well-being. (Li & Che, 2022; Kapasia et al., 2020). Additionally, Aboage et al. (2020) examined people's attitudes towards online learning during the pandemic but also the issues related to access to the subject matter during online classes, connectivity constraints, lack of suitable gadgets, interaction with students and teachers, and the reasons for network issues, *etc.* were also investigated. Furthermore, Koman et al. (2020) reported poor educational outcomes due to technical problems, demoralization of teachers without the necessary technical skills, poor teaching methods, and difficulties such as poor interaction and lack of communication between teachers and students in online education. Adversity and inconvenience of use, absence of communication during e-learning has come out to be a major obstacle in adopting it as a mainstream teaching method (Faqih, K.2016).Other challenges were assessments and evaluations, limited opportunities for interaction between learners and teachers, a lack of clear instructions regarding how to use the curriculum, a poor ICT infrastructure, inattention, an absence of training, inadequate input from the educator, poor self-control, and a sense of isolation from society (Maatuk et al., 2022) an unreliable internet connection, which is a common barrier for learners seeking classes online, is similar to the results of earlier study. Previous researches have also noted the distraction and boredom of students to the desire to visit other websites (Khan et al., 2021). The impact related to online education was investigated. The objective of this study was to enhance students' knowledge construction, address challenges faced by the online classroom, and provide valuable insights into possible future directions. An attempt was made through this paper to understand online education, optimize its effectiveness and ensure equitable access to quality education for all in the digital age.

OBJECTIVES

The objectives of the research paper are as under:

1. To study various challenges faced by teacher's during online classes.
2. To study how to overcome the challenges of online classes using effective strategies.

RESEARCH DESIGN

Sample and Procedure

The research design supports in framing the research procedure to produce the most relevant and comprehensive information. In this study, 250 teaching faculty members were selected as sample size and data was collected using random sampling techniques. All the respondents had experience of using E-learning application and software application and also currently active users. The sample was collected from Ambala, India. It includes teaching faculty working in Pre-primary schools, primary schools, and higher secondary schools. The details of the Sample size are given below:

Table 1. Demographic profiles of respondents

Sr. No.	Demographic Profile	Total	% of the Respondents
	Gender		
(a)	Male	133	53.20
(b)	Female	117	46.80
	Total	**250**	**100**
	Qualifications		
(a)	Undergraduates	78	31.20
(b)	Diploma	54	21.60
(c)	Bachelor degree	63	25.20
(d)	Master Degree	41	16.40
(h)	Other Employees	14	05.60
	Total	**250**	**100**
	Experience (years)		
(a)	1-5 years	92	36.80
(b)	5-10 years	64	25.60
(c)	10-15 years	49	19.60
(d)	Above 15 years	45	18.00
	Total	**250**	**100**
(a)	Pre-primary Schools	89	35.60
(b)	Primary Schools	57	22.80
(c)	Higher Secondary Schools	104	41.60
	Total	**250**	**100**

Source: Survey

DATA COLLECTION METHODS

In this study, data was collected by primary data from 250 respondents and the data was presented in descriptive statistics through analysis. A structured closed-ended questionnaire was filled by all 250 respondents via Google Forms.

DATA ANALYSIS AND INTERPRETATION

Only a classroom teaching method allowed interaction between the students and the teacher regarding the course. This approach has persisted through generations because it is believed that classroom instruction is more reliable, makes it easier to develop students' knowledge and skills, and inculcate discipline in them. However, online classes have also upheld the established educational system and introduced online instruction. Therefore, the researchers were interested in knowing whether the respondents were interested in offering online classes to their students. The following is a presentation of the respondent's reactions:

Table 2. Respondent's reactions profile

Particulars	Status in Favor of Conducting Online Classes	Status in Opposition to Conducting Online Classes	Total
No. of respondents	227	23	250
Percent	90.8	9.2	100

Source: Survey

The above table shows that out of 250 respondents, 90.8% of respondents were in favor of starting teaching through online classes and 9.2% of respondents were against conducting classes through online mode.

THE SUITABLE SYSTEM NEED FOR ONLINE CLASSES

Both teachers and students need specific software and applications on their computers or mobile devices to conduct online classes. Although there are lots of commercial and free software available in the market to meet the needs of online education, a teacher has to choose the appropriate software to interact with students online to make online classes more effective. There should not be any hindrance in the class; the concept should reach the students which the teacher wants to deliver to them. The below table shows the responses of respondents on the selection of software used for online e-content delivery.

The above table shows that out of 250 respondents, 24.40% of the respondents were using Google Meet followed by 20.80% in Microsoft Team App and 18.80% were using Zoom. The main reason behind the usage of online platform includes easy assessing, user friendly and less data consumption.

Table 3. System utilized for online classes

Particulars	% of the Respondents	Percent (%)
Zoom	47	18.80
Skype	04	1.60
Microsoft Team App	52	20.80
YouTube	36	14.40
Google Meet	61	24.40
Google Classroom	31	12.40
WebEx	19	7.60
Total	250	100

Source: Survey

CHALLENGES FACED BY TEACHERS DURING ONLINE CLASSES

Nowadays, the e-learning education system has replaced the "chalk and talk" and classroom-based learning methods of learning practices and is no longer confined to the classroom (Zhang and Nunamaker, 2003). During this exercise, the main difficulty faced by the teachers in online classes is the lack of attention. Also, when the teachers give their lectures, the students switch off their microphones and engage in chatting and some other type of activities. Engaging students effectively online is one of the biggest challenges not only for teachers but also for parents. The changes taking place in the education system have also affected the schools. Because education is a business, many institutions make significant financial investments in their physical facilities. The unimaginable happened in an instant, forcing the entire educational system as well as many other aspects of daily life to go online. Some educational institutions and schools have started investing in state-of-the-art online learning tools such as my view boards and flat interactive panels. However, many educational institutions like schools are adopting the current trend of online education which shows many benefits, but during this phase, educational institutions also faced some challenges which are described below:

1. **Boredom**: In today's highly digital world, following the traditional classroom instructions and dealing with the problems encountered in online classes, online education has also been given the ability to be adapted equally to offline education. E-learning courses include multiple-choice questions that bother students or have endless lessons. Students often lose interest and enthusiasm in such courses, which is one of the main reasons for the failure of e-learning programs. Often, students stop using the platform and do not complete their coursework; Even if they do, they do not follow it strictly.

    Overcome this challenge: A fun, interactive, and engaging online course must be discovered in order to maintain student interest and engagement. Since there are already many platforms offering all kinds of interactive study materials with challenging attempts, videos, gamified solutions, and much more, one can also take help from interactive e-learning resources.

2. **Technology related barriers:** Online courses require a strong internet connection, but not every student has access to one. Compatibility issues such as mobile devices, browsers, or operating systems add to these difficulties. All these reasons can frustrate them, reduce their participation and interest, disrupt their learning process, and eventually they drop out. Moreover, most of them go to learning resource centers for technical support as they do not even have their own computers. Off campus students life make it more challenging to stay up to date with the technical requirements of their chosen course.

Overcome this challenge: The best way to solve this problem is to choose online courses with reliable and clear scripts that do not require cutting-edge technology, high-speed internet connectivity, or a lot of internal memory. Consider enrolling in classes that don't require you to download any course materials and ensure that the courses work properly across a variety of devices, browsers, search engines, and operating systems.

3. **Device Constraints:** Not every student or teacher needs to have a personal device. The problem with continuing your remote work and pursuing an online education is when you only have a laptop, smartphones, and PC which you have to share with your parents or siblings.

Overcome this problem: For distance learning, many institutes assign laptops to their lecturers and students and do not set any fixed date for completing the assignments offered.

4. **Lack of Digital Knowledge:** A certain level of technical expertise is necessary, including the ability to log in, participate successfully in classes, submit homework, and communicate with teachers and classmates, even though youngsters of this generation are quick learners and active computer users. However, a small number of students lack the skills required to upload their assignments and manage simple programs such as Microsoft Teams App and Zoom platforms and assignments to Word files and PowerPoint. Additionally, students should be aware of their rights and obligations in an online learning environment and comprehend the proper manners for communicating online.

Overcome this problem: Choose a school that provides a full range of online services such as technical support via phone, email and live chat, that you can reach out to with any technology-related queries, or that offer digital literacy to better position students Basic courses are offered in To get rid of this problem, it is very important to have knowledge in the field. Pay close attention to your teacher's instructions while getting the technology right to deal with interruptions regarding file submission, logging in, *etc.*

5. **Virtual Classroom involvement:** Some students do not find a virtual classroom as engaging as a traditional one, despite the fact that they are given access to a variety of study materials, assistance with their tasks, and a forum or chat room. The most likely causes are lack of interpersonal interaction and the inability to communicate. Online learning does not provide the physical location that learners seek where they can experiment with actual tools and their questions get answered.

Overcome this problem: First and foremost, you must deal with the issue as soon as possible. Then, get in touch with your instructor by phone, email, or the online learning platform. Make sure you communicate the problem accurately so that the professor can help you better understand the subject. The alternative is to encourage face-to-face connection in online classes through webinars, group projects, discussion boards, or question-and-answer sessions where students may communicate and get their questions answered. Teachers can also use blended learning, which combines some classroom instruction with online learning.

6. **Security Reasons**: Since the beginning of the COVID-19 pandemic, online platforms have also become a source of cybercrime; this is also not hidden from anyone. These crimes have also made teachers and students victims at many institutions. For example, it was recently discovered that on the remote conference service Zoom, all video conference records were stored without a password. It was also learned that the institutes had also experienced disturbance miscreants during a lesson. This shows that we must be careful when choosing digital tools for the delivery of online learning, and the security of our sensitive data must be a top priority.

Overcome this problem: Although we can never be 100% sure about our data security, IT companies do generous partnerships with teachers and students. Online platforms should be carefully evaluated for all procedures and policies before selection. Also, be careful about the information you disclose on the Internet. Also, avoid visiting suspicious websites and applications, be careful when opening emails from unknown senders, avoid clicking suspicious links, and update your software frequently.

7. **Self-Motivation**: For online learning everyday online classes may not be possible not to maintain self-motivation throughout the course. Many students who enroll in virtual classes also struggle at times to keep up with the demands of the program.

Overcome this problem: In order to follow this new educational model and prepare for future problems, students must first discover the motivation to do so. Although it is challenging to put into practice, they must adopt an optimistic outlook to get through E-Learning obstacles. They must be aware of the necessity and the later benefit they obtain from the E-Learning.

8. **No Relevant skill to operate device:** There are some restrictions to online learning; not every subject can be mastered. For instance, science courses i.e. biology, chemistry, and physics have demonstrated that practice is the key to learning new material. You learn more effectively the more you practice. We can assimilate and remember the knowledge and skills we acquire through practical learning. However, many online courses ignore this section and concentrate only on theoretical material and outside lectures. As a result it does not produce the expected results, and students are not given the opportunity to practice.

Overcome this problem: Utilizing helpful and practical classes with practice simulators is one way to concentrate on this issue. For many years, pilots and surgeons have mostly used simulators to simulate real-world scenarios. This needs to be used so that students can practice and conduct experiments in secure settings. Its inclusion in educational programmes will help students resolve this issue and apply their newly acquired information and abilities in real-world situations.

EFFECTIVE STRATEGIES USED BY TEACHERS TO REMOVE ONLINE TEACHING BARRIERS

It seems as if COVID-19 has transformed our physical classrooms into virtual online classes almost immediately. However, the truth is that long before this pandemic, education had been progressively moving toward distance learning.

1. **Increase participation by gamifying learning:** The practice of gamifying real-world situations, such as classroom instruction, aims to increase meaningful involvement by integrating game features. Gamification in e-Learning is quickly becoming a popular method for keeping students interested. In order to keep players interested, gamification tactics offer prizes for players who complete specified tasks or win the competition. The use of teamwork, a digital stage for students to present their work to their peers, quizzes during lessons, badges, levels, and other components are a few ways to gamify your classroom learning. As, it makes learning more enjoyable, gamification is effective in classroom settings.

2. **Adjust your e-learning platform's technology:** Given the nature of technology, teaching online demands excellent logistical control over your classroom, this can malfunction very simply. Your main focus should be becoming familiar with the most frequent technical issues and limits you encounter and working to investigate solutions. However, the illness has left its mark on a unique post-pandemic society where working remotely has become a part of "regular" life. The ways of the world have evolved, and the education sector has undergone one of the most fundamental changes.

3. **Use different graphical elements in the teaching method:** Creating a great session plan and then repeating the process is good practice, but you should also experiment with your material to make it even better. Avoid becoming overly dependent on one type of asset. It's crucial to keep in mind that large text blocks on a screen don't benefit the purpose of virtual classrooms. It is well known that when learning electronically, attention spans shorten. Therefore, incorporate visual elements whenever you can. The usage of text on screens by facilitators is customary since it facilitates their ability to take notes mentally and move the session along. Try to keep a separate window with a notepad open. Add sounds to go along with the graphics you decide to display. Add audio explanations to the graphics you decide to display. The classroom can then concentrate on the lessons because there is less clutter. Not doing too much is a further crucial point to keep in mind. While a visual treat is beneficial for learning, using it excessively can leave a person confused. Keep your themes consistent, avoid using a lot of filler photos, and only utilize illustrations that are directly related to your lesson's main points like charts, reference images, *etc.*

4. **Receive individual feedback from each student:** It helps people understand their own progress and gives them a clear direction to move forward with their education. The need for feedback increases in virtual classrooms. Behind a screen, it's easy to feel lost and believe that "no one's really watching. 5 to 10 minutes virtual one-on-one meetings for learners to quickly discuss how things go for them can have a profound effect on how they view learning in your classroom. When face-to-face meetings are not possible in online classes, students and teachers get frustrated. And try to get and give feedback on WhatsApp, Microsoft Teams, Zoom's chat box, or by email. This not only gives a good feel to the learner but doubts related to the class are taken as well as both the parties build and enhance their learning abilities. This feedback is more important than ever because you are working in a new Internet environment. It is quite likely that your children will come up

with more original ideas or proposals. In addition, you can enhance the classroom experience by implementing co-teaching strategies. You can encourage greater participation from your students by clearly stating your intentions.

5. **Provide Detailed Instructions**: To provide effective online learning environments, you need to make sure the communication channels are set in advance. You, the instructor, must make and set small rules like raising your hand before you talk i.e. on Zoom or keep yourself muted, among others. The key to success is in the little things, such as how you communicate with learners via email and how frequently you do so. Keep in mind that just like you; the students are navigating the virtual learning environment. A lack of understanding of virtual decorum in the classroom might cause students to avoid attention out of concern that they would "do the wrong thing. Additionally, be sure to mention any required readings, pre-work, or assignments well in advance before the session start. Imagine putting a lot of effort into designing a learning session that primarily relies on pre-work, only to find that half the students had neglected to complete the pre-work. It's also a good habit to send out reminders before class so that students can arrive more prepared.

6. **Arrange your classes ahead of time:** There is no doubt that physical classroom management is simpler than online classroom management. In a real classroom, there is plenty of flexibility for applying an improvised fix when a scheduled session goes awry. The environment in virtual classrooms can become chaotic very quickly. You cannot see your students in person, and it is unlikely that they will ever be online at the same time. Planning is therefore essential for an online learning environment. Your students will have greater faith in you as a result since you will come across as more assured and knowledgeable.

7. **Improve virtual awareness:** A crucial characteristic of an excellent online teacher is awareness in a virtual classroom. Although it is not easy to recognize student behavior in a physical classroom (someone dozing off, some busy with the cute bird outside the window), it is more challenging in an online session than in an offline classroom. It usual makes students to become distracted in the middle of a lesson. Try to meaningfully engage each student rather than making it seems like a terrible thing and telling the student to "come back to the class."

8. **Be flexible and simple**: It is very important for the learners to understand the instruction of the teacher which is experienced by the learners and the teacher in the online class. The typical process starts with a group interaction, which is followed by an endless barrage of questions from the students. So, it is crucial to create distant learning courses with extremely clear instructions and a limited number of materials. Keep in mind that even simple structures require careful work, less detailed tasks frequently promote the best higher-order thinking since students must decide what to accomplish within predetermined boundaries.

CONCLUSION

In this paper, various challenges faced by students opting for online education and teachers and students while attending online classes were discussed and some strategies to optimize online education were identified which are helpful in attending online classes. This includes instructional and customized online class design, support for students and their families, and technical infrastructure so that we can grow and improve. Nowadays due to the advancement of technology, presence in employment and a strong desire to earn money among students is playing a significant role in increasing the popularity of online learning as a result. However, researchers are now working with more interest in developing new e-learning approaches that can work according to the preferences and interests of the learners. In today's time, the behavior of the learner, their learning style, and the online activities of the learner studying search criteria to predict interest. This transition to e-learning methods from conventional classroom activities must be accepted by both teachers and students as a result this digital divide can be closed by creating a safe online environment that encourages collaboration and offers opportunities to learn how to use various technologies. Additionally, it can lessen educational deference, resulting in an efficient e-learning experience. Further supporting teachers and students in e-learning environments is the creation of relevant, purposeful, and defined courses that include educational, social, and cultural components. The technological, cultural, and skill obstacles of e-learning must be understood in order to successfully adopt an e-learning system to manage the knowledge and educational needs of higher education organizations. To overcome these challenges, it is vital to construct technology infrastructure, set technological standards, and draw on the e-learning experiences of industrialized nations. Additionally, an appropriate culture must be established in order to familiarize teachers and students with the creation and application of an e-learning system.

IMPLICATIONS FOR FUTURE SCOPE

Thus, the findings of the study encourage institutions and educational institutions to tackle online-based learning even better by implementing the latest and most up-to-date methods of online instruction and continually educating learners and instructors using new technology inspire. The process of learning and instruction becomes more enjoyable as well as efficient. In addition, better guidelines should also be drawn up for educators and policymakers to make decisions regarding the integration of online education into educational systems that work for all. Additionally, this study may be beneficial in the development of online education infrastructure, framework, and course materials for successful learning.

REFERENCES

Aboagye, E., Yawson, J. A., & Appiah, K. N. (2021). COVID-19 and E-learning: The challenges of students in tertiary institutions. *Social Education Research*, 1–8.

Ali, W. (2020). Online and remote learning in higher education institutes: a necessity in light of COVID-19 pandemic. *Higher Education Studies*, *10*(3), 16–25.

Allen, I. E., & Seaman, J. (2017). *Digital Learning Compass: Distance Education Enrollment Report 2017*. Babson Survey Research Group.

Andriivna, O. (2021). Psychological Difficulties during the COVID Lockdown: Video in Blended Digital Teaching Language, Literature, and Culture. *Arab World English Journal*. https://ssrn.com/abstract=3851685

Apriliyanti, D. L. (2021). Teachers' Encounter of Online Learning: Challenges and Support System. *Journal of English Education and Teaching*, *5*(1), 110–122. doi:10.33369/jeet.5.1.110-122

Atmacasoy. (2018). Blended learning at pre-service teacher education in Turkey: a systematic review. *Education Information Technology, 23*(6), 2399-2422.

Baloran, E. T., Hernan, J. T., & Taoy, J. S. (2021). Course satisfaction and student engagement in online learning amid COVID-19 pandemic: A structural equation model. *Turkish Online Journal of Distance Education, 22*(4), 1–12. doi:10.17718/tojde.1002721

Bernard, R. M., Abrami, P. C., Borokhovski, E., Wade, C. A., Tamim, R. M., Surkes, M. A., & Bethel, E. C. (2009). A meta-analysis of three types of interaction treatments in distance education. *Review of Educational Research, 79*(3), 1243–1289. doi:10.3102/0034654309333844

Bolliger, D. U. (2004). Key factors for determining student satisfaction in online courses. *International Journal on E-Learning, 3*(1), 61–67.

Coman, C., Țîru, L. G., Meseşan-Schmitz, L., Stanciu, C., & Bularca, M. C. (2020). Online teaching and learning in higher education during the coronavirus pandemic: Students' perspective. *Sustainability (Basel), 12*(24), 10367. doi:10.3390u122410367

Doherty, I. (2010). Agile project management for e-learning developments. *International Journal of E-Learning & Distance Education/Revue internationale du e-learning et la formation à distance, 24*(1), 91-106.

Faqih, K. M. (2016). Which is more important in e-learning adoption, perceived value or perceived usefulness? Examining the moderating influence of perceived compatibility. *4th global summit on education GSE.*

Holle, D. (2020). Student engagement and blended learning: Portraits of risk. *Computers & Education, 54*(3), 693-700.

Huber, S. G., & Helm, C. (2020). COVID-19 and schooling: Evaluation, assessment and accountability in times of crises reacting quickly to explore key issues for policy, practice and research with the school barometer. *Educational Assessment, Evaluation and Accountability, 32*(2), 237–270. doi:10.100711092-020-09322-y PMID:32837626

Joshi, A., Vinay, M., & Bhaskar, P. (2021). Impact of coronavirus pandemic on the Indian education sector: Perspectives of teachers on online teaching and assessments. *Interactive Technology and Smart Education, 18*(2), 205–226. doi:10.1108/ITSE-06-2020-0087

Kapasia, N., Paul, P., Roy, A., Saha, J., Zaveri, A., Mallick, R., & Chouhan, P. (2020). Impact of lockdown on learning status of undergraduate and postgraduate students during COVID-19 pandemic in West Bengal, India. *Children and Youth Services Review, 116*, 105194. doi:10.1016/j.childyouth.2020.105194 PMID:32834270

Khan, M. A., Kamal, T., Illiyan, A., & Asif, M. (2021). School students' perception and challenges towards online classes during COVID-19 pandemic in India: An econometric analysis. *Sustainability (Basel), 13*(9), 4786. doi:10.3390u13094786

Levy, Y. (2007). Comparing dropouts and persistence in e-learning courses. *Computers & Education, 48*(2), 185–204. doi:10.1016/j.compedu.2004.12.004

Li, J., & Che, W. (2022). Challenges and coping strategies of online learning for college students in the context of COVID-19: A survey of Chinese universities. *Sustainable Cities and Society*, *83*, 103958. doi:10.1016/j.scs.2022.103958 PMID:35620298

Li, W., Gillies, R., He, M., Wu, C., Liu, S., Gong, Z., & Sun, H. (2021). Barriers and facilitators to online medical and nursing education during the COVID-19 pandemic: Perspectives from international students from low-and middle-income countries and their teaching staff. *Human Resources for Health*, *19*(1), 1–14. doi:10.118612960-021-00609-9 PMID:33980228

Maatuk, A. M., Elberkawi, E. K., Aljawarneh, S., Rashaideh, H., & Alharbi, H. (2022). The CO-VID-19 pandemic and E-learning: Challenges and opportunities from the perspective of students and instructors. *Journal of Computing in Higher Education*, *34*(1), 21–38. doi:10.100712528-021-09274-2 PMID:33967563

Martinez, R. A., Bosch, M. M., Herrero, M. H., & Nunoz, A. S. (2007). Psychopedagogical components and processes in e-learning. Lessons from an unsuccessful on-line course. *Computers in Human Behavior*, *23*(1), 146–161. doi:10.1016/j.chb.2004.04.002

Means, B., Toyama, Y., Murphy, R., & Baki, M. (2013). The effectiveness of online and blended learning: A meta-analysis of the empirical literature. *Teachers College Record*, *115*(3), 1–47. doi:10.1177/016146811311500307

Moore, M. G., & Kearsley, G. (2012). *Distance education: A systems view of online learning*. Cengage Learning.

Mutakinati, L. (2020). The Impact of Covid-19 to Indonesian Education and Its Relation to the Philosophy of Merdeka Belajar. *Studies in Philosophy of Science and Education*, *1*(1), 38–49. doi:10.46627ipose.v1i1.9

Nouri, J. (2020). Covid-19 and Crisis-Prompted Distance Education in Sweden. Technology, Knowledge and Learning, 26, 443-459. doi:10.100710758-020-09470-6

Oduma, C. A., Onyema, L. N., & Akiti, N. (2019). E-learning platforms in business education for skill acquisition. *Nigerian Journal of Business Education*, *6*(2), 104–112.

Picciano, A. G. (2017). Theories and frameworks for online education: Seeking an integrated model. *Online Learning : the Official Journal of the Online Learning Consortium*, *21*(3), 166–190. doi:10.24059/olj.v21i3.1225

Roca, J. C., & Gagné, M. (2008). Understanding e-learning continuance intention in the workplace: A self-determination theory perspective. *Computers in Human Behavior*, *24*(4), 1585–1604. doi:10.1016/j.chb.2007.06.001

Rossman, M. H., & Rossman, M. E. (1995). Facilitating Distance Education. Jossey-Bass Inc., Publishers.

Salloum, S. A., Alhamad, A. Q. M., Al-Emran, M., Monem, A. A., & Shaalan, K. (2019). Exploring students' acceptance of e-learning through the development of a comprehensive technology acceptance model. *IEEE Access : Practical Innovations, Open Solutions*, *7*, 128445–128462. doi:10.1109/AC-CESS.2019.2939467

Selvaraj, A., Radhin, V., Nithin, K. A., Benson, N., & Mathew, A. J. (2021). Effect of pandemic-based online education on teaching and learning system. *International Journal of Educational Development, 85,* 102444. doi:10.1016/j.ijedudev.2021.102444 PMID:34518732

Simonson, M., Smaldino, S., Albright, M., & Zvacek, S. (2019). *Teaching and learning at a distance: Foundations of distance education.* Information Age Publishing.

Sitzmann, T., Kraiger, K., Stewart, D., & Wisher, R. (2006). The comparative effectiveness of Web-based and classroom instruction: A meta-analysis. *Personnel Psychology, 59*(3), 623–664. doi:10.1111/j.1744-6570.2006.00049.x

Smedley, J. (2012). Implementing e-learning in the Jordanian Higher Education System: Factors Affecting Impact. *International Journal of Education and Development using ICT, 8*(1). https://www.learntechlib.org/p/188017/

Smith, D. (2015). Comparing social isolation effects on learner's attrition in online versus face-to face courses in computer literacy. *Issues in Informing Science and Information Technology, 12,* 11–20. Retrieved from http://iisit.org/Vol12/IISITv12p011-020Ali1784.pdf

Song, L., Singleton, E. S., Hill, J. R., & Koh, M. H. (2004). Improving online learning: Student perceptions of useful and challenging characteristics. *The Internet and Higher Education, 7*(1), 59–70. doi:10.1016/j.iheduc.2003.11.003

U.S. Department of Education, Office of Planning, Evaluation, and Policy Development. (2010). *Evaluation of Evidence-Based Practices in Online Learning: A Meta-Analysis and Review of Online Learning Studies.* Author.

VillaD. (2020). Secondary Teachers' Preparation, Challenges, and Coping Mechanism in the Pre-Implementation of Distance Learning in the New Normal. *IOER International Multidisciplinary Research Journal, 2*(3), 144 – 154. https://ssrn.com/abstract=3717608

Wagner, N., Hassanein, K., & Head, M. (2008). Who Is Responsible for E-Learning Success in Higher Education? A Stakeholders' Analysis. *Journal of Educational Technology & Society, 11*(3), 26–36. Retrieved January 14, 2023, from https://www.learntechlib.org/p/75266/

Wang, Y. S., Wang, H. Y., & Shee, D. Y. (2007). Measuring e-learning systems success in an organizational context: Scale development and validation. *Computers in Human Behavior, 23*(4), 1792–1808. doi:10.1016/j.chb.2005.10.006

Zhang, D., & Nunamaker, J. F. (2003). Powering e-learning in the new millennium: An overview of eLearning and enabling technology. *Information Systems Frontiers, 5*(2), 207–218. doi:10.1023/A:1022609809036

Zhang, Y., & Ma, Z. F. (2020). Impact of the COVID-19 Pandemic on Mental Health and Quality of Life among Local Residents in Liaoning Province, China: A Cross-Sectional Study. *International Journal of Environmental Research and Public Health, 17*(7), 2381. doi:10.3390/ijerph17072381 PMID:32244498

Chapter 9
Impact of Technological Innovations and Online Social Capital on Education

Blessing Foluso Adeoye
iD https://orcid.org/0000-0002-9142-0048
Dilla University, Ethiopia

ABSTRACT

The author of this chapter explored the social capital knowledge regarding education in the following four theoretical contexts presented by Mikiewicz, the tradition of James Coleman's social exchange theory, the tradition of Robert D. Putnam's theory of civil society, the tradition of Pierre Bourdieu's theory of cultural structuralism, and the tradition of network theory. This chapter also presented the effective use of the research on social capital and the impact of technological innovations and online social capital on education. The author pooled literature from different parts of specializations, especially in education. It documented that co-creation and social learning are essential components of knowledge productivity; therefore, by working together and leveraging the power of social networks, individuals can achieve more than they ever could on their own, leading to profound improvements in organizational and societal outcomes.

INTRODUCTION

It is essential first to understand how social networks evolved. Before humans decided to form online social communities, social networking and relationship-building were part of the human experience. As various communities grew and technology was involved, the quality of those interpersonal relationships became increasingly essential and progressively complex. Technological innovations and online social capital are having a significant impact on teaching and learning at all levels. The roles of the learning environments are also critical in the successful implementation of educational programs. The learning environment is supportive and productive. It promotes independence, interdependence, and self-motivation;

DOI: 10.4018/978-1-6684-8953-6.ch009

students' needs, backgrounds, perspectives, and interests are reflected in this environment. With social capital, learning connects strongly with communities and practices beyond the classroom.

This chapter explores the social capital knowledge regarding education, especially the research on social capital and the impact of technological innovations and online social capital on education. The information gathered will benefit students and educators because by working together and leveraging the power of social networks, students and instructors can achieve more than they ever could on their own, leading to profound improvements in teaching and learning.

METHODOLOGY

I thoroughly examined previous research published mainly in peer-reviewed journals about social capital and education. The databases used were Education Source, ScienceDirect, SAGE Journals, Taylor & Francis Online, and ProQuest Central. Education Sources and research reports from Google Scholars retrieved the highest number of relevant articles, so I searched that database to gather perspectives across various disciplines. I complimented the search by using the Yahoo search engine to locate articles using the exact keywords I used in the databases. The keywords and phrases used in the search included information and communication technology, ICT, digital media, Technological innovations, Online Social capital, Education, Digital Tools, Educational Technology, and Social Networking. Only articles that followed rigorous measures for research quality were considered for this review.

Digital tools, educational technology, social networking, and other emerging technologies have transformed educational systems worldwide. Understanding the impact of technological innovations and online social capital on education is critical to academic development in the 21st century. Social networks have expanded with digital technology in many disciplines, especially education. Teaching and learning have been transformed with the birth of the Internet, digital communication platforms, and social media. This transformation has enabled teachers and students to achieve much in critical times. Teachers could teach well, and students could learn effectively. The students and teachers could design, share information, and interact through websites, blogs, webinars, podcasts, social media sites, and smartphones. Teachers, students, and parents have connected in ways never before imagined. Social capital has enabled such connections and has contributed enormously to supporting educational innovation. Social capital refers to the networks, relationships, and norms facilitating cooperation and trust among individuals and groups. It is an intangible asset derived from social relationships and networks. According to Blessinger, Sengupta, and Meri-Yilan (2023), individuals and groups, including higher education, form networks and establish personal and professional collaborative relationships. They seek to collaborate with others because they can achieve personal and group goals in ways not possible to achieve alone (Blessinger et al. 2023). According to Blessinger et al. (2023), the benefits of these social networks in higher education include, among other things, sharing intellectual resources, co-development of knowledge, and joint research. Therefore, teachers and students often form networks because it serves their interests, and when their interests align, the relationships benefit everyone.

Salimi, Heidari, Mehrvarz, and Safavi (2022) examined the hypothesis that online social capital can improve students' academic performance, as one of the leading educational goals, through the mediation of knowledge sharing in the online environment. Three hundred seventy-six graduate engineering students from five universities in Iran participated in their study. Salimi et al (2022) found that bridging online social capital positively and significantly affected the cognitive and social integrative benefits of online knowledge sharing. They also indicated that the integrative social and personal integrative benefits of online knowledge sharing influenced academic performance. The social and emotional integrative benefits mediated the relationship between bridging online social capital and academic performance (Salimi et al., 2022). According to Salimi et al. (2022), one of the factors affecting academic performance is the benefits of online knowledge sharing, which can also be influenced by online trust-based social capital; as a result, the social capital can affect the student's academic performance both directly and indirectly through the benefits of online knowledge sharing.

The benefits of online social capital have also been reported in business, social development, education, healthcare, and psychology, as well as in achieving sustainable development goals. Social capital is critical in promoting educational innovation by facilitating cooperation, trust, and access to resources necessary for implementing and sustaining new practices. Raza, Qazi, and Umer (2016) analyzed the influence of Facebook usage on building social capital among 560 university students in Karachi by using a modified framework of the technology acceptance model. Important information was gathered with an organized questionnaire containing items of Facebook intensity, social self-efficacy, perceived ease of use, perceived usefulness, perceived playfulness (independent variables), intention to continue use (mediating variables), bridging social capital, and bonding social capital (dependent variables). The procedures utilized as a part of their study are reliability analysis, confirmatory factor analysis, and partial least square-structural equation modeling to check the impact of these factors on the building of social capital. Findings show that Facebook intensity, perceived ease of use, usefulness, playfulness, and social self-efficacy positively and significantly impact intention to continue use (Raza, Qazi, & Umer, 2016). In contrast, the choice to continue using has a positive and significant impact on both dependent variables bridging social capital and bonding social capital, concluding that social networking sites (Facebook) help build and maintain social capital by creating an intention to continue using them (Raza, Qazi, & Umer, 2016).

Social media allows students to connect with learning groups and other educational systems that make education convenient. Social network tools afford students and institutions multiple opportunities to improve learning methods. Although social media empowers everyone, including parents, teachers, and students, it is also an effective way to share information to build a community (dTobin, 2023).

Conceptualizations of the Social Capital

In the field of social sciences, there are several conceptualizations of social capital; however, the empirical applications can be reduced to four theoretical traditions:

(1)   The tradition of James Coleman's social exchange theory
(2)   The tradition of Robert D. Putnam's theory of civil society
(3)   The tradition of Pierre Bourdieu's theory of cultural structuralism
(4)   The tradition of network theory

James Coleman's concept originates from the tradition of economic sociology, the theory of exchange, according to which social structures result from petrifying interpersonal relations as conditions for the effective action of individuals (Mikiewicz, 2021). An individualistic concept places individual actors' actions in specific action structures at the center of analysis. Key elements of social capital as features of the collective are shared values and norms, multidimensional social relationships, and effective social control. According to Mikiewicz (2021), these are structural conditions that lead to trust, based on which social actors can act in a given structure.

The fundamental principles of the Coleman approach can be summarized as follows:

- Capital is a feature of the community, although it is analyzed in terms of its use by individuals.
- It highlights bonds, relationships, trust, and a structure enabling individuals to act effectively.
- The more substantial the bonds, the better—the more closed a community is, the denser the network it has, and the more active it is in civic life, the more capital it represents. In such circumstances, people tend to cooperate more for the common good.
- Capital is an unexpected result of purposive action—people do not act to build social capital but to achieve specific goals. If they work together, they create social structures that help them meet their needs (Mikiewicz, 2021).

The second, most prominent tradition of social capital research has been built based on Robert D. Putnam's studies of the community and democracy. As in the case of the Coleman tradition, Putnam treats social capital as a community resource. It is a collective characteristic that diagnoses citizens' involvement in activities for the public good (Putnam 1993, 2000). Social capital equals the level of social involvement of the inhabitants. It seems that it is the most popular way of studying social capital, based on quantitative measurements of the frequency of association membership, knowledge about local self-government authorities, and time spent on social life. The greater the social involvement and the more significant and better the knowledge of political mechanisms and neighbors, the greater the social capital is (Putnam 1993, 2000).

The social structuralism of Pierre Bourdieu founds the third tradition. In Pierre Bourdieu's theory, the concept of social capital is based on a different assumption than the two previous traditions. The critical difference indicates that social capital is a unique resource and not a structural feature (Bourdieu, 1998; 2005, Portes, 1998). To better understand the concepts of social capital from this perspective, it is essential to bear in mind the necessity to consider it as part of a broader theory in conjunction with other important concepts such as habitus, field, symbolic violence, and, of course, capital (Bourdieu, 1998; 2005, Portes, 1998). The French sociologist distinguishes three forms of capital: economic, cultural, and social. Bourdieu gradually developed a fundamental distinction between social and symbolic capital and identified social and cultural capital as specific forms of this symbolism. It considered cultural capital the most critical and social capital to be a subsidiary, although it also pointed to specific situations in which social capital became a central explanatory concept (Bourdieu, 1998; 2005, Portes, 1998).

For Bourdieu, social activities occur in socially constructed interaction fields (Bourdieu, 1998; Bourdieu & Passeron, 1990). Generally speaking, the basic assumptions can be summarized as follows:

- Actors in the field are equipped with various resources that can be recognized and used as capital in a game with other actors to gain an advantage in certain conditions.
- The actors recognize the field and the resources/capitals through their habitus, socially shaped nature, and disposition to interpret the world and act.
- Depending on the social position and the biographically shaped habitus, the actors recognize the field differently and apply their actions to it. The result is a hierarchy of influence and power in the field and a balance between the benefits of playing in the field. (Bourdieu, 1998; Bourdieu & Passeron, 1990).

Cultural capital is the competence of using cultural symbols, functioning in three forms: embodied, institutionalized and objective. Social capital, on the other hand, is belongingness to a group and social relations that can become the basis for providing social legitimation to an individual in his or her actions to achieve a specific goal in a given field. *Social capital* is a relationship that can be referred to or gives access to other resources—economic and cultural. Thus, the greater the economic, cultural, and symbolic resources of the group to which an individual belongs and to which it can refer, the greater the social capital he/she possesses (Bourdieu, 1998).

The fourth source of social capital conceptualization is the network theory, derived from the concept of the strength of the weak ties by Granovetter (1973). It was transformed and expanded by Nan Lin, who used Ronald Burt's economic theory of structural holes (see: Burt, 1992, 1997; Lin, 2001). This concept arises from the research on getting a job and locating oneself in the professional structure. Therefore, it is firmly rooted in the tradition of economic research on the processes of status achievement. Lin and Burt's analyses concerned the strategy of employees in the labor market or the activities of corporate members. These authors tried to show how economic players can use their networks to gain valuable information—to change jobs or to win in a market game. In this tradition, social capital is a resource an individual has access to through networks of relationships with others. A distinction is made between individual capital—resources held by the individual—and social capital—resources held by others to which the individual has or can have access because of their relationships with them. Mikiewicz (2021) also indicated that in the core of the educational studies, we could observe two kinds of reductionism; a focus on individual characteristics of actors in education (pupils' values, attitudes, aspirations, habitus, etc.) and the structural factors determining educational performance and status attainment (educational structures, processes of selection and allocation).

APPLICATION OF DIFFERENT CONCEPTUALIZATIONS IN EDUCATIONAL RESEARCH

Educational research from the perspective of James Coleman's theory focuses on formal education as a tool for shaping human capital—building competencies, skills, and knowledge. The effects of this process can be measured in the school results and other educational and professional careers. The difference in school achievements of young people may be determined by the difference in the features of the social structure in which students operate (Coleman & Hoffer, 1987). The features of this structure are characterized by the family model, different levels of parents' involvement in helping a child in education, the quality of contact with relatives, and the degree of control over the child. According to Coleman and Hoffer (1987), if one looks at social capital outside the family, one should pay attention to social networks, organization membership, and religious practices. In addition, we can also look at the quality of the school and the perceived quality of the neighborhood.

Educational Benefits of Social Capital

In the light of Robert D. Putnam's theory, the relationship between social capital and education is two-way. Social capital resources are the basis for specific educational achievements—the level of passing exams, school drop-out, and the length of school years. Also, theory, education, and its expansion can be seen as a tool for raising the level of civic participation, strengthening political activity, and increasing and building a participatory culture (Putnam, 1993). The greater the culture of civic participation in the community (commune, region, country), the better the educational results, and at the same time, the better the educational conditions, the greater the culture of participation (Halpern, 2005).

Education is one of the institutions established to respond to social needs, and its effectiveness depends on the level of citizenship. Through participation in civic activity networks, citizens influence the institution and make it more effective in meeting its needs (Putnam, 1993). In their studies of classroom strategies in the education market, Lareau (2003) and Ball (2003) stressed the importance of social capital as a tool used by middle-class parents to ensure the reproduction of their social position by providing their children with an adequate level of education. Social capital is fundamental to mobilizing the cultural and economic resources of the family or individual; therefore, the social capital analyses in the light of Bourdieu's theory are always the "status" and the "class" analyses (Bourdieu, 1998).

According to Lin (2001), education was of little interest to either Lin or Burt in applying the network theory. For the former, education as an indicator of the level of human capital appears in the model primarily as an independent variable—it determines the achieved status determines the level of social capital both available and mobilized (Lin, 2001, pp. 97–98, 116–117). Educational research inspired by network theory is primarily quantitative in nature. The network nomenclature makes it possible to track the actors' connections with the items enabling access to educational and institutional support resources.

DIFFERENT SOCIAL CAPITAL CONCEPTUALIZATION AND ITS USAGE IN EDUCATION

People learn so much about the relations between education and social structure through different conceptualizations of social capital. The use of different concepts of social capital revealed a different view of reality, which is imposed by the theoretical background of the category of social capital. To understand social capital better, we choose a theoretical background that suggests what questions about the relationship between education (schooling) and social structure are worth asking; consequently, we learn various things about school and society.

Table 1 presents various theoretical backgrounds; Social exchange theory (James Coleman), theory of civil society (Robert D. Putnam), theory of cultural structuralism (Pierre Bourdieu), and network theory (Nan Lin). Each of the theories defined and described what social capital means to it and what functions it performs. Each of them allows us to see certain conditions determining people's actions and to understand how the effects of education and the functioning of individuals in education are connected with their functioning in different social systems. Within each theoretical tradition, research procedures are constructed, and empirical findings are collected, which can then be compared with those resulting from applying a different model.

Table 1. Critical elements of different social capital conceptualization and its usage in education

Theoretical Background	Collective or Individual Feature	Key Elements	How Social Capital Is Created	The Meaning of Social Capital as a Resource	How Social Capital Is Used in Education (Schooling)
Social exchange theory (James Coleman)	Collective	• Shared values and norms, • Multidimensional social relationships	Unintended consequences of purposive actions in the community	Affects the structural conditions of individuals' actions	• Conditions the process of shaping a culture of engagement in education • Conditions effective control and students in the process of gaining knowledge
Theory of civil society (Robert D. Putnam)	Collective	• Trust • Reciprocal norms • Citizenship	Unintended consequences of purposive actions in the community	Affects the structural conditions of individuals' actions	• Conditions of effective control over educational institutions • Conditions support the local community in the activities of educational institutions
Theory of cultural structuralism (Pierre Bourdieu)	Individual	• Social relations giving access to other forms of capital: cultural and economic • Membership in the group gives the legitimation and the credit	Intentional individual actions to get legitimation from and credit from the (elitist) group	It is a tool in the purposive action of individuals	• Enables the use of symbolic capital in the form of group authentication in the educational field • Facilitates the conversion of capital—the exchange of economic capital into cultural capital and thus determines students' school achievements • Provides social support from the group of origin in school field activities
Network theory (Nan Lin)	Individual	• Network of the relations with its characteristics: network density, • network span (how wide our contacts extend) • the highest available social status thanks to the networks	Intentional individual action to build the network and use social ties	It is a tool in the purposive action of individuals	• Enables access to valuable helpful information in the process of social mobility

Source: Adopted from Mickiewicz (2021)

THE IMPACT OF TECHNOLOGICAL INNOVATIONS AND ONLINE SOCIAL CAPITAL ON EDUCATION

The concept of social capital is a valuable tool for understanding differences among student learning outcomes. It refers to the networks, relationships, and norms that facilitate cooperation and trust among individuals and groups within a society. The role of social capital in supporting educational innovation has been enumerated by West (2021). West indicated that social capital:

- Provide access to resources and expertise necessary for implementing and sustaining innovative practices. For example, education innovators may rely on social networks to identify potential collaborators, secure funding, share knowledge and best practices.

- Promote the adoption and diffusion of educational innovation. Positive social norms and trust among educators, policymakers, and other stakeholders can reduce resistance to change and increase willingness to experiment with new approaches.
- Create opportunities for community engagement and partnerships that support innovation. For example, schools and districts with strong ties to local businesses, non-profits, and community organizations may be better positioned to leverage these resources to support student learning.
- Is critical in promoting educational innovation by facilitating cooperation, trust, and access to resources necessary for implementing and sustaining new practices.

Managerial and Practical Implications Through Cocreation and Social Learning

According to West (2021), the important impact of social capital on educational innovation is also through co-creation and social learning.

Co-creation is creating something together, which involves sharing ideas, skills, and knowledge (West, 2021). The concept of co-creation is prominent with the use of various social media. West (2021) enumerated ways to use social media in education as listed below:

1. **Facebook Pages** - Facebook can support education in many ways. West indicated that it could be used to broadcast updates, send alerts, and by individuals or groups to conduct research or work on a group project. A class page can be created for a class where students can collaborate on group assignments. Also, the Facebook Group page can be used to present live lectures and host discussions. Instructors can create Facebook Groups for each of their classes, and within these groups, class announcements can be made, discussion questions can be posted, and live lectures and other homework can take place. Facebook Group page can keep students engaged during school breaks by posting reminders and assignments to avoid having to review once class resumes from the break. According to West (2021), when using social media for education, it is essential to ensure a professional boundary, so when setting up a Facebook Group, teachers do not need to send friend requests. Also, with a Facebook Group, it is possible to email both parents and students a direct link to the Facebook Group for access.
2. **Twitter** - Twitter is becoming popular in educational use. It can be great for a class discussion board or message board. Teachers can create a single Twitter handle per class and reuse it yearly or create a new one each school year. The 280-character limit makes students think critically about communicating concisely and effectively. Teachers can also use Twitter to post reminders for assignment due dates or share inspirational quotes and helpful links to practice quizzes or resources.
3. **Instagram** - Instagram is a content-sharing platform. It helps teachers to showcase their student's work. It can also be used as a digital bulletin board to recognize students. Instagram enables people to present a series of photos or graphics visually appealingly. It enables students to practice digital storytelling in ways other social media platforms may fall short.
4. **Create a class blog for discussion** - For writing and publishing blogs, many different platforms are available, such as WordPress, Squarespace, Wix, Blogger, Tumblr, or Medium. Blogging gives students an outlet for digital content that they can easily link back to class social channels. Teachers can also create a class blog to post assignments, class notes, course syllabi, updates, and resources needed by students.

5. **Assign blog posts as essays** - Having students create their own blogs for essays or short-form writing is another strategy for combining social media and learning. This can improve students' writing and critical thinking. The use of social media in education can be transferred across all subjects.

6. **Create a class-specific Pinterest board** - Pinterest is a great social media platform teachers can use to prepare and organize resources, lesson plans and worksheets for their classes in one place. According to West (2021), instructors can create Pinterest boards for each of their classes and save pins that are relevant to lessons. They can create boards according to class or subject, and create sub-topic boards for weekly units or all worksheets. Pinterest can also be useful for students to curate a digital bibliography for research projects, papers or group assignments. Students can pin websites, books or videos to a board on a single topic and refer back to it when it's time to write.

7. **Social media links on school website** - Many parents and prospective students often check a school's website first when they are looking for information about a school. It makes it easy for parents and students to find school's social media profiles by adding links to the website's main navigation or creating a social media directory that house- social media attract new students and parents to various schools. They can share photos and events around campus to showcase what to expect. Highlighting events and extracurriculars can make your school stand out from the rest. While school and university websites tend to follow the same mold, social media allows you to be more unique and casual.

8. **Create interest-based Facebook groups** - Many people, especially university alumni, want to be involved in their schools even after they leave. Creating Facebook Groups for current students and alumni can increase engagement and school spirit. Alumni groups, groups for different graduating classes or departments, and groups for various extracurriculars allow students to engage and meet others with common interests. Groups can be closed or secret, meaning that they're only viewable by invitation or by the approval of a group admin, or they can be open so that potential students can check out the types of conversations and events these groups have before requesting to join (West, 2021).

9. **Create a social media crisis strategy** - Social Media enables institutions to communicate with the entire campus during emergencies. They can incorporate social media into their crisis communication plan, whether a fire, tornado or other immediate campus emergency. Many campuses have automated messaging alerts, but using social media will keep even more people updated and informed.

10. **Manage your accounts all under one roof** - Social media marketing for your schools or universities should focus exclusively on making institutions seem like the best option for prospective students or parents. All that is needed is a social media management tool that makes publishing content for each school's social media platforms easy. A tool like Sprout Social can help make social media management a breeze. Multiple users can use the Sprout platform to create content with consistent messaging and schedule posts across all networks.

Together, cocreation and social learning can produce knowledge, generating new ideas and insights that ultimately contribute to improved outcomes. The benefits of co-creation and social learning are numerous. A collaborative spirit encourages open communication and exchanging of ideas when individuals come together to create something. This generates a sense of ownership and accountability for the outcomes, leading to higher commitment and motivation. Social media and technology are integral parts of daily life, and integrating these into the classroom is more natural than before, given how acclimated many students are. Each social media platform offers many different ways to be used in the school, from sharing announcements to holding live lectures and so much more.

THE USE OF SOCIAL MEDIA IN EDUCATION

Social media allows students to connect with others and allow access to more educational resources. Social network tools afford students and institutions multiple opportunities to improve learning methods. Social media empowers students, teachers, and parents by providing opportunities to share information and build a community. It allows students to get more helpful information, access better resources, and network with learning groups and other educational systems that make education convenient. Social network tools afford students and institutions multiple opportunities to improve learning methods.

Parmelee (2021) presented innovations at the World Economic Forum that transform education's future and facilitate cooperation and trust among individuals and groups within educational institutions. The innovations by Parmelee are enumerated below:

Learnable - Learnable is an augmented teaching assistant that allows teachers to compose and distribute dynamic, interactive lessons via a dedicated mobile app and WhatsApp. Lessons can be saved offline, so students do not need constant internet access.

Nomad Education - Nomad Education is a free mobile app that offers 350 academic certificates that helps more than 1 million francophone children succeed every year, regardless of their social, geographic, or educational background.

Pan-African Robotics Competition - The Pan-African Robotics Competition (PARC) is the largest robotics competition in Africa and has educated more than 1000 African youth in Science, Technology, Engineering & Math (STEM) while also offering a Virtual Learning Platform (VLP) to enable the African youth to learn to code, design and build their robots virtually. It also integrates a feature for collaboration and knowledge exchange.

StanLab - StanLab is a cloud-based, 3D virtual laboratory platform providing near real-life laboratory experience for students without access to physical laboratories.

UCT Online High School - UCT Online High School's mission is to turn physical limitations into digital opportunities for Africa's children to access aspirational, quality secondary school education. Its purpose-built online school and free online curriculum pave the way for high-quality, online, and blended learning to be delivered at scale and stimulate the digital transformation of the education systems on the continent.

Call-A-Kahaani - Emotional intelligence, critical thinking, and problem-solving are vital skills for the future of work. Call-a-Kahaani is Udhyam Learning Foundation's Interactive Voice Response (IVR) platform to empower youth with entrepreneurial mindsets, leveraging engaging interactive storytelling.

Ekatra - Ekatra is a tool for educators and organizations to deliver learning at scale, using text (including SMS and WhatsApp) message-based micro courses targeted to improve understanding, with the mission to bring essential knowledge to people no matter their circumstances.

Rocket Learning - Rocket Learning supports parents with crucial early years of education, including teaching children to recognize letters and numbers. It helps build vibrant digital communities of parents and teachers to support foundational learning for some of the world's most underprivileged children. It also helps 20,000 teachers reach over 200,000 parents daily with contextualized content in their local language via WhatsApp groups.

#GenEducators - An initiative of Generation Peace, this solution aims to empower educators to reinvent how they teach. The web-based learning platform is designed to help Indonesian educators encourage innovation in their classrooms – and raise the next generation of critical thinkers. It offers practical tools, proven strategies, and best practices worldwide to inspire future change-makers.

Komerce - Komerce is transforming the lives of rural Indonesian communities by unlocking e-commerce potential through education. The innovative platform teaches Indonesian youth e-commerce skills. It connects them with small and medium-sized enterprises in their rural towns to boost the local economy and provide opportunities for young people.

Scaling Skills That Matter - An innovation of The Posify Group, The Posify Academy is a student-led, evidence-based combined well-being and career development platform, arming youth with a sense of purpose and equipping them with future skills, so they can navigate this rapidly evolving world with confidence, and uncover and deliver their unique potential (Tandi, (2021).

Tech-Voc Career Accelerator Program - An initiative of Edukasyon.ph, Tech-Voc Career Accelerator drives youth not in education, employment, and training (NEET) in the Philippines to the frontlines of jobs by transforming their interest into a passion for technical-vocational work through holistic skills development, industry training and linkages, and continuous learning (Parmelee, 2021).

Social learning fosters a culture of continuous improvement, whereby individuals learn from each other's experiences and build on their collective knowledge. This can lead to new insights and breakthroughs in many areas, increasing productivity and more significant innovation. Overall, co-creation and social learning are essential components of knowledge productivity. Through collaboration and leveraging the power of social networks, individuals can achieve more than they ever could on their own, leading to profound improvements in organizational and societal outcomes and knowledge productivity, which involves sharing ideas, skills, and knowledge. On the other hand, social learning focuses on learning by interacting with others in a social context. Together, these two processes can lead to knowledge production, which generates new ideas and insights that ultimately contribute to improved outcomes (West (2021).

The benefits of co-creation and social learning are numerous. A collaborative spirit encourages open communication and exchanging of ideas when individuals come together to create something. This generates a sense of ownership and accountability for the outcomes, leading to higher commitment and motivation.

Overall, co-creation and social learning are essential components of knowledge productivity.

POSITIVE INTERVENTIONS TO SUPPORT PROFESSIONALS IN INNOVATION WORK

The following are positive interventions to support professionals in innovation work:

1. **Encourage a creative and flexible work environment**: This work environment could include providing flexible working hours, allowing employees to work remotely, or providing them with access to creative spaces.

2. **Set clear goals and deadlines**: Professionals who work in innovation must have clear objectives and deadlines to strive towards. This keeps them focused and motivated and helps ensure their work is aligned with the company's goals.

3. **Provide tailored training to staff**: Innovation requires various skills, including problem-solving, creativity, and strategic thinking. Providing customized training to staff can help them develop more valuable skills.

4. **Recognize and reward creativity and innovation**: Rewarding employees for their innovative ideas can motivate them to be more productive.

5. **Encourage collaboration and teamwork**: Collaboration is essential for innovation, as it allows professionals to bounce ideas off each other and create new solutions. Creating a collaborative work environment can support innovative work and foster a sense of teamwork.

6. **Provide access to innovative tools and resources**: Providing employees with access to innovative tools and resources, such as software, research, and data, can support their work and help them to be productive and competitive in their field.

7. **Offer mentorship and coaching**: Providing support through mentorship and coaching can help to develop talent within the organization and provide professionals with guidance and support as they navigate the challenges of innovation work.

CONCLUSION

Most of the studies cited in this review indicated that bridging online social capital had a positive and significant effect on the cognitive and social integrative benefits of online knowledge sharing (e.g., Hidayat, Febrianto, Purwohedi, Rachmawati, & Zahar, 2023). Also, that various factors can influence and improve academic performance, such as using new technologies and social media (Edmunds et al., 2021). Educational institutions have learned much about better educational practices, and more is needed to know about processes for implementing new procedures. According to Frank, Zhao, and Borman (2004), the standard diffusion model suggests that people change perceptions about innovation's value through communication, which drives implementation. But implementation can be affected by more instrumental forces. As a result, educational institutions share the institutions' common fate and affiliate with the standard social system of the institution. Frank, Zhao, and Borman (2004) article characterized informal access to expertise and responses to social pressure as manifestations of social capital. Using longitudinal and network data in a study of the implementation of computer technology in six schools, Frank et al. found that the effects of perceived social pressure and access to expertise through help and talk were at least as significant as the effects of traditional constructs. By implication, change agents should attend to local social capital processes for implementing educational innovations or reforms (Frank, Zhao, & Borman, 2004).

REFERENCES

Blessinger, P., Sengupta, E., & Meri-Yilan, S. (2023). *How students and faculty can build their social capital.* Retrieved from https://www.universityworldnews.com/post.php?story=20230314110328688

Bourdieu, P. (1998). *Distinction. A social critique of the judgment of taste.* Harvard University Press.

Bourideu, P., & Passeron, J. C. (1990). *Reproduction in education, society, and culture.* Sage Publications.

Burt, R. S. (1992). *Structural holes. The social structure of competition.* Harvard University Press. doi:10.4159/9780674029095

Coleman, J. S., & Thomas, H. (1987). *Public and private high schools: The impact of communities.* Basic Books. Retrieved at https://www.psychreg.org/social-media-education

Edmunds, J. A., Gicheva, D., Thrift, B., & Hull, M. (2021). High tech, high touch: The impact of an online course intervention on academic performance and persistence in higher education. *The Internet and Higher Education, 49,* 100790. doi:10.1016/j.iheduc.2020.100790

Frank, K. A., Zhao, Y., & Borman, K. (2004). Social capital and the diffusion of innovations within organizations: The case of computer technology in schools. *Sociology of Education, 77*(2), 148–171. Advance online publication. doi:10.1177/003804070407700203

Granovetter, M. S. (1973). The strength of weak ties. *American Journal of Sociology, 78*(6), 1360–1380. doi:10.1086/225469

Hidayat, S., Febrianto, Z., Purwohedi, U., Rachmawati, D., & Zahar, M. (2023). Proactive personality and organizational support in television industry: Their roles in creativity. *PLoS One, 18*(1), e0280003. doi:10.1371/journal.pone.0280003 PMID:36626372

Mikiewicz, P. (2021). Social capital and education – An attempt to synthesize conceptualization arising from various theoretical origins. *Cogent Education, 8*(1), 1907956. doi:10.1080/2331186X.2021.1907956

Parmelee, M. (2021). *Twelve innovators that are transforming the future of education.* Retrieved from https://www.weforum.org/agenda/2021/09/education-innovation-uplink-skills-work-edtech

Portes, A. (1998). Social capital: Its origins and applications in modern sociology. *Annual Review of Sociology, 24*(1), 1–24. doi:10.1146/annurev.soc.24.1.1

Putnam, R. D. (1993). *Making democracy work.* University Press.

Putnam, R. D. (2000). *Bowling alone: The collapse and revival of American community.* Simon & Schuster.

Raza, S. A., Qazi, W., & Umer, A. (2016). Facebook is a source of social capital-building among university students. *Journal of Educational Computing Research.* Advance online publication. doi:10.1177/0735633116667357

Salimi, G., Heidari, E., Mehrvarz, M., & Safavi, A. A. (2022). Impact of online social capital on academic performance: Exploring the mediating role of online knowledge sharing. *Education and Information Technologies, 27*(5), 6599–6620. doi:10.100710639-021-10881-w PMID:35075344

Tandi, M. (2021). *Arming youth with a sense of purpose to navigate this rapidly evolving world of education - Today in Bermuda.* https://todayinbermuda.com/mukesh-tandi-arming-youth-with-a-sense-of-purpose-to-navigate-this-rapidly-evolving-world-of-education

West, C. (2021). *Twelve ways to use social media for education.* Retrieved from https://sproutsocial.com/insights/social-media-for-education

ADDITIONAL READING

Astone, N. M., Nathanson, C., Schoen, R., & Kim, Y. (1999). Family demography, social theory, and investment in social capital. *Population and Development Review, 25*(1), 1–31. doi:10.1111/j.1728-4457.1999.00001.x

Bailey, M., Cao, R., Kuchler, T., & Stroebel, J. (2018). The economic effects of social networks: Evidence from the housing market. *Journal of Political Economy, 126*(6), 2224–2276. doi:10.1086/700073

Baker-Doyle, K. J., & Yoon, S. A. (2011). In search of practitioner-based social capital: A social network analysis tool for understanding and facilitating teacher collaboration in a US-based STEM professional development program. *Professional Development in Education, 37*(1), 75–93. doi:10.1080/19415257.2010.494450

Baker-Doyle, K. J., & Yoon, S. A. (2020). The social side of teacher education: Implications of social network research for professional development design. *International Journal of Educational Research, 101*, 101563. doi:10.1016/j.ijer.2020.101563

Borgatti, S. P., Jones, C., & Everett, M. G. (1998). Network measures of social capital. *Connections, 21*, 27–36.

Bourdieu, P. (1980). Le capital social [Social capital]. *Actes de la Recherche en Sciences Sociales, 31*, 2–3. doi:10.3406/arss.1979.2654

Chetty, R., Jackson, M. O., Kuchler, T., Stroebel, J., Hendren, N., Fluegge, R. B., Gong, S., Gonzalez, F., Grondin, A., Jacob, M., Johnston, D., Koenen, M., Mudekereza, F., Rutter, T., Thor, N., Townsend, W., Zhang, R., Bailey, M., Barberá, P., ... Wernerfelt, N. (2022). Social capital I: Measurement and associations with economic mobility. *Nature, 608*(7921), 108–121. doi:10.103841586-022-04996-4 PMID:35915342

Coppe, T., Thomas, L., Pantić, N., Froehlich, D. E., Sarazin, M., & Raemdonck, I. (2022). The use of social capital in teacher research: A necessary clarification. *Frontiers in Psychology, 13*, 866571. Advance online publication. doi:10.3389/fpsyg.2022.866571 PMID:35756242

Goddard, R. D. (2003). Relational networks, social trust, and norms: A social capital perspective on students' chances of academic success. *Educational Evaluation and Policy Analysis, 25*(1), 59–74. doi:10.3102/01623737025001059

KEY TERMS AND DEFINITIONS

Digital Tools: Digital tools are online platforms or software applications leveraged by businesses or individuals to perform quick and optimized functions that ordinarily could be difficult.

Educational Technology: Educational Technology is the field of study investigating the process of analyzing, designing, developing, implementing, and evaluating the instructional environment, learning materials, learners, and the learning process to improve teaching and learning.

Online Social Capital: Online social capital is defined as accessibility to ties on an online network that promote networking and group norms.

Social Capital: Social capital is about the value of social networks, bonding with similar people, and bridging between diverse people with norms of reciprocity.

Social Networking: Social networking refers to using internet-based social media sites to connect with friends, family, colleagues, or customers.

Technological Innovations: Technological Innovation focuses on a product or service's invention or technological aspects.

Technology: The branch of knowledge that deals with the creation and use of technical means and their interrelation with life, society, and the environment, drawing upon such subjects as industrial arts, engineering, applied science, and pure science.

Chapter 10
Influence Maximization and Online Social Capital for Entrepreneurs:
Leveraging Social Networks to Achieve Business Goals.

M. Venunath
Pondicherry University, India

Pothula Sujatha
Pondicherry University, India

Prasad Koti
Sarada Gangadaran College, India

Srinu Dharavath
Annamalai University, India

ABSTRACT

Social networks are vital for businesses today, enabling them to reach a wider audience, engage with customers, and conduct market research. Influence maximization and online social capital are key to entrepreneurs' success, helping them strategically build and leverage networks to achieve specific goals. They can identify and engage with influencers, create high-quality content, and use tools to expand their reach. Social capital provides access to resources, builds reputation and credibility, and offers support and motivation. Successful businesses like Nike, Coca-Cola, Airbnb, and Tesla demonstrate the power of social networks in building customer relationships and promoting products. Overall, influence maximization is crucial for entrepreneurs to increase visibility, credibility, and influence in the digital age, helping them achieve their goals effectively.

DOI: 10.4018/978-1-6684-8953-6.ch010

INTRODUCTION

In recent years, researchers from various disciplines have contributed to a multitude of research problems centered on social networks (SNs). These include influence maximization, information diffusion (Chen et al., 2013), recommender systems (Amigó et al., 2023), rumor prediction (Xiang et al., 2023), opinion leader detection (Fournier-Viger et al., 2022), and many more SNs have become an integral part of our daily lives, providing an excellent platform for sharing ideas, opinions, and performing various online activities. They virtually connect people worldwide and serve as ideal platforms for promoting ideas, products, and businesses. A social network is a constantly evolving network where users produce and consume vast amounts of content. It can be represented as a graph g=(V,E), where V represents a set of people or entities present, and E denotes edges. An edge connects two nodes if both nodes have a social connection such as friendship, follow-followee, co-authorship, and so on.

Social media platforms such as Twitter, Facebook, Instagram, and Siena-Weibo have a significant impact on shaping public perceptions and raising awareness. Due to their massive global user base, these platforms are widely recognized for their low-cost marketing and business promotion benefits. In network science, influence maximization (IM) is a well-researched problem that aims to identify a small number of seed users, known as influential nodes, who can maximize the spread of information through diffusion cascades to the optimal number of nodes in the system (Banerjee et al., 2020). This is an optimization problem, and Kempe et al. (2003) demonstrated that obtaining an optimal solution is NP-hard under conventional information diffusion models. Mathematically, the IM problem can be stated as follows: "Given a social network G=(V,E), an information propagation model M, and a small positive integer k, the objective is to select a set s of k users as the seed set to maximize the information spread, subject to the condition that for any other seed set s* of k users satisfying $\sigma_{G,M}(s^*) < \sigma_{G,M}(s)$ where $S \subseteq V(G), S^* \subseteq V(G)$, and $\sigma_{G,M}(s)$ is the expected number of users influenced or infected by the users in set S."

Influence maximization (IM) is widely used for viral marketing (He et al., 2019; Nguyen et al., 2016) due to its commercial potential, where a company seeks to promote or adopt a product by targeting a few initially selected influential users and utilizing a "word-of-mouth" strategy through social connections. This triggers a large cascade of further adoptions (Leskovec, Adamic, & Huberman, 2007). Viral marketing is a powerful tool for promoting businesses as it is based on social relationships and mutual trust between users. Recommendations from known or trusted individuals are an effective method of advertisement and form the basis of viral marketing. Advertisers follow a similar approach to influence buyers by targeting influential nodes known as seed nodes. Therefore, e-commerce companies aim to target influential users to conduct successful advertisements and achieve maximum product publicity through viral marketing. IM and Online social capital are two related concepts that play a critical role in the success of entrepreneurs (Chen et al., 2010). Social capital refers to the network of relationships that individuals and organizations have, which provides them with access to valuable resources such as information, support, and opportunities. Meanwhile, influence maximization refers to the process of strategically building and leveraging one's social network to achieve specific goals or objectives, such as increasing visibility, driving sales, or securing funding. And also Finding influential nodes in social networks has many other applications, such as handling rumors, containing outbreaks of disease, maximizing opinions, political campaigning, and social recommendation.

Numerous influence maximization methods have been proposed in the literature, including node centrality, greedy-based, and metaheuristic optimization techniques (Banerjee et al., 2020). Node centrality-based approaches are simple and computationally efficient, but lack theoretical guarantee in performance and can produce varied results depending on the chosen network. In contrast, greedy-based approaches offer better results with a theoretical guarantee but are computationally intensive. Community structure-based influence maximization algorithms assume independence between communities and use node centrality or a greedy-based approach. Recently, deep learning-based techniques have been applied to the problem of influence maximization and have shown promising results (Tian et al., 2020).

Deep learning has demonstrated its capabilities in various domains such as computer vision, pattern recognition, and natural language processing with remarkable performance (Bhowmik et al., 2021). Transfer learning is a popular application of deep learning, which involves using a pre-trained model's informational gain, trained on one dataset, for a different dataset .Transfer learning has been extensively explored in computer vision and NLP, but limited work has been done in social network analysis, particularly for problems like influence maximization, link prediction, and community detection.

In social network analysis, transfer learning can be used to train a complex model on a large dataset to capture task-specific details for the model and maintain the dataset-independent nature of the model. The trained model can then be applied to real-life networks for various applications such as influence maximization, link prediction (Kumar et al., 2020; Yang et al., 2015), and community detection (Shang et al., 2015, 2016).

The paper's remainder is structured as follows. In Section 2, we review previous research in the field of influence maximization, Social Capital for Entrepreneurs focusing on the role of information diffusion. The details of our proposed approach are presented in Section 3. Section 4 explains the experimental setup that we used and discusses the results that we obtained through our experiments. Our work concludes in Section 5.

RELATED WORK

Social capital refers to the ability of individuals or groups to access resources within their social networks, such as favors or new information, by engaging in social interactions and anticipating future social benefits. It can be categorized as "bridging" or "bonding." Bridging social capital connects different clusters in a network, enabling the exchange of novel information and diverse perspectives. These connections, often weaker ties, provide access to resources beyond what stronger ties based on trust and intimacy can offer. Platforms like Facebook have both strong and weak ties, but this study specifically focuses on bridging social capital and examines how Facebook facilitates greater access to resources from weaker ties, which may not be available through other communication channels (Ellison et al., 2014).

Social capital plays a significant role in various domains, including economics, politics, education, and public health. Notable references such as "Bowling Alone" by Putnam (Putnam, 2000) explore the decline of social capital in the United States and its consequences for communities and democracy. Lin's "Social Capital" (Lin, 2001) provides a comprehensive framework discussing dimensions, measurement, and effects on individuals and communities. Putnam's "Making Democracy Work" (Raffaella et al., 1994) compares regional governance in Italy, demonstrating that higher social capital leads to more effective governance. Ruef's (Ruef, 2010) "The Social Capital of Entrepreneurial Newcomers" investigates the impact of social capital on entrepreneurship. "Social Capital and Health" (Kawachi et al., 2008) explores its influence on health outcomes, including access to resources, social support, and health behaviors. Further research is needed to deepen our understanding of the complexities of social capital.

Online social capital plays a crucial role in today's interconnected world, offering a wide range of benefits to individuals and communities. Firstly, it provides easy access to a wealth of information and knowledge through social networks and online communities. This allows individuals to stay informed, learn from diverse perspectives, and gain insights into various topics of interest. Secondly, online social capital facilitates networking and relationship building, enabling individuals to connect with people from different backgrounds and industries. These connections can lead to new opportunities, collaborations, mentorship, and career advancements.

Engaging in online social capital activities also contributes to professional and personal development (Hamilton et al., 2023). Participating in professional forums, attending webinars (Al-Naabi, 2023), or joining interest-based communities provides valuable learning opportunities, allowing individuals to acquire new skills, seek advice, and share experiences. Moreover, online social capital fosters a sense of support and belonging. It offers a platform for individuals to connect with like-minded people, share thoughts and experiences, seek guidance, and receive emotional support, particularly during challenging times.

Furthermore, online social capital empowers individuals to amplify their voice and extend their influence beyond their immediate circles (Saenz, 2023). Through social media platforms, blogs, or online communities, individuals can share their ideas, perspectives, and expertise with a broader audience. This has the potential to make a significant impact on discussions, movements, or social causes. For entrepreneurs and business professionals, online social capital is particularly advantageous. It provides access to potential customers, partners, investors, and mentors. Effectively leveraging online social capital can help entrepreneurs promote their businesses, gather feedback, and secure funding.

Additionally, online social capital has played a pivotal role in facilitating social change and activism (Li, Fabbre, & Gaveras, 2023). It allows individuals to connect, organize, and mobilize around shared causes and issues. Online platforms serve as spaces for raising awareness, coordinating efforts, and advocating for positive societal transformations. In summary, online social capital offers access to information, facilitates networking and relationship building, supports personal and professional development, amplifies voice and influence, fosters support and emotional well-being, opens doors for entrepreneurship and business opportunities, and drives social change. Effectively utilizing online social capital can lead to numerous benefits and opportunities for individuals and communities in the digital age.

Online social capital plays a crucial role for entrepreneurs in the digital era, providing them with unique opportunities and advantages. Here are some key points highlighting the importance of online social capital for entrepreneurs:

Access to Resources (Hossain et al., 2023): Online social capital expands an entrepreneur's network, connecting them to a wider range of individuals, organizations, and knowledge sources. It facilitates access to valuable resources such as funding, mentorship, expertise, and business partnerships.

Knowledge and Information Exchange (Ali et al., 2023): Online platforms enable entrepreneurs to tap into diverse communities and engage in knowledge sharing. By leveraging online social capital, entrepreneurs can access industry insights, market trends, and innovative ideas, fostering learning and keeping them informed about the latest developments in their field.

Building Trust and Reputation (Itani et al., 2023): Online social capital allows entrepreneurs to establish and enhance their reputation through digital interactions. Positive online interactions, endorsements, and recommendations from their network can contribute to building trust and credibility, attracting potential customers, investors, and collaborators.

Collaboration and Co-Creation (Entrepreneurial enactment as social value creation, 2022): Online social capital enables entrepreneurs to connect and collaborate with like-minded individuals, fostering opportunities for co-creation, joint ventures, and collective problem-solving. It facilitates the formation of virtual teams and communities, promoting innovation and synergy.

Marketing and Branding (Hossain et al., 2023): Online social capital offers entrepreneurs an effective platform for marketing their products or services. Through their social networks, entrepreneurs can reach a wider audience, engage with potential customers, and leverage word-of-mouth marketing, all of which can significantly enhance their brand visibility and reputation.

Support and Feedback (Mallios & Moustakis, 2023): Online social capital provides entrepreneurs with a supportive ecosystem where they can seek advice, feedback, and emotional support from their peers and mentors. It creates a sense of belonging to a community of entrepreneurs who understand the challenges and opportunities associated with starting and growing a business.

Global Reach (Fan & Zhai, 2023): Online platforms break down geographical barriers, allowing entrepreneurs to connect with individuals and markets worldwide. Online social capital empowers entrepreneurs to expand their reach, explore international collaborations, and tap into a global customer base.

Overall, online social capital provides entrepreneurs with an extensive network, access to resources, knowledge exchange, collaboration opportunities, and a platform to build their brand and reputation. Leveraging online social capital can significantly enhance an entrepreneur's chances of success in the digital age.

In this paper, our focus is on the importance of online social capital as an effective platform for entrepreneurs to market their products or services. Online social capital provides entrepreneurs with the opportunity to reach a wider audience and engage with potential customers through their social networks. By leveraging online platforms, entrepreneurs can benefit from word-of-mouth marketing, which can have a significant impact on their brand visibility and reputation.

Through their online social capital, entrepreneurs can tap into their network's connections and extend the reach of their marketing efforts. They can share information, promotions, and updates about their products or services, reaching individuals who may have not been accessible through traditional marketing channels.

Engaging with potential customers through online social capital allows entrepreneurs to build relationships and establish trust. Positive interactions and endorsements within their network can lead to increased credibility and a stronger reputation for their brand. This, in turn, can attract more customers and create a positive image of the entrepreneur and their offerings.

Word-of-mouth marketing is a powerful tool that online social capital enables for entrepreneurs. When satisfied customers share their positive experiences with their own networks, it creates a ripple effect, spreading awareness and generating organic interest in the entrepreneur's products or services. This form of marketing is often trusted and influential, as it comes from individuals who have first-hand experience with the offerings.

So, online social capital provides entrepreneurs with an effective platform for marketing their products or services. By leveraging their social networks, entrepreneurs can reach a wider audience, engage with potential customers, and benefit from word-of-mouth marketing (Buyya et al., 2023). This can significantly enhance their brand visibility and reputation, leading to increased business opportunities and success.

Indeed, in order to effectively market their products or services through online social capital, entrepreneurs can benefit from identifying influential users within their online social networks. This concept is commonly referred to as influence maximization. It focuses on identifying individuals who have a significant impact on the behavior and opinions of others within a social network. These influential users have the potential to shape the attitudes, preferences, and actions of their connections, making them valuable targets for entrepreneurs looking to promote their offerings. By identifying and targeting influential users, entrepreneurs can leverage their social capital to maximize the reach and impact of their marketing efforts. These influential users can serve as brand ambassadors, spreading positive word-of-mouth, and generating interest and engagement among their network connections.

There are various approaches and algorithms available for influence maximization (Li, Cheng, Wang et al, 2023; Singh et al., 2022), which aim to identify the most influential users within a social network. These methods often take into account factors such as the number of connections a user has, the strength of their relationships, and their past behavior in influencing others. By using these techniques, entrepreneurs can strategically focus their marketing efforts on the individuals who are most likely to amplify their message and drive conversions.

Overall, influence maximization within online social networks is a valuable strategy for entrepreneurs to leverage the power of online social capital in marketing their products or services. By identifying influential users and engaging them effectively, entrepreneurs can tap into the potential of word-of-mouth marketing and significantly enhance the visibility and success of their brand.

Influence Maximization Methods

Influence maximization can be classified into three main types: simulation-based methods, heuristic methods, and optimization-based methods. Here, we provide a brief overview of some notable methods within each type:

Simulation-based approaches in influence maximization have several advantages. Firstly, they provide realistic modeling of influence propagation by considering factors such as network structure, user behavior, and the dynamic nature of influence spreading. This enables researchers to better understand the real-world mechanisms of influence diffusion. Secondly, simulation-based approaches offer flexibility in modeling various scenarios. Researchers can customize parameters to simulate different influence dynamics and study their effects on the spread of influence. This flexibility allows for a deeper exploration of the underlying processes involved in influence propagation. Additionally, simulation-based approaches demonstrate scalability and can handle large-scale social networks with numerous nodes and edges, capturing the spread of influence across the entire network.

However, simulation-based approaches also have certain disadvantages. First, they can be computationally intensive and time-consuming, especially when simulating influence propagation in large networks. The need for multiple iterations to accurately estimate influence spread probabilities can limit their suitability for real-time applications. Second, simulation-based approaches do not guarantee finding the globally optimal set of influential users. The selection of influential users is based on observed outcomes from simulations, which may not always result in the maximum possible influence spread.

Moreover, simulation-based approaches are sensitive to parameter settings, making it challenging to determine the optimal parameter values for a given scenario accurately. Lastly, the generalizability of results obtained from simulation-based approaches is limited to the specific models and assumptions used, as their effectiveness may vary depending on the characteristics of the network and the chosen models.

In conclusion, simulation-based approaches provide a realistic and flexible means of studying influence propagation in social networks. While they offer advantages such as realistic modeling, flexibility, and scalability, they also have drawbacks including computational intensity, lack of global optimization, sensitivity to parameter settings, and limited generalizability. Researchers must carefully consider these factors when employing simulation-based approaches for influence maximization in order to make informed decisions and draw accurate conclusions.

These methods rely on simulating the spread of influence in a social network to estimate the influential users. The few most well-known algorithms in this category are:

The objective function of the Influence Maximization (IM) problem, considering both the Independent Cascade (IC) and Linear Threshold (LT) models, exhibits two important properties. Firstly, it is monotone, meaning that adding more nodes to a seed set S will not decrease its current influence spread. Secondly, it is sub-modular, indicating that the marginal gain in influence for each successive iteration cannot exceed the gain achieved in the previous iteration (Kempe et al., 2015). Taking advantage of this sub-modularity, Leskovec et al. introduced an optimization approach called Cost Effective Lazy Forward (CELF), which proved to be significantly faster than the original Greedy algorithm, with a speed improvement of approximately 700 times. This computational efficiency was further enhanced by 35-55% with the introduction of CELF++. However, subsequent research by Arora et al. showed that CELF and CELF++ exhibit nearly identical computational times. They also highlighted that while these simulation-based approaches offer improved solution accuracy, they still require exhaustive Monte Carlo simulations, making them inefficient for large real-world networks (Arora Akhil, 2017; Goyal et al., 2011; Leskovec, Adamic, & Huberman, 2007).

Heuristic approaches: These algorithms utilize heuristics or rules of thumb to identify influential users. These methodologies in influence maximization have several advantages and disadvantages. One of the key advantages is their efficiency in providing faster solutions compared to simulation-based methods. These approaches aim to find a near-optimal set of influential nodes without requiring exhaustive computations. This efficiency makes heuristic approaches well-suited for large-scale networks and real-time or near-real-time applications where time is a critical factor. Additionally, heuristic approaches demonstrate scalability, as they employ efficient algorithms and strategies to search for influential nodes, enabling them to handle complex network structures effectively. Another advantage of heuristic approaches is their ability to approximate optimal solutions. While they do not guarantee finding the globally optimal set of influential nodes, they aim to provide near-optimal solutions. Heuristic approaches leverage techniques such as greedy algorithms or local search strategies to iteratively select nodes with high potential for influence spread. This approximation capability allows heuristic approaches to achieve reasonably good results within a reasonable amount of time, striking a balance between solution quality and computational resources.

However, heuristic approaches also come with some disadvantages. One of the main drawbacks is the limited guarantee of solution quality. As heuristic approaches rely on approximation techniques, the selected set of influential nodes may not always result in the maximum possible influence spread. The quality of the solution can vary depending on the specific algorithm and parameters used, making it important to carefully consider their selection. Moreover, heuristic approaches are often dependent on input parameters, such as the number of iterations or the scoring mechanism for node selection. Calibrating these parameters accurately is crucial, as suboptimal parameter values can lead to suboptimal or less accurate results. Additionally, heuristic approaches face challenges in handling dynamic networks where the network structure or influence probabilities change over time. Adapting heuristic approaches to capture the dynamics of influence propagation in such scenarios can be difficult and may impact their effectiveness.

Some prominent heuristic algorithms include: Several meta-heuristic approaches have been applied to solve the influence maximization problem in social networks. These approaches include Simulated Annealing (SA) (Jiang, Song, Cong, Wang, Si, & Xie, 2011; Li et al., 2017), Genetic Algorithm (GA) (Cheng, 2020; Zhang et al., 2017), Discrete Particle Swarm Optimization (DPSO) (Rameshkumar et al., 2005; Singh et al., 2019; Tang, 2019), Ant Colony Optimization (ACO) (Singh et al., 2020), Evolutionary Algorithm (EA) (Cui, 2018), Memetic Algorithm (MA) (Gong et al., 2016), Gray Wolf Optimization (GWO) (Cheng, 2020), and Discrete Shuffled Frog-Leaping Algorithm (DSFLA) (Tang et al., 2020). Jiang et al. (Jiang, Song, Cong, Wang, Si, & Xie, 2011) introduced the Expected Diffusion Value (EDV) measure to estimate the influence power of a candidate solution and utilized SA as a meta-heuristic to find the optimal subset of influential nodes. This work was significant as it was the first application of a meta-heuristic approach to solve the influence maximization problem in social networks.

In overview, heuristic approaches in influence maximization offer efficiency and scalability, making them suitable for large-scale networks and real-time applications. They provide approximate solutions and can handle complex network structures effectively. However, they lack a guarantee of solution quality, rely on carefully chosen parameters, and may face challenges in handling dynamic networks. Researchers should consider these factors when selecting and applying heuristic approaches for influence maximization.

Miscellaneous approaches: Apart from the well-established approximation and heuristic approaches, there are distinct optimization strategies found in the literature. Notably, community-based (Li et al., 2018) and MCDM-based (Mugnolo et al., 2015) approaches have emerged. In community-based approaches, social networks are divided into non-overlapping communities, and influential nodes are selected from each community. While these approaches reduce overlapping influence spreads, they lack diversity in solution generation and struggle to find non-overlapping communities in real-life cases. Conversely, MCDM-based approaches consider multiple centrality metrics to rank influential nodes. Mesgari et al. (Mugnolo et al., 2015) utilized the TOPSIS method to rank nodes based on a combination of centrality metrics. However, simply selecting the top-k nodes does not account for overlapping influences. Zareie et al. (Zareie et al., 2018) improved upon this by incorporating more criteria and distances among nodes to minimize overlapping influence. Jalayer et al. (Jalayer et al., 2018) combined community detection with TOPSIS, while Ko et al. (Ko et al., 2018) proposed a hybrid approach merging community detection with a path-based heuristic. Despite their strengths, these approaches often lack diversity in solutions and can become trapped in local optima.

It is important to note that the effectiveness of these algorithms can vary depending on the specific characteristics of the social network and the objectives of the influence maximization problem. Researchers continue to explore and develop new algorithms and variations within these categories to improve the accuracy and efficiency of influence maximization in social networks.

METHODOLOGY

The identification of influential nodes in complex networks is a crucial challenge when analyzing spreading dynamics. Existing methods often focus on either local or global information of nodes, overlooking the interplay between them. A recently proposed centrality measure called gravity centrality addresses this by combining both local and global information to capture the node interactions. However, gravity centrality relies solely on node degree as the local information metric, disregarding the connectivity of neighboring nodes. To overcome this limitation, an enhancement is introduced by utilizing Laplacian centrality to optimize the initial gravity centrality, resulting in a centrality measure known as Laplacian gravity centrality. By incorporating the Laplacian centrality, the Laplacian gravity centrality aims to overcome the shortcomings of node degree parameters in the original gravity centrality approach.

Laplacian Gravity Centrality (LGC)

Gravity centrality is a centrality measure that assigns node degree as the mass parameter in the gravitational formula. However, relying solely on node degree may not accurately identify influential nodes, particularly when a node connects to numerous low-degree nodes. The ability to influence other nodes is a crucial characteristic of influential nodes in network spreading. If a node primarily connects to 1-degree nodes, it might be situated in the center of a cluster, limiting its influence on nodes outside the cluster. Considering that network spreading affects nearby nodes incrementally, the degree of neighboring nodes is an important indicator that should not be overlooked. To address the issue of being trapped in cluster centers in the original gravity centrality method, we introduce Laplacian centrality, which incorporates the degrees of neighboring nodes.

Laplacian centrality (LC) is a method that utilizes the Laplacian matrix of a network to measure node centrality. Let $A=(a_{ij})$ represent the adjacency matrix of the network G, and $K=\text{diag}(k_i)$ be a diagonal matrix with the degrees of nodes on the diagonal. The Laplacian matrix of network G can be obtained as L = K - A. Qi et al. (Qi et al., 2013) introduced the Laplacian centrality method by calculating the change in Laplacian energy resulting from the removal of nodes.

The Laplacian energy of network G is defined as $E(G) = \sum_{i=1}^{n} \lambda_i^2$ in which λ_1, λ_2,...,λ_n; are the eigen values of L. The Laplacian energy loss after the removal of node i, or Laplacian centrality of node i, can be defined as:

$$LC(i) = \Delta E(i) = E(G) - E(G)_{-1} \tag{1}$$

By analyzing the change in Laplacian energy, Laplacian centrality identifies the importance of nodes in the network based on their impact on the overall network structure and connectivity.

In Eq. (1), G_{-1} is the network G without node i and edges linking to it. By the connection between matrix eigenvalues and trace in linear algebra, it is easy to proof $E(G) = \sum_{i=1}^{n} K_i^2 + \sum_{i=1}^{n} K_i$ from the definition of Laplacian energy.

By the definition of Laplacian centrality in Eq. (1), after the removal of node i, all neighboring nodes have a degree loss of 1. So, we can deduce that

$$LC(i) = E(G) - E(G)_{-1}$$

$$= K_i^2 + K_i + \sum\nolimits_{j \in \Gamma i} \left[K_j^2 - \left(K_{j-1} \right)^2 \right] + K_i$$

$$= K_i^2 + K_i + \sum\nolimits_{j \in \Gamma i} 2K_j - K_i + K_i \qquad (2)$$

$$= K_i^2 + K_j + 2\sum\nolimits_{j \in \Gamma i} K_j$$

According to the findings presented in (Zhao et al., 2022), Eq. (2) demonstrates that K_i represents the degree of node i, while Γ_i denotes the collection of adjacent nodes to node i. The Laplacian centrality, as demonstrated, relies solely on the node's degree and the cumulative degree of its neighboring nodes. This method operates through node removal.

We used a novel method (Zhang et al., 2022), Laplacian gravity centrality (LGC), which utilizes Laplacian centrality as a substitute for node degree in gravity centrality. This innovative approach aims to identify influential nodes within a network more accurately and effectively. By incorporating Laplacian centrality into LGC, we provide a powerful tool for determining influential nodes.

In order to introduce LGC, we first define the Laplacian gravitational force between a pair of nodes (i, j) as $\lg f(i, j) = \dfrac{LC(i)LC(j)}{d_{ij}^2}$, where LC(i) represents the Laplacian centrality of node i, calculated using Eq. (2), and d_{ij} denotes the topological distance between nodes i and j. If node j is isolated and not part of the connected component in the network, d_{ij} is considered to be infinity, resulting in a Laplacian gravitational force of zero between them. It is worth noting that the square of the topological distance in the denominator, originating from Newton's gravity formula, remains unchanged in our proposed method. This choice is justified by its ability to effectively describe the decay of influence with distance in a reasonable and scientifically sound manner.

The definition of LGC can be expressed as follows: It involves adding the Laplacian gravitational forces of node pairs whose topological distance falls within a specified truncation radius. By summing these Laplacian gravitational forces, we obtain the Laplacian gravity centrality (LGC) value for a given node.

$$LGC(i) = \sum\nolimits_{j \neq i, d_{ij} \leq (d)/2} \lg f(i, j) = \sum\nolimits_{j \neq i, d_{ij} \leq (d)/2} \frac{LC(i)LC(j)}{d_{ij}^2} \qquad (3)$$

Gravity centrality: Gravity centrality (Li et al., 2019) adapts the concept of gravitational force between objects to complex networks. In the gravity formula, the mass and distance between objects determine the strength of the force. Similarly, in gravity centrality, the degree of vertices serves as the mass, and the shortest path length acts as the distance. The initial equation for gravity centrality (GC) can be expressed as follows:

$$GC(i) = \sum\nolimits_{j \neq i} \frac{k_i k_j}{d_{ij}^2} \qquad (4)$$

In Equation (4), the variables k_i and d_{ij} represent the degree of node i and the topological distance between node i and j, respectively. To address the challenges of time complexity in large-scale networks and minimize the impact of noise from distant nodes, an enhanced version of the GC method has been devised. This improved GC method focuses solely on interactions between nodes that fall within a pre-determined truncation radius. By setting the truncation radius to half of the average path length (d), the improved GC can be precisely defined as follows:

$$GC(i) = \sum_{j \neq i, d_{ij} \leq (d)/2} \frac{k_i k_j}{d_{ij}^2} \tag{5}$$

Gravity centrality stands out from other existing methods due to its unique combination of node degree and topological distance information. By incorporating both local and global information, it provides a comprehensive understanding of node importance within a network. Our proposed method builds upon the optimization of LGC, and further details can be found in this Section

In Eq. (3), (d) represents the average topological distance between nodes in the network. Upon comparing Eqs. (5) and (3), it becomes apparent that our LGC method combines the GC and LC methods, employing node LC as a substitute for node degree in the GC method. The algorithm for the LGC method is presented in Algorithm 1.

RESULTS

Data Sets and Comparison Algorithms

In this paper, we provide the five social data sets from the real world that were culled from the SNAP(snap.stanford.edu/data/). shown in Table 1.

Table 1. Datasets description

Network	V	E	Avg Degree
NetHEPT	15233	58891	4.23
Wiki-Vote	7115	103689	29.15
CA-GrQc	5242	28980	11.06
CA-HepPh	12006	237008	39.48
Com-Youtube	1134890	2987624	5.27

Figure 1. Algorithm 1

Input:G=(N,E)-- A network contains N nodes and E edges

Initialize information

for each $i \in N$ do

    for each $i \in N$ do

Compute topological distance d_{ij} using Dijkstra or Floyd algorithm

    end for

end for

for each $i \in N$ do

Compute LC(i) using Equation (2)

  for each $i \in N$ do

  if $d_{ij} \leq 0.5(d)$

      Compute LGC(i) using Equation (3)

  end if

  end for

end for

Output: LGC(i)

Running Time Comparison

The accuracy of the proposed algorithm in identifying prominent individuals is higher than that of the other methods, as shown in Figure 2, even though the run time of the proposed algorithm is slower than that of other algorithms. Even if the parameters of the suggested algorithm have an effect on its performance, the proposed algorithm nevertheless produces results that are much superior to those produced by other algorithms. Even though the proposed approach offers a wide range of solutions, it complicates the optimization process and increases the program's runtime in some circumstances. In most cases, the proposed algorithm performs more effectively with regard to efficiency.

In terms of execution time, The PMIA and LGC have very low running time, and the DD and DDSE has high than the others. Certainly, the PMIA and LGC running time results are very close to each other. Likewise, the introduced LGC approach has reduced running time after DD. Generally, the running time of the approaches from low to high is arranged as LGC,IMA, DDSE,DD.

Figure 2. Running time comparison of proposed CB-IM and four other algorithms under IC model

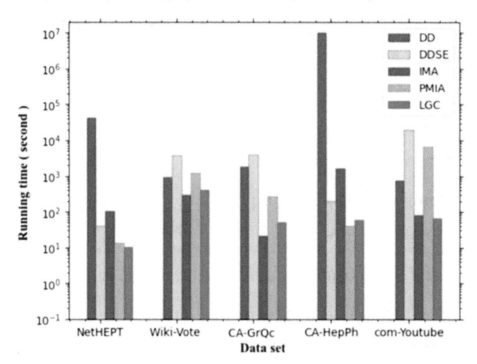

CONCLUSION AND FUTURE DIRECTIONS

In conclusion, social capital, both in offline and online contexts, plays a crucial role in connecting individuals and communities, facilitating access to resources, fostering learning and collaboration, and driving social change. Online social capital, in particular, offers unique advantages and opportunities in the digital age. It provides individuals with easy access to information, networking platforms, and support systems, enabling them to learn, connect, and thrive. For entrepreneurs, online social capital is especially valuable as it expands their networks, facilitates resource access, enhances their reputation, and offers avenues for marketing and growth. Leveraging online social capital can significantly contribute to an entrepreneur's success by increasing brand visibility, reaching a wider audience, and harnessing the power of word-of-mouth marketing. Furthermore, influence maximization within online social networks presents a strategic approach for entrepreneurs to identify and engage influential users who can amplify their message and drive conversions. Overall, understanding and effectively utilizing online social capital can open doors to numerous opportunities and benefits for individuals and communities in the digital era.

Future Scope: While the importance of online social capital for entrepreneurs has been established, there are several areas for future research and exploration. Firstly, further studies can delve into the dynamics of online social networks and the factors that contribute to the formation and maintenance of social capital within these networks. Understanding how relationships develop, evolve, and influence resource access and collaboration can provide insights into optimizing online social capital for entrepreneurial success.

Additionally, investigating the role of online social capital in different industries and sectors can offer valuable insights. Each industry has its unique characteristics and challenges, and understanding how online social capital can be leveraged effectively within specific contexts can guide entrepreneurs in maximizing their opportunities and overcoming industry-specific obstacles.

Furthermore, the ethical implications of online social capital and its potential risks deserve attention. As online platforms continue to shape our social interactions, privacy concerns, information security, and the potential for social manipulation and misinformation become critical areas of investigation. Examining the ethical considerations and developing guidelines for responsible use of online social capital can help ensure that its benefits are harnessed while mitigating potential harms.

Lastly, the advancement of technology and the emergence of new online platforms present opportunities for exploring novel ways to leverage social capital. Investigating the potential of emerging technologies such as blockchain, virtual reality, and artificial intelligence in enhancing online social capital can uncover innovative approaches for entrepreneurs to connect, collaborate, and market their products or services.

By addressing these areas of future research, we can deepen our understanding of online social capital and its implications for entrepreneurs, enabling them to navigate the digital landscape effectively and harness its full potential for success.

REFERENCES

Al-Naabi, I. (2023). Did They Transform Their Teaching Practices? A Case Study on Evaluating Professional Development Webinars Offered to Language Teachers during COVID-19. *International Journal of Higher Education*, *12*(1), 36. doi:10.5430/ijhe.v12n1p36

Ali, Balta, & Papadopoulos. (2023). Social media platforms and social enterprise: Bibliometric analysis and systematic review. *Int. J. Inf. Manage.*, *69*, 102510. . doi:10.1016/j.ijinfomgt.2022.102510

Amigó, E., Deldjoo, Y., Mizzaro, S., & Bellogín, A. (2023). A unifying and general account of fairness measurement in recommender systems. *Information Processing & Management*, *60*(1), 103115. doi:10.1016/j.ipm.2022.103115

Arora Akhil, S. R. (2017). *Debunking the Myths of Influence Maximization: An In-Depth Benchmarking Study*. ACM.

Banerjee, S., Jenamani, M., & Pratihar, D. K. (2020). A survey on influence maximization in a social network. *Knowledge and Information Systems*, *62*(9), 3417–3455. doi:10.100710115-020-01461-4

Bhowmik, N. R., Arifuzzaman, M., Mondal, M. R. H., & Islam, M. S. (2021). Bangla Text Sentiment Analysis Using Supervised Machine Learning with Extended Lexicon Dictionary. *Nat. Lang. Process. Res.*, *1*(3–4), 34. doi:10.2991/nlpr.d.210316.001

Chekkai, N., & Kheddouci, H. (2022). TOP-Key Influential Nodes for Opinion Leaders Identification in Travel Recommender Systems. In P. Fournier-Viger, A. Hassan, L. Bellatreche, A. Awad, A. Ait Wakrime, Y. Ouhammou, & I. Ait Sadoune (Eds.), *Advances in Model and Data Engineering in the Digitalization Era* (pp. 149–161). Springer Nature Switzerland. doi:10.1007/978-3-031-23119-3_11

Chen, W., Lakshmanan, L. V. S., & Castillo, C. (2013). Information and Influence Propagation in Social Networks. *Synthesis Lectures on Data Management*, *5*(4), 1–177. doi:10.1007/978-3-031-01850-3

Chen, W., Wang, C., & Wang, Y. (2010). Scalable Influence Maximization for Prevalent Viral. *16th ACM SIGKDD Int. Conf. Knowl. Discov. data Min.*, 1029–1038.

Cheng. (2020). Identification of influential users in social network using gray wolf optimization algorithm. *Phys. A Stat. Mech. its Appl.*, *142*(1), 112971. . doi:10.1016/j.eswa.2019.112971

Cui. (2018). DDSE: A novel evolutionary algorithm based on degree-descending search strategy for influence maximization in social networks. *J. Netw. Comput. Appl.*, *103*, 119–130. . doi:10.1016/j.jnca.2017.12.003

Ellison, N. B., Vitak, J., Gray, R., & Lampe, C. (2014). Cultivating social resources on social network sites: Facebook relationship maintenance behaviors and their role in social capital processes. *Journal of Computer-Mediated Communication*, *19*(4), 855–870. doi:10.1111/jcc4.12078

Entrepreneurial enactment as social value creation: An exploration of the Aberdeen entrepreneurial ecosystem. (2022). Academic Press.

Fan, Z., & Zhai, X. (2023). The Performance Improvement Mechanism of Cross-Border E-Commerce Grassroots Entrepreneurship Empowered by the Internet Platform. *Sustainability (Basel)*, *15*(2), 1178. doi:10.3390u15021178

Gong, M., Song, C., Duan, C., Ma, L., & Shen, B. (2016). An Efficient Memetic Algorithm for Influence Maximization in Social Networks. *IEEE Computational Intelligence Magazine*, *11*(3), 22–33. doi:10.1109/MCI.2016.2572538

Goyal, A., Lu, W., & Lakshmanan, L. V. S. (2011). CELF++: Optimizing the greedy algorithm for influence maximization in social networks. *Proceedings of the 20th International Conference Companion on World Wide Web, WWW 2011*, 47–48. 10.1145/1963192.1963217

Hamilton, W., Duerr, D. E., Hemphill, C., & Colello, K. (2023). Techno-capital, cultural capital, and the cultivation of academic social capital: The case of adult online college students. Internet High. Educ., 56, 100891. doi:10.1016/j.iheduc.2022.100891

He, Q., Wang, X., Lei, Z., Huang, M., Cai, Y., & Ma, L. (2019). TIFIM: A Two-stage Iterative Framework for Influence Maximization in Social Networks. *Applied Mathematics and Computation*, *354*, 338–352. doi:10.1016/j.amc.2019.02.056

Hossain, M. A., Yesmin, N., Jahan, N., & Reza, S. M. A. (2023). Effect of Social Presence on Behavioral Intention to Social Commerce Through Online Social Capital. *International Journal of e-Collaboration*, *19*(1), 1–23. doi:10.4018/IJeC.315779

Itani, O. S., Badrinarayanan, V., & Rangarajan, D. (2023, January). The impact of business-to-business salespeople's social media use on value co-creation and cross/up-selling: The role of social capital. *European Journal of Marketing*, *57*(3), 683–717. doi:10.1108/EJM-11-2021-0916

Jalayer, M., Azheian, M., & Agha Mohammad Ali Kermani, M. (2018). A hybrid algorithm based on community detection and multi attribute decision making for influence maximization. Comput. Ind. Eng., 120, 234–250. doi:10.1016/j.cie.2018.04.049

Jiang, Q., Song, G., Cong, G., Wang, Y., Si, W., & Xie, K. (2011). Simulated annealing based influence maximization in social networks. *Proc. Natl. Conf. Artif. Intell.*, 1, 127–132. 10.1609/aaai.v25i1.7838

Kawachi, I., Subramanian, I. V., & Kim, D. (2008). *Social capital and health*. Soc. Cap. Heal. doi:10.1007/978-0-387-71311-3

Kempe, D., Kleinberg, J., & Tardos, É. (2003). Maximizing the spread of influence through a social network. *Proceedings of the ACM SIGKDD International Conference on Knowledge Discovery and Data Mining*, 137–146. 10.1145/956750.956769

Kempe, D., Kleinberg, J., & Tardos, É. (2015). Maximizing the spread of influence through a social network. *Theory Comput.*, *11*(1), 105–147. doi:10.4086/toc.2015.v011a004

Ko, Y. Y., Cho, K. J., & Kim, S. W. (2018). Efficient and effective influence maximization in social networks: A hybrid-approach. *Information Sciences*, *465*, 144–161. doi:10.1016/j.ins.2018.07.003

Kumar, Singh, Singh, & Biswas. (2020). Link prediction techniques, applications, and performance: A survey. *Phys. A Stat. Mech. its Appl.*, *553*, 124289. doi:10.1016/j.physa.2020.124289

Leskovec, J., Adamic, L. A., & Huberman, B. A. (2007). The dynamics of viral marketing. *ACM Transactions on the Web*, *1*(1), 5. Advance online publication. doi:10.1145/1232722.1232727

Li, D., Wang, C., Zhang, S., Zhou, G., Chu, D., & Wu, C. (2017). Positive influence maximization in signed social networks based on simulated annealing. *Neurocomputing*, *260*, 69–78. doi:10.1016/j.neucom.2017.03.003

Li, Q., Cheng, L., Wang, W., Li, X., Li, S., & Zhu, P. (2023). Influence maximization through exploring structural information. *Applied Mathematics and Computation*, *442*, 127721. Advance online publication. doi:10.1016/j.amc.2022.127721

Li, X., Cheng, X., Su, S., & Sun, C. (2018). Community-based seeds selection algorithm for location aware influence maximization. *Neurocomputing*, *275*, 1601–1613. doi:10.1016/j.neucom.2017.10.007

Li, Y., Fabbre, V. D., & Gaveras, E. (2023). Authenticated social capital: Conceptualising power, resistance and well-being in the lives of transgender older adults. *Culture, Health & Sexuality*, *25*(3), 352–367. doi:10.1080/13691058.2022.2044519 PMID:35235503

Li, Z., Ren, T., Ma, X., Liu, S., Zhang, Y., & Zhou, T. (2019). Identifying influential spreaders by gravity model. *Scientific Reports*, *9*(1), 1–7. doi:10.103841598-019-44930-9 PMID:31182773

Lin. (2001). *Social Capital: A Theory of Social Structure and Action*. Academic Press.

Mallios & Moustakis. (2023). *Social Media Impact on Startup Entrepreneurial Intention : Evidence from Greece*. Academic Press.

Mesgari, I., Kermani, M. A. M. A., Hanneman, R., & Aliahmadi, A. (2015). Identifying Key Nodes in Social Networks Using Multi-Criteria Decision-Making Tools. In D. Mugnolo (Ed.), *Mathematical Technology of Networks* (pp. 137–150). Springer International Publishing. doi:10.1007/978-3-319-16619-3_10

Nguyen, H. T., Thai, M. T., & Dinh, T. N. (2016). Stop-and-Stare: Optimal sampling algorithms for viral marketing in billion-scale networks. *Proc. ACM SIGMOD Int. Conf. Manag. Data*, *26*(20), 695–710. 10.1145/2882903.2915207

Putnam. (2000). *Bowling Alone: The Collapse and Revival of American Community*. Academic Press.

Qi, X., Duval, R. D., Christensen, K., Fuller, E., Spahiu, A., Wu, Q., Wu, Y., Tang, W., & Zhang, C. (2013). Terrorist Networks, Network Energy and Node Removal: A New Measure of Centrality Based on Laplacian Energy. *Social Networking*, *02*(01), 19–31. doi:10.4236n.2013.21003

Raffaella, Putnam, & Leonardi. (1994). *Making Democracy Work: Civic Traditions in Modern Italy*. Academic Press.

Rameshkumar, K., Suresh, R. K., & Mohanasundaram, K. M. (2005). Discrete particle swarm optimization (DPSO) algorithm for permutation flowshop scheduling to minimize makespan. *Lect. Notes Comput. Sci.*, *3612*(3), 572–581. doi:10.1007/11539902_70

Ruef. (2010). *The Social Capital of Entrepreneurial Newcomers: Bridging*. Status-power, and Cognition.

Saenz, C. (2023). Corporate social responsibility strategies beyond the sphere of influence: Cases from the Peruvian mining industry. *Resour. Policy*, *80*, 103187. doi:10.1016/j.resourpol.2022.103187

Shang, R., Luo, S., Li, Y., Jiao, L., & Stolkin, R. (2015). Large-scale community detection based on node membership grade and sub-communities integration. *Phys. A Stat. Mech. its Appl.*, *428*, 279–294. doi:10.1016/j.physa.2015.02.004

Singh, S. S., Kumar, A., Singh, K., & Biswas, B. (2019). LAPSO-IM: A learning-based influence maximization approach for social networks. *Applied Soft Computing*, *82*, 105554. doi:10.1016/j.asoc.2019.105554

Singh, S. S., Singh, K., Kumar, A., & Biswas, B. (2020). ACO-IM: Maximizing influence in social networks using ant colony optimization. *Soft Computing*, *24*(13), 10181–10203. doi:10.100700500-019-04533-y

Singh, S. S., Srivastva, D., Verma, M., & Singh, J. (2022). "Influence maximization frameworks, performance, challenges and directions on social network: A theoretical study," *J. King Saud Univ. -. Comput. Inf. Sci.*, *34*(9), 7570–7603. doi:10.1016/j.jksuci.2021.08.009

Tang, J. (2019). Identification of top-k influential nodes based on enhanced discrete particle swarm optimization for influence maximization. *Phys. A Stat. Mech. its Appl.*, *513*, 477–496. doi:10.1016/j.physa.2018.09.040

Tang, J., Zhang, R., Wang, P., Zhao, Z., Fan, L., & Liu, X. (2020). A discrete shuffled frog-leaping algorithm to identify influential nodes for influence maximization in social networks. *Knowledge-Based Systems*, *187*, 104833. doi:10.1016/j.knosys.2019.07.004

Tian, S., Mo, S., Wang, L., & Peng, Z. (2020). Deep Reinforcement Learning-Based Approach to Tackle Topic-Aware Influence Maximization. *Data Science and Engineering*, *5*(1), 1–11. doi:10.100741019-020-00117-1

Venunath, M., Sujatha, P., & Koti, P. (2023). Identifying Top-N Influential Nodes in Large Complex Networks Using Network Structure. In R. Buyya, S. M. Hernandez, R. M. R. Kovvur, & T. H. Sarma (Eds.), *Computational Intelligence and Data Analytics* (pp. 597–607). Springer Nature Singapore. doi:10.1007/978-981-19-3391-2_45

Xiang, T., Li, Q., Li, W., & Xiao, Y. (2023). A rumor heat prediction model based on rumor and anti-rumor multiple messages and knowledge representation. *Information Processing & Management*, *60*(3), 103337. Advance online publication. doi:10.1016/j.ipm.2023.103337

Yang, Y., Lichtenwalter, R. N., & Chawla, N. V. (2015). Evaluating link prediction methods. *Knowledge and Information Systems*, *45*(3), 751–782. doi:10.100710115-014-0789-0

Zareie, A., Sheikhahmadi, A., & Khamforoosh, K. (2018). Influence maximization in social networks based on TOPSIS. *Expert Systems with Applications*, *108*, 96–107. doi:10.1016/j.eswa.2018.05.001

Zhang, K., Du, H., & Feldman, M. W. (2017). Maximizing influence in a social network: Improved results using a genetic algorithm. Phys. A Stat. Mech. its Appl., 478, 20–30. doi:10.1016/j.physa.2017.02.067

Zhang, Q., Shuai, B., & Lü, M. (2022). A novel method to identify influential nodes in complex networks based on gravity centrality. *Information Sciences*, *618*, 98–117. doi:10.1016/j.ins.2022.10.070

Zhao, J., Wen, T., Jahanshahi, H., & Cheong, K. H. (2022). The random walk-based gravity model to identify influential nodes in complex networks. *Information Sciences*, *609*, 1706–1720. doi:10.1016/j.ins.2022.07.084

Chapter 11
Exploring Managerial Perspectives:
Digital Transformations and Virtual Workforce Management in the Modern Workspace

Roma Singh

https://orcid.org/0000-0003-0683-1051

Tezpur University, India

Runumi Das

Tezpur University, India

ABSTRACT

In today's highly competitive global business environment, the efficient management of a "scattered" or "distance" workforce is critical for the success of any organisation. The purpose of this chapter is to look into how the debate on digital transformation and leadership has changed in recent years. The approach is mixed. The first section is a review of the literature on digital advancements in various sectors of the economy as well as new trends in virtual workforce management. The second section summarises the conclusions of empirical study based on interviews with managerial representatives from IT, operations, and sales. The study was conducted in Tier 1 cities in India. The results show that managers have adjusted into this new era of employee management from distant places and have undergone necessary training for skill development. However, the rising use of technologies has brought a new set of challenges that need to be dealt with.

DOI: 10.4018/978-1-6684-8953-6.ch011

INTRODUCTION

The fourth industrial revolution has been mainly discussed in terms of how advancements in technology and digital transformations have led to the shift from a market economy to a knowledge-based economy. Technology has become increasingly ubiquitous in all aspects of life, including work, social interactions, and civic engagement (Kolade et al., 2021). Likewise the impact of "technological innovation" is primarily seen in altering how a company conducts its operations by putting forward a notion for a new product or elements into an organization's course of service operation (Torres & Augusto, 2019), leading to "organizational innovation" at large by necessitating new approaches in management, corporate strategy, and business models (Matt et al., 2015).

This emerging digital transformations that affect interpersonal communication is causing employees to face increased demands and pressure in an environment that is constantly evolving (Biedenbach et al., 2022), demanding for a digital transformation strategy which can assist organisations in managing the transformations occurring due to the integration of digital technologies (Matt et al., 2015). Despite such rapid advancements occurring, and challenges encountered in practice, very less is known about employees and organisational respond to such disruptive technologies specially in developing economies (Trenerry et al., 2021).

Similarly, when the world experienced an unforeseen outbreak of coronavirus in 2020, resulting in a staggering death toll of over five million people in two years and causing unprecedented damage to businesses and other institutions. In such circumstances, the ability to bounce back, or resilience, was undoubtedly a crucial trait that decided the endurance of individuals, companies, and the entire mankind in coping with the difficulties (Biedenbach et al., 2022). That is when end number of businesses and institutions all round the globe went virtual, adapting a new form of working in order to sustain itself and survive the catastrophe. This work practice popularly known as remote working or work from home (WFH) mainly "concerns any intellectual work carried out outside the normal place of work, whose effects are sent to the employer using information and communication technologies" as cited by Pokojski et al., (2022) (Battisti et al., 2022). Likely, it was also predicted that more than 85% of the employed professionals were part of certain type of virtual team (e.g, Dulebohn & Hoch, 2017; Raghuram et al., 2019; Morrison-Smith & Ruiz, 2020). This rise in remote employment has been largely welcomed by certain policymakers in low- and middle-income nations, as well as organisations concerned with economic development (Wood et al., 2018). Regardless of these virtual team benefits, researchers show that they deliver a number of challenges when conferred to in- person teams (Dulebohn & Hoch, 2017 ; Alsharo et al., 2017; Morrison-Smith & Ruiz, 2020). Such drawbacks include difficulties in communication and cooperation, as well as complications in monitoring and managing virtual workforce's. Subsequently, the struggles of managing virtual workforce's have acquired considerable attention in both scholastic and practitioner publications (Hoch & Kozlowski, 2014; Raghuram et al., 2019). Therefore, empirical investigations revealed that adopting computerisation might contribute in boosting remote monitoring, speeding up work, filling in gaps between tasks, and tracking locations beyond the traditional workplace during working hours (Pokojski et al., 2022). Surprisingly this burgeoning recognition and interest in these teams, has not led to much of the knowledge about successful virtual team management yet (Dulebohn & Hoch, 2017; Ford et al., 2017; Chamakiotis et al., 2021). Therefore, the current study aims to learn about their perspectives on rapidly changing management dynamics, as well as the effects of digital transformations on managerial activities in the modern management era. Recent studies have defined this transformation as a process that "aims to improve an entity by triggering significant changes to its properties through combinations of information, computing, communication, and connectivity technologies" (Vial, 2019).

Our research has a specific focus on the adoption of innovation and virtual technologies within a particular industry in India (Hilmersson et al., 2022). The purpose of this is to enhance comprehension of how technology is implemented and developed in developing nations, by examining the surrounding circumstances and conditions. (Ozuem et al., 2019; Hilmersson et al., 2022).

In this paper, the researchers will begin by discussing those writings that informed the study. Next, they will describe the research background and methodology, and then produce and analyze the results. Finally, they will culminate by summarizing their addition and the practical implications of their findings. The chapter will discuss the study's shortcomings and offer areas for future research (e.g., Klessova et al., 2022; Trabucchi et al., 2017; Chichkanov et al., 2019; Kaulio et al., 2017; Hilmersson et al., 2022; Seclen-Luna et al., 2022; Pantano, 2016).

BACKGROUND OF THE STUDY

Statement of Problem

Two of the major challenges that firms were facing in coordinating with this transition and will have to, in a post-pandemic scenario will be that, how tasks and control mechanisms are delineated when work is physically distributed, and how digital technologies are opted to overcome social distancing, could be adopted in interaction with the new work arrangements and to improve work effectiveness, productivity and employee wellbeing. COVID19 has led to new emerging challenges in the way of strategic HRM practices by extending new shifts in understanding how the online/ WFH trend influences employee behaviour, highlighting the need for tactical practices as well. The pandemic has been witnessed throwing various impacts on employees, organisation and its other stakeholders, making the HR practices a vital element in contributing to the overall operational and strategic success of the firm (Collings et al., 2021). Because of COVID, the expansion of remote working has expedited some trends that were already underway, such as teamwork connection and virtualization, which has influenced the management style necessary in scattered organisations (Wang et al., 2021).

Objective and Research Questions

In order to lead a remotely distributed workforce, new and more complicated methods of communication, performance management, training, and relationship building must be implemented. Therefore, this particular objective will try to find out the problems encountered in adoption and implementation of such modern management practices by managers/Team Leaders, specially in supervising digital workforces scattered remotely and its impact on their managerial productivity.

RQ.1 To find out managerial perception on the adaption of modern management culture and increased delegation of duties?

RQ.2 To identify the challenges encountered while managing/ leading virtual teams ?

RQ.3 To know the trainings/courses undergone and the new skillset adopted for increasing managerial effectiveness ?

RQ.4 To explore the use of different softwares and Artificial Intelligence tools in managing distance workforces and their implications?

RQ.5 To find out the job expectations from managers and its affect on their productivity ?

RQ.6 To explore the most preferred leadership style ?

Need/Purpose of the Study

Technology's actual potential may be better tapped through continuous study and practitioner discussions. According to authors, research on themes such as social isolation, group and team behaviour, and management practices in teleworking, should be done. To understand more about how to manage this new method of working, research that thoroughly explored teleworking and e-leadership, as well as the causes for success and failure, are required (Contreras et al., 2020). The academic writings still have little to say on topics such as how to best handle training, development and advancement opportunities for remote workers or how to constructively look into practical, psychological and managerial aspects in leading remote teams (Popovici & Lavinia Popovici, 2020).

Terms like Work From Home/ Remote/ Hybrid work, Online/ Management/Networking etc., has gained immense importance in recent COVID times and has become feasible to some extent due to the joint efforts of HR complimented by AI tools and techniques in the global context. Reports argue about the changed mindset needed in the organisation and current culture before adoption of any digital tool or technology, otherwise the inability of senior leaders to focus on their business strategy, or recognise employee's fear of job polarization before any kind of innovative investments, might lead to more destruction than transformation (Tabrizi et al., 2019). The rise in digitisation has no doubt raised many other concerns. Apart from its security issues, the creation of a complex work environment has exposed new challenges compelling the tenacity to learn digital strategies in order to guide the new form of digital workspace (Vallo Hult & Byström, 2021). In the past, researchers mainly investigated product and process innovations in manufacturing industries, SME's and micro firms with a particular focus on product-related patents. It was suggested that future researchers expand on this neglected areas by examining process innovations in other sectors such as service and digital industries (Walker et al., 2015; Pantano, 2016; Dan et al., 2018; Heredia Pérez et al., 2019 ; Torres & Augusto, 2019;Seclen-Luna et al., 2022; Hilmersson et al., 2022).

Therefore, the main purpose of this study is to explore the challenges occurring while managing virtual teams and the employee expectations and types of trainings or skillsets acquired by them in order to lead the teams and be future ready in meeting the work expectations of a fast changing market culture with new innovations every second, which can have diverse effects on the managerial productivity and their Work Life Balance as well.

LITERATURE REVIEW

Tech Innovations

There will be more technology-driven change during the coming two decades than it happened in the first ICT revolution. Applying these technologies may bring all sort of accelerating changes, there are cybersecurity threats and safety issues involved in the use and implementation of tech innovations like

Artificial Intelligence (AI) as well as the presence of numerous gaps in digital governance which needs to be filled up by proper R&D along with setting up clear policies (Manning, 2020). The initial set of research studies focused on how innovation spreads and is embraced in developing nations, which was in the 1960s (Hasan et al., 2020). Undoubtedly, the innovation contention is still of great interest to both scholars and professionals, who are actively engaged in research and development from diverse viewpoints. There is ongoing promotion of innovation research to better understand and advance this field (Han & Gao, 2019), because technological advancements are solely linked to the growth and implementation of novel technologies, which are derived from the outcomes of new technological advancements, fresh amalgamations of pre-existent technologies, or utilization of other learnings obtained by the organisation (Han & Gao, 2019; Seclen-Luna et al., 2022). However, studies have still not sought the direct affect of technological innovations on a single sub factor of organisational innovation which is the new management practices, whether complimented or adversely affected by tech innovations. It is crucial to investigate how firms frame their digital transformation strategies under specific cultural and institutional environments (Černe et al., 2013; Walker et al., 2015). Different types of innovation occur, and their impact on survival can vary, being more or less significant (Cefis & Marsili, 2018). It is widely understood that innovations that significantly alter industries can modify competitive advantages and jeopardize the sustainability of existing organizations and economic structures (Trabucchi et al., 2017). Therefore, innovation researches in the past have emphasized the importance of categorizing innovation into various types, and a significant distinction among them is between technological and non-technological innovation (Černe et al., 2013; Han & Gao, 2019; Heredia Pérez et al., 2019). Such studies have given more focus on non-technological innovations such as managerial innovations, besides product and process innovations. (Cefis & Marsili, 2018; von Delft & Zhao, 2021). In the realm of non-tech innovations, modifications in organizational and marketing approaches were included. Such innovations had a close association with technological innovations, particularly in service-oriented industries (Cefis & Marsili, 2018). The majority of research has prioritized examining innovation in advanced economies, resulting in less attention given to studying innovation in emerging markets. This has led to a deficiency in conducting comprehensive investigations of the innovative disruptions in emerging economies (Walker et al., 2015). Various theories and models later on have attempted to explain technology acceptance behavior in developing countries, but they have limitations in their ability to fully explain all the factors involved (Hasan et al., 2020). The discoveries and deductions stipulate that there are requirement for strategies and initiatives focused on encouraging originality, while taking into account distinctive attributes of each nation and business domain (Heredia Pérez et al., 2019). According to studies, investigating the highlighted aspects related to both digital transformation and psychological-behavioural drivers (such as job satisfaction and techno-stress), which are important in the decision to continue working remotely after the COVID-19 pandemic requires a focus from the perspective of individuals (Battisti et al., 2022).

Virtual Teams and E-Leadership

"Virtual teams are work arrangements in which team members are geographically dispersed, have limited face-to-face contact, and collaborate to achieve common goals using electronic communication media" (Ford et al., 2017). On the other hand, Avolio & Kahai (2010, p. 239) defined e-leadership as "E-leadership is a process of social influence that takes place in an organizational context where a significant amount of work is supported by information technology". Therefore, previous researches have looked at Actor Network Theory (ANT) to investigate how digital platforms and developments affect communication (Tahirkheli, 2022).

Large-scale networks of computers, people and objects were the results of disruptive technologies like mobile computing and virtual reality which erode formerly defined limits between online and offline settings (Schwarzmüller et al., 2018).

The teleworking literature recognised the significance of technology dependence in remote work and the call for supportive infrastructure, but it did not empirically investigated the inherent processes through which technology components perform this role (Raghuram et al., 2019). Although virtual teams have been around for more than two decades, the Covid-19 has resulted in a worldwide transition into virtual networking, also known in the literature as remote or distributed working. Also, it has rekindled interest in how ICTs might cause work reconfigurations, enabling novel working arrangements and requiring additional research (Chamakiotis et al., 2021).

Scholars are paying more attention to cross-cultural leadership and how it applies to global organisations when communication happens through electronic means. However, the effects of virtual working and team management on team leaders or managers, especially when the work is done in a totally virtual setup, are still not well understood (Tahirkheli, 2022).

Such studies mainly focus to develop and implement cutting-edge technological capabilities and creative business strategies in entrepreneurial business models of developing economies (Kolade et al., 2021).

In her research, Ellington (2023) recognised the difficulties that leaders encountered in the digital world, as well as the tactics that were crucial to the development of creative teaching methods for digital adults. However, the focus of this article was on the andragogical leadership component, and the publication restricted its review to the educational field.

The transformations in HRM activities that have been seen on digital platforms (Waldkirch et al., 2021) demand for a focus on the organisational leadership elements of digital problems and creative solutions. This emphasis is necessary because of the changes that have been observed in various leadership activities and as per Barley's (2015) suggestion that was mentioned by Ellington (2023) in her paper that, although digital technology has become almost as infrastructural as electricity, there is a surprising lack of research on how it is altering work systems or the work that people do. This emphasis is necessary because of the changes that have been observed in different leadership activities.

METHODOLOGY

Research Design

The study relies on primary sources, which have been cross-checked to enhance the credibility and strength of the conclusions. (Trabucchi et al., 2017). It is qualitative in nature, the authors chose to use purposive sampling as it aligned with their phenomenological hermeneutics approach, and they specifically selected individuals or contexts that were believed to provide valuable insights (Ozuem et al., 2019). This research primarily aims to shed light on the managerial practices involved in implementing computer-mediated management in the private sector of India. The research was guided by a pre-existing understanding of the subject matter, which helped in formulating relevant questions for the respondents. To investigate this perspective, semi-structured interviews were conducted with managers from different organizations to gain insight into their experiences (Trabucchi et al., 2017; Dattée et al., 2018).

Table 1. Demographic profiling of respondents

Age	Work Experience	Job Location
35 years	10 yrs	From Home
35 years	15 yrs	From Home
41 years	19 yrs	Anywhere Remotely
32 years	10 yrs	From Home
45 years	20 yrs	Hybrid

Source: Author's compilation

Data Collection and Analysis

The area studied is a part of the researcher's thesis, hence efforts have been made to acquire more interviews to get a better managerial perception. However, due to the hectic work schedule of managerial professionals the collection process was time consuming and responses were attained at certain time gaps between the months of October 2022 and January 2023.

The authors have labeled their five respondents as "R1" "R2" "R3" "R4" and "R5" for privacy reasons. This professionals belong to top-level and middle managers from organisations that are global leaders in the private sector, respectively. The paper's main focus was on the private sector industry, as they have been the pioneers in embracing these advancements.

A semi-structured interview was conducted after identifying and approaching the targeted audiences via linkedIn and other social media platforms. Around 15 managerial employees were approached and asked for participation, out of which only 5 corporate professionals, representing different strata responded, and helped us uncover the necessary insights. This respondents included, have a virtual working experience. The perspective of managers on the modern management culture and its effect on their productivity were explored through this interview and information regarding various tech innovations and their uses were further questioned. Below steps were followed to analyse the collected data:

A. Prepared the interview transcriptions to create homogeneity among the datasets
B. A coding table was prepared based on the first impression from the transcripts and codes were created from the most important interview texts or phrases.
C. Finally, interviews were categorised based on certain themes and those texts were added under the categories, which resulted in creation of various themes/ elements representing their concerned headings.

The following basic keywords were used in our initial search: "Technological innovations" OR "Tech Innovations" AND "AI tools" AND "Virtual workforce management" OR "Distance workforce management" OR "hybrid Managerial/ leadership positions." The topic chosen was based on the given selection criterion; title, abstract, and keywords. without any more limitations on choosing. Since the subject is addressed by a number of disciplines, the authors chose to search publications published in fields other than management. An initial sample of 4,375 Web of Science articles was produced using these parameters. Table 2 presents the number count of documents published within the ten years time frame (2013- 2022) in the area of Management, which resulted into 140 documents. Similarly, Figure 1 depicts how the discussion has grown in 2013, and how it significantly expanded since 2018.

Later the search was made based on certain inclusion and exclusion criteria provided in Figure 2 for Web of Science database, which resulted into 84 documents focusing on the Management subject area, with 35 open Access articles. Out of which, 11 such articles not in sync with the aim of the chapter were excluded. However, upon closer examination of these articles, the researchers realised that they needed more relevant works to effectively conduct the review. This prompted to broaden the search including additional databases (von Delft & Zhao, 2021). The final count of articles thus reached to 49, mostly during the time frame of 5-10 years (Walker et al., 2015). During which the two- fold rise in technological innovations and online networking/virtual team management was witnessed.

Table 2. Tabular representation of number of publications between 2013- 2022

Publication Years	Record Count	% of 140
2022	16	11.429
2021	15	10.714
2020	20	14.286
2019	20	14.286
2018	13	9.286
2017	9	6.429
2016	13	9.286
2015	14	10.000
2014	9	6.429
2013	11	7.857

Source: WOS database

Figure 1. Graphical representation of publication frequency between 2013-2022

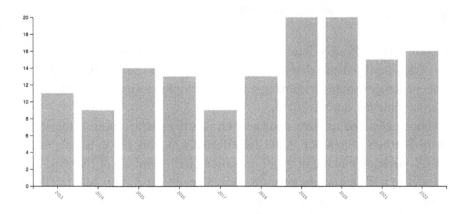

Figure 2. Inclusion and exclusion criteria

Type	Specification
Inclusion	I1 Paper's including Technological innovations & Virtual teams
	I2 Article providing empirical data
	I3 Open Access
	I4 Full Text Articles
	I5 Articles In Press
	I6 Articles within the time frame of 2013-2022
Exclusion	E1 Paper written in other languages apart from English
	E2 Non peer-reviewed Paper (e.g., dissertation thesis)
	E3 Paper not in relation with at least one of the research theme

Source- Morrison-Smith & Ruiz, 2020; de Souza et al., 2015

Innovation and Modern Management Practice: The Combined Perspectives

Mezias and Starbuck (2003) defined perception "as the entirety of information that managers cognitively interpret and utilize in their decision-making process" (Seclen-Luna et al., 2022).

THEME 1: MODERN ERA MANAGEMENT PRACTICES

One idea expressed is that effective implementation of TIAs (Technological Innovation activities) is linked to the use of decentralised knowledge management practices (Bello-Pintado & Bianchi, 2020). An organization that encourages strategic thinking among its employees can adapt more quickly to changes in the business environment (Aaltola, 2018).

Disruptive technologies and modern management practices have changed the style of managerial activities performed earlier, not restricting the daily decision making power to only managerial roles, in order to embark fast decision making in the organisation (Bello-Pintado & Bianchi, 2020).

Idealized influence, inspirational motivation, individual consideration, and intellectual stimulation are characteristics of transformational leadership. This type of leadership enables followers to maximise their performance and reach their full potential (Morrison-Smith & Ruiz, 2020. All the managers were seen preferring this style of leadership in exchange of the traditional one. Figure 3 highlights those major practices of managers by their response on modern era management practices.

Figure 3. Modern era management

THEME 2: VIRTUAL MANAGEMENT CHALLENGES

For technological advancements to be fully utilized and implemented within an organization, consistent changes and innovations must be made in the administrative and management systems, serving as an indispensable requirement (Černe et al., 2013). Many organisations, specially in developing countries have started facing all new set of challenges in managing their remotely scattered teams, due to absence of necessary infrastructure, strategies to develop employee belongingness.

Virtual leadership can improve team collaboration by administering guidance, training, resources, coaching, and facilitation of building bonds (Morrison-Smith & Ruiz, 2020). The complications of developing adequate practises to unveil and resolve cross-distance conflicts, and monitor members' performance is difficult enough to do when everyone is in the same place, but resolving conflicts in virtual teams takes a special skill (Dulebohn & Hoch, 2017; Ford et al., 2017). The leader is also the task manager, who sets up task objectives and role requirements that assign responsibility for completion of mission by individual members (Ford et al., 2017). Therefore, the management functions where managers faced challenges in the remote setup was in; Effective team building, Conflict resolution and Coordination of tasks as mentioned in Figure 4.

Unexpectedly, developed countries also lack an understanding of the required e-leadership skills for managing productive virtual teams under challenging job situations. Thus, how can e-leaders build effective virtual teams is a pertinent leadership obstacle (Contreras et al., 2020).

Figure 4. Challenges in virtual management

THEME 3: MANAGERIAL TRAININGS AND ADAPTED SKILLSETS

Notable publication are existence with pioneering ideas about the switching nature of work, and there is a rising demand for managerial training to prepare leaders for the digital age (Larson & DeChurch, 2020).

Remote/ Virtual work did not only arouse the need for training and ups killing of non- managerial employees, but also affected the same to those on leadership positions. In the realm of fulfilling their team requirements, managers went through trainings like Managerial Performance, Stakeholder centred Coaching and started using collaborative apps to stay connected online with teams mentioned in Figure 5.

On one hand where few managers could manage time for their upskilling with ease, those at top level hierarchies struggled in doing so due to their high level commitments and workload. Research has indicated that that having the necessary internal abilities in fostering innovation makes it easier to recognise and learn from external information, leading to better overall performance (Heredia Pérez et al., 2019).

The managers mentioned that the most vital skills they had for managing virtual teams were effective communication and listening to the queries of their team members without any bias or pre assumption of the matter shared, which made virtual management effective.

The leader should frequently communicate with all team members, both individually and collectively, about the task, what role each member is expected to play in completing the team's mission, how the team goals are the means to the organisation mission, and what progress is being made. This is because the leader's role as the communication hub is so crucial (Ford et al., 2017).

Figure 5. Trainings and certifications acquired

Preferred AI Tools and Technology

Telepresence systems have made employees resilient to virtual operations without heavily relying on physical presence to perform their collaborative activities and team meetings using technology such as video conferencing (e.g., Zoom and Skype) text messaging (e.g., Slack and Microsoft Teams) and collaboration tools (such as Slack, Google Hangouts, or Microsoft Yammer) (Raghuram et al., 2019; Morrison-Smith & Ruiz, 2020).

Leading technology companies recognise the value of using enterprise for virtual work and the below Table2, shows which are the tools and softwares used by our respondents in their role of supervising/ managing virtual teams. Today, tracking of total working hours, processing holiday requests are done automatically, Eventually even in self-service for employees. The clerk's manual form of recording time is no longer required (Schwarzmüller et al., 2018)

Although email and telephone have been cited as the most common modes of online communication in the literature on telecommuting (Raghuram et al., 2019), same was noticed for the sales manager responsibilities where instead of AI tools, telephonic communication was the major mode of collaboration, still there has not been much differentiation between the types of technology used for work.

Table 3. Major tools and technology used during managing virtual teams

Job Title	Applicant Tracking Software Preferred in Remote Hiring	Employee Surveillance Software Used	Telecommunication Channel
Renewals Manager	Oracle Taleo	Zoho People	Zoom Meeting
Operations Manager	Oracle Taleo	Infor Talent Management	E-mails
Sales Manager	Not used	Not used	E-mails
Associate Manager,	Avature	Company internal	Microsoft Teams
Chief Information Officer (CIO)	Not used	Not used	Microsoft Teams

Source: Authors Compilation

THEME 4: IMPLICATIONS OF AI TOOLS AND TECHNOLOGY ON VIRTUAL MANAGEMENT

The defining factor separating those who win and those who fail in the AI era may be how managers employ AI: "Brilliant machine advances will astound us, but they will only transform the lives of senior executives if managerial advances allow them to" (Larson & DeChurch, 2020).

Furthermore, the digital transformation is creating highly dynamic markets, putting pressure on employees for constant adaption of evolving circumstances and surging their desire for flexibility. circumstantially, making long- term learning more important: 'Lifelong learning' is a necessity (Schwarzmuller et al., 2018). In the advent of technological innovations and virtual team management, learning of certain tech tools became a necessity. Initially, managers found found it to be stressful, later on making it sorted. It was noticed that technology in the sales managerial role did not have much functions apart from a mobile networking, as the teams mostly operated in the field or client locations for pitching their products or services.

The algorithmic method of work quality control is distinguished from Taylorist types of informational management as it operates at the conclusion of the labour process rather than during it by judging on the basis of final completion rather than the whole working pattern (Wood et al., 2018).Furthermore, previous researches have recommended that as the magnitude of communication within virtual teams increases, it may hinder the performance by resulting into excessive irrelevant information distracting from needful informational exchange. This impact may worsen with increased level of virtuality, because an increase in communication frequency is likely to take the form of high volume e-mails or messages via other virtual modes. Categorising through these e-mails may result in information overload (Marlow et al., 2017)

Major hurdles which they had to frequently undergo during online mentoring were unschedule interactions, at times this exposed them to 24*7 availability, as in so much that it blurred the boundaries between work- non work hours. Virtual management has surely increased their dedicating hours for listening and conveying task demands to the teams, this at times also depended on the nature of work and employee presence at same time. The jobs more tech savvy in nature called for extra hours of instructions and mentoring compared to non- tech ones. Previous research also discovered team communication to be one of the most significant challenges associated with virtuality (Morrison-Smith & Ruiz, 2020).

According to research, successful electronic communication necessitates a degree of trust and confidence between all parties involved, as well as a readiness to exchange information (Ford et al., 2017; Ozuem et al., 2019). Trust in the business literature, is defined as a psychological state that implies to a person's expectation that there shall be no selfish act by their team member at the expense of the person's welfare, which increases readiness to accept vulnerability. Team trust has a remarkable impact on team performance and is the "glue" that holds group collaborations (Alsharo et al., 2017; Ford et al., 2017; Morrison-Smith & Ruiz, 2020). One out of five respondents found that there was a lack of mutual trust while virtually managing teams, on the contrary three of them faced no such trust issues. Similarly one of them suggested the use of JIRA software for issue tracking and easy collaborations of teams under project management roles. Fig 6 depicts the positive and negative implications of technology on managerial practices in current era of software centric human resource management.

Figure 6. Tech implications

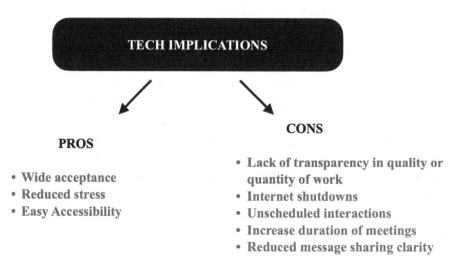

EMPLOYEE EXPECTATIONS AND MANAGERIAL PRODUCTIVITY

They shared that their teams had to be trained in; interpersonal communication skills and ICT skills specially, to perform their tasks with ease during virtual working.

A surprising fact which was witnessed during interview was that, even though their workload and job expectations did not increased compared to traditional style, still it led to job burnouts sometimes because there was an increase in management hours just like the non- managerial employees, who in past studies have reported high involvement time in a virtual setup.

An intriguing case observed here was that, the application of innovative management practices did not affect the work/life balance of nearly all respondents, unlike few, whose WLB did get affected sometimes. Yet, it never hindered their managerial productivity, rather assisted in fulfilling their team expectations even virtually. Few out of which were coded as; open communication and meaningful mentoring, quality and frequent feedback regarding performance and essentially to introduce modern IT technology and infrastructure to support new era work requirements. A good deal of the research has focused on technology as a barrier to overcome, because it creates ambiguity and uncertainty when compared to face-to-face communication. Telecommuters, according to researchers, struggle to create bonds with their co-workers or supervisors, share tacit knowledge, and collaborate because the ability to have meaningful exchanges through lean communication media is quite less (Raghuram et al., 2019)

Regardless of all types of challenges faced in online mentoring, the managers were able to meet there job expectations most of the time and lead the team effectively, also because the organisation provided with necessary managerial resources. Besides that, their answer about future work space preferences came in favour of hybrid or remote working.

FINDINGS AND SUGGESTIONS

Table 4 presents the leadership choices of respondents. Managers preferred to transformational leadership style instead of the transactional one as they were very much aware of the notion that current management era demands for change in the style of working and handling teams in order to retain talented employees by making them part of certain decision making process.

Table 4. Preferred leadership style by managers

Job Profile	Preferred Leadership Style
Renewals Manager	Transformational leadership style
Operations Manager	Transformational leadership style
Sales Manager	Transformational leadership style
Associate Manager,	Transformational leadership style
Chief Information Officer (CIO)	Transformational leadership style

Source: Author's compilation

Our findings indicate which innovative credentials are acquired by managers in developing their adaptive capabilities required to address and handle new work environments. Innovative managerial strategies could be crucial especially in multinational corporations (MNCs) to even tackle cultural conflicts between the home country and host country and to advance technological innovation (Černe et al., 2013).

Technology today is used for both construction and destruction of the goodwill of any firm. Having both the "smarter side" on one hand which helps in prompt decision making and problem solving of employees, whereas on the contrary a "darker side" which gives every possible opportunity and power to tarnish the image of the organisation via various online and digital media platforms, replacing the traditional workplace surveillance system (Holland & Bardoel, 2016). There is a common notion among employees nowadays, witnessed all over social media and other platforms, claiming the idea that executives at managerial positions need not necessarily face any sort of challenges or crisis in any form and are rather always stress free or inattentive to their demands. These mindset may vary from person to person also depending on the organisational culture as the managerial employees are said to serve as a chain of communication between the individual contributors and top level authorities. Which is regarded as a rewarding position in the corporates but, at times might be most challenging ones due to their role of supervising and leading diverse teams at the same time being answerable for all the actions of their teams. This again depends on the type of leader or managers and their leadership style.

The impact of technology can be examined based on its intended purpose, as well as the way it was created and put into use. Unlike traditional media such as newspapers, radio, and television, the internet does not simply provide an additional means of communication or interpretation of real-life events. Rather, it creates a new virtual world that runs parallel to our daily lives and face-to-face interactions. Computer networks do not just enable us to reflect on society; they actively shape social relationships and construct a new reality. Where, the managers need to have the ability to blend two aspects, exploration which pertains to technological advancements and exploitation which relates to non-technological innovations (Contreras et al., 2020; Chamakiotis et al., 2021; Heredia Pérez et al., 2019). Such digital transformations challenges has added to the rise in managerial expectations to some extent. The innovation process is typically complex because it involves a significant level of uncertainty. Therefore, successful innovation also requires the company to effectively coordinate its organisational knowledge and expertise (Chichkanov et al., 2019). It is also essential for both companies and policymakers to comprehend the origins of organisational change in order to be able to respond rapidly and effectively to catastrophes that spread quickly in a globalised and interconnected environment. Because, Previous research suggests that companies that innovate are more likely to survive, based on evidence before the 2007 financial crisis. Additionally, other studies suggest that innovators receive an added advantage for survival during difficult times when environmental pressures unexpectedly intensify and become extreme. This is referred to as an "adaptive premium" (Pantano, 2016; Cefis & Marsili, 2018)

Implications and Future Research

Diverse empirical studies conducted in different regions of the economy were found to be in favour of the current findings of algorithmic controls in management under the Indian context. The outcomes of this research also aligned with the views expressed by Aaltola (2018), who suggests that agile development practices can be advantageous in facilitating executive decision-making, promoting innovation, and fostering collaboration within organizations.

Overcoming barriers is essential for managers to successfully implement innovation. These barriers can stem from various sources, such as financial concerns (such as cost and funding risks), organizational issues (such as inflexibility and centralization), informational challenges (such as access to market and technology information), and other factors. Despite this, previous research has predominantly emphasized financial obstacles (Heredia Pérez et al., 2019).

The current research and observation helped us in revealing such facts by considering the managerial point of view and seeking their perception on this new era virtual teams led by them, where they need to be fully equipped with skills and training, tools and technology and necessary infrastructure in order to effectively lead their teams in the modern workspace.

This research is relevant for policymakers as it not just addresses the ongoing debate on the impact of innovation on employment, rather adds to the affects of recurring technological innovations introduced in the field of management and the need for continuous upskilling of managers. It provides insight on the intricate relationship between innovation and employment, which goes beyond the immediate effects of replacing or compensating workers. Our findings, in conjunction with prior studies, emphasize the favorable influence of innovation on the company's workforce development (Bello-Pintado & Bianchi, 2020).

There are some limitations to this study. The findings are based on the collective insights and experiences of participants from diverse organizations. Consequently, the research does not delve deeply into the intricacies of any particular organizational context (Aaltola, 2018). It is hard to determine which industries have not been influenced by digitalization; further research needs to be conducted in industries that are not as complex and do not contain as many components (Dattée et al., 2018). One of the major hurdles undergone during the time span of the study was the collection of responses from managerial professionals specially in the corporate sector, a vital reason being the policy structure and guidelines of such organisations regarding outside surveys, as many organisations have their personalised R&D departments for conducting any necessary surveys. Also the busy schedule of employees at managerial positions affected the time span of the study.

REFERENCES

Aaltola, P. (2018). Investing in strategic development. *Qualitative Research in Accounting & Management*, *15*(2), 206–230. doi:10.1108/QRAM-05-2017-0044

Alsharo, M., Gregg, D., & Ramirez, R. (2017). Virtual Team Effectiveness: The role of knowledge sharing and trust. *Information & Management*, *54*(4), 479–490. doi:10.1016/j.im.2016.10.005

Bello-Pintado, A., & Bianchi, C. (2020). Workforce education diversity, work organization and innovation propensity. *European Journal of Innovation Management*, *24*(3), 756–776. doi:10.1108/EJIM-10-2019-0300

Biedenbach, G., Biedenbach, T., Hultén, P., & Tarnovskaya, V. (2022). Organizational resilience and internal branding: Investigating the effects triggered by self-service technology. *Journal of Brand Management*, *29*(4), 420–433. doi:10.105741262-022-00275-9

Cefis, E., & Marsili, O. (2018). Good times, Bad Times: Innovation and survival over the business cycle. *Proceedings - Academy of Management*, *2018*(1), 17783. doi:10.5465/AMBPP.2018.17783abstract

Černe, M., Jaklič, M., & Škerlavaj, M. (2013). Decoupling management and technological innovations: Resolving the individualism–collectivism controversy. *Journal of International Management*, *19*(2), 103–117. doi:10.1016/j.intman.2013.03.004

Chamakiotis, P., Panteli, N., & Davison, R. M. (2021). Reimagining e-leadership for reconfigured virtual teams due to covid-19. *International Journal of Information Management*, *60*, 102381. doi:10.1016/j.ijinfomgt.2021.102381 PMID:34934257

Chichkanov, N., Miles, I., & Belousova, V. (2019). Drivers for innovation in KIBS: Evidence from Russia. *Service Industries Journal, 41*(7-8), 489–511. doi:10.1080/02642069.2019.1570151

Contreras, F., Baykal, E., & Abid, G. (2020). E-Leadership and Teleworking in Times of COVID-19 and Beyond: What We Know and Where Do We Go. *Frontiers in Psychology, 11*(590271), 590271. Advance online publication. doi:10.3389/fpsyg.2020.590271 PMID:33362656

Dan, S. M., Spaid, B. I., & Noble, C. H. (2018). Exploring the sources of Design Innovations: Insights from the computer, communications and Audio Equipment Industries. *Research Policy, 47*(8), 1495–1504. doi:10.1016/j.respol.2018.05.004

Dattée, B., Alexy, O., & Autio, E. (2018). Maneuvering in poor visibility: How firms play the ecosystem game when uncertainty is high. *Academy of Management Journal, 61*(2), 466–498. doi:10.5465/amj.2015.0869

Dulebohn, J. H., & Hoch, J. E. (2017). Virtual teams in organizations. *Human Resource Management Review, 27*(4), 569–574. doi:10.1016/j.hrmr.2016.12.004

Ford, R. C., Piccolo, R. F., & Ford, L. R. (2017). Strategies for building effective virtual teams: Trust is key. *Business Horizons, 60*(1), 25–34. doi:10.1016/j.bushor.2016.08.009

Han, C., & Gao, S. (2019). A chain multiple mediation model linking strategic, management, and technological innovations to firm competitiveness. *Revista Brasileira de Gestão de Negócios, 21*(4), 879–905. doi:10.7819/rbgn.v21i5.4030

Hasan, M. R., Shams, S. M. R., Rahman, M., & Haque, S. E. (2020). Analysing pro-poor innovation acceptance by income segments. *Management Decision, 58*(8), 1663–1674. doi:10.1108/MD-09-2019-1301

Heredia Pérez, J. A., Geldes, C., Kunc, M. H., & Flores, A. (2019). New approach to the innovation process in emerging economies: The manufacturing sector case in Chile and Peru. *Technovation, 79*, 35–55. doi:10.1016/j.technovation.2018.02.012

Hilmersson, M., Pourmand Hilmersson, F., Chetty, S., & Schweizer, R. (2022). Pace of innovation and speed of small and medium-sized enterprise international expansion. *International Small Business Journal, 41*(2), 181–203. doi:10.1177/02662426221085193

Hoch, J. E., & Kozlowski, S. W. (2014). Leading virtual teams: Hierarchical leadership, structural supports, and shared team leadership. *The Journal of Applied Psychology, 99*(3), 390–403. doi:10.1037/a0030264 PMID:23205494

Holland, P., & Bardoel, A. (2016). The impact of technology on work in the twenty-first century: Exploring the smart and dark side. *International Journal of Human Resource Management, 27*(21), 2579–2581. doi:10.1080/09585192.2016.1238126

Kaulio, M., Thorén, K., & Rohrbeck, R. (2017). Double ambidexterity: How a Telco incumbent used business-model and Technology Innovations to successfully respond to three major disruptions. *Creativity and Innovation Management, 26*(4), 339–352. doi:10.1111/caim.12246

Klessova, S., Engell, S., & Thomas, C. (2022). Assessment of the advancement of market-upstream innovations and of the performance of Research and Innovation Projects. *Technovation*, *116*, 102495. doi:10.1016/j.technovation.2022.102495

Kolade, O., Atiase, V., Murithi, W., & Mwila, N. (2021). The business models of Tech Hubs in Africa: Implications for viability and Sustainability. *Technology Analysis and Strategic Management*, *33*(10), 1213–1225. doi:10.1080/09537325.2021.1947492

Larson, L., & DeChurch, L. A. (2020). Leading teams in the digital age: Four perspectives on technology and what they mean for leading teams. *The Leadership Quarterly*, *31*(1), 101377. doi:10.1016/j.leaqua.2019.101377 PMID:32863679

Manning, R. A. (2020). *Emerging Technologies. New Challenges to Global Stability*. Atlantic Council. Available at: https://www.jstor.org/stable/resrep26000

Marlow, S. L., Lacerenza, C. N., & Salas, E. (2017). Communication in virtual teams: A conceptual framework and research agenda. *Human Resource Management Review*, *27*(4), 575–589. doi:10.1016/j.hrmr.2016.12.005

Morrison-Smith, S., & Ruiz, J. (2020). Challenges and barriers in virtual teams: A literature review. *SN Applied Sciences*, *2*(6), 1096. Advance online publication. doi:10.100742452-020-2801-5

Ozuem, W., Howell, K. E., & Lancaster, G. (2019). Consumption and communication perspectives of it in a developing economy. *Technology Analysis and Strategic Management*, *31*(8), 929–942. doi:10.1080/09537325.2019.1574971

Pantano, E. (2016). Benefits and risks associated with time choice of innovating in retail settings. *International Journal of Retail & Distribution Management*, *44*(1), 58–70. doi:10.1108/IJRDM-03-2015-0047

Raghuram, S., Hill, N. S., Gibbs, J. L., & Maruping, L. M. (2019). Virtual work: Bridging research clusters. *The Academy of Management Annals*, *13*(1), 308–341. doi:10.5465/annals.2017.0020

Schwarzmüller, T., Brosi, P., Duman, D., & Welpe, I. M. (2018). How does the digital transformation affect organizations? key themes of change in work design and leadership. *Management Review*, *29*(2), 114–138. doi:10.5771/0935-9915-2018-2-114

Seclen-Luna, J. P., Fernandez, P. M., Güenaga, J. B., & Ferrucci, L. (2022). Innovation in micro firms builders of machine tool? effects of T-KIBS on technological and non-technological innovations. *Revista Brasileira de Gestão de Negócios*, *24*(1), 144–158. doi:10.7819/rbgn.v24i1.4163

Tabrizi, B., Lam, E., Girard, K., & Irvin, V. (2019). Digital transformation is not about technology. *Harvard Business Review*, *13*(March), 1–6.

Torres, P., & Augusto, M. (2019). Understanding complementarities among different forms of innovation. *European Journal of Innovation Management*, *23*(5), 813–834. doi:10.1108/EJIM-01-2019-0012

Trabucchi, D., Pellizzoni, E., Buganza, T., & Verganti, R. (2017). Interplay between technology and meaning: How music majors reacted? *Creativity and Innovation Management*, *26*(4), 327–338. doi:10.1111/caim.12234

Vallo Hult, H., & Byström, K. (2021). Challenges to learning and leading the Digital workplace. *Studies in Continuing Education, 44*(3), 460–474. doi:10.1080/0158037X.2021.1879038

von Delft, S., & Zhao, Y. (2021). Business models in Process Industries: Emerging Trends and Future Research. *Technovation, 105*, 102195. doi:10.1016/j.technovation.2020.102195

Waldkirch, M., Bucher, E., Schou, P., & Grünwald, E. (2021). Controlled by the algorithm, coached by the crowd – how HRM activities take shape on digital work platforms in the gig economy. *International Journal of Human Resource Management, 32*(12), 2643–2682. doi:10.1080/09585192.2021.1914129

Walker, R. M., Chen, J., & Aravind, D. (2015). Management innovation and firm performance: An integration of research findings. *European Management Journal, 33*(5), 407–422. doi:10.1016/j.emj.2015.07.001

ADDITIONAL READING

Battisti, E., Alfiero, S., & Leonidou, E. (2022). Remote working and digital transformation during the COVID-19 pandemic: Economic–financial impacts and psychological drivers for employees. *Journal of Business Research, 150*, 38–50. doi:10.1016/j.jbusres.2022.06.010 PMID:35706830

de Souza, É. F., de Falbo, R., & Vijaykumar, N. L. (2015). Knowledge Management Initiatives in Software Testing: A mapping study. *Information and Software Technology, 57*, 378–391. doi:10.1016/j.infsof.2014.05.016

Drive employee engagement with Dynamic Learning. Infor. (n.d.). https://www.infor.com/resources/infor-talent

Ellington, L. M. (2023). Leading through Digital Andragogy. *Advances in Human and Social Aspects of Technology*, 290–305. doi:10.4018/978-1-6684-7832-5.ch015

Liden, R. (1998). Multidimensionality of leader-member exchange: An Empirical Assessment through scale development. *Journal of Management, 24*(1), 43–72. doi:10.1016/S0149-2063(99)80053-1

Matt, C., Hess, T., & Benlian, A. (2015). Digital Transformation Strategies. *Business & Information Systems Engineering, 57*(5), 339–343. doi:10.100712599-015-0401-5

Pokojski, Z., Kister, A., & Lipowski, M. (2022). Remote work efficiency from the employers' perspective—What's next? *Sustainability (Basel), 14*(7), 4220. doi:10.3390u14074220

Popovici, V., & Popovici, A.-L. (2020). Remote work revolution: Current opportunities and challenges for Organizations. EconPapers. https://stec.univ-ovidius.ro/html/anale/RO/2020/Section%203/35.pdf

Tahirkheli, S. K. (2022). E-leadership theory – a more than ever virtually connected world needs a virtually theorized leadership in a globally cross-cultural network space. Social Sciences &amp. *Humanities Open, 6*(1), 100299. doi:10.1016/j.ssaho.2022.100299

Taleo. Oracle. (n.d.). https://www.oracle.com/human-capital-management/taleo/

Trenerry, B., Chng, S., Wang, Y., Suhaila, Z. S., Lim, S. S., Lu, H. Y., & Oh, P. H. (2021). Preparing workplaces for digital transformation: An integrative review and framework of multi-level factors. *Frontiers in Psychology*, *12*, 620766. Advance online publication. doi:10.3389/fpsyg.2021.620766 PMID:33833714

Tyran, K. M., & Tyran, C. K. (2008). The role of Leadership in Virtual Teams. Encyclopedia of E-Collaboration, 540–546. doi:10.4018/978-1-59904-000-4.ch082

Vial, G. (2019). Understanding digital transformation: A review and a research agenda. *The Journal of Strategic Information Systems*, *28*(2), 118–144. doi:10.1016/j.jsis.2019.01.003

Wood, A. J., Graham, M., Lehdonvirta, V., & Hjorth, I. (2018). Good gig, Bad gig: Autonomy and algorithmic control in the global gig economy. *Work, Employment and Society*, *33*(1), 56–75. doi:10.1177/0950017018785616 PMID:30886460

KEY TERMS AND DEFINITIONS

Avature: Application tracking system helps the community of hiring managers with their every-day hiring needs, making strategic HR possible by assisting in hiring projects such as getting information about competitors and improving service.

Infor's Workforce Management: Software helps companies put the right people in the right jobs by using behavioural and performance data, empowering people with strategy execution tools, and driving employee engagement with dynamic learning.

Oracle Taleo: Taleo's products are largely focused on recruiting (talent acquisition), performance management, pay management, and learning & development, all of which work together to deliver a deeper degree of insight into applicants and employees. Taleo provides its human resource management system (HRMS / HRIS) solutions exclusively as a software-as-a-service (SaaS) model, with all software and data residing in Taleo-operated and protected data centres. Later, in 2012 these corporation was acquired by Oracle.

Zoho People: Is a cloud-based human resources software designed to nurture people, respond to changes rapidly, and make HR management nimble and successful. Simplify HR procedures, retain people, and create a high-performing staff by prioritising the employee experience.

Chapter 12
Quantifying Information Propogation Rate and Geographical Location Extraction During Disasters Using Online Social Networks

Anbalagan Bhuvaneswari
iD https://orcid.org/0000-0001-6651-2031
Vellore Institute of Technology, Chennai, India

Leela Rachel J. Julanta
Vellore Institute of Technology, Chennai, India

ABSTRACT

The pervasive popularity of social networking facilitates the propagation of trending information and the online exchange of diverse opinions among socially connected individuals. In order to identify events from the density ratio of real-time tweets, the authors suggest a new underlying quantification model, and morphological time-series analysis is performed using information entropy to ascertain the rate of news coverage of crisis situations. To further get insightful patterns in events, the event-link ratio is evaluated. In this study, the authors utilize data collected from Twitter to evaluate how far news of these events has spread. The study concludes by demonstrating the effectiveness of the proposed framework in a case study on the disasters events where it successfully captured critical information and provided insights into the dissemination of information during the disaster. The suggested approach detects events faster and with 94% accuracy than state-of-the-art methods. Comparing all location references, unambiguous location extraction has 96% accuracy.

DOI: 10.4018/978-1-6684-8953-6.ch012

1. INTRODUCTION

During disaster events, the ability to quickly and accurately disseminate information is crucial in ensuring public safety and minimizing the impact of the disaster (Ma et al. (2022)). The use of online social networks, notably Twitter, as major sources of information during natural disasters is a relatively recent development. During catastrophes, social media data is abundant, making it difficult to retrieve vital information (Gao et al., 2021). Social media data contains massive amounts of event and opinion data. This data assists public safety during catastrophes (A. Zhang et al. 2020). Lee et al. (2015) used social networks to examine the real-time consequences of catastrophic occurrences. The platform's user-friendly services enable content creation in response to the large volume of information. Non-geotagged data sometimes contains additional information from automated bots, location fabrication, and human mistakes, whereas geotagged data is limited. Many studies want to understand how geo-tagged tweets diffuse differently on Twitter. Events fluctuate temporally and spatially. Imran et al. (2015) found that Twitter and Facebook can detect earthquakes, floods, and landslides. These platforms enable rapid recuperation. Hughes et al. (2009) say geographically situated social streaming data can identify catastrophes and analyzed reaction following large emergency situations. Disasters use social media mining. Its public sentiment analysis helps disaster relief models. Filtering is needed due to the volume of social data streams.

Disasters may be identified by activity surges and meaning by content changes. Disaster studies have examined social media usage. During Hurricane Sandy, Kryvasheyeu et al. (2016) discovered that Twitter was excellent in spreading information and connecting people to supplies. However, the incident created a lot of data, making it hard to extract relevant information quickly. Other research have used machine learning and NLP to extract disaster-related social media data. Imran et al. (2015) suggested a method for automatically recognizing interesting tweets during disasters. They classified disaster-related tweets using machine learning and natural language processing. Kumar et al. (2011) developed a technique to automatically recognize tweets concerning disaster-related road closures. It's hard to track information on catastrophe victims' true social connections, implicit behavioural profiles, and social roles. Liu et al. 2013 and Kim et al. 2013 found that core heterogeneity Social Networks and user behavioural patterns affect information propagation. "Temporal series" data measures user behaviour. This research examines retweeting by "popular" Twitter users (Li, Y., & Li, J. (2021). Information sharing may reduce damage and save lives during disasters. Twitter is used to share information during such incidents (Mishra et al. 2022). Twitter allows users to post real-time crisis bulletins, calls for support, and offers of aid. Twitter helps people find supplies and information during disasters.

Sun et al. (2020) and Rahman et al. (2021) developed a Twitter crowd behavior-based geo-social event identification method. Geographic uniformities derived from crowd behaviour patterns discovered aberrant geo-social events despite sparse geo-tags. Wang and Zhang (2021) used weather and seasonal trends to assess user interest distribution based on trip history. A probabilistic-based topic model identifies user commonalities on the subject. The research used geo-tagged Flickr photos from eleven Chinese cities. Zhang et al. (2021) developed a framework to reduce noise, investigate the diffusion process's fundamental structure, and examine geo-tagged tweets' geographical patterns and land-use categories. The researchers used two phrases, 'flu' and'movie Ted', to collect Twitter data from four US areas. This was done to assess and categorise various subjects and locales. Li and Zhai (2020) found various pivot characteristics in geo-tagged twitter streams' query windows using a cross-modal expert measure. This method was used for real-time local event detection without precision. Ding and Shen (2021) examined Twitter retweeting behaviours among geographically susceptible people. The disaster-induced cluster was examined using Twitter-based linkages. The research found that the general public shared locally-focused tweets on disaster help. Khattak et al.'s (2020) hybrid method uses Twitter content and network information as model features. Gaussian mixture models were used to map the unprocessed model properties onto a predicted domain.

The present document is structured in the following manner. Section 2 provides a discussion of the related work pertaining to various event detection techniques. Section 3 contains a discussion on Information Propagation Rate Evaluating Metrics. Section 4 of the document presents a discussion of Proposed Entropy Based Quantification Methodology. Section 5 discusses of the experimental evaluation and its corresponding results and the rate of event detection. Section 6 presents a discussion on the conclusion and potential future work.

2. RELATED WORK

Various approaches have been developed to analyze social media data to create support models for predictive analysis. Twitter tweets are used to study catastrophe information flow structure. Castillo et al. (2013) presented a social media-based natural catastrophe identification and monitoring paradigm. Machine learning algorithms classified disaster-related tweets and extracted geographical information. The architecture successfully detected and monitored natural catastrophes. Liu et al. (2017) suggested a system for retrieving disaster-related location data from social media. Tweet location information was extracted using natural language processing and named entity recognition. The system successfully extracted location information from social media data during a crisis. Hu et al. (2019) suggested leveraging social media data to identify and monitor real-time events. The system tracked occurrences in real time using machine learning and spatial information extraction. The framework detected and tracked events in real-time. Nguyen et al. (2018) presented a framework for Twitter location extraction during disasters. The article examined all constraints-based automated user grouping and filtering options. Based on Twitter data before and after the Japan earthquake, their new technique could categorized people by traits with high accuracy compared to the prior methods. Technology has advanced these procedures. One method (Dashun Wang et al. 2011) uses supervised machine learning algorithms to categorize disaster-related tweets and extract key information like location and sentiment. Bag-of-words, word embedding and subject modelling may do this. Unsupervised machine learning algorithms can cluster tweets by content and discover patterns (Nguyen et al. 2017). This may reveal catastrophe information flow tendencies and social media influencers.

According to Hasan et al. (2019), there have been proposed approaches for data extraction to enhance the precision of location extraction from social media data in times of disaster. The utilisation of location extraction APIs enables the automatic identification of location information from social media data. The author mentions two approaches to address natural disasters: developing frameworks to identify critical information and real-time detection of natural disasters using social media data. The frameworks mentioned in the text, a blend of natural language processing techniques and machine learning algorithms to cluster tweets and extract pertinent data instantly. Lee et al. (2015) proposed a framework to process social media data in real-time during a disaster event. The study employed a framework that incorporated qualitative observations, as well as methods of quantification or optimal scaling to analyse events that occurred during disasters in Japan. The Hayashi methods (first and second) are utilised to analyse a scenario where an external criterion exists. These methods are employed to forecast the potential impacts of the factors that are being studied. The HQM and MDS results were utilised to analyse the data, specifically focusing on the first and second component.

Ma et al. (2022) presented a framework that aims to identify crucial information in the context of natural disasters through the analysis of social media data. The analysis of tweets that contain URLs is based on their collective "retweeting" behaviour. Of the various aspects under consideration, the dissemination mechanisms of particular information fragments, encompassing investigations into corpus sequencing and viral diffusion patterns, bear the closest relevance to our research. The study revealed the existence of several discrete classifications of retweeting behaviour on the Twitter platform, including automated or robotic activity, dissemination of noteworthy information, promotional and advertising efforts, campaign-related activity, and parasitic advertising. The findings indicate that the suggested framework demonstrated efficacy in discerning crucial information in the context of natural calamities. The process of event detection involves the utilisation of various modules such as event-prediction, event-related query identification, event assignment, and event archive in Table 1. These modules are based on clustering and classification algorithms. The two common tasks in event detection are retrospective event detection (RED) and new event detection (NED). The main focus of RED is to identify events that have not been previously detected from historical data, whereas NED is centred around identifying new events from live streams in (near) real-time.

Gao et al. (2021) presented a methodology for extracting geolocation data from social media during times of disaster. The methodology employed a hybrid model consisting of convolutional neural networks and graph convolutional networks to extract salient features from tweets and forecast the geographical origin of the calamity. Bhuvaneswari et al. (2019) utilised a two-feature approach to classify content based on the user response it elicits, resulting in the successful differentiation of various activities. Y.Lin et al. 2020, Suh et al. 2021, and Y.Wu et al. 2020 suggested classical methods to identify events for defined temporal and geographical closures, even though events of different sizes usually occur simultaneously. Starbird, K et al. (2010) investigated multi-scale event detection for data similarity graph computation. A graph-based clustering approach detects events of various sizes. Wang et al. (2021) suggested a framework for real-time catastrophe social media data analysis. The insight research uses 2011 Tohoku earthquake Twitter data. An early warning system using an automated method to discover relevant corpus for catastrophe monitoring was studied.

3. INFORMATION PROPAGATION RATE EVALUATING METRICS

This research proposes using the following data to understand user behaviour at key moments. Targeted users' tweets and retweets follow temporal trends. In particular, users associate their impulsive reaction during disasters with Social Media Timeline (SMT), news feeds where users post (PT), tweet (TW), reply (RE), retweet (RT), share (S), and mention (MT) images and videos to draw attention to disaster sources. Emergency situations need immediate judgements to preserve lives. Thus, social networks are employed as a rich supply of user-generated data and information. During a tragedy, social media generates a lot of data, making it hard to find relevant information quickly. Social media analytics reveal current events and hidden concerns. This makes it difficult to determine the most important information propagating. This research focuses on Twitter data streams with the following goal.

Table 1. Type, detection method, detection task, and application for state-of-the-art references

Author	Event Type		Event Detection Methodology			Event Detection Task		Pivot Application
	Specified	Unspecified	Supervised	Unsupervised	Hybrid	NED	RED	
Yin, J et al. (2012).		√		√			√	Disaster Events
Y. Wu, et al. (2020)		√	√		√	√		Query-based Event Retrieval
Y. Lin, et al. (2020)	√			√		√		Query-based Event Rescue
Sakaki *et al.* 2010)	√		√			√		Crisis-related Sub-event Detection
Suh, A., et al. (2021).		√		√		√		Disaster
Selvan, A.et al. (2021		√		√		√		Disaster
S. Ye et al.(2021)		√	√		√	√		Crisis-related Sub-event Detection
S. Saha et al.(2021)	√		√			√		Event detection in streaming data
S. Gao, J. Liu, and Y. Zhao *et al.* (2019)		√		√		√		Query-based Event Retrieval
Olteanu, *et al.* (2015)	√		√			√		Crime Events
Nguyen *et al.* (2017)	√		√				√	Event Photo Identification
Mishra *et al.* (2021)	√			√			√	Breaking News
M. Imran, *et al.* (2015)	√			√			√	Geo-Social Event Detection
Liu *et al.* (2012)		√		√		√		Disaster
Liu *et al.* (2013)	√			√		√		Breaking News
Kumar *et al.* (2011)		√	√				√	Trend Detection
Rumi Ghosh *et al.* (2011)	√			√		√		Emergent topics
Nguyen *et al.* (2015)	√						√	Event Detection Twitter
Castillo *et al.* (2013)	√		√				√	Disaster Crisis-related Streaming sub-event detection
Bhuvaneswari *et al.* (2019)		√	√			√		Disaster Events

The objective of this study is to develop an innovative quantification model for the identification of disaster-related events. Our framework utilizes machine learning and natural language processing techniques to analyze data collected from Twitter during a disaster event. The proposed model is designed to detect events that occur across multiple temporal and spatial scales by computing the Event Link Ratio (ELR). Additionally, the model is capable of effectively handling uncertain and noisy data through the use of a change-point-detection algorithm. Furthermore, this research proposes a system for evaluating information dissemination and extracting geographical locations during a catastrophe by leveraging online social networks.

3.1. Identifying Change Point Detection

Using RuLSIF - change point detection, the event burst distribution can be identified by continuously observing Twitter. In addition, the method of setting up an immediate alert for immediate attention is implemented whenever a real-time unexpected event is detected. It can be measured based on the density of comparable tweets that erupt between t and t seconds. In particular, the aggregate frequency of tweets containing the word wi during a given interval is directly proportional to the occurrence of the event Ej during the interval. The moment at which the density of tweets exceeds a certain threshold during a peak period and reaches saturation is known as the change-point. The formula for the relative tweet density-ratio estimator is f (Y), and the – relative Pearson(PE-divergence) can be approximated using Eq. (1).

$$\widehat{PE_\alpha} = -\frac{\alpha}{2n}\sum_{i=1}^{n}\widehat{f}\left(Y_i\right)^2 - \frac{1-\alpha}{2n}\sum_{j=1}^{n}\widehat{f}\left(Y'_j\right)^2 + \frac{1}{n}\sum_{i=1}^{n}\sum_{i=1}^{n}\widehat{f}\left(Y_i\right) - \frac{1}{2} \tag{1}$$

$0 \leq \infty < 1$ is a parameter used for our experiments, a change point detection algorithm based on Relative unconstrained Least-Squares Importance Fitting (RuLSIF) is used to directly estimate the relative tweet density-ratio.

3.2. Probability Distribution of Tweets

Based on the aforementioned parameters, it has been determined that the likelihood of a Twitter event burst in times of disaster conforms to a binomial distribution, as described by Equation 2. To calculate the probability of the overall count of tweets that include a specific term w_k at time $T(w_j)$, can be denoted as $P(n_{j,k})$, as mentioned below:

$$P\left(n_{j,k}\right) = \binom{N}{n_{j,k}} p_k^{n_{j,k}} \left(1 - p_k\right)^{N-n_{j,k}} \ni W_i \tag{2}$$

The analysis process the total number of tweets in a specific time period, where N is the total number of tweets. Despite the fact that Ni is the number of tweets that fluctuate in each time interval ti, it may be re-scaled in all time intervals by uniformly normalising the frequency of words responsible for the event burst. P_ki is the estimated probability of tweets containing the word wk in a randomly selected time period based on the aforementioned distribution. As a result, the average of the observed probability of the word wk in all time periods containing wk, defined as

$$p_k = \frac{1}{C}\sum_{i=0}^{C}P_0\left(n_{j,k}\right) \ni W_k \tag{3}$$

where C is the number of time-intervals containing w_k and $P_0(n_{j,k})$.

The burstiness of a word, w_k, is ascertained by contrasting its observed probability of occurrence within the time-interval $T(w_j)$ with its anticipated probability, pk, of appearing in a stochastic interval (t, Δt). When the computed value of $P_0(n_{j,k})$ exceeds the anticipated likelihood of the term wk (pk), it is evident that the term wk demonstrates an aberrant pattern during the designated period $T(w_j)$. Moreover, it is apparent that the term "w_k" functions as a bursty word (tweet) at a specific time point $T(w_j)$.

Figure 1. Probability of tweet follows binomial distribution

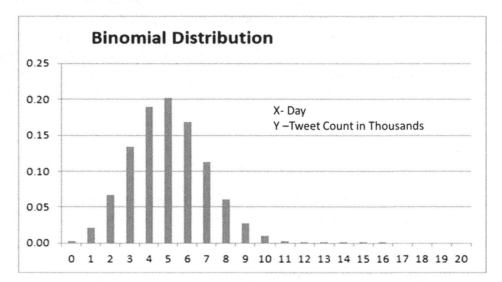

4. PROPOSED ENTROPY BASED QUANTIFICATION METHODOLOGY

4.1. Event Detection and Quantifying Models

The present study aims to discern disaster-related incidents through the analysis of a tweet corpus and subsequently assess the patterns of tweeting activity that emerge during such events. The working proposed model is depicted in Figure 2. The frequency of the corpus of tweets is analysed over a specific time interval. The system comes equipped with a disaster corpus word library that serves as a point of reference for detecting burst words. The automated system is designed to filter tweets and identify change points through the utilisation of RuLSIF's Change-Point Detection technique. The system employs a methodology that involves the computation of three key metrics, namely the Temporal Burst Ratio, Homogeneity Index, and Event Link Ratio, in order to accurately identify the occurrence of an event and its corresponding location within the tweets corpus. Upon surpassing the temporal tweet threshold, the event is detected and its corresponding geographic location is determined based on the density of tweets. The correlation between a user's tweet frequency, time interval, and location is utilised to differentiate between human users and bots. The tweets' similarity is computed, and Markov clustering is utilised to group diverse occurrences.

The proposed model for quantifying information propagation rate and geographical location extraction during disasters using online social networks consists of several key components. Firstly, the model utilizes a data collection mechanism that can capture relevant information from social media platforms in real-time during disasters. This mechanism uses machine learning algorithms to identify and extract critical data such as location information, hashtags, and keywords related to the disaster. Secondly, the model employs a network analysis tool that can track the flow of information through the social network. The model analyzes the dissemination patterns of information, including the speed of propagation and the most influential nodes in the network. Thirdly, the model incorporates a geolocation extraction module that can accurately identify the location of the social media users who post information related to the disaster. This module analyzes the content of the posts and identifies any location information that may be present, including GPS coordinates or location tags. Finally, the model includes a visualization component that can display the results of the analysis in real-time. This component uses interactive maps and graphs to provide disaster response teams with a clear and concise understanding of the flow of information and the areas most affected by the disaster.

Figure 2. Proposed event detection model

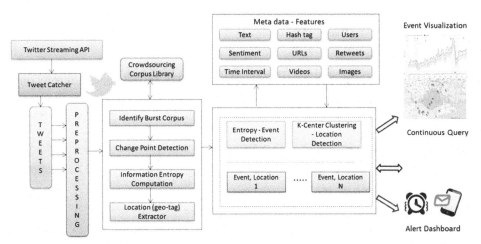

Calculating time-interval entropy turns Twitter user actions into an information theoretic technique. Our tests also assess user entropy for a URL and Mentions on tweets containing photos and videos. This may characterise comparable tweets and users based on their tweets. Twitter Retweet (RT) and Reply (RE) concentrate on URL-only tweets. Using modified Ghosh's technique, we calculate entropy by picking topic-word-specific characteristics. Entropy is used to assess the predicted quantity of information transmitted in the time-interval (t, t) owing to the spread of subject terms Wi. The "Novelty Evaluation Epoch" determines word-occurrence similarity between the selected interval and average of K previous intervals. For given N traces how do we dynamically characterize and categorize the tweets is more significant in real-time. The procedure includes computing *time-interval entropy, user entropy, hashtag entropy, similar user entropy and sentiment score* for a specific event with the topic word in trend. Let the set of all posts on a specific topic word be represented as P_{word}, the set of users who tweet that topic word can be represented as U_{word}. The set of posts of a user $u \in U$ with a topic word is represented as $P_{u,word} \in P_{U,word}$ and $n_{u,p}$ be the total number of posts by users. Let b is used to representing the type of post where b=1 indicate normal tweets, b=2 indicate retweet (RT) and b=3 indicate reply (RE). The regularity of the traces of tweets is measured using *time-interval entropy* on topic words. The frequency of word (*W*) in given time-interval $\Delta t_{u,p,t}$ is calculated as follows.

The dynamic characterszation and categorisation of tweets in real-time is of great importance when dealing with a set of N traces. The methodology entails the computation of various entropies, namely time-interval entropy, user entropy, hash-tag entropy, and similar user entropy, as well as the sentiment score, for a particular event that pertains to a trending topic word. The collection of all posts pertaining to a particular topic word can be denoted as P_{word}, while the assemblage of users who compose tweets on that same topic word can be denoted as U_{word}. Let $P_{(u,word)} \in P_{(U,word)}$ denote the set of posts authored by a user $u \in U$ on a given topic word. Additionally, let n(u,p) represent the aggregate count of posts contributed by users. The variable "b" is utilised to denote the category of a post, where "b=1" signifies a regular tweet, "b=2" signifies a retweet (RT), and "b=3" signifies a reply (RE). The temporal duration of posts made by a specific user, denoted as u, and pertaining to a particular topic word, The time-interval of particular user u's posts p with topic word W expressed as $\Delta t\_(u,p,t)$ where $\Delta t\_(u,p,0)=0$ because the first post is assumed to be at zeroth starting time.

$$N_{u,p,t} = \frac{\Delta t_{u,p,t}}{r} \ni W, r = 1, 2, \ldots, n_{u,p} \ni W_i \tag{4}$$

where r is the parameter to determine the unit of time-interval. The time-interval entropy on topic words can be derived using following equations.

$$H_{T_{u,p}} = -\sum_{k=0}^{m_{u,p}} p_{\Delta T}\left(\Delta N_{u,p,t}\right) \log_2\left(p_{\Delta T}\left(\Delta N_{u,p,t}\right)\right) \ni W \tag{5}$$

Information Entropy $H_{T_{u,p}}$ is calculated to quantify the degree of user dispersion, referred to as user entropy, with respect to topic-specific terms. The random variable D is utilised to denote a unique user within the trace Ti, where the set of all feasible values is $\{d_1, d_2, \ldots d_{nD}\}$. Consider the quantity of retweets generated by a given user Ui within the trace Ti. The symbol pF denotes the probability density function of D, where $P_F(d_i)$ signifies the likelihood of a retweet being produced by user fi. The frequency of user $a \in U$ posting b to user $c \in U$ can be mathematically represented by the given equation.

$$H_{User} = -\sum_{c=1}^{n} p_F\left(n_{abc}\right) \log_2\left(p_{\Delta FT}\left(n_{abc}\right)\right) \ni W \tag{6}$$

Using the following formula, we can compute the normalised hashtag entropy H(X) on subject terms based on the frequencies of occurrence of the given hashtag mention by different users throughout a continuous set of time-interval by j, as follows.

$$H(X) = -\frac{\sum_{j=0}^{X} P(X_j) \log_2\left(P(X_j)\right)}{\log_2\left(|X|\right)} \ni W \tag{7}$$

where $P(x_j) = \frac{Ch(j) + 0.01}{\sum_{j=0}^{X} Ch(j) + 0.01|X|} \tag{8}$

The given equation assures that the probability computations are normalised and that the entropy for hashtags is limited. For fuzzy crisp dataset values, the value 0.01 is used to normalise the entropy. In our research, high-entropy dataset findings on hashtags that arises with uniform frequency throughout time. Furthermore, Similar User - Entropy is derived by analysing the burst terms in tweets that are regularly retweeted more than 100 times by the same set of users. It is critical to compare the similarities of various tweets about the same incident. We assess the similarity between each pair of tweets T_a and T_b as in our baseline event detection technique.

$$\text{Sim}\left(T_a, T_b\right) = \begin{cases} \text{sim}_{\text{tf-idf}}\left(T_a, T_b\right), & if\ time\left(T_a, T_b\right) \le T_t\ and\ dist\left(T_a, T_b\right) \le T_d \\ 0, & otherwise \end{cases} \tag{9}$$

where $time(T_a, T_b)$ and $dist(T_a, T_b)$ are the time difference and locality difference between tweet pairs (T_a, T_b) respectively. The thresholds T_t and T_d represent the locality of the events and enforce the constraints of tweets restricted to a spatio-temporal boundary. The function $sim_{tf-idf}\left(T_a, T_b\right)$ represents the similarity in text of T_a and T_b where the cosine angle between the vector representations of any similar tweets using the term frequency inverse document frequency (tf–idf) weighting method.

4.2. Information Entropy Maximization Problem

The motivation towards event detection problem in online social media is twofold: first, maximizing entropy will minimize the overall prior knowledge established in distribution of tweets; second, the proposed computation system models will tend to move forward towards maximum entropy configuration over a period of time. The inference we chosen is detecting an event in social network depends on the frequency of tweet terms and increase the information gain about an event. Prior knowledge can promptly integrate into our inference technique as constraints for optimization of our problem. In this paper, two prior knowledge is considered as follows.

- Tweeters and Re tweeters:

In terms of tweets and retweets, social media users are thought to be a wealth of information. They broadcast the event at any time interval T, with an emotion score S.

- Entropy Distribution:

Ei is the trending event propagation entropy distribution from source i. Due to network size, density, and followers' desire to retweet disasters, users will instinctively have more influence.

With the prior knowledge, our technical contribution is to detect a disaster event in social network. We formulate this event detection problem as entropy maximization problem which is identified to be a solution of convex optimization problem. An appropriate model to perform optimization process is shown in Figure 3. The user tweets and re tweets are taken as data for detecting event. The process of identifying and expressing the inference model using mathematical terms can be done using objective function, entropy parameters and constraints. In our study, we constrained the optimization problem to have non-negative and non-zero values for entropy measures where μ_E is the tuning parameter for set of tweets that maximize the overall entropy.

Figure 3. Baseline inference model

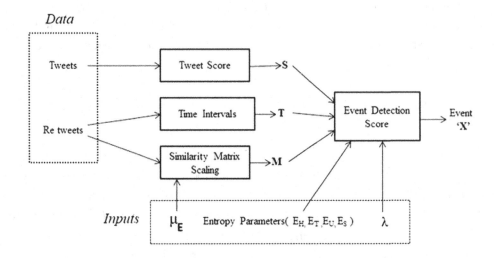

The threshold for entropy parameters is fixed for sentiment score(S), entropy(E) and time intervals(T). Using the similarity matrix (M) is constructed. Our final convex-constrained entropy optimization formulation is:

$$\text{Maximize}\left(\left\{H_{ht}\left(E\right)+H_{user}\left(E\right)+H_{time}\left(E\right)\right\}+\mu_E M+\lambda X\right) \qquad (10)$$

subject to H(E)≠0 where λ is the tuning parameter. . The objective of our problem is a quantitative measure of entropy {$H_{ht}(E)$, $H_{user}(E)$, $H_{time}(E)$} that we want to maximize with available information obtained from the disaster tweets. The entropy variables or parameters are the components of the proposed system to be calculated. The function that determine the allowable values for the parameters are the constraints or threshold values of the problem.

4.3. Tweet Analyzing Parameters

The Document Incidence (DI) is the number of Tweets that include the term. The Global Frequency Rate (GFR) is the total number of times the term occurs in the tweet dataset between the first and last intervals (FI and LI). BR stands for Burst Ratio. It is calculated by dividing the frequency of the word in the specified period by the average frequency of the word across all intervals. A high z-score indicates that the term is unusually more common and so likely to be a suitable descriptive word for innovative or otherwise uncommon things covered within the period. The percentage number that shows the degree to which tweets throughout surrounding periods mention a fresh subject is measured by novelty. The originality of 0% implies that all of the terms in the chosen interval were the same as those in other intervals. In the other direction, 100% indicates that every term in that interval differed from other intervals as indicated by the burst term model selection. The percentage figure that shows the degree to which tweets within that period employ the same terms is known as homogeneity.

$$H(t, \Delta t) = \begin{cases} 0\% - 30\%, & \text{where every tweet within that interval has distinct content} \\ 31\% - 70\%, & \text{where every tweet in that interval is similar in content} \\ 71\% - 100\%, & \text{indicate heavy retweeting activity of similar content} \end{cases} \quad (11)$$

Event Link Ratio is the number of tweets that have links to disasters as a percentage of the overall number of tweets for that time period. The ELR goes from 0 to 1. When the value of ELR is low, the number of links between events is low, and the opposite is true when the value is close to 1. The number of tweets that spread fake information about an event to a large number of people is called the false panic rate. In our tests, these tweets are labelled as coming from bots. Temporal Burst Ratio (TBT) is a not-so-easy way to find out how events are linked during a disaster. It is the measure of how new something is to how often it happens in time interval (t, t).

$$TBR(t, \Delta t) = \frac{\text{Homogeneity}}{\text{Burstiness}} = \frac{\text{Tweets in time discuss same topic words}}{\text{Topic word suddenly becomes popular}} \quad (12)$$

5. IMPLEMENTATION AND RESULTS

5.1. Quantifying Metrics Relevant to Disaster Event Dataset

A training dataset of around 3.2 million tweets gathered in the aftermath of significant disasters from 2014 to 2020 is used for deployment. The Assam Floods, the Utt.nd Landslide, the Chennai Floods, the Odisaa Cyclone, the Tripura Wildfires, and the Manglore Heavy Rainfall are monitored for the sake of implementation. The statistical trends that emerged in the aftermath of India's deadliest natural catastrophes. The tweets are brought together using the Twitter Streaming API in order to discover the corpus or phrase that suddenly arises in order to detect a tragic incident. In reality, the collection consists of tweets written in a variety of indigenous Indian languages. The phrase is important in event clusters, according to the information supplied by the word index. The study done by the suggested technique is both effective and efficient for exploring and examining the geographical distribution of Twitter users. The time stamp associated with each message reflects the time at which the messages were posted, providing an estimate of when an event occurred. The variables, which include location and hashtag, are obtained initially from tweets sent within a certain time period. The following Mapper and Reducer algorithms are utilised in event detection processing inside the MapReduce architecture.

The implementation of RuLSIF utilising relative Pearson divergence α within the range of 0.7 to 0.9 has been established. The detection of a change point serves as evidence of the presence of dynamics within social streams. The dataset was obtained using a non-uniform sample of 19,313 tweets. Stratified sampling was employed to obtain a well-proportioned data-set comprising 10127 tweets. The surge in the aggregate volume of tweets pertaining to the Assam flood and the ratio of tweets containing embedded URLs are being taken into account. In order to detect the occurrence of floods in Assam, a change point detection method is employed whereby Twitter is utilised as a monitoring tool for identifying disaster-related topic words. Upon analysing the data sets, the experimental findings indicate that the flood-related tweets originating from Assam exhibit a 3% level of novelty, an 85% level of homogeneity, and an event link ratio of 0.81.

During the incident, individuals used mostly nasty terms in their tweets. 3% uniqueness indicates a unique subject similarity throughout and across periods. Twitter users send flood keywords with 85% lexical similarity. Event Link Ratio of 0.78 (81%) suggests that more than 80% of tweets are about Assam flood. Temporal burst ratio and false panic rate assessed event burst distribution detection studies. Our burst detection technique has a 91% BDR and 4.1% FPR, according to experiments.

Table 2. Quantifying metrics relevant to disaster event dataset

Quantifying Metrics	Event Datasets					
	Assam Floods	Utt.nd Landslide	Chennai Floods	Odisaa Cyclone	Tripura Wildfires	Manglore Heavy Rainfall
Homogeneity	0.90	0.88	0.78	0.90	0.67	0.67
Event Link Ratio (ELR)	0.85	0.87	0.64	0.67	0.88	0.80
Temporal Burst Ratio (TBT)	0.66	0.71	0.88	0.88	0.67	0.67
Burst Ratio(BR)	0.86	0.70	0.67	0.60	0.86	0.80
Z-score	0.56	0.77	0.87	0.87	0.56	0.90
Local-to-Global Ratio	0.79	0.80	0.71	0.70	0.79	0.67

Table 3. Evaluation of entropy (Class A vs. Class B)

User Name	Time. Int. Ent.		RT-Time. Int. Ent.		User Ent.		RT User Ent.		HashTag Ent.		HashTag RT Ent.		Similar User Ent.	
CLASS	A	B	A	B	A	B	A	B	A	B	A	B	A	B
Sovinko	2.89	4.02	6.10	8.04	3.20	5.21	2.84	3.20	2.45	4.00	3.10	5.68	5.26	7.20
News7	2.45	4.25	1.04	3.56	2.74	3.84	3.74	5.36	0.89	1.25	0.98	2.01	0.00	1.36
CNN News	1.75	2.04	3.41	5.95	5.12	7.51	3.41	4.12	2.10	4.26	4.52	6.24	1.98	3.20
Bloombrg	0.04	0.12	0.00	0.20	0.00	0.00	0.00	0.00	0.00	0.00	0.00	0.00	0.00	0.00

Naïve Bayes classifies tweets into two classes: Class A (tweets without multimedia content) and Class B (multimedia tweets). Table 3 reveals that people retweet more multimedia tweets than text tweets. Bloombrg, a bot user page, has significantly low entropy compared to prominent Twitter userpage. Low-entropy hash tags are light and short-term. We categorised hashtags by entropy: less than 0.5 (Entropy A) and larger than 0.5 (Entropy B). As time passes, higher-entropy hash tags stay relevant while low-entropy tags go away. Class B (multimedia material with a tweet) has a greater entropy value than Class A (without multimedia content). Our studies show that the algorithm can forecast Twitter catastrophe news sources and quantify their importance for news spread. During disasters, entropy-based user screening determined if a user was human (unbiased) or robotic (biassed to automate).The suggested technique achieves 94% accuracy compared to 73% for the Ghosh quantification model. The quantification model detects flood disasters with 96% accuracy. A desktop computer with basic hardware (one i5 CPU, 8

GB RAM) collects twitter datasets of 3 GB with n=12000 tweets and computes word index statistics in non-linear time. Our implementation scales huge problems faster than theoretical O(n log n).

5.2. Event Detection Rate

Twitter data stream simulations of the Assam Flood (2016), Uttrakand Flood (2016), and Chennai Flood (2015) are used to estimate the processing delay time required to start monitoring and verifying incident detection. 750 tweets per minute are arriving. Sample intervals are 2, 4, and 6 minutes. Setting the location threshold to 300 and the hashtag threshold to 700 sends the data stream to Hadoop MapReduce. With an average node latency of 75 seconds, the MapReduce framework identified the event faster. MapReduce detects events faster than Hasan, M et al. 2019, which takes 200 seconds.

Table 4. Evaluation of event detection rate

Time Interval	Proposed MapReduce Framework		Hasan et al. (2019)
	Processing Start Time	Event Confirmation Time (Seconds)	Event Confirmation Time (Seconds)
2 minutes	121.24	192.4	324.7
4 minutes	240.8	283	456.1
6 minutes	361.4	401.4	566.1

Table 4 shows that the time taken to confirm an event between the start of event detection and the time at which the event detection is confirmed.

Figure 4. Performance evaluation: Event detection rate

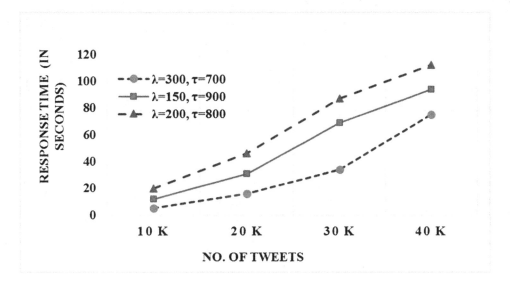

Nguyen et al. (2015) took 200 seconds to confirm an event, whereas the MapReduce framework recognised it in 75 seconds. Results reveal that the suggested MapReduce architecture delays event extraction from the initial time period to validate event detection. The suggested system averages 192 seconds to analyse the first tweet data stream. Comparing genuine timestamps, the system validates event detection after 75 seconds.

5.3. Geographical Location Extraction Method

For the purpose of determining whether or not location detection algorithms are effective, we employ the following metrics. Within the framework of the experiment, we made use of the Random Method (RDM), the Trivial Method (TVM), and the K-Center Clustering (KCC) method. We choose the point in the circle that has the most location references for each individual user and make that point the centre of the circle. The tolerance value is the radius of the circle, which is the same as N in the Accuracy_N formula but 30 miles when N=0 is used.

- **Average Error Distance (AED).** The typical distance separating a user's real location from their anticipated location based on other users' locations. ACC stands for "accuracy." The proportion of users within a city that have correctly predicted locations when compared to the total number of users. The value of tolerance has been set to zero.
- **Accuracy within N miles (ACC_N).** The proportion of times when projected locations are found to be within N miles of the actual place. For instance, the ACC_50 metric calculates the proportion of projected places that are less than 80 kilometres (50 miles) away from the current location of the user profile.

Table 5. Comparison of accuracy of various location ident cation models to identify location of a user

Method	Unambiguous Location References				All Location References			
	ACC	ACC_25	ACC_50	ACC_75	ACC	ACC_25	ACC_50	ACC_75
SAMPLE - 1500 Tweets								
RDM	0.453	0.513	0.524	0.532	0.551	0.561	0.570	0.581
TVM	0.515	0.539	0.561	0.582	0.592	0.621	0.629	0.678
KCC	**0.568**	**0.677**	**0.698**	**0.779**	**0.790**	**0.810**	**0.822**	**0.837**

Table 6. Effect of time on location detection

Time After Event Detection (in Secs)	15 Secs	30 Secs	45 Secs	60 Secs	75 Secs
Accuracy - RDM	0.447	0.565	0.616	0.756	**0.560**
Accuracy - TVM	0.567	0.675	0.766	0.856	**0.671**
Accuracy - KCC	0.554	0.745	0.781	0.831	**0.854**
% of tweets with location detail	33%	54%	66%	79%	**81%**

The metrics employed to determine the precision of a given measurement within distances of 25, 50, and 75 miles are denoted as ACC_25, ACC_50, and ACC_75, respectively. The tolerance value denoted by N has been computed and recorded in Table 5. The accuracy of unambiguous location references is reasonably obtained within a range of 50 to 75 miles. When considering various location references, the highest level of accuracy, reaching up to 83%, is achieved at a distance of 75 miles. Table 6 presents the impact of time on the accuracy of location detection and the proportion of location detail. The KCC algorithm exhibits the highest level of accuracy in detecting location, as per observations. Nonetheless, the precision of the RDM and TVM techniques exhibits a diminished level of accuracy when it comes to identifying the location of crisis events.

6. CONCLUSION AND FUTURE WORK

This paper focused on the detection of catastrophes in social media in real time and reported the levels of information disseminated during disasters via Twitter activities with time constraints. By calculating the entropy in time-interval distributions, similar user, hashtags, and sentiment score, we characterise the dynamics of tweeting activity associated with social media. The results classify visitors as either actual humans or machines. The proposed entropy-based quantification method identified prominent users and hash tags, allowing us to analyses actual human voices in the form of tweets during natural disasters. Indeed, it demonstrates the perception of social media becoming a news media platform. Our system detected three significant flood events between 2014 and 2020 with a detection rate of 94%, which is an acceptable level. The system can be expanded to detect impending natural disasters as early as feasible in order to alert users via prominent news broadcasting accounts. The proposed MapReduce framework detected the event in 75 seconds, which is more efficient than the current standard of 200 seconds. Based on experimental findings, the dynamical quantification method that considers multiple feature sets can classify users in a social network with a higher rate of accuracy than the conventional technique, while maintaining the ability to detect alerts for unanticipated disaster events. Observed, when comparing the unambiguous location references to all location references, a maximal accuracy of 83% is obtained at 75 miles. The KCC algorithm identifies the effect of time on location detection with the maximum degree of precision, 75%.

In future work, the proposed model is expected to automate the identification of various natural and man-made disasters, such as earthquakes, tsunamis, and terrorist attacks, in a distributed real-time environment.

REFERENCES

Bhuvaneswari, A., & Valliyammai, C. (2019). Information entropy based event detection during disaster in cyber-social networks. *Journal of Intelligent & Fuzzy Systems*, *36*(5), 3981–3992. doi:10.3233/JIFS-169959

Bhuvaneswari, Jones, Thomas, & Kesavan. (2020). Embedded Bi-directional GRU and LSTM Learning Models to Predict Disasters on Twitter Data. *Procedia Computer Science, 165C*, 101-106.

Castillo, C., Mendoza, M., & Poblete, B. (2013). Information credibility on Twitter. *Proceedings of the 20th International Conference on World Wide Web*, 675-684.

Choi, H. J., & Park, C. H. (2019). Emerging topic detection in twitter stream based on high utility pattern mining. *Expert Systems with Applications*, *115*, 27–36. doi:10.1016/j.eswa.2018.07.051

Dabiri, S., & Heaslip, K. (2019). Developing a Twitter-based traffic event detection model using deep learning architectures. *Expert Systems with Applications*, *118*, 425–439. doi:10.1016/j.eswa.2018.10.017

Di Marco, M., Chong, M. N., Piciucco, A., Cresci, S., & Petrocchi, M. (2021). Covid-19 on Twitter: Analyzing misinformation in tweets with topic modeling and supervised classification. *IEEE Access : Practical Innovations, Open Solutions*, *9*, 68504–68516.

Gao, S., Liu, J., & Zhao, Y. (2019). Quantifying Information Propagation in Disaster Response on Social Media. *IEEE Transactions on Computational Social Systems*, *6*(2), 337–349.

GhoshR.SurachawalaT.LermanK. Entropy-based Classification of 'Retweeting' Activity on Twitter. Social and Information Networks, Computers and Society,2011, arXiv:1106.0346v1.

Guo, L., Wang, H., Chen, H., & Zeng, D. (2013). Identifying and analyzing topical authorities in micro-blogs. *Proceedings of the 2013 IEEE/ACM International Conference on Advances in Social Networks Analysis and Mining*, 613-617.

Hasan, M., Orgun, M. A., & Schwitter, R. (2019). Real-time event detection from the Twitter data stream using the TwitterNews+ Framework. *Information Processing & Management*, *56*(3), 1146–1165. doi:10.1016/j.ipm.2018.03.001

Hughes & Palen. (2009). Twitter Adoption and Use in Mass Convergence and Emergency Events. *Int. J. of Emergency Management, 6*, 248–260.

Imran, M., Castillo, C., Diaz, F., & Vieweg, S. (2015). Processing social media messages in mass emergency: A survey. *ACM Computing Surveys*, *47*(4), 67–105. doi:10.1145/2771588

Imran, M., Elbassuoni, S. M., Castillo, C., Diaz, F., & Meier, P. (2015). Practical extraction of disaster-relevant information from social media. *Proceedings of the 24th International Conference on World Wide Web*, 1023-1028.

Kim, M., Newth, D., & Christen, P. (2013). Modeling Dynamics of Diffusion Across Heterogeneous Social Networks: News Diffusion in Social Media. *Entropy (Basel, Switzerland)*, *15*(12), 4215–4242. doi:10.3390/e15104215

Kryvasheyeu, Y., Chen, H., Obradovich, N., Moro, E., Van Hentenryck, P., Fowler, J. W., & Cebrian, M. (2016). Rapid assessment of disaster damage using social media activity. *Science Advances*, *2*(3), e1500779. doi:10.1126ciadv.1500779 PMID:27034978

Kumar, S., Barbier, G., & Abbasi, M. A. (2011). TweetTracker: An analysis tool for humanitarian and disaster relief. *Proceedings of the 3rd International Conference on Web Science*, 1-8.

Li, L., Li, J., Li, X., & Liu, J. (2019). Real-time Geographical Location Extraction during Disasters Using Social Media. *International Journal of Geographical Information Science*, *33*(8), 1543–1561.

Li, Y., & Li, J. (2021). A deep learning based framework for real-time disaster event detection from social media. *International Journal of Disaster Risk Reduction, 65*, 102402.

Lin, Y., Xu, C., Zhu, Y., & Chen, Z. (2020). Quantifying Information Propagation on Twitter during Hurricane Harvey. *Natural Hazards, 104*(3), 2073–2092.

Liu, S., Yamada, M., Collier, N., & Sugiyama, M. (2013). Change-point detection in time-series data by relative density-ratio estimation. *Neural Networks, 43*, 72–83. doi:10.1016/j.neunet.2013.01.012 PMID:23500502

Liu, S. B., Chen, H., & Zhu, X. (2012). Mining social media data for public health surveillance and monitoring. *Health Information Science and Systems, 2*(1), 1–11.

Luo, T., Zhou, C., & Zhao, Y. (2021). Uncovering flood-related topics in social media using topic modeling and clustering analysis. *International Journal of Disaster Risk Reduction, 64*, 102464.

Mishra, A., Padhi, S. S., Kumar, S., & Swain, S. (2022). An efficient deep learning-based approach for disaster event detection using Twitter data. *Information Processing & Management, 59*(1), 102737.

Nguyen, D. T., & Jung, J. E. (2017). Real-time event detection for online behavioral analysis of big social data. *Future Generation Computer Systems, 66*, 137–145. doi:10.1016/j.future.2016.04.012

Olteanu, A., Vieweg, S., & Castillo, C. (2015). What to expect when the unexpected happens: Social media communications across crises. *Proceedings of the 18th ACM Conference on Computer Supported Cooperative Work & Social Computing*, 994-1009. 10.1145/2675133.2675242

Saha, S., Mondal, S., & Saha, S. (2021). Quantifying Information Propagation Rate in Disaster-affected Areas through Social Media Analysis. *International Journal of Disaster Risk Reduction, 55*, 102027.

Sakaki, T., Okazaki, M., & Matsuo, Y. (2010). Earthquake shakes Twitter users: real-time event detection by social sensors. *Proceedings of the 19th International Conference on World Wide Web*, 851-860. 10.1145/1772690.1772777

Selvan, A., Ramesh, V., & Natarajan, S. (2021). A novel hybrid approach for effective disaster response using social media and machine learning. *Sustainable Cities and Society, 72*, 103110.

Starbird, K., Palen, L., Hughes, A. L., & Vieweg, S. (2010). Chatter on the Red: What hazards threat reveals about the social life of microblogged information. *Proceedings of the ACM 2010 Conference on Computer Supported Cooperative Work*, 241-250. 10.1145/1718918.1718965

Suh, A., Kim, S., Kim, Y., & Kim, S. (2021). Monitoring and prediction of wildfire using social media and deep learning models. *Information Processing & Management, 58*(5), 102566.

Wu, Y., Song, Y., & Kafai, M. (2020). Identifying Geographical Locations and Quantifying Information Propagation during Disaster Events on Social Media. *Journal of Contingencies and Crisis Management, 28*(1), 58–69.

Ye, S., Jiang, H., & Guo, H. (2021). Quantifying Information Propagation and Opinion Evolution in Social Media during Natural Disasters. *Journal of Disaster Research*, *16*(4), 602–614.

Yin, J., Lampert, A., Cameron, M., Robinson, B., & Power, R. (2012). Using social media to enhance emergency situation awareness. *IEEE Intelligent Systems*, *27*(6), 52–59. doi:10.1109/MIS.2012.6

Zhang, A., Li, Y., & Li, L. (2020). A Novel Method for Extracting Geographical Locations from Social Media during Disasters. *Journal of Cleaner Production*, *247*, 11926–11938.

Chapter 13
Exploring Online Social Networking Patterns and the Growth of Social Capital Among Rural Maritime Community Members

Marhaini Mohd Noor
Universiti Malaysia Terengganu, Malaysia

Azizan Zainuddin
Universiti Technology MARA, Malaysia

Nor Aziah Alias
🆔 https://orcid.org/0000-0002-6405-1400
Universiti Technology MARA, Malaysia

Nor Hafizah Mohamed Harith
🆔 https://orcid.org/0000-0002-7503-8770
Universiti Technology MARA, Malaysia

ABSTRACT

This research investigates the creation of social capital among members of the online community. In this case, social networking refers to interpersonal connections among members of a rural maritime community. The major goal of this study is to determine how much the maritime community uses social online networking and how social capital grows within the community via the internet. The study applied a triangulation method to analyze data from participants with several points of view and to engage people appropriately for a better understanding of the phenomenon. Main findings extracted from the interviews have been categorized into three themes: (1) patterns of online social networking and social media use, (2) social networking and trust, and (3) social capital development. Hence, it is apparent that online networking can be used to reduce the social capital divide between urban and rural communities in Malaysia.

DOI: 10.4018/978-1-6684-8953-6.ch013

INTRODUCTION

The proliferation of social networks as a result of the rapid development of technology is inevitable; social networking is widely used at every level by various groups. There is no doubt that social networking is a global phenomenon that moves dynamically in line with its progress and the society's needs around it. It affects every aspect of the users' lives in terms of education, communication, social relationship, and personal productivity (Matthew, Adedamola & Sarhan, 2019). Social networking application is used as one of the channels to reach various sources of information through digital networks around the world. It is also a platform used to build an online community and the individuals who use it can share information, interests, and activities across political, economic, and geographical borders. This study is particularly significant, given that more rural maritime community users are increasingly communicating actively on the Internet wherever they may be.

In the Malaysian context, the number of internet users in 2018 was reported to be at almost 79% of the Malaysian population (Ili, 2018)., 75% of the population were using social media services and spent an average of three hours a day on social media sites then. The 2018 Digital Report showed that Malaysia ranked 9th among the most active countries in the world on social media sites. Two years on, the press reports were boasting, a shocking increase of 28 million users or 86% of the population using social media sites in 2020 as a result of the Covid-19 outbreak which limited the community movement to remain at home during the Movement Control Order (MCO) period (BH Online, 2021). Most urban and rural communities use the internet to obtain information about a product or service, download digital media, software, applications or send and receive emails as well as make phone calls. The applications in this platform have somehow become more apt, dynamic and unique to user needs and thus, can attract social network users to use it rigorously.

Like other technologies, social networking applications also have different effects on their users. The challenges, as well as the positive and negative effects of the use of these technologies, have had various consequences. Nevertheless, the question which arises is *to what extent the community utilizes the existing social networks and how do they view the use of these social networks towards social capital development.*

Figure 1. Number of internet users in Malaysia from 2010 to 2020 and forecast up to 2025 (in millions)
Source: Statista Digital Market Outlook @ Statista 2022

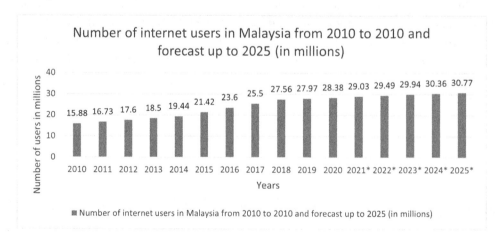

Therefore, the main purpose of this chapter is to report the experiences of social network users, consisting of rural communities who are living near the maritime areas in Malaysia. Specifically, the study seeks to illustrate the activities performed by the users while using existing social networks and how they view trust and security aspects of their online activities. In essence, it answers the following research question:

To what extent do maritime community members in Malaysia utilize social online networking and how does social capital develop within the community through the online platform?

The chapter is restricted to reporting on the viewpoints of selected community members. In this study, social capital is operationally defined as assets and resources provided to the community to foster social networking. Despite the limited scope of the research, which precluded generalisation, the thorough investigation allowed others to benefit from the findings and apply them to a comparable setting.

Review of Literature

This section defines the terms social network concept and theory, social capital concept, social network behaviour, and community development in the context of this study. A phenomenon of real-world circumstances in rural locations is reviewed in earlier works. In contrast to their human capital, rural communities often have strong social bonds and large levels of social capital (Beggs, et al, 1996; David & Stephan, 2013). To enhance their quality of life, these people require social networks and social capital. Malaysian rural areas, however, have received little research. Aside from a few studies like those by Kamal Chandra Paul et al. (2014), Abdul Hakim et al. (2010), and Marhaini (2018), more research is needed to understand how social networks and social capital function in rural areas that are less reliant on ICT and in an era of pervasive internet use.

In order to analyse the various viewpoints and experiences of participants, who spent the majority of their lives as members of rural coastal villages and were "forced to go online during the epidemic," this study investigates the concepts and delves into the pertinent theory. This section also included links to other concepts and theories that could improve the study, such as the social network concept, the theory of weak relationships, the diffusion of innovation, and social network behaviour, all of which are related to the growth of social capital.

Social Network Concept

An information, resource, and capability source are a network. The expertise, reputation, and network that the rural seafaring communities have created. This is the advantage of social connections. Bad information, resources, and mechanisms can have a bad reputation. Social networks can be helpful in a variety of ways, including to promote discovery, exchange information, connect with others who share your interests, and share new information and concepts. Social networks are crucial because they enable people to establish connections with people they might not have otherwise been able to meet.

A social network is a way for people to connect and communicate with one another over the Internet and in virtual communities by creating, sharing, and occasionally exchanging ideas, photographs, videos, and other content. Thoughts can be formed and exchanged quickly on social media platforms like Facebook, Twitter, and blogs. The community is impacted by social networking in a positive and connected way. This had consequences for families and friends, including the virtual world becoming a virtual society (Agarwal, 2019). With a surge from 85.6% in 2018 to 93.3% in 2020, social networking is now the second most popular online activity in Malaysia among Internet users. Using the internet to communicate for social purposes is the most popular online activity, accounting for 98% of all usage (MCMC, 2020).

Clubhouse is the name of a brand-new social network that was unveiled in April 2020. As an alternative to another social network, this software offers live streaming audio conversation that is only ever present in real time (Perez, 2021). In chat rooms, users can start conversations and listen to others. The COVID-19 pandemic cases and problems that people around the world are dealing with can also be solved by this clubhouse. As a result, while contemporary technology does help individuals communicate more, it also makes them feel more isolated and alone (Gkritsi, 2021; Faisal et al., 2021; Jiang et al., 2021).

Social networks can take on a variety of needs and difficulties by engaging in app development, which is quite intriguing. It has been reported that this has caused data leakage from Clubhouse audio discussions, thus the problem has to be addressed (Russon, 2021). With the help of supporting theories and a social networking component, the notion is used in this study to improve digital abilities. This discusses how rural communities are currently dealing with the COVID-19 pandemic and the need for more businesses to boost networking while also generating revenue.

Social Network Theory

In order to convey information, channel personal or media influence, and facilitate attitudinal or behavioural change, social interactions are key in social network theory. The social media era and social networking sites are the main topics of this philosophy. The quick development of media technology alters how people conduct themselves and affects the social order. When a result, as this model is developed, many ties, various actors, and multiple levels of networks are created. This is relevant to new media technology since it allows users to obtain content from a variety of sources and create a wide range of media (Wenlin et.al, 2017). The relationship between the notion of weak links and social networks illustrates how technology adoption alters peoples' lifestyles.

Theory of weak ties. In rural marine communities, the degree of weak relationships influences how ideas and information are spread across social networks. The degree of intimacy shared in a relationship as well as the frequency with which people communicate as well as the amount of time and effort people put into maintaining their social networks are all used to gauge a relationship's strength. Weak relationships have a higher propensity than strong ties to deliver novel insights and original data. In terms of the relationships that unite a community or a group, this idea is comparable to bridging networks or capital. As an illustration, the community might be one that uses social media extensively and is located in the countryside, however they still received the same information. As a result, the quantity of connections is irrelevant to the strength of weak bonds. Hence, social media has increased the number of weak online links (Granovetter, 1973). Thus, in this study, social connections and social media among rural communities help to strengthen weak linkages in the online social network.

Diffusion of innovation. Diffusion of innovation is "the process by which invention is disseminated over time among the members of a social system through specific routes," according to Rogers (2010). According to the social network theory, creativity comes from outside sources and spreads through social networks into communities. The most powerful medium is social networking sites and media, which shape how the public perceives innovation and adoption patterns (Wenlin et.al, 2017). The strength of rural community members' connections in social networks was examined in this study using data from both the social network theory and the diffusion of innovation theory.

Social Capital

Social trust, norms, and networks are together referred to as social capital and are resources that individuals can use to address common issues. In particular, between sociology and economics, social capital provides a highly significant conceptual innovation for cross- and inter-disciplinary theoretical integration. A solution to a variety of social issues, including rural poverty and crime, economic underdevelopment, and ineffective government, has been embraced: the construction of social capital (Nieman, 2006; Putnam, 2000; 2017). The ideas vary but are generally agreed to be social interactions and resources produced by social networks (formal and informal relationships).

Trust and trustworthiness. Social capital has relationship qualities that include trust and dependability. For people to feel confident and have solid connections with one another, trust is necessary. The local community develops close links with its associations and learns to trust those they do not know. Trust is defined as a relationship between people, social networks, and the reciprocity and dependability rules that result from that. Without trust and reliability, social networking is practically impossible; yet, it is feasible to preserve calm and stable social ties for group behaviour and action. Building trust can either take place within a community or outside of it; these two types of trust are referred to as "thick" and "thin," respectively (Grafton, 2005; Tristan, 2020). Social capital is produced by interpersonal relationships, social networks, and membership in non-profit organisations (Coleman 1988; Putnam 1993). Individual values are positively correlated with individual social trust, per a study by Seung & Sangmook (2021). A higher level of social trust is produced by older, better educated, and more financially successful persons.

Long-lived asset. In the long run, social capital and social trust are a long-lasting advantage to the community since they are viewed as productive resources. It focuses on interpersonal relationships and is intangible, making it community property as ownership cannot be transferred. The tools will expand social networking to different communities and won't lose value over time, allowing users access to a wider network (Lin, 2001; Humnath & Kumi, 2009).

The Behaviour of Social Network

The absence of social/family bonds and low engagement in social activities are two things that constitute social detachment. It is separate from subjective loneliness and has unfavourable health consequences, such as early mortality.

Too much time spent staring at a screen, for example, causes people to lose sight of the distinction between being alone and being lonely when it comes to disconnection in modern society. Technology typically has a detrimental impact on a person's ability to engage with others; it makes people more socially awkward and lonely (Kushlev, Proulx & Dunn, 2017). The desire to expand social networks and be a part of communities is urgent, particularly for rural residents who relied on such connections before to the advent of pervasive technology and the epidemic. But research has shown that social networks can also strengthen community, particularly among the elderly and those who live in rural areas. It helps new generations have a tremendous respect for the value of elder generations while also giving older folks a feeling of purpose.

Less depression, improved physical health, and increased levels of life satisfaction will result from this. They typically have more optimism for the future and are happier with their current situation (Paul, 2011; Matthew et. al, 2019). The well-being of the elderly is recognised to be influenced by social networks, although Zheng and Chen (2020) stress that there is uncertainty when comparing urban and rural areas and older people. Their findings further demonstrate the need for this study to be carried out in a different environment, which is why Malaysia's coastal and marine rural populations were chosen.

Social Network and Community Development

Building relationships, enhancing communications, documenting development efforts, sharing information in real-time, and informing and reaching a larger audience than was previously possible are all made possible by the use of social media and networking. This is significant as a tool for community development (Peter, 2016).

This is a sign that social networking sites and social capital are growing positively. Applications for social networking have been used in these communities for socioeconomic activities like politics, business, healthcare, and social contact. The way that people communicate, work, learn, and live their lives has altered as a result of social networking (Matthew et.al, 2019). But rural areas still have a low level of digitalization compared to urban areas, which is still insufficient (Podgorskaya & Shitov, 2021).

The justification and theoretical foundation for this investigation are explained in the preceding section. Because of their low online social network usage but high levels of social capital, Malaysia's marine communities in three of its states were chosen. In the section that follows, a brief summary of these communities will be given.

METHODOLOGY

Research Design

The research is mostly based on an interpretivist or social constructionist philosophical stance. The interpretive epistemological approach, in accordance with Merriam & Tisdell (2016), presupposes that reality is socially produced. Instead of using the etic technique, this study will focus on the emic strategy (Creswell, 2007). The research was particularly interested in learning new information or discovering new themes that were inspired by key informants' perceptions of social trust and networking in rural communities along East Coast Malaysia. To concentrate on the targeted informants and gather more detailed information, a qualitative technique was adopted. During the pandemic, data was gathered.

Sampling Technique

This study adopted a purposeful sampling technique to select its key informants. Purposive sampling method is a method in which the required essential criteria were preselected and was utilized to choose the appropriate population or sites to be studied (Patton, 2002) as cited in Merriam, 2009). In this study, the type of purposeful sampling adopted is maximum variation sampling that would involve identifying and seeking out those who represent the widest possible range of the characteristics for the study (Merriam, 2009).

On Peninsular Malaysia's East Coast, the study's focus was on members of a rural maritime community. Residents of the community must develop their digital skills and overall wellbeing because they are being left behind in the growth process. In locations where the main economic resources are concentrated, the government is devoted to the development of rural maritime communities. The fact that they come from diverse educational backgrounds, lifestyles, social classes, and cultural origins, as well as geographic areas, is one of the hallmarks of rural marine communities. In terms of social & psychological qualities, rural populations are more homogenous. The variety of socioeconomic situations present in each village or district must be acknowledged if rural regions are to be revitalised.

Sample Size

The decision of how many informants to use was made based on the saturation of the data. The study's informant's demographic profile is displayed in Table 3.1. Merriam thought it was a good idea to use 12 informants (2009). In this study, there were seven communities and five managers. According to Meriam, "what is needed is an adequate number of informants, places, or activities to answer the questions provided at the outset of the study. In order to study subjects in-depth within the constraints of time and using methods that directly relate to the research issues, qualitative researchers always deal with small samples of individuals nested in their setting (Miles and Huberman, 1994). Small size, according to Bloomberg and Volpe (2008), is acceptable because it denotes deeper information. During the fifth interview, the saturation was attained.

Interview Protocol

Semi-structured interviews were used to get the data. By specialists in the fields of sociology and policy studies, a set of interview questions was created and evaluated. The interviews were place in the homes or offices of the different informants and lasted one to two hours. The interview questions focused on the informants' opinions on social trust and networking when utilising social media like WhatsApp, Facebook, and Twitter for communication, online banking, and conducting business. The utilisation of social networks and the growth of social capital were influenced by this.

There were two phases to the interviews. From June 3 through June 12, 2021, the managers were involved in semi-structured interviews as part of phase one. Google Meet was used to conduct these online interviews. The researcher first intended to visit the managers and perform in-person interviews, but owing to the Covid-19 outbreak, the researcher was forced to alter the plan and ultimately conduct the interviews electronically. It can be fairly challenging to approach managers at first. However, the researcher's network has helped to support and made it possible for the interviews to occur. During the interviews, the key informants gave their complete cooperation and dedication. Here is an example of a manager interview question:

"What do you understand about social network?"

"How do communities increase their networking?"

"How does ICT network build trust among the rural maritime community?"

Focus group discussions were used in phase two among the communities. The researcher was forced to split the conversation into two groups. Beginning on June 28 and concluding on July 4, 2021, is the focus group discussion (FGD). The FGD was carried out via Google Meet online. By using the managers and snowball techniques, the researcher reached the communities. Thus, the search for the target informants is made simpler by the physical and virtual networking that is already in place. Here is an example of a community interview question:

"How often do you use social media?"

"Why do you trust people online?"

"How frequent do you communicate with people online?"

Data Analysis

The interview transcripts in this study were analysed using a thematic approach. Thematic analysis is a method for encoding qualitative data, according to Boyatzis (1998). Thematic analysis, on the other hand, was described by King & Horrocks (2010) as "recurring and distinctive elements of participants' stories, identifying particular perceptions and experiences, that the researcher considers pertinent to the research topics. The study's research questions served as the primary guidance for the analytic procedure, which used a technique that included three key stages: a) descriptive coding; b) interpretative coding; and c) overarching themes (King & Horrocks, 2010).

Table 1. Demographic profile

Participant Code	Marital Status	Employment Status	State
(P5, 66 years old, NGO)	Divorcee	NGO	Terengganu
(L2, 26 years old, businessman)	Bachelor	Self-Employed	Kelantan
(P7, 24 years old, businesswoman)	Bachelor	Self-Employed	Kelantan
(P6, 32 years old, businesswoman)	Married	Self-Employed	Kelantan
(P8, 30 years old, student)	Bachelor	Student	Kelantan
(P9, 43 years old, businesswoman)	Married	Self-Employed	Terengganu
(P10, 44 years old, businesswoman) (L1, Tok Janggut, Kelantan, Manager)	Married Married	Self-Employed Public sector	Terengganu Kelantan
(P1, Balok, Pahang, Assistant Manager)	Married	Public sector	Pahang
(P2, Telaga Daing, Terengganu, Assistant Manager)	Married	Public sector	Terengganu
(P3, Sg Petai, Kelantan, Assistant Manager)	Married	Public sector	Kelantan
(P4, Sg Petai, Kelantan, Manager)	Married	Public sector	Kelantan

The demographic breakdown of the key informants is shown in Table 1. Without hesitation, each informant gave their agreement and took part in the study. The in-depth interviews performed gave an understanding of the activities of the informants, who were from the maritime populations living along the coasts of three states in Malaysia. Ten of the twelve informants whom were female. They shared the same race and religion as the informants. Each informant's profile is provided in the table. According to the description, the bulk of the informants were entrepreneurs who shared the resources necessary to establish and strengthen their social networks. This also holds true for the "Clubhouse" idea, which was used by maritime communities to boost networking and generate income.

Validity and Reliability

Several methods of ensuring validity and reliability of data analysis were adopted in the study. First, the data triangulation method is used to increase the credibility of the findings. Triangulation using multiple sources of data means comparing and cross-checking data collected (Merriam & Tisdell, 2016). Thus, in the study, the interview data was collected from people with different perspectives. The data triangulation occurs when data were collected from both the rural community members and the managers. Further triangulation was ensured by having multiple investigators collecting and analysing data of qualitative interview.

Second, adequate engagement in data collection is another strategy adopted in the study. According to Merriam & Tisdell (2016), the adequate engagement with informants is to get as close as possible to informants' understanding of a phenomenon and to decide how many people need to be interviewed. They explain the best rule of thumb is that the data and emerging findings must feel saturated; that is, your long engagement with the interviewers. Therefore, to ensure this, in the study the interviews were conducted for more than an hour and questions were asked until the interviewer felt no new information surfaced from the informants' responses.

FINDINGS AND DISCUSSIONS

This section describes the findings from the in-depth interviews with the informants. The findings will be divided into two subsections which are findings from (1) interviews with community members and (2) interviews with the managers of internet centres located in the communities. Besides, the subsections also discuss the findings in relation to the theories and previous research in the field.

Based on the data analysis, three themes were formulated and analysed through the existing frameworks: 1) Patterns of Online Social Networking and Social Media Use, 2) Social Networking and Trust, and 3) Social Capital Development.

Patterns of Online Social Networking and Social Media Use

Contrary to earlier pre-pandemic hunch, the informants were regular users of the internet; they spent a substantial amount of time using their mobile phones and being online. Being entrepreneurs, they attributed their online business as the main reason why they were online or checking their phones for orders that might come in. The student basically was browsing the internet all the time. Seeking information was another reason for such use of the internet. This has shown the role of social relationships in social network theory, whereby the use of social network sites and social media to develop networking.

In terms of social media use, the informants reported similar patterns since the social media has grown to be a popular platform for promoting their online businesses. The entrepreneurs whose businesses were not online sought social media for information and rarely updated their activities or profiles as compared to those doing business online. The informant who was a member of an NGO in particular, used the social media frequently to stay updated with the organization's activities and to contribute as well. The social media platforms most cited were Facebook and WhatsApp. Instagram and Twitters were less used. The entrepreneurs nonetheless utilize Tweets to connect with youngsters as they believe Twitters are more popular among the youths. This applies to diffusion of innovation which the use of social media from external sources create innovation in social network, as stated: "the process in which innovation is communicated through certain channels over time among the members of a social system" (Roger, 2010).

The informants relayed their sharing and/or uploading of information was mostly due to business needs (promotion, updating product info) and sharing the latest issues for the purpose of community awareness. The informants also shared recipes; the student limited her sharing to friends and acquaintances only. This was also apparent among entrepreneurs who were not doing online business- most were lurkers and sought the social media for general information from certain groups of which they were members of.

A noticeable and expected observation among the informant was the purposeful use of social media and the internet in general. The online entrepreneurs were basically avid users while the rest were less active. Besides, a few informants were socially disconnected with minimal participation in social activities.

Social Networking and Trust

In view of the regular use of online platforms and online tools among the informants, further probes into their views on the networking and trust in online transactions and interactions were conducted.

The informants were requested to share how they transmit information and use of social media influence their social networking. The informants view personal or one-to-one online sharing such as through social media is basically safe, unlike those that are posted in groups. The informants are quite wary of group postings thus they limit the sharing to general and common information. They were, however, agreeable to the fact that they need to be on an online network especially during the pandemic. They put trust in government websites and they are in the view that they are organizations protecting them from cyber threats. They believe that evidence from online and electronic transactions are traceable through documented processes and audit trails, thus making them safer. The informants also stressed that as individuals, they were also responsible for assuring safety when doing transactions and other business operations. One should know the parties involved in an online interaction or transactions along with knowledge of cues, tools (such as passwords) and have the ability to identify and filter scams and threats. Each informant, however, had a preference on the category of social media they feel safer with or the kind of transaction they were more comfortable doing online. The idea of having a face-to-face transaction was still appealing to some of the informants.

The informants agreed that there needs to be trust between parties who are interacting and having business dealings online. They termed 'good thoughts' as a must have attribute while keeping vigil on shady requests and suspicious online messages. All informants agreed that the need for online networking and interacting on social media is more critical now (with the pandemic) than ever.

It is via the internet that we get to know people, to widen our network. From not being acquainted to getting to know each other. In this case, when someone organises an activity, we would request to send our members as well. this is utterly required of us now, this is good. (Participant 1, NGO)

Businesses too have to be advertised and conducted online; even studying is performed online. The informants cited conducting meetings, buying stuff, promoting their products and communicating with family and friends as the common things they do online. All these save time and money, on top of them being able to scale the sale of their merchandise. The dimension of distance is reduced via online interactions and the idea of choices or options is heightened through the multitude of sources informants can shop from when online. Informants also quoted to gain cheaper bargains when shopping online. They particularly welcomed the leisure of choosing the merchandise from different vendors; some of whom would offer prices that are better suited to their budget.

One interesting feature of social networks that emerged through online buying and selling was the concept of supporting and helping each other. The entrepreneurs saw the online platform as a duct to help other entrepreneurs as well.

I like online (buying and selling) because we are actually helping each other, right. (Participant 4, entrepreneur)

Similar themes echoed when the informants were asked regarding selling items online. The entrepreneurs saw a wider pool of customers; also, a dynamic one as more groups can be connected to the seller. The range of items could also be expanded easily as there's no constraint of space as in the four walls of a general store or number of workers necessary to entertain customers coming in. Going online meant networks and more networks could be established beyond the location where the entrepreneurs lived. With such networks, authentic products are sourced from one state and made available in many other states.

In terms of communications, the informants communicate frequently with families and friends. The informant who was from an NGO communicated according to the activities planned for the week. Those who were entrepreneurs made good use of the online platforms and social media to communicate with their customers. They established ties that allowed them to offer better prices to regular customers.

The above findings allowed us to synthesize the prominent subthemes extracted from the three main themes and the maritime community members which are regulated internet utilization, high acceptance of online networking, business benefit of social networking and social benefit of online networking.

The internet was seen as a must. It was in fact regarded as a challenge if a person was not well versed in the use of the internet. The informants did not doubt information searching and sharing, widening access to others, connecting with friends and learning as the reasons to be on the internet. In terms of social capital, the development of relationships as described by the participants who were entrepreneurs contributed to more efficient flow of information, services and products. By having a broad range of connections, their online businesses are expected to thrive. As Mozer (2006) stated,

The central premise of social capital is that individuals benefit from various norms and values that a social network fosters and produces, such as trust, reciprocity, information, and cooperation.

Such a situation was apparent in the interviews with the informants. The findings revealed a development of both bonding and bridging social capital was apparent among the maritime community social network users. Despite being maritime community members who did not live in big bustling cities, the informants were very much connected to networks that mattered to them.

Hence these findings support the theory of weak ties that explains the strength of weak ties through the amount of efforts the maritime community invest in social relationships, their social support within the group of entrepreneurs and outside the community. The ties also delivery new knowledge and original information among the entrepreneurs. This concept is similar to bridging capital.

In addition, the use of social media and networking is significant as a community development tool. This is a positive sign of social capital development and social networking sites. As a result, the social networking has changed the maritime community lifestyle.

Social Capital Development

The findings on social networking and social capital from the earlier interviews were further supported by in-depth interviews with the managers and assistant managers of rural internet centres from three different states in Malaysia. Four of the five informants engaged were female. Both the informants' race and religion were the same. The managers oversee ICT services and operations. They participate in social networking as well as helping the community develop its digital abilities. The purpose of the interviews was to assess the informants' perceptions on social networks and social capital as well as their contributions to the growth of the community.

Basically, the informants had a clear perspective of social network, be it online or offline. They understood the dynamics of the community and how different groups interact to support and complement each other. According to the managers, the community they were in were close knit with members knowing each other well. It is interesting to note that the informants found bonding, bridging and linking social capital to emerge within the communities and inter-communities. They noted that communication was the most pertinent element and they were also aware of the differences in the way the community clusters communicated.

Different groups have different ways of communicating; the students, the fishermen, the post-secondary youths, teachers – the centre acts a reference point and link them to resources and government offices. (Assistant Manager L1)

The pandemic and the demand for online education, according to the informants, served as a catalyst for community members to engage in online networking, including parents, instructors, and students. The managers understood how crucial it was for their centres to serve as a conduit between businesses and consumers. They viewed the centres as "one-stop centres" that facilitated networking, linking, and bonding. The managers saw themselves as well as the centres as a dependable resource used by the community's residents, including parents, teachers, company owners, job seekers, and others. The informants claimed that the neighbourhood they lived in already had a strong sense of community. The accessibility of the online platform improved social networking, community member cooperation, and the growth of social capital in rural maritime communities.

Thus, the social capital is accepted to be social interactions and resources created through social networks (thick and thin ties or relationships). These findings support with previous studies on Lin 2001; Putnam, 2017; and Tristan 2020. This can be illustrated as in

Figure 2. Relational dimensions of social capital

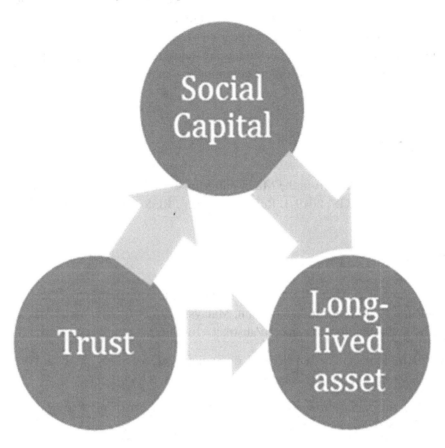

Trust is the dimension of social capital, which the maritime communities learn to trust people they do not know and build strong ties with their communities. This relational dimension is the connection between individuals, social network and trustworthiness. Hence, building trust could be within the community (bonding) or outside the community (bridging).

Additionally, social capital has a long-lived asset component. Social capital and trust are an asset over the long term. It is impossible to transfer ownership of an intangible asset. The resource is thus the maritime community's property. Social trust and relationships are its main points of emphasis. As social networking spreads to more communities, it cannot be devalued.

CONCLUSION

In contrast to the idea of rural communities have trouble accessing the internet and staying online, social online networking patterns do have important influences on the development of social capital among rural maritime community members in the three East Coast states studied. The pandemic is believed to act as a catalyst to staying connected and building online network. First and foremost, online networking facilitates the generation of more economic opportunities, especially among rural entrepreneurs. Second, online networking enables the widening and strengthening of participants' social ties; thus, overcoming time and geographical limitations. Third, participants' access to, and sharing of, information online, also enable knowledge to be generated and circulated among other members of the rural communities. Hence it is apparent that online networking can be used to reduce the social capital divide between urban and rural communities in Malaysia. Further studies are required to establish the appropriate conduit and support system in order to develop the online community social capital and sustain a more robust rural development.

ACKNOWLEDGMENT

This work has received funding from the Malaysian Ministry of Higher Education under Fundamental Research Grant Scheme (FRGS) 2019-1. Reference code: FRGS/1/2019/SSI10/UMT/02/1.

REFERENCES

Abdul-Hakim, Russayani, & Abdul-Razak. (2010). The Relationship between Social Capital and Quality of Life Among Rural Households in Terengganu, Malaysia. *OIDA International Journal of Sustainable Development, 1*(5), 99-106. https://ssrn.com/abstract=1671066

Adams, O. K. (2016). Impact of Social Network on Society: A Case Study of Abuja. *American Scientific Research Journal for Engineering, Technology, and Sciences, 21*(1), 1–17.

Agarwal, S. (2019). *Are social networks good for our society?* Christ University. https://www.researchgate.net/publication/339780597

Aras, Abdulkadir, & Serpil. (2017). Social Networking Sites as Communication, Interaction, and Learning Environments: Perceptions and Preferences of Distance Education Students. Anadolu University, Turkey. *Journal of Learning for Development, 4*(3), 348-365.

Beggs, J. J., Haines, V. A., & Hurlbert, J. S. (1996). Revisiting the Rural-Urban Contrast: Personal Networks in Nonmetropolitan and Metropolitan Settings. *Rural Sociology, 61*(2), 306–325. doi:10.1111/j.1549-0831.1996.tb00622.x

Bhandari, H., & Yasunobu, K. (2009). What is Social Capital? A Comprehensive Review of the Concept. *Asian Journal of Social Science, 37*(3), 480–510. doi:10.1163/156853109X436847

Bloomberg, L. D. & Volpe, M. (2008). *Completing Your Qualitative Dissertation: A Roadmap from Beginning to End.* Sage Publications.

Boyatzis, R. E. (1998). *Transforming Qualitative Information: Thematic and Code Development.* Sage Publications.

Coleman, J. S. (1988). Social capital in the creation of human capital. *American Journal of Sociology, 94*(Supplement), S95–S120. doi:10.1086/228943

Creswell, J. W. (2007). *Qualitative inquiry and research design: Choosing among five approaches* (2nd ed.). Sage Publications, Inc.

Creswell, J. W. (2009). *Research design: Qualitative, quantitative, and mixed methods approaches* (3rd ed.). Sage Publications, Inc.

Debertin & Goetz. (2013). *Social Capital Formation in Rural, Urban and Suburban Communities*. University of Kentucky Staff Paper 474.

Faisal, R. A., Jobe, M. C., Ahmed, O., & Sharker, T. (2021). Mental health status, anxiety, and depression levels of Bangladeshi university students during the COVID-19 pandemic. *International Journal of Mental Health and Addiction*, 1–16. doi:10.100711469-020-00458-y PMID:33424514

Gkritsi, E. (2021). *Clubhouse invites for sale on Alibaba's used goods app*. Available at: https://technode.com/2021/02/02/clubhouse-invites-for-sale-on-alibabas-used-goodsapp

Grafton, R. Q. (2005). Social capital and fisheries governance. *Ocean and Coastal Management, 48*(9–10), 753–766. doi:10.1016/j.ocecoaman.2005.08.003

Granovetter, M. S. (1973). The strength of weak ties. *American Journal of Sociology, 78*(6), 1360–1380. doi:10.1086/225469

Jiang, Y. (2021). Problematic Social media usage and anxiety among university students during the COVID-19 pandemic: The mediating role of psychological capital and the moderating role of academic burnout. Frontiers in Psychology, 12, 612007. https://dx.doi.org/ doi:10.3389/fpsyg.2021.612007

Kim, S. H., & Kim, S. (2021). Social trust as an individual characteristic or societal property? *International Review of Public Administration, 26*(1), 1–17. doi:10.1080/12294659.2020.1834677

Kostadin, K., Proulx, J. D. E., & Dunn, E. W. (2017). Digitally connected, socially disconnected: The effects of relying on technology rather than other people. *Computers in Human Behavior, 76*(November), 68–74.

Lin, N. (2001). *Social Capital: A Theory of Social Structure and Action*. Cambridge University Press. doi:10.1017/CBO9780511815447

Marhaini, M. N. (2018). Rural Community Digital Technology Connectedness: Does Ict In Rural Areas Contributes To Rural Development In Malaysia? *Social Sciences*.

Matthew, Sadiku, Adedamola, Omotoso, & Musa. (2019). Social Networking. Roy G. Perry College of Engineering, Prairie View A&M University, Prairie View. *International Journal of Trend in Scientific Research and Development, 3*(3). www.ijtsrd.com

Merriam, S. B. (2009). *Qualitative research: A guide to design and implementation*. Jossey-Bass.

Merriam, S. B. (2009). *Qualitative Research: A Guide to Design and Implementation* (2nd ed.). John Wiley & Sons.

Merriam, S. B., & Tisdell, E. J. (2016). *Qualitative Research A Guide to Design and Implementation* (4th ed.). Jossey Bass.

Miles, M. B., & Huberman, A. M. (1994). *An Expanded Sourcebook: Qualitative Data Analysis* (2nd ed.). Sage Publications.

Mozer, P. (2006). Social network analysis and social capital. *International Relations and Security Network*. https://www.files.ethz.ch/isn/130867/ISN_Special_Issues_Jun.2006.pdf

Nieman, A. (2006). Social Capital and Social Development. *Social Work/Maatskaplike Werk, 42*(2). https://socialwork.journals.ac.za/

Paul, K. C., Hamzah, A., Samah, B. A., Ismail, I. A., & D'Silva, J. L. (2014). Value of Social Network for Development of Rural Malay Herbal Entrepreneurship in Malaysia. *Procedia: Social and Behavioral Sciences, 130*, 59–64. doi:10.1016/j.sbspro.2014.04.008

Paul, L. (2011). The Use of Social Networking in Community Development. Academic Press.

Perez, S. (2021). *Social audio app Clubhouse has topped 8 million global downloads*. Available at: https://techcrunch.com/2021/02/18/report-social-audio-app-clubhouse-has-topped-8-million-global-downloads

Peter, M. (2016, July). Social media, community development and social capital. *Community Development Journal: An International Forum, 51*(3), 419–435. doi:10.1093/cdj/bsv040

Podgorskaya, S., & Schitov, S. (2021). The role and importance of social capital in rural development. *E3S Web Conf., 273*, 08072. doi:10.1051/e3sconf/202127308072

Punch, K. F. (2005). *Introduction to Social Research: Quantitative and Qualitative Approach* (2nd ed.). SAGE Publications.

Putnam, R. D. (1993). Making democracy work: civic tradition in modern Italy. Princeton University Press.

Putnam, R. D. (2000). Bowling Alone: The Collapse and Revival of American Community. New York: Simon & Schuster.

Putnam, R. D. (2017). *Social Capital Primer. Bowling alone*. Professor Putnam's Harvard webpage.

Rogers, E. M. (2010). *Diffusion of innovations* (4th ed.). Free Press.

Russon, A.-M. (2021). *Clubhouse confirms data spillage of its audio streams*. Available at: https://www.bbc.com/news/business-56163623

Statista. (2022). *Statista Digital Market Outlook @ Statista 2022*. https://www.statista.com/outlook/digital-markets

Tristan, C. (2020). *Trust and trustworthiness: An aspect of the relational dimension of social capital*. Social Capital Research. https://www.socialcapitalresearch.com/trust-and-trustworthiness/#comment-25209

Wenlin, L., Anupreet, S., Amanda, M. B., & Thomas, V. (2017) Social Network Theory. University of Southern California. doi:10.1002/9781118783764.wbieme0092

Zheng, Z., & Chen, H. (2020). Age sequences of the elderly' social network and its efficacies on well-being: An urban-rural comparison in China. *BMC Geriatrics, 20*(1), 372. doi:10.118612877-020-01773-8 PMID:32993525

Chapter 14
Role of Technological Innovations in the Development of an Indian Banking Sector

Mohamed Syed Ibrahim
iD https://orcid.org/0009-0006-3546-275X
Government Arts College (Autonomous), Periyar University, India

ABSTRACT

With the advent of information technology, there has been an opening up of new markets, new products, and improved productivity and efficiency in the banking sector. Commercial banks in India are now becoming vibrant markets, and technology allows banks and financial institutions to create what looks like a branch in a business building's lobby without having to hire for manual operations. Today, the banks are running in the concept of 24X7 working, made possible by the use of technological innovations. Almost all financial institutions and banks in India are using the advanced technological innovations like ATM, mobile banking, digital money using debit and credit cards, etc. This study is attempting to evaluate the vibrant usage of information/technological innovations. The study is diagnostic and exploratory in nature and makes use of secondary data. The study finds and concludes that the commercial banks in India have significantly improved their working performance with the help of information technology.

INTRODUCTION AND BACKGROUND OF THE STUDY

Banking system plays a vital role in the economic development of a country. The structure of the banking system in India consists of two parts: (i) unorganized sector and (ii) organized sector. The unorganized sector comprises moneylenders and indigenous bankers. The organized sector consists of commercial banks, cooperative banks and regional rural banks. Besides the above institutions which provide mainly short-term credit to business, there are a number of specialized terms lending institutions which provide long-term requirements of industry, agriculture and foreign trade. Post office savings bank which is 110 years old is another segment of the banking system. The Reserve Bank of India, the central bank of the country is at the apex of the banking structure in India.

DOI: 10.4018/978-1-6684-8953-6.ch014

The information technology using by the banks are providing better and speedy services to its customers. Most importantly, the latest technology delivering channels like ATM, Debit and Credit Cards, Internet Banking Mobile Banking etc. Indian government started implementation of varied policies for development of technology. As of now, technology and innovations have a good impact on overall economic growth. Technology occupies enormous sectors like banking and finance, medical advancements and communication sector etc.

Review of Related Literature

Considerable amount of research has been done in the area of role of information technology in the development of banking sector. The literature obtained by the investigator is briefly reviewed in this part.

Mega Jain and Popli.G.S. (2012), tiled in their paper "Role of Information Technology in the Development of Banking Sector in India" concluded that the efficient use of technology has facilitated accurate and timely management of the increased transaction volume of banks which comes with larger customer base and Indian banking industry is greatly benefited with the advent of information technology and innovations.

Vinay Numar (2016) studied and elaborately discussed how innovations helped the development of banking sector.

Anbalaghan.G (2017) in his paper analyzed the examined with all innovations and new technological changes in the banking sector.

Rajesh Kannan.S and Neeraja Basker.B (2018) in their paper concluded that technology in banking sector eliminates people as well as bank efforts, cost and time.

Ravi.B and Shanbulingappa F. Nallanavar (2021), in their study highlighted the new innovations in the banking sector at the state and national level banks.

Objectives of the Study

The study aims to gain insights into the concept of information technology and innovations in development of an Indian Commercial Banks. The following broad objectives are laid down for the purpose of the study.

(a)   to assess the performance with regard to the Automated Teller Machines (ATM) of selected and leading public and private sector banks;
(b)   to analyze the performance in terms of debit and credit card issuance by the banks.

Research Methodology and Tools Applied

This research covers the selected and leading public and private sector banks in India using innovative banking services like ATM, Mobile Banking Debit and Credit Cards etc., Data and information gathered from secondary sources which included books, journals, research studies, published data from various issues of RBI and relevant websites.

The collected data and information have been processed on computer. To reach certain relevant results, the data collected from all resources have been tabulated, analyzed and interpreted with the help of appropriate statistical techniques. In order to analyze the data and draw conclusions in this study, various statistical tools like Descriptive Statistics. including Z-Score Values and One-Way ANOVA have been applied using through SPSS Software.

Data Analysis and Interpretation

1.   Automated Teller Machine (ATM)

Automated Teller Machine (ATM) is an amalgam of several inventions. It enables the customers to withdraw their money 24 hours a day 7 days a week. ATMs are used by the customers not only to withdraw their cash, but it can be used for payments and fund transfer. ATMs are playing an important role in providing remote services to customers. The year-wise installation of ATMs (both on-site and off-site) by the selected public sector banks are provided in Table 1.

Table 1. ATMs installed by selected and leading public sector banks

Years	State Bank of India	Punjab National Bank	Canara Bank
March, 2018	59541	9668	9395
March, 2019	58415	9255	8851
March, 2020	58555	9168	8772
March, 2021	62617	13781	13452
March, 2022	65539	13354	12210
AVERAGE	60933	11045	10536
SD	3081.55	2315.19	2153.95
C.V. (%)	5.05	20.96	20.44

Source: Data extracted from the Reserve Bank of India (RBI) Data Base.

It has been observed from the above table that the number of ATMs installed and operated by the State Bank of India (SBI) from 59,541 in 2018 to 65,539 in 2022 which is very encouraging sign. The increase over the period was 1.1 times. In the case of Punjab National Bank (PNB), the number of ATMs installed from 9,668 in 2018, and it went up to 13,354 in 2022.The increase over the period was 1.4 times. The number of ATMs installed and operated by the Canara Bank was 9,395 in 2018 which further amplified to 12,210 in 2022 which is also significant sign of growth.

By comparing the performance on the basis of the mean value for the period, it has been noted that the number of ATMs installed and operated by the SBI is high as the mean value is 60933. Next is the place of Punjab national Bank (PNB) whose mean value is 11045, and it is lowest in the case of Canara Bnak as it is 10536. The degree of variation is very low in SBI as the CV (%) is 5.05 and the variation is very high in case of both the banks (PNB & CB) as per the per cent of CV are 20.96 and 20.44 respectively. It is found to be more consistent as the CV of the ATMs installed by the SBI is less than that of ATMs installed by both the banks i.e., PNB and CB during the study period.

To test the differences in the installation and operations of ATM among the three public sector banks, 'One-Way ANOVA' has been applied and for which the following hypothesis has been framed and tested.

Null Hypothesis (H0)

There is no difference in the installation of and operations of ATMs among the three public sector banks namely SBI, PNB & CB.

Alternative Hypothesis (H1)

There is difference in the installation of and operations of ATMs among the three public sector banks namely SBI, PNB & CB.

The test results are given in the following Table.

Table 2.

ANOVA					
ATM					
	Sum of Squares	**df**	**Mean Square**	**F**	**Sig.**
Between Groups	8.382E9	2	4.191E9	644.886	.000
Within Groups	7.798E7	12	6498552.667		
Total	8.460E9	14			

Table above shows the F test values along with degrees of freedom (2, 12) and significance of 0.000. Given that $p < 0.05$, we can reject the null hypothesis (H0) and accept the alternative hypothesis (H1) that there is a significant difference of ATM installation and operations among the three public sector banks chosen in the study, $F_{(2,12)} = 644.886$, $p < .05$.

Figure 1 Means Plot is a pictorial representation of means scores of dependent variables for each group. Here, the Means Plot shows the means of ATMs installed and operated by the three public sector banks. A closer examination of the Means Plot reveals that the mean scored by SBI bank is 60933 whereas for PNB bank it is 11045; the mean scored by CB is 10536. Therefore, it is concluded that the SBI is having high difference in mean score as compared to that of other tow public sector banks (PNB & CB).

Figure 1.

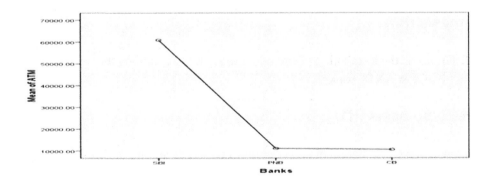

Table 3 exhibits the year-wise installation of ATMs (both on-site and off-site) by the selected and leading private sector banks.

Table 3. ATMs installed by selected and leading private sector banks

Years	HDFC Bank Ltd	ICICI Bank Ltd	AXIX Bank Ltd
March, 2018	12635	14367	13814
March, 2019	13160	14987	11801
March, 2020	14061	17430	17477
March, 2021	14779	16803	17043
March, 2022	18130	16577	16922
AVERAGE	14553	16033	15411
SD	2162.59	1295.19	2489.84
C.V (%)	14.8	8.1	16.1

Source: Data Extracted from Reserve Bank of India (RBI) Data Base.

Table 3 exhibits that the number of ATMs installed and operated by the HDFC Bank from 12,635 in 2018 to 18,130 in 2022 which has increased constantly and is very encouraging sign. The increase over the period was 1.4 times. In the case of ICICI Bank, the number of ATMs installed from 14,367 in 2018, and it increased up to 16,577 in 2022.The increase over the period was 1.1 times. The number of ATMs installed and operated by the AXIX Bank was 13,814 in 2018 which was greater than before to 16,922 in 2022 which is also a significant sign of growth.

By comparing the performance on the basis of the mean value for the period, it has been noted that the number of ATMs installed and operated by the ICICI Bank is high as the mean value is 16033. Next is the place of AXIX Bank whose mean value is 15411, and it is slightly lowest in the case of HDFC Bank as it is 14553. The degree of variation is very low in ICICI Bank as the CV (%) is 8.1 and the variation is very high in case of both the banks (HDFC & AXIX Bank) as per the per cent of CV are 14.8 and 16.1 respectively. It is found to be more consistent as the CV of the ATMs installed by the ICICI Bank is (8.1) less than that of ATMs installed by both the selected private sector banks i.e., HDFC & AXIX Bank during the period of study.

To test the differences in the installation and operations of ATM among the three private sector banks, 'One-Way ANOVA' has been applied and for which the following hypothesis has been framed and tested.

Null Hypothesis (H0)

There is no difference in the installation of and operations of ATMs among the three private sector banks namely HDFC, ICICI & AXIX banks.

Alternative Hypothesis (H1)

There is difference in the installation of and operations of ATMs among the public sector banks namely HDFC, ICICI & AXIX banks.

The test results are given in Table 4.

Table 4.

ANOVA					
ATM					
	Sum of Squares	**df**	**Mean Square**	**F**	**Sig.**
Between Groups	5521327.600	2	2760663.800	.660	.535
Within Groups	5.021E7	12	4184564.000		
Total	5.574E7	14			

Table 4 shows the F test values along with degrees of freedom (2, 12) and significance of .535. Given that p > 0.05, we can accept the null hypothesis (H0) and reject the alternative hypothesis (H1) that there is no significant difference of ATM installation and operations among the three private sector banks in India, $F(2,12) = .660$, p >.05.

Figure 2.

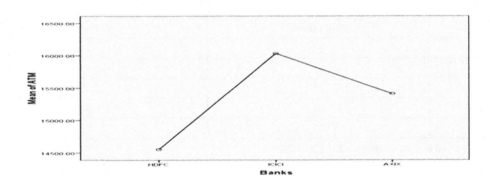

Figure 2 Means Plot is a pictorial representation of means scores of dependent variables for each group. Here, the Means Plot shows the means of ATMs installed and operated by the three private sector banks. A closer examination of the Means Plot reveals that the mean scored by HDFC bank is 14553 whereas for ICICI bank it is 16033; the mean scored by AXIX bank is 15411. Therefore, it is concluded that there is a small difference in mean score by three private sector banks.

2.   Debit and Credit Card

The credit card industry has grown tremendously in India. There are many developments happening in the space, with varied innovations and changes in technology. Table 4 exhibits the year-wise number of active credit and debit cards of SBI which is one of the leading public sector banks in India.

Table 5. Number of active credit and debit cards of SBI card in India from financial year 2018 to 2022 (in millions)

Years	State Bank of India	Z-Score Values
2018	6.26	-1.3149
2019	8.27	-.6326
2020	10.55	0.1412
2021	11.82	0.5722
2022	13.77	1.2341

Source: Data Extracted from the Reserve Bank of India (RBI) Data Base.

It is observed from Table 5 that the number of active credit and debit cards of SBI which has increased from 6.26 in 2018 to 13.77 in 2022. The increase over the period was 2.19 times which good sign of performance is. The Z scores with minus sign represent observations that are below the mean for the sample. Whereas, the Z scores with plus sign represent observations that are above the mean for the sample. It is, therefore, concluded that the recent three years (2020, 2021 & 2022) the SBI registered with positive score and the performance in this regard are highly eye-catching.

Table 6 provides the data about the Credit Card Industry in India during the study period.

Table 6. Credit card issuance (in millions)

Years	Credit Cards	Z-Score Values
2018	37	-1.3162
2019	47	-0.5930
2020	57	0.1301
2021	62	0.4917
2022	73	1.2872

Source: RBI Data and PwC Payments Hand Book 2021-2022.

Table 6 exhibits that the number of credit card issued in the country which raised 37 million in 2018 to 73 million in 2022. The increase over the period was 1.9 times which a good sign of growth is. The Z scores with minus sign represent observations that are below the mean for the sample. Whereas, the Z scores with plus sign represent observations that are above the mean for the sample. It is, therefore, inferred that the recent three years (2020, 2021 & 2022) witnessed the positive score and the performance in this regard are highly noticeable.

Findings of the Study

a. Analysis of ATM installation and operations by the selected and leading public sector banks reveal that State Bank of India (SBI) stands first place during the period of study. It is found to be more consistent as the CV of the ATMs installed by the SBI is less than that of ATMs installed by both the banks i.e., PNB and CB during the study period.

b.   As far as the private sector banks are concerned, banks chosen in the study that ATM installation and operations by the selected and leading private sector banks reveal that ICICI Bank stands first place and the statistical analysis reveals that the CV of the ATMs installed by the ICICI Bank is (8.1) less than that of ATMs installed by both the selected private sector banks i.e., HDFC & AXIX Banks. Hence, the ICICI bank is found to be more consistent during the study period.

c.   The statistical analysis reveals that that there is a significant difference in ATM installation and operations among the three public sector banks (SBI, PNB & CB).

d.   Mean Plot depict that the SBI is having high difference in mean score as compared to that of other tow public sector banks (PNB & CB).

e.   The statistical analysis reveals that that there is no significant difference in ATM installation and operations among the three private sector banks (HDFC, ICICI &AXIX Banks).

f.   Pictorial representation of Mean Plot put across that there is a small difference in mean score by three private sector banks.

g.   The study found that the number of active credit and debit cards of SBI which has constantly increased and the increase over the period was 2.19 times which good sign of performance is.

h.   The study visualized that the number of credit card issued in the country which raised 37 million in 2018 to 73 million in 2022. The increase over the period was 1.9 times which an excellent sign of growth is.

CONCLUSION

A development in the field of information technology and innovations powerfully supports the growth and inclusiveness of the entire banking system by facilitating inclusive growth of an Indian economy. The important innovations in the field of information technology in the Indian Banking sector are;

Debit/Credit Cards in late 1980s and 90s
Electronic Clearing Services (ECS) in late 1990s
Electronic Fund Transfer (EFT) in early 2000s
Real Time Gross Settlement (RTGC) in 2004
National Electronic Fund Transfer (NEFT) in 2005
Cheque Truncation System (CTS) in 2007.

Technology has changed the face of the Indian banking sector through the computerization with the advent of information technology. Though private sector and foreign sector banks have an edge at present, yet public sector banks have also made a significant growth in this regard.

Limitations of the Study

The study is based on secondary data as published in various publications of RBI and other reports. The study, as limitations, is confined only to the selected indicators and the selected and leading banks from public and private sector and the study is confined only for the period of five years.

Scope of Further Research

This research paper and its findings may be of considerable use to banking institutions, policymakers and the academic researchers in the area of banking performance evaluation with special reference to the information technology and innovations.

REFERENCES

Anbalagan, G. (2017). New technological changes in Indian banking sector. *International Journal of Scientific Research and Management*. doi:10.18535/ijsrm/v5i9.11

Customer satisfaction towards internet banking with special reference to North Chennai. (2019). *International Journal of Recent Technology and Engineering, 8*(4S3), 284–286. doi:10.35940/ijrte.D1058.1284S319

Customers' perception towards mobile banking with reference to Chennai city. (2019). *International Journal of Recent Technology and Engineering, 8*(4S3), 312–315. doi:10.35940/ijrte.D1066.1284S319

Deshpande, B. N. (2018). Digitalization in banking sector. *International Journal of Trend in Scientific Research and Development*, 80–85. doi:10.31142/ijtsrd18677

Harchekar, M. J. S. (2018). Digitalization in banking sector. *International Journal of Trend in Scientific Research and Development,* 103–109. doi:10.31142/ijtsrd18681

Jain, M., & Popli, G. S. (2012). Role of information technology in the development of banking sector in India. SSRN *Electronic Journal*. doi:10.2139/ssrn.2151162

Wewege, L. (2017). *The Digital Banking Revolution: How financial technology companies are rapidly transforming the traditional retail banking industry through disruptive innovation*. Scribl. https://economictimes.indiatimes.com/nation-world/heres-the-story-of-atms-over-the-years/worldwide-launch/slideshow/55511212.cms

Chapter 15

Study of the Dark Web With Reference to the Indian Banking System and Black Market and Fraud Scenarios

Devendra Singh

Amity University, Greater Noida, India

Sumitra Singh

Amity University, Greater Noida, India

ABSTRACT

The dark web as a technology has shown great potential and has grown tremendously. We have everything on our tips. This type of environment is also very fruitful and dangerous at the same time. Where everything is available on sale for the highest bidder, dark web plays as a role of intermediary in the sale. This chapter aims to highlights the use of TOR, and other dark webs, and their related activities which leads to the frauds happening in India and to study the connection between dark web, black markets, and banking fraud in India (if any). This chapter attempts to understand the working of the dark web and the illegal transactions.

1. INTRODUCTION

We live in times where, no one is left from the touch of the technology in this era. From banking to meeting people internet plays a very vital role in today's time. Every data is available on the Internet. This area is where the dark web is a very dangerous tool for the right and highest buyer. Dark Web unlike any other web has very deep roots on the internet. The normal web where only 10-15% of the information is available, the rest of the information is available on the Dark Web. It allows anonymous searches, or else it changes the servers from country to country making it untraceable to locate the servers of the users. Now we are living in the ages of Data, where is the new key to everything. This is the new

DOI: 10.4018/978-1-6684-8953-6.ch015

currency. Because of this strong system, the banking frauds, black markets, corporate espionage, and other illegal activities such as extortion have grown. The transactions are untraceable which motivates and promotes the use of these illegal activities. Terrorist organizations like Taliban, Al-Qaeda receive funding through the dark web.

Since the beginning of the Internet, Dark web has existed as a reality. A load of information is being indexed on the web which is easily accessible by any person having internet connectivity irrespective of geography, there is a lot more information and data on the web, as it is hidden and requires a special privilege to access. This unchartered portion of the web is called Dark Web.

2. BACKGROUND (REVIEW OF LITERATURE)

The Internet from what it was before to what it is now, the picture has taken a 360-degree turn. No one would have ever thought of how just a few commands a lot can be done from your laptop and world can be changed from world governments toppling. This is possible because of the help of Dark Web. Dark Web can be understood as just the space of the ocean unexplored and with lots of information with no trace. Very few scholars have attempted to study on the dark web have and have conducted very less study with relation to the banking area. Dark Web is as similar as Black hole in the space which is known to humans but it is unexplored till date, hence no actual limit. One such software which not only achieves the privacy preservation objectives but also offers potential anonymity is the onion router (Tor) browser. David Chuam of University of California. (Chaum, 1981) was developed a model for "Untraceable Electronic Mail, return addresses and digital fictitious name (pseudonyms) and observed that technique related to public key cryptography allows an electronic mail system to hide sender details and as well as contents of the mail. Rajesh E. (2019) observed in his study dark web is growing rapidly specially to transact illegal actives and TOR have created new platform to perform criminal actives and payment gateways for such kind of criminal act. The various literary works enable for the improvement of research, and as a result, the TOR routing with the other concepts is provided with the aid of the numerous US intelligence systems (Navara & Nelson, 2007). It makes it possible for the Dark Network system to be utilized for both unlawful and legal purposes. The privacy of the program is conveniently illustrated for the purpose of analyzing the data, and study is also continued with the help of the ISI testing frameworks. In a separate study by Barnett et al., the role of spiders, defined as computer programs used to browse information on the World Wide Web, and the simplicity of access that can be obtained through registration are studied, allowing the precise and necessary information on the various forms to be easily gathered. As a result, all the researches till date have focused on General issues of Dark web that is the human trafficking, human life-threatening crimes etc but our paper deals with a very important and tries to uproot the financial crimes and throw light on this topic. The dark web is just like an octopus hands which a lot of branches which if unidentified can help other crimes to make place for them. According to a research, trade on the internet dark markets cost India $18.5 billion in 2017. This is a four-fold rise from $4.2 billion in 2014, per a March 2019 research by the Indian Council on Global Relations, think tank, Gateway house. The UN office on Narcotics and Crime (UNODC) reports that India is particularly affected by the worldwide trend of purchasing drugs through dark net trade platforms utilizing cryptocurrency. This practice has already extended throughout South Asia. After adopting the usage of cryptocurrency, the Indian anti-narcotics agency saw an increase in the activities of drug traffickers using the dark web in India in 2017.

3. CONNECTION BETWEEN DARK WEB AND BANKS IN INDIA

A major cause of worry for governments and companies worldwide is the dark web, a portion of the internet that is virtually unknown. In India, the dark web has had an impact on the banking sector, raising questions about the security of financial data and customer privacy. With all the data being available, anything which is linked to internet can be hacked and can get remote access. Indian banks are particularly vulnerable to cyberattacks originating from the dark web, as the country has one of the highest per capita internets uses in the world and the financial sector has been slower to adopt security measures and technologies than other sectors. Furthermore, the Indian Government has not taken sufficient measures to protect citizens from cybercrime, allowing cybercriminals to target banks with relative weak audience. The implications of this breach are wide-ranging, with the potential for identity theft, account hijacking, money laundering, and other financial crimes now more likely.

4. IMPACT OF DARK WEB

Impact of dark web has grown to a very great extent in these times for illegal activities, they are a safe haven for all the hackers, be it white or gray. While browsing on the open web, all the footprints are traced back to the IP of the users, but while working on the Dark Web, no single activity is shown, it hides the digital footprints of the users, just like the inner most layer of an onion. The system acts like a very well-connected array of computers wherein the address jumps from one system to another therefore allowing criminals to anonymously work. Now, dark web is not only associated with heinous crimes, but also with financial crimes as well. Dark Web has become a hotspot for these finance crimes as well. From Money laundering, terrorist financing, phishing, bribery, market manipulation, insider trading etc.

With the new system of block chain, and bitcoins, the payment activities are now more discrete, and therefore work in hindsight. It anonymizes the users true IP. Now since the internet is available around the world, everything is accessible to everyone. Therefore, some of the services are unavailable on the open web, now to access these services Dark Web comes into the picture. The browsers of the dark web, helps in accessing these sites to the full extent and with anonymity. This anonymity means that information about the host, location and even the content is hidden. Recent the of dark web have been drastically increase specially in the banking & financial system -

5. BANKING FRAUD AND ITS IMPACT BY DARK WEB

The most populous democracy in the world is also becoming into a hotspot of innovation and startup creation, China is the only other country with a population close to 12 million. According to the research and consulting firm McKinsey Digital, China had the most internet customers in September 2018 with 560 million, followed by India. Indians downloaded 12.3 billion more applications in 2018 than any other nation save China, and they spent 17 hours more each week on social media than Americans and Chinese users combined. The report continues: Thanks in major part to the percentage of Indian adults with at least one digital financial account has more than doubled since 2011 to 80% because to the government's Jan-Dhan Yojana initiative for widespread financial inclusion. Interestingly, the country seems to be advancing towards the financial future nearly in lockstep with the chronology of cryptocurrencies themselves, but there has been one significant hurdle: the Indian government. Bans on regulated financial services supporting firms dealing in cryptocurrencies issued by the R.B.I. in 2018 stunted growth and angered many. Although cryptocurrency was never prohibited in the country, certain people who used it to develop the economy found it very difficult to operate legally and effectively. The embargo has finally been lifted, at least temporarily, and the industry is once again in the spotlight. But what about that part of the internet that disregards governmental orders? The Narcotics Control Bureau of India recently reported the arrest of Dipu Singh, 21, to whom the NCB's deputy director general Rajesh Nandan Srivastava described as "a key participant on the darknet." He has listings on one of the biggest and most famous darknet markets, namely Empire Market and Majestic Garden. The significant dark web arrest, according to sources, had been an Indian first. The allegedly committed offence by Singh involves shipping psychotropic drugs to as far away as the United States while passing them off as treatments for erectile dysfunction. CNN station News18 cites Srivastava as saying: "The operators exploited the payment gateways of cryptocurrencies like Bitcoins and Litecoin to disguise the transactions from regulatory bodies." In fact, more individuals in India than ever before have access to technology that may be exploited for dark web commerce. India has the highest percentage of people worldwide who "have used technologies that allow access to the dark web," according to information gathered in February of last year from 23,227 interviewees. The report elaborates: "This statistic presents the share of internet users who have used technologies, such as the anonymity network Tor, that allow access to the dark web as of February 2019, sorted by country. 26 percent of respondents from India said they have utilised such technology throughout the poll period.

5.1. The Stolen Data Case

The large data infringement on the Dark Web originated from a hacked server of the Juspay digital payment gateway, which is situated in Bengaluru. An unauthorized attempt on our servers was discovered on August 18, 2020, and it came to an abrupt halt. No card numbers, encryption credentials, or purchase information, according to an organization spokeswoman's statement.

Rajaharia, however, said that the information was being offered for sale on the Dark Web for an unknown sum through crypto.

"However, the encrypted card number will be decrypted if the hackers have ability to discover the Hash technique habituated to create the card fingerprint. As according Rajaharia, all 100 million cardholders are at risk in this circumstance.

No card numbers and other financial information were accessed since they are kept in a separate, separated system. No transactional or order-related data was stolen, according to a business spokeswoman. Juspay, which was established in 2012, in its series B fundraising round last year, the company raised $21.6 million. Vostok Emerging Finance (VEF), a Swedish company, took the lead in the round with a $13 million investment in the technology company, its first in the nation.

The dark web has been used to spread personal information of 7 million Indians, containing their phone numbers and email address, who use ATM and credit cards. Data from the years 2010 through 2019 might be extremely beneficial to fraudsters and hackers. Rajaharia stated in a statement to IANS. The PAN details for five lakh cardholders are also included in the stolen information, according to the internet security expert.

Although the authenticity of the data of 70 lakh individuals has not been confirmed, Rajaharia has validated the data of select users and discovered that the details provided in many of the areas are accurate. This data was made public and sold at the highest bid, since it is of financial nature.

5.2. Credit, Debit Card Data of Half a Million Indians Up for Sale on Dark Web:[1] (Dasgupta, Feb 07, 2020)

Indian cyber security officials have alerted the Reserve Bank of India (RBI) and all Indian banks that such data was being sold on the dark web, a senior official in a department handling cyber security said, asking not to be named.

According to cyber security analysts, the breach is the most catastrophic in at least the past 12 months and involved the credit and debit card information of over 500,000 Indians. The website in question is a prominent source for financial crime.

According to Group IB, a Singapore-based cyber security company, the data, which was Listed for sale on Joker's Stash, the confidential material includes, beside the card numbers which range from 14 to 16 digit, expiry dates, CVV/CVC codes, customers' names, and even email addresses in certain circumstances. Together, these may be utilized to conduct digital banking transactions without the need for additional authentication procedures.

"This is the second significant card leak involving Indian banks that the Group-IB threat intelligence team has discovered in recent months…The head of Group-cybercrime IB's investigation section, Dmitry Shestakov, said to HT in an email, "In the present situation, we are dealing with so called fulls, who have data on the cardholder's name, card number, expiration date, CVV/CVC, and other sensitive information.

The dark net is used by the internet black markets, which deal in the selling of illegal goods such child pornography, unlicensed medications, cyber weaponry, stolen credit card information, counterfeit money, and fake papers.

5.3. Darknet and P2P Crypto Utility for Evading State Violence

It cannot be denied that dark web markets are utilised for immoral, violent, and even disgusting objectives. This fact is demonstrated by the newly revealed darknet offer of more than 460,000 payment card details from Indian banks. The less-discussed reality is that illicit activities also take place in state-approved marketplaces and official organisations, and they do so on a considerably larger scale. One need only consider high-level Department of Defence connections to child pornography, which go largely unmentioned in the public discourse, or Purdue Pharma's infamous Oxycontin drug scam, which openly contributed to the US opioid crisis. The importance of parallel markets, peer-to-peer cryptocurrency trading, and the dark web in alleviating the de facto violence that governments and financial regulators perpetrate against the poor and everyday people trying to conduct business peacefully and maintain economic viability is not frequently mentioned in mainstream media.Many people in India are now in financial danger due to a plague of bank closures, withdrawal restrictions, and cash shortages. Utilizing cryptocurrencies is one method to maintain value in such a situation, but even this requires caution since Indian banking users have had to learn how to conceal the fact that their transactions involve cryptocurrencies in order to escape financial repression. While the RBI's decision to reverse its crypto ban may help to ease some of the pressure in this area, nations like Lebanon, where international transfers are restricted and the state-mandated exchange rate effectively deducts 40% from customer withdrawals, demonstrate that bitcoin has been a safe haven compared to government volatility and that parallel markets can flourish despite laws.

5.4. Banking Frauds under Indian Banking System

The foundation of the Indian economy is banks. The banking industry relies heavily on cash, making it particularly vulnerable to fraud. Fraudsters are changing as new technology becomes more prevalent. The Indian Banking System has experienced several scams, whether they include technological frauds or conventional loan mortgage frauds. (As in the Nirav Modi scam)

It is deemed immoral or unlawful for a person or group to seek to get property illegally or to obtain money from a bank. It covers a wide range, from small-scale cheque theft to major credit card skimmer. As well as impersonating a bank or other financial organization in order to potentially gain money, assets, or any other properties possessed by depositors.

Frauds occur when there is no proper mechanism in place. The banks lacks control over the use of money, and it is not checked by the fiscal's end. Proper documentation lacks. Banks frequently lack the technical knowledge necessary to assess a project. Due to a lack of industry expertise among bankers, initiatives are not being evaluated by a third party. The project report is often completed by the bank's investment banking division when the concerned bank takes part in the financing. There is a very obvious conflict of interest with this system. One of the main causes of the rise in frauds has been revealed to be corruption among bank employees.

Practice of name lending is common in India. Bank risk and credit analyst teams do not challenge the relationship, and fail to complete the background checks and ask right questions. In contrast to loans and advances, balance sheet lines like guarantees have revealed that banks have a considerably laxer approach for approving them items.The RBI has interconnected databases and information systems to improve fraud monitoring and detection. By January 2021, it is anticipated that NBFCs' online fraud reporting systems and SCBs' CFR portal with enhanced capabilities would be active.

5.5. Indian Banks Review Leak After Details of 1.3 Million Cards Surface on Dark Web.[2] (Nair, 01 Nov 2019)

Indian banks have begun reviewing stolen card data that was recently leaked on the dark web for sale. The RBI had sent instructions to the banks after the leak was reported on Oct. 29, the people said on the condition of anonymity as details are not public yet. Details of more than 1.3 million cards issued by Indian banks were put on a website called Joker Stash, a notorious marketplace for cybercriminals to buy and sell card details, on the dark web. Uploaded information called "card dumps" can lead to cloning of credit or debit cards, allowing hackers to withdraw money from ATMs anywhere in the world. Technology website ZDNet first reported the leak hours after security researchers at the Singapore-based Group-IB detected it.

The article claims that the card information was being sold for $100 per item, putting the entire tranche at $130 million. The card information is no longer accessible on Joker Stash, according to Dilip Asbe, managing director and chief executive officer of National Payments Corporation of India, who spoke to BloombergQuint. "Now that the card details are out in the public, banks should be proactive and immediately deactivate all these cards, and then issue new cards," Prashant Mali, advocate and cyber lawyer, said. "Since the leaked details have the serial numbers, it is fairly easy for the banks to swiftly block these cards from usage."

This is the second major breach of card details of Indian customers in three years. After malware was placed in the State Bank of India's ATM network in October 2016, hackers were able to steal the data from around 32 lakh credit and debit cards.

6/ CURRENT SCENARIO OF DARK WEB -

"The Notorious market on the Dark Web", This is well known that Dark Web is the place for the highest bidder for the data buyer. The highest buyer has all the access to the data. Since the starting the online payments the data of cards (Debit and Credit) is stored on the web. Therefore, making the consumers vulnerable to fraud. There have emerged many new techniques of online frauds such as obtaining OTPs and E-Mail frauds. This leads to theft of money from the accounts. Now these financial details are obtained from many ways. These methods include 'phishing', 'skimming', malware and data leaks. Dark Web has very deep roots on the internet, it has numerous sources. The normal web browser contains around 4.5 billion websites, the Dark Web is thousand times larger. The Data, like usernames, passwords, banking credentials are the most asked for on the Dark Web.

6.1. Sells in Dark Web Markets in 2020

60% of the Information for Sale on the Dark Web Can Damage a Business

When formulating their cyber security strategy, the majority of IT professionals immediately take Dark Web dangers like stolen password data or other types of ransomware into account. However, the Dark Web makes it simple to find a variety of information that might harm enterprises, such as:

- Payment Card Information – Stolen or skimmed credit card data (and the software to capture it) is a perennial bestseller.
- Research Data – Medical research including information about new drugs and therapies is a hot commodity, especially COVID-19 data.[3] (AGENT, July 02, 2020)
- Trade Secrets & Formulas – Proprietary manufacturing information is both popular and easy to sell.
- Blueprints & Security Plans– From buildings to networks, all kinds of schematics and planning data is useful for bad actors.
- Medical Records – They're especially popular for blackmail and spearfishing ammunition.
- Financial Records – This multipurpose data is desirable for money laundering, blackmail, spearfishing, and identity theft.[4] (SOCRadar, March 11, 2021)
- Intelligence Reports – International espionage is a big market that's high-danger but high-reward.
- Government Secrets – Investigations, communication, programs, budgets, documents, and more sell fast.[5] (AGENT, What Sells in Dark Web Markets in 2020?, July 02, 2020)

"As a Service" Offerings Are the New "It" Category

Why just sell your password when you can keep making money by selling your services? "As a Service" transactions on the Dark Web are proliferating, and that creates big dangers for every company.[6] (AGENT, What Sells in Dark Web Markets in 2020?, July 02, 2020) Malicious insiders can make a fortune by selling their services to support other cybercrimes if they have access to specialized data, systems, or organizations.

Dark Web markets aren't just focused on selling data, passwords, and hacking services.[7] (AGENT, What Sells in Dark Web Markets in 2020?, July 02, 2020) Additionally, there is a thriving market for illicit, hazardous, and repulsive products including firearms, drugs, stolen goods, plundered artifacts, illegal goods, endangered animals, child labour, and child pornography in addition to some seemingly innocent but odd items.

7. TOR (THE ONION RING): ANONYMITY NETWORK

Tor is a free and open source program that enables anonymous communication by routing internet traffic over a free, volunteer, global overlay network with more than 7,000 relays. It is more challenging to link a user's online activities, such as "visits to websites, online posts, instant chats, and other communication forms," when they utilize Tor."[8] Tor's intended use is to protect the personal privacy of its users, as well as their freedom and ability to conduct confidential communication by keeping their Internet activities unmonitored.[9] (Wallet, May 17, 2021). The TOR browser uses different relays to hide the IP address. While using the TOR, no one can trace the activity and the digital footprint of yours, and instead of real IP address, an explicit identity will be shown.

Encryption at Stack of networking protocols' application layer, which is layered like the onion's layers is employed to create onion routing.[10] (Valentine, 2016) Tor transfers the data over a virtual circuit while repeatedly encrypting it, including the IP address of the next node's destination comprising successive, random-selection Tor relays.[11] (TAYLOR, AUGUST 25, 2020) Each relay decrypts a layer of encryption to reveal the next relay in the circuit to pass the remaining encrypted data on to it.[12] (KrebsonSecurity, February 10, 2020) Without disclosing or being aware of the originating The final relay, using the target's IP address, decrypts the innermost layer of encryption and delivers the original data. So because of communication's path was partially obscured at every point along the Tor circuit, this method eliminates any single place where the communicating associate may be identified by network monitoring, which depends on knowing the communication's origin and destination.

7.1. TOR Operating Mechanism and Online Service Protocol

Tor Browser routes all your web traffic through the Tor network, anonymizing it. As the images below illustrate, Tor consists of a three-layer proxy, like layers of an onion (hence Tor's onion logo).[13] (CSO, 2018) Tor Browser connects at random to one of the publicly listed entry nodes, bounces that traffic through a randomly selected middle relay, and finally spits out your traffic through[14] (Porup, 2019) the third and final exit node.

Figure 1.
Source: Porup, CSO INDIA (2019)[15]

7.2. Working of TOR, Use of TOR

Step 1: As a result, don't be surprised if Google or another service greets you in a foreign tongue.[16] (Porup, What is the Tor Browser? And how it can help protect your identity, 15 OCTOBER 2019) These services look at your IP address and guesstimate your country and language, but when using Tor, you will often appear to be in a physical location halfway around the world.[17] (Porup, What is the Tor Browser? And how it can help protect your identity, 15 OCTOBER 2019)

Figure 2.
Source: Porup, CSO INDIA (2019)[18]

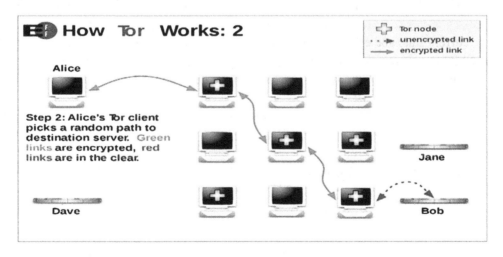

Step 2: If you live in a regime that blocks Tor or need to access a web service that blocks Tor, you can also configure Tor Browser to use bridges. Unlike Tor's entry and exit nodes, bridge IP addresses are not publicly listed, making it difficult for web services, or governments, to blacklist those IP addresses.[19] (Secur, September 30, 2020)

Figure 3.
Source: Foundation (2005)[20]

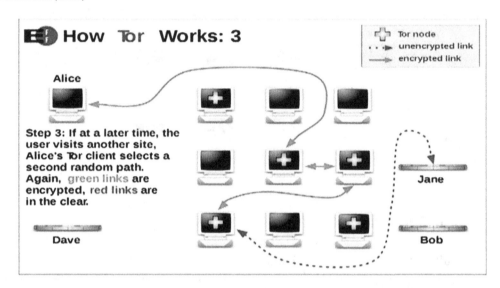

Step 3: The Tor network routes TCP traffic of all kinds but is optimized for web browsing. Tor does not support UDP, so don't try to torrent free software ISOs, as it won't work.[21] (Porup, What is the Tor Browser? And how it can help protect your identity, 15 OCTOBER 2019)

8. SEVEN RECENT BANKING FRAUDS THAT HAVE SHOCKED INDIA

A look at the current state and effects of the main financial scams, from the Nirav0Modi- PNB controversy to the PMC Bank problem. In the past two years, there have been a number of financial scams, and NPAs continue to be a problem despite the economy's decline.

Here are some major scandals:

Some examples: -

Triangulation/site cloning: Customers enter their card details on fraudulent shopping sites.[23] (GUDUP, 2016)These details are then misused.

Table 1. Table showing some major scandals in Indian Banking System (Panchal, 2019)

Date	Entity	Nature of Scandal	Status	Impact
February 2018	Punjab National Bank(PNB)- Nirav Modi	A handful of PNB banks staffers at Bradys House branch issued fake bank guarantees in excess of ₹13,8000 crore, over the years, aiding companies of two jewellery groups-led by diamond magnate Nirav Modi and his uncle Mehul Choksi. They received credit from overseas banks to fund their business/ imports. The CBI arrested eight PNB officials in connection with the case	The CBI has declared Nirav Modi and his brother Neeshal as offenders and is busy attaching their properties in India. Modi is in judicial custody in London (Wandsworth prison) after being arrested by Scotland Yard on an extradition warrant in March 2019. A trail is expected in May 2020	In March 2018, the RBI scrapped banking instruments such as the letter of undertaking. The government has also approved the Fugitive tve Economic Offenders Bill to stop economic offenders from escaping Indian law.
February 2018	Gitanjali Group	Mehul Choksi, Nirav Modi's uncle and owner of the group, is among those named in the PNB fraud	Choksi, who has an Antiguan citizenship, might be repatriated soon, as the Antigua government is set to revoke his citizenship	The gems and jewellery sector continues to be hurt by constrained access to bank finance since 2015, amid weaker demand
2013 to 2019	Bank NPAs	A mix of aggressive and carefree lending, alongside wilful loan defaults/ frauds and economic slowdown resulted in a rapid rise in bank NPAS. Not a single public or private sector bank has been spared	Gross NPAS of public sector banks rose nearly four times to ₹8.06 lakh crore in March 2019 from ₹1.30 crore in March 2014. Those for scheduled commercial banks rose to ₹9.49 lakh from ₹1.42 lakh crore in the same period	The impact after six years is acute: From operation concerns such as higher provisions for bad loans and lower profitability, there have been deeper problems like leadership crisis and shifts across several banks and an inability to lend in a major way
September 18	IL&FS	One of the largest shadow banking firms started defaulting early last year and a company which has multiple businesses and highest ratings was unable to pay its loans; 26 percent of the loan book consist of the top 10 group exposures. The rating agencies stated that the company's NPA had increased to ₹816 crore by the end of March 2018 from ₹410 crore during the previous year, a whopping 99 percent increase	Uday Kotak is chairman of IL&FS which has been reconstituted by the government. It is pursuing asset sales to realise funds and pay off the debt on its book. A debt of ₹1500 crore has been restructured. The group has a total of external debt of ₹94,216 crore.	The entire banking system witnessed the biggest liquidity freeze in India due to collapse of IL&FS. The liquidity shortage across banks and NBFCs has led to a situation where most NBFCs are now struggling for survival
March 2018	IDBI BANK	Former Aircel promoter C Sivasankaran, his son and companies controlled by them- Axcel Sunshine Ltd and WinWin D Oy-were accused by the CBI of defaulting on loans worth ₹600 crore from IDBI bank. Fifteen bank officials-including then MD and CEO Kishor Kharat, who worked when the loans were sanctioned(2010-2014) to Sivasankaran's companies-were named in FIR registered on a complaint from the Central Vigilance Commission	Sivasankaran who has denied any link with the fraud, has moved the Madras High Court against a lookout circular issued against him by the Bureau of Immigration	The government has indicated indirectly that it is not keen to provide additional capital to the loss-making IDBI Bank. The bank has said it requires ₹7,000 crore as regulatory requirements
September 2019	Laxmi Vilas Bank	Financial services firm Religare Finvest has accused the bank management of misappropriating ₹790 crore (which it kept as fixed deposit), in a report filed with the Economic Offences Wing	Police investigation is on. The bank management has said it will take appropriate legal measures	The RBI has intensified its "fit and proper" checks on the management of the bank and Indiabulls, with whom a merger is sought
September 2019	Punjab and Maharashtra Cooperative (PMC) Bank	Cooperative lender PMC is in midst of a scam for under-reporting NPAs. The managing director of the firm, in his confession letter, claimed that the bank had created new accounts to keep its loan to real estate firm HDIL as standard loans which had ideally become NPAS. The bank has lent nearly 70 percent capital to the developer which is against RBI norms	RBI and other agencies are investigating the matter.	Existing bank account holders are allowed to withdraw ₹10,000 per month from their account.

8.1. Internet Banking and Related Frauds

- While the majority of advance-related fraud was the majority (64 percent) fraud contributes for of the total value, approximately 65 percent of all Technology-related fraud cases were those that banks reported, including those that involved ATMs, credit/debit/prepaid cards, internet banking, and other payment methods.
- **Hacking:** Hackers/fraudsters obtain unauthorized access to the card management platform of banking system. Counterfeit cards are then issued for the purpose of money laundering.[24] (GUDUP, 2016)
- **Online fraud:** Card information is collected during an online transaction. Fraudsters then use the card details to conduct online transactions or adopt identities of others.
- **Lost/stolen card:** It describes the use of a lost card for unauthorized or criminal activities by the lawful account holder.
- **Skimming of debit cards:** When users utilize their cards at an ATM, a device or camera is installed to collect card details and PINs.
- **ATM fraud:** A fraudster uses a customer's card and/or PIN to access the machine and withdraw money.
- **Social engineering:** A thief may persuade a worker to let him access the premises, or he may persuade a victim over the phone or in writing that he is entitled to get certain information.
- **Dumpster diving:** When employees discard documents holding confidential information carelessly, they risk giving individuals who search the company's garbage access to sensitive information.
- **False pretenses:** Someone with the intent to steal corporate information can get a job with a cleaning company or other vendor specifically to gain legitimate access to the office building.[25] (analytics, 2019)
- **Computer viruses:** A business runs the danger of having its systems compromised by malicious software that is designed to gather data from the corporate servers with every internet click.

Statistics reflecting fraudulent activities in Indian Banking System

Table 2. Table showing a comparative picture of total number of fraud cases and amount involved as on March 31, 2013 for scheduled commercial banks, NBFCs, Urban Cooperative banks, and Financial Institutions [26] *(Chakrabarty, 2013)*

(No. of cases in absolute terms and amount involved in ` crore)

Category	No. of Cases	Amount Involved
Commercial Banks	169190	29910.12
NBFCs	935	154.78
UCBs	6345	1057.03
FIs	77	279.08
	176547	31401.01

Table 3. Table showing a year-wise break up of fraud cases reported by the banking sector together with the amount involved [27] (Chakrabarty, 2013)

(No. of cases in absolute terms and amount involved in ` crore)

Year	No. of cases	Total Amount
2009-10	24791	2037.81
2010-11	19827	3832.08
2011-12	14735	4491.54
2012-13	13293	8646.00
Total frauds reported as of March 2013	169190	29910.12

Table 4.

(No. of cases in absolute terms and amount involved in ` Crore)

Bank Group	No. of cases	% to Total Cases	Amount Involved	% to Total Amount
Nationalised Banks including SBI Group	29653	17.53	24828.01	83.01
Old Pvt. Sector Banks	2271	1.34	1707.71	5.71
New Pvt. Sector Banks	91060	53.82	2140.48	7.16
Sub Total (Private Banks)	93331	55.16	3848.19	12.87
Foreign Banks	46206	27.31	1233.92	4.12
Total	169190	100	29910.12	100

8.3. About 84,545 Bank Fraud Cases Reported During 2019-2020, Says RBI, in Reply to RTI[28]

Around 84,545 fraud cases - involving about Rs 1.85 lakh crore - were reported by scheduled commercial banks and select FIs during 2019-20, an RTI activist said, citing information received[29] (NewsClick, 27 Jul 2020)from the RBI. RTI Abhay Kolarkar, an activist, asserted that he addressed a number of banking-related queries to the RBI in Mid-2020 and that he recently obtained the responses.

The RBI said that during Fiscal Year 2019–20, Scheduled Commercial Banks and Selected FIs revealed a total of 84,545 frauds, with a total financial loss of Rs. 1,85,772.42 crore.[30] (NewsClick, 84,545 Bank Fraud Cases Worth Rs 1.85 Lakh Cr Reported During 2019-20, 27 Jul 2020) However, it should be highlighted that during FY 2019–20, SCBs and Select Financial Institutions reported a total of 2,668 frauds allegedly perpetrated by personnel, totaling Rs. 1,783.22 billion, the Reserve Bank Stated. The RTI also sought to know how many consumer complaints received by the RBI's 15 ombudsmen offices during April 1, 2019 to March 31, 2020.[31] (Newsclick, 27 Jul 2020). From 2019 July 1, through 2020 March, there were around 2,14,480 complaints. SBI got the most complaints—63,259—followed by HDFC bank, 18,764; ICICI bank, 14,582; Punjab National Bank, 12,469; and Axis bank, 12,214.

In response, the central bank stated that it has received 56,493 complaints between April 1 and June 30, 2019. The RTI query also sought information on number of branches exited by banks and those closed after merger during April 1, 2019 to March 31, 2020.[32] (IndiaTimes T. E., July 28, 2020). According to the RBI, there were 438 branches that were merged with other branches of the same bank in 2019–2020, including 130 branches of SBI, 62 branches of the Central Bank of India, 59 branches of Allahabad0Bank, and other branches. 194 branches in all, comprising 78 SBI branches and 25 other branches, were closed in 2019–20 of Fino0payments0Bank0limited.[33]

9. THE WORLD GOVERNMENT'S STAND ON THE DARK WEB

If we look at the regulations all around the globe, or even in India, there are very few laws to regulate the Dark Web. Bharat has no specific laws to deal with Cyber Violence. The amendment of 2008, of IT act, Sec. 66F deals with cyber terrorism. Section 66F is the sole law that recognises and covers any act performed with the purpose to undermine India's unity, integrity, security, or sovereignty. Now the Section 66 also deals with hacking, sending offensive messages, identity theft, punishment for cheating personation, cyber terrorism, etc.

When we take a closer look at the laws that are mention under the IT act, there is no specific mention to regulate the working of the Dark Web. The TOR browser leaves no trace of your digital footprint. This promotes more criminal activities all along. One of the major problems for the regulation of Dark Web is its encryption and anonymity. The encryption method and anonymity of the dark web present the greatest barrier to law enforcement and policymakers when trying to regulate it. Cyberterrorism is difficult to define as there is no single definition to define it, which makes it more difficult to find solutions of it. Strong rules and regulation for dark web are required to curb down the illegal activities on the web.

9.1. The Legal and Technological Framework on the Dark Web

Now the legal implications of the dark web are delicate and tricky in nature. While using the dark web itself is not illegal or unlawful in itself, but for the evident reasons, carrying the activities are of illegal nature. Now the legality of the Dark Web can be controversial. The legality may depend on country to country laws. When the legality comes to India, the government does not have any restrictions on its surfing. The political institution considers this as only surfing as part of the internet. But the problems arise when we come to accessing and downloading the content on the web. The restricted content becomes a problem when it is downloaded or accessed. India has no specific legislation to deal with Cyber terrorism and the financial crimes.

The Section 66F is the provision of Information Technology Act, 2000 deals with and covers any act committed with the intent to threaten unity, integrity, security or sovereignty of India. There is nowhere mention of using the Dark Web in this section. Because mere surfing does not violate the following points of the act and therefore does not comes under the ambit of this act. The section 66 and its subsections of the IT acts deal with hacking, sending offensive messages, punishment of identity theft, cheating, personation, cyber terrorism. The act deals with the broad topics and scopes in general. And there is no specific mention of the web.

The following guidelines are suggested for better improvement:

9.2. As a Result, the Following Guidelines Are Offered for the Early Detection of Scams

1) **Autonomous specialized cadre:** The administration can take into account creating a separate, autonomous cadre of officers, akin to the all India services, who have the finest monetary and legal knowledge to identify financial crimes and are able to conduct an efficient and timely inquiry into such schemes. The government may decide to create this cadre in the near future by lateral hiring a group of commercial bankers, RBI, and CBI personnel.

2) **Know your markets:** Each bank needs a specialized unit to evaluate the business or corporation receiving a loan as well as the macroeconomic climate of the relevant sector of the economy or market where goods are sold. Many Chinese-imported manufacturing enterprises in India were unable to begin their projects and create cash flow, which had an impact on the banks from whose loans were obtained.

3) **Internal rating agency:** Banks ought to create a capable internal rating agency that assesses expensive projects before approving loans. The rating company must adhere rigorously evaluate the project on the basis of business model/plan of project without being influenced by brand name or credit worthiness of the parent company, considering current macro-economic situation and exposure of the sector to the global economy. In case ratings of internal and external agencies are not similar then an investigation must be conducted to establish the causes for such differences. Also, bank should seek services of at least 2-3 independent auditors in evaluation of such projects so as to prevent chances of any possible collusion.

4) **Use of latest technology:** In order to ensure the effective implementation of the red flagged account (RFA) and early warning signals (EWS) framework recommended by the RBI, which would help in a better customer profiling by analyzing patterns of their exchanges, the banks should make use of the best IT systems and information analytics available today and rendering a near real time monitoring possible for banks. Also, we recommend that the Institute for Development and Research in Banking Technology (IDRBT) could consider incentivizing development of relevant software for commercial banks at affordable costs. This is vital to enhance their monitoring of suspicious and fraudulent transactions within the branches of their banks.

5) **Tracking unusual movement at the regional level:** The RBI may think about extending its monitoring ambit and scope, and should monitor the outlier movements of transactions at regional level on the lines of SEBI's circuit breaker, which might be effective in tracking the earliest possible signs of financial frauds.

6) **Severe Penalties for Third Parties:** The government ought to think about inspecting the role of third parties such as chartered accountants, advocates, auditors, and rating agencies that figure in accounts related to bank frauds, and put in place strict punitive measures for future deterrence. There is also a case to be made to question the certification/credentials of third parties like auditors to decide their competence in evaluating accounts containing potentially fraudulent entries.

7) **Strong legal protections against false financial reporting:** The present legislation can be strengthened in a number of areas to increase the responsibility of auditors with regard to their work.

    I.   **One of them might be tightening KYC standards.:** OECD regulations for trust and corporate service providers (TCSPs), which helped broaden responsibility for deceptive misconduct in these organization to include auditors and attorneys, can be used as a standard in this situation. Similar reporting of suspicious transactional actions is required of NBFCs in India, however due to the existing weakness of the legislation, this is not done efficiently. ii. The legislation against intentional default, which ought to be declared a crime, is another that may be tightened. Currently, it is a civil infraction in India but it is a criminal violation elsewhere.

II. **Ground intelligence assets:** Financial institutions should have some sort of intelligence collecting agency on hand that may be used to monitor borrower activity and assist the bank in assuring real-time compliance and early fraud identification. Banks should build up a specific fraud monitoring agency with highly qualified/trained personnel. A specialist investigative agency with knowledge from organizations like the CBI, RBI, SEBI, and commercial banks is also required.

8) **Dedicated department for handling fraud cases:** Every corporate branch of a PSB should have a specialized department with legal support that acts as a one point of contact investigative authorities and makes it simple to retrieve pertinent records.

9) **Financial literacy:** The employees frequently has to be trained on this topic because they frequently do not grasp the precise meaning of fraud. As a result, staff members should regularly get training sessions on best practices for early fraud detection and prevention from around the world. Regular e-modules with updates and downloadable e-certifications are possible.

10) **Transparent hiring and adequate compensation:** Corporate governance must be upheld to the highest standards by banks. The top management must establish standards and regulations for moral behavior throughout the organization and provide an example of zero tolerance for carelessness and dishonesty. In light of the functions and responsibilities of senior management, attention should be placed on a proper recruiting process at this level, with a preference for at least three years of service as a minimum and an accountability provision. Additionally, modifications to incentive programs are required to maintain a balance between short-term and long-term goals.

CONCLUSION

Even though aberrant behavior on the Dark Web has been the primary focus of this investigation, it is essential to keep in mind that this represents only a small portion of the content that can be found on the Dark Web as a whole. It's the equivalent of using fan fiction to symbolize the entirety of the internet.

The financial cost of frauds can be quite large when considering the likelihood of disruption to the market, financial institutions, and payment system as well as the impact of dark web crimes on organizations such as banks. In addition to undermining the economy's stability and integrity, frauds considerably erode consumers' faith in the economic system, which further exacerbates the problem. It could interfere with the ability of the central bank to supervise, it could bring down banks, and it could possibly lead to social unrest, political disturbance, and other unwelcome outcomes. As a result of recent advancements in technology, financial institutions are increasingly more susceptible to fraud. The paper focuses mostly on scams perpetrated by financial institutions and the currency industry, as well as on money laundering, financial crimes, hacking, one-time passcodes, and other related topics. Despite this, it is important to recognize the numerous arenas in which the Dark Web serves as a catalyst for other types of criminal activity. The trafficking of people, the selling of drugs and illicit weapons, and most significantly, the illegal sale of personal information, all take place over the internet. As was mentioned previously, the data is the new key to unlock new sorts of criminal activity, or what might be called modern-day warfare. The laws pertaining to information technology that govern the operation of this environment and put a stop to the crimes of today.

REFERENCES

Agent. (2020). What Sells in Dark Web Markets in 2020? *AGENT*, 3.

Chakrabarty, K. C. (2013). *Frauds in the Banking Sector: Causes, Concerns and Cures.* Delhi: Reserve Bank of India (RBI Bulletin).

Chaum, D. (1981, Feb). *Untraceable electronic mail, return addresses, and digital pseudonyms.* Retrieved from Digital Library: https://dl.acm.org/doi/10.1145/358549.358563

CSO. (2018). What is the Tor Browser? How it works and how it can help you protect your identity online. *CSO*, 1-8.

Dasgupta, B. (2020). Credit, debit card data of half a million Indians up for sale on dark web. *Hindustan Times*, 1-2.

Foundation, E. F. (2005). *Torproject.* Retrieved from Torproject: https://www.torproject.org/about/overview.html.en

Ganguly, S. (2019). India Loses $18.5 Bn Due To Illegal Business Done Over Darknet. *Inc42*, 1-2.

Gudup, M. S. (2016). The study of frauds and safety in e-banking. *NIL: Anveshana's International Journal of Research in Regional Studies, Law, Social Sciences.*

IndiaTimes. (2020a, Dec. 9). Data of 70 lakh Indian cardholders leaked on dark web. *The Economic Times(CIO) IndiaTimes.*

IndiaTimes. (2020b, July 28). About 84,545 bank fraud cases reported during 2019-2020, says RBI, in reply. *The Economic Times(BFSI) IndiaTimes*, 1-2.

KrebsonSecurity. (2020). U.S. Charges 4 Chinese Military Officers in 2017 Equifax Hack. *krebsonsecurity*, 1-6.

Nair, A. R. (2019). ndian Banks Review Leak After Details Of 1.3 Million Cards Surface On Dark Web . *Bloomberg (bqprime)*, 1-2.

News, B. (2021). 10 crore Indians' card data selling on Dark Web. *BFSI.com(from The Economic Times)*, 1-3.

News, C. (2020). Data of 70 lakh Indian cardholders leaked on dark web. *CIO.Com(From Economic Times)*, 1-2.

NewsClick. (2020). 84,545 Bank Fraud Cases Worth Rs 1.85 Lakh Cr Reported During 2019-20. *NewsClick*, 1-2.

Porup, J. (2019). What is the Tor Browser? And how it can help protect your identity. *CSO INDIA*, 2-7.

Salil Panchal, P. S. (2019). *Seven recent banking frauds that have rocked India*. Retrieved from Forbes India: https://www.forbesindia.com/article/leaderboard/seven-recent-banking-frauds-that-have-rocked-india/55613/1

Secur. (2020). Understanding How To Use Tor. *Secur*, 2-6.

SOCRadar. (2021). Under the Spotlight: Most Popular Dark Web Marketplaces (DWMs). *SOCRadar(Your Eyes Beyond)*, 2.

Taylor, C. (2020). Tor Browser. *CyberHoot*, 1-2.

Valentine. (2016). Tor Explained-ish. *Anonymity*, 1-2.

Wallet, B. (2021). We are donating to Tor! *blockwallet.medium*, 1-3.

ENDNOTES

[1] The news source updated on FEB 07, 2020 11:55 PM IST *available at:* https://www.hindustantimes.com/india-news/credit-debit-card-data-of-460k-indians-up-for-sale-on-dark-web/story-qUjfpRK-dHPk9raKSVq4NgP.html (Visited on March 12, 2021 at 9:25 PM IST)

[2] The news last updated on NOV 01, 2019 1:07 PM IST *available at:* https://www.bloombergquint.com/business/indian-banks-review-leak-after-details-of-13-million-cards-surface-on-dark-web (Visited on March 12, 2021 at 11:00 PM IST)

[3] https://www.idagent.com/blog/what-sells-in-dark-web-markets-in-2020/

[4] https://socradar.io/under-the-spotlight-most-popular-dark-web-marketplaces-dwms/

[5] Ibid

[6] https://www.idagent.com/blog/what-sells-in-dark-web-markets-in-2020/

[7] Ibid

[8] https://www.omertadigital.com/blogs/post/mask-your-internet-usage-configuring-tor-to-use-with-signal-web-browser/

[9] https://blockwallet.medium.com/we-are-donating-to-tor-b977d52a320a

[10] https://0x00sec.org/t/anonymity-tor-explained-ish/739

[11] https://cyberhoot.com/cybrary/tor-browser/

[12] https://krebsonsecurity.com/2020/02/u-s-charges-4-chinese-military-officers-in-2017-equifax-hack/

[13] https://www2.cso.com.au/article/643723/what-tor-browser-how-it-works-how-it-can-help-protect-your-identity-online/

[14] https://www.csoonline.com/article/3287653/what-is-the-tor-browser-how-it-works-and-how-it-can-help-you-protect-your-identity-online.html

[15] https://images.idgesg.net/images/article/2018/07/how_tor_works_1-100763523-orig.jpg

[16] https://www.csoonline.com/article/3287653/what-is-the-tor-browser-how-it-works-and-how-it-can-help-you-protect-your-identity-online.html

[17] Ibid

[18] https://images.idgesg.net/images/article/2018/07/tor-2-100763518-orig.jpg

[19] https://www.secur.cc/understanding-how-to-use-tor/

[20] https://upload.wikimedia.org/wikipedia/commons/a/a1/How_Tor_Works_3.svg

21   https://www.csoonline.com/article/3287653/what-is-the-tor-browser-how-it-works-and-how-it-can-help-you-protect-your-identity-online.html

22   The source published on FORBES INDIA dated Oct 7, 2019 12:38:47 PM IST *available at*: https://www.forbesindia.com/article/leaderboard/seven-recent-banking-frauds-that-have-rocked-india/55613/1 (Visited on March 13, 2021 at 10:00 AM IST)

23   http://publications.anveshanaindia.com/wp-content/uploads/2016/09/THE-STUDY-OF-FRAUDS-AND-SAFETY-IN-E-BANKING.pdf

24   Ibid

25   https://issuu.com/chmanalytics/docs/types_of_banking_frauds_in_india.pp

26   The Reserve Bank of India: https://m.rbi.org.in//scripts/bs_viewbulletin.aspx?id=14351 (Visited on March 13, 2021 at 11:00 AM IST)

27   The Reserve Bank of India: https://m.rbi.org.in//scripts/bs_viewbulletin.aspx?id=14351 (Visited on March 13, 2021 at 11:11 AM IST)

28   The news updated on DEC 09, 2020 16:16 IST *available at*: https://cio.economictimes.indiatimes.com/news/digital-security/data-of-70-lakh-indian-cardholders-leaked-on-dark-web/79643154 (Visited on March 12, 2021 at 10:45 PM IST)

29   https://www.newsclick.in/84545-bank-fraud-cases-worth-Rs-1.85-lakh-Cr-reported-2019-20-RBI

30   https://www.newsclick.in/84545-bank-fraud-cases-worth-Rs-1.85-lakh-Cr-reported-2019-20-RBI

31   Ibid

32   https://bfsi.economictimes.indiatimes.com/news/banking/about-84545-bank-fraud-cases-reported-during-2019-2020-says-rbi-in-reply-to-rti/77212770/

33   https://www.moneycontrol.com/news/

Chapter 16
Digital Era in Papua New Guinea (PNG):
Novel Strategies of the Telecom Service Provider Companies

Arun Kumar Singh

Papua New Guinea University of Technology, Papua New Guinea

ABSTRACT

A revolution in wireless communication refers to a significant advancement or breakthrough in the field of wireless communication technology. This can include the introduction of new technologies, the development of faster and more efficient communication methods, and the widespread adoption of wireless communication in various industries and sectors. One example of a revolution in wireless communication is the development of 5G technology. 5G, or fifth-generation wireless technology, promises faster data speeds, lower latency, and improved network capacity compared to previous generations of wireless technology. This is expected to enable a wide range of new applications and use cases, such as the internet of things (IoT), autonomous vehicles, and virtual reality. Overall, the revolution in wireless communication has led to significant advancements in the way we live, work, and communicate, and is expected to continue to shape the future of communication. In this chapter, the authors discuss the services and the quality with basic comparison between the different telecom companies.

INTRODUCTION

Papua New Guinea is a country located in the southwestern Pacific Ocean, comprising the eastern half of the island of New Guinea and numerous smaller islands. It is the world's second-largest island country, and the largest in the Oceania region. The country has a diverse population, with over 800 indigenous languages spoken, and a mix of traditional and modern cultures. The official languages are English and TokPisin. Papua New Guinea is rich in natural resources, including minerals, timber, and oil. Its economy is heavily dependent on the export of these resources, particularly gold and copper. Agriculture is also

DOI: 10.4018/978-1-6684-8953-6.ch016

an important sector, with the majority of the population engaged in subsistence farming. The country has a diverse geography, ranging from tropical forests to snow-capped mountains (R Anand Kumar et al., 2022). It is home to a wide variety of plant and animal species, many of which are found nowhere else in the world. Papua New Guinea is also known for its rich cultural heritage, with traditional customs and practices still widely practiced today.

There are several telecommunications service providers companies in Papua New Guinea. Some of the major ones include:

1. Bmobile-Vodafone: This is a joint venture between Vodafone and the state-owned telecommunications company, Bmobile. They offer a range of services including mobile phone services, internet, and fixed-line services.
2. Digicel: This is a regional telecommunications company that operates in several countries in the Pacific and Caribbean regions. They offer mobile phone services, internet, and fixed-line services in Papua New Guinea.
3. Telikom PNG: This is the state-owned telecommunications company in Papua New Guinea. They offer a range of services including fixed-line services, internet, and mobile phone services.
4. Telikom PNG Wireless: This is a subsidiary of Telikom PNG that offers wireless services such as 3G and 4G internet.
5. DataCo: This is a state-owned company that manages and regulates the country's telecommunications infrastructure. They are responsible for the operation and maintenance of the national fiber-optic network and international gateways.

These providers also offer services such as data center, cloud computing, and other enterprise services. With the increasing use of internet and mobile services, the demand for telecom services is expected to grow in the future.

Telecommunication is – according to Article 1.3 of the International Telecommunication Union´s (ITU) Radio Regulations (RR) – defined as "Any transmission, emission or reception of signs, signals, writings, images and sounds or intelligence of any nature by wire, radio, optical or other electromagnetic systems." This definition is also identical to those contained in the Annex to the Constitution and Convention of the International Telecommunication Union (Geneva, 1992).Telecommunication is the transmission of information over a distance, typically via electronic means. It is the process of sending, receiving, and processing information using various technologies such as telephone, radio, television, and the internet. Telecommunication technologies include a wide range of devices and systems, such as telephones, cell phones, satellite systems, and fiber-optic networks. These technologies have revolutionized the way people communicate, allowing for instant and seamless communication across the globe. Telecommunication is a vital part of modern society and has a significant impact on various industries such as business, education, healthcare, and entertainment. It has enabled new forms of communication and has made it possible for people to stay connected with each other regardless of their location. Telecommunication also plays a critical role in the development of new technologies such as the Internet of Things (IoT) and 5G networks (Singh et al., 2022), which have the potential to bring about a new level of automation and connectivity to various industries (Holzinger et al., 2014).

KEY CONCEPTS OF TELECOMMUNICATIONS:

Telecommunications

- Transmission: The process of sending information from one location to another, typically via electronic means such as telephone, radio, television, or the internet.
- Network: A system of interconnected devices, such as telephones, computers, and servers, that allows for the transmission of information.
- Protocols: Standards and guidelines that govern the transmission of information over a network, such as the Transmission Control Protocol (TCP) and the Internet Protocol (IP).
- Bandwidth: The amount of data that can be transmitted over a network in a given period of time, typically measured in bits per second (bps).
- Frequency: The number of oscillations or cycles of a wave per unit of time, typically measured in hertz (Hz).
- Signal: An electrical or electromagnetic wave that carries information over a network.
- Modulation: The process of varying a signal's characteristics, such as amplitude, frequency, or phase, to carry information.
- Multiplexing: The process of combining multiple signals into one for transmission over a network.
- Coding: The process of converting information into a format suitable for transmission over a network.
- Security: Measures taken to protect information transmitted over a network from unauthorized access or interference.

These concepts are fundamental to the operation and design of telecommunications systems and networks, and are critical to understanding the underlying technology and infrastructure that enables modern communication (Singh, 2017).

Telecommunication Network

Telecommunication networks are critical to modern society, enabling seamless and instantaneous communication, connecting people and organizations, and enabling the development of new technologies and services. Telecom companies are building and expanding their networks to keep up with the increasing demand for internet and mobile services, with the advent of new technologies like 5G and IoT, the network is expected to be more complex and sophisticated in the future. A communications network is a collection of transmitters, receivers, and communications channels that send messages to one another. Some digital communications networks contain one or more routers that work together to transmit information to the correct user. An analog communications network consists of one or more switches that establish a connection between two or more users (Jordan & Mitchell, 2015, p 255-260). For both types of network, repeaters may be necessary to amplify or recreate the signal when it is being transmitted over long distances. This is to combat attenuation that can render the signal indistinguishable from the noise. Another advantage of digital systems over analog is that their output is easier to store in memory, i.e. two voltage states (high and low) are easier to store than a continuous range of states.

Communication Channels

In the telecommunications industry, communication channels refer to the different methods and mediums through which information is transmitted between devices and networks. Some common communication channels in the telecommunications industry include:

- Circuit-switched: A communication channel in which a dedicated connection is established between two devices for the duration of the communication. Examples include traditional telephone networks and PSTN (Public Switched Telephone Network).
- Packet-switched: A communication channel in which information is broken into small packets and transmitted over a shared network. Examples include the internet and mobile data networks.
- Cellular: A communication channel that uses radio waves to transmit information between mobile devices and cellular networks. Examples include 2G, 3G, 4G, and 5G cellular networks.
- Satellite: A communication channel that uses satellites to transmit information between devices on the ground and in space. Examples include satellite phones, satellite internet, and satellite television.
- Optical: A communication channel that uses light waves to transmit information over fiber-optic cables. Examples include FTTx (Fiber to the x), which refers to the installation of fiber-optic cables to residential and business locations.
- Radio: A communication channel that uses radio waves to transmit information over the airwaves. Examples include traditional radio, WiFi, and WiMAX (Worldwide Interoperability for Microwave Access)
- Hybrid: A combination of different communication channels, such as circuit-switched and packet-switched, or cellular and satellite.

Telecommunication companies use a variety of communication channels to provide services to their customers, and the choice of channel can have a significant impact on the quality, speed, and cost of the service. The telecom industry is constantly evolving, and new technologies and channels are being developed to improve the efficiency and capabilities of communication systems.

Modulation

Modulation is the process of varying one or more characteristics of a signal, such as amplitude, frequency, or phase, to carry information. Modulation is used in telecommunications to convert a baseband signal, which is a signal with a limited frequency range, into a passband signal, which is a signal that can be transmitted over a wider frequency range (Naim & Malik, 2022). There are different types of modulation techniques, each with their own advantages and disadvantages. Some common types of modulation include:

- Amplitude Modulation (AM): The process of varying the amplitude of a carrier signal to transmit information. AM is used in traditional radio broadcasting.
- Frequency Modulation (FM): The process of varying the frequency of a carrier signal to transmit information. FM is used in FM radio and some forms of wireless communication.
- Phase Modulation (PM): The process of varying the phase of a carrier signal to transmit information. PM is used in some forms of wireless communication, such as Phase Shift Keying (PSK)

- Quadrature Amplitude Modulation (QAM): A digital modulation scheme that combines amplitude and phase modulation to transmit multiple bits of information with each symbol. QAM is used in digital television and digital subscriber line (DSL) internet.
- Orthogonal Frequency-Division Multiplexing (OFDM): A digital modulation scheme that divides a high-bandwidth signal into multiple narrowband subcarriers, each of which can be modulated independently. OFDM is used in digital television, wireless local area networks (WLANs) and 4G mobile networks.

Modulation is a crucial process in telecommunications, as it allows for the efficient and reliable transmission of information over a distance. The choice of modulation technique depends on the specific requirements of the application and the characteristics of the communication channel (Le Cun et al., 2015).

Factsheet of Telecom Companies in Papua New Guinea

Mobile Phone Companies or Operators in Papua New Guinea (Source: https://tech.pngfacts.com/2018/04/mobile-phone-companies-or-operators-in.html)

There are three Mobile Phone Companies or operators in Papua New Guinea (PNG). These companies are Digicel, Bmobile-Vodafone and Telikom PNG. Below is the description of each of the companies.

Bmobile-Vodafone

Bemobile Limited is a 100% Government of Papua New Guinea owned company since November 2016, through Kumul Consolidated Holdings (KCH) and has been operating in PNG since 1997. They are Papua New Guinea's very own and first-ever mobile carrier with operations in Papua New Guinea and Solomon Islands (since 2009) In 2014, Bemobile Limited partnered with the world's largest mobile operator, Vodafone. The new entity, bmobile-Vodafone's vision is to be the leading provider of mobile voice and data services in Papua New Guinea and the Solomon Islands. They now offer high-speed data, reliable voice and SMS across Papua New Guinea and the Solomon Islands. They footprint is growing rapidly and similarly their innovation of products into the market (Purchasing of electricity, Voluntary contribution to Superannuation, Insurance, Buying airline tickets) regardless of the type of handset that a customer owns.

Products and Services:

- Variety of Smart Phones
- Data and Voice calls
- Broadband internet
- Wifi Internet
- 3G/4G internet network

Cons: Their coverage is mainly in the major centers of the country. Rural areas are not covered.

Bmobile-Vodafone is the largest telecommunications service provider in Papua New Guinea. The company is a joint venture between Vodafone, one of the world's largest telecommunications companies, and the state-owned telecommunications company, Bmobile. Bmobile-Vodafone offers a range of services including mobile phone services, internet, and fixed-line services. They have a significant market share in the country, and their network coverage is extensive, reaching many remote and rural areas of the country. They also have a wide range of plans, services, and offers for both personal and business users.

Figure 1. Mobile coverage
Source: https://www.bmobile.com.pg/NetworkCoverage

MOBILE COVERAGE MAP

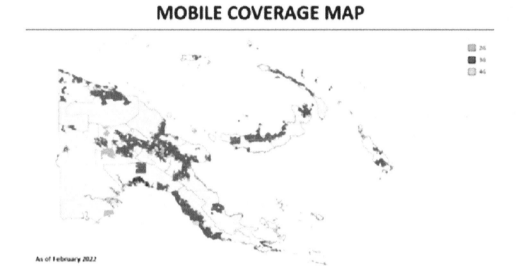

As of February 2022

Digicel

Digicel is a mobile phone network provider operating in 31 markets across the Caribbean, Central America, and Oceania regions. The company is owned by the Irish billionaire Denis O'Brien, is incorporated in Bermuda, and based in Jamaica. Digicel first entered Papua New Guinea in 2006. The company rolled out its services the following year 2007. Digicel is a telecommunications company that operates in several markets in the Caribbean, Central America, and Oceania regions. The company was founded in 2001 by Irish businessman Denis O'Brien, and it has grown to become one of the largest mobile phone service providers in the Caribbean and Central American regions. Digicel operates in over 30 markets, including Jamaica, Haiti, Trinidad and Tobago, and Papua New Guinea. The company offers a variety of services including mobile phone service, broadband, and television services. It has grown rapidly since its founding, and as of 2021, Digicel has over 13 million customers across its markets. Like most telecom companies (Singh, 2021), Digicel's financial performance can be influenced by a variety of factors such as economic conditions, competition, and regulations.

You can check their annual report or financial statement to get the specific data on their growth.

Product and Services-Digicel provides the following services:

- Broadband Internet
- Wifi
- Voice and data Services

- 3G/4G network
- Cover most parts of the country.

Cons: Many customers on the company's network have complained of poor customer service and disappearing data and credits. Their data rates are expensive compare their competitors. They also offer ridiculuscombos services from midnight 12 am - 6 am

Figure 2.
Source: ESG2021 Environmental Social Governance Report-Digicel

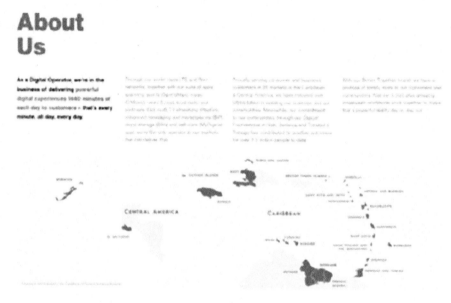

Figure 3.
Source: ESG2021 Environmental Social Governance Report-Digicel

Figure 4.
Source: https://www.digicelfoundation.org/png/en/home/programmes/about/our-achievement-date.html

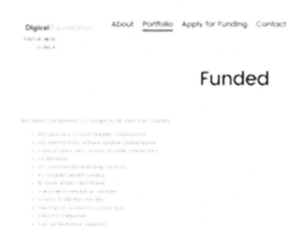

Telokom

Telikom PNG is the leading telecommunications company with a telecommunications system that is among the most modern in the South Pacific region. Telikom offers retail business of voice and data broadband services along with wholesale business of these voice and data services. Its network is entirely digital, extensive and a well established combination of microwave radio, satellite and intra-city optical fiber transmission systems that connect to a nationwide network through telephone exchanges and data switches while linking PNG worldwide with it Optical Ground Wire system and submarine cables through PPC-1 PIPE in Madang and APNG 2 at Ela Beach. With its proud history of service spanning over six decades, Telikom is into the business of providing advanced innovative communication solutions in PNG and clients in the region. New products are also available to help families and businesses alike have more reliable access to telephone and internet. The aim is to continue the increase in the number of homes connected to the national network, where fixed line local calls are still the cheapest option for staying in touch. Services currently available feature landline, Telikom mobile service, fixed wireless voice & data, Wimax broadband, VSAT, PABX, IPLAN, VPN, hotspot, and video conference. Telikom Mobile, a product of Telikom PNG provides mobile service with competitive call and data rates with coverage available to most urban centers around the country. In terms of mobile service, Telikom's shares in bemobile have been transferred to the Independent Public Business Corporation, thus bemobile is a separate entity from Telikom since 2008. Radio broadcaster Kalang Advertising is one or two subsidiary companies with Telikom staking 100 percent ownership and 54 percent share for PNG directories. Telikom business offices are established across the country to assist valued customers with sales for product and service maintenance along with a 24/7 Customer Care Call Center. (Source: https://www.telikompng.com.pg/index.php?option=com_content&view=category&layout=blog&id=79&Itemid=478)

Figure 5. Investment to date
Source: https://www.digicelfoundation.org/png/en/home/programmes/about/our-achievement-date.html

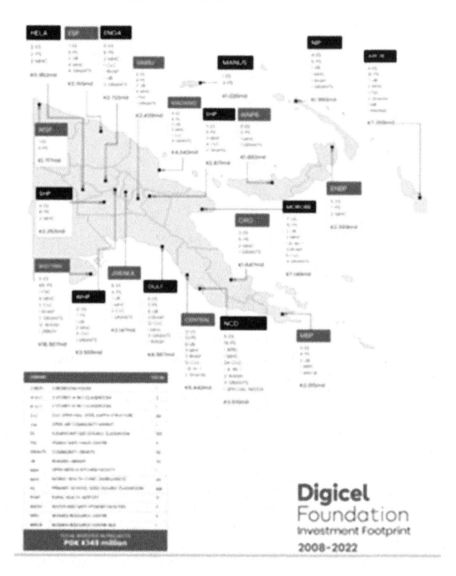

With its proud history of service spanning over six decades, Telikom is into the business of providing advanced innovative communication solutions in PNG and clients in the region. New products are also available to help families and businesses alike have more reliable access to telephone and internet. The aim is to continue the increase in the number of homes connected to the national network, where fixed line local calls are still the cheapest option for staying in touch. Services currently available feature landline, Telikom mobile service, fixed wireless voice & data, Wimax broadband, VSAT, PABX, IPLAN, VPN, hotspot, and video conference. Telikom Mobile, a product of Telikom PNG provides mobile service with competitive call and data rates with coverage available to most urban centers around the country.

In terms of mobile service (Singh et al., 2022), Telikom's shares in bemobile have been transferred to the Independent Public Business Corporation, thus bemobile is a separate entity from Telikom since 2008. Radio broadcaster Kalang Advertising is one or two subsidiary companies with Telikom staking 100 percent ownership and 54 percent share for PNG directories.

Cons: Telikom does not cover the rural areas.

Welcome To Broadband

Telikom PNG provides Internet services throughout the country through its high speed network infrastructure. This service is designated with an aim to enable as many Papua New Guinean Individuals, Businesses, and communities to connect and enjoy the super high speed internet at competitive rates. Telikom PNG's internet is accessible through Telikom's existing high speed network infrastructure, spawn across the country. Where there is coverage of broadband DSL network, WiMAX, VSAT, GSM, IPVPN and Lease Line, it is possible to connect to the Internet (Singh, 2019, 2021).

Landline Telephony (Fixed Line)

Telikom deploys Fixed Line telephone services throughout PNG via its extensive network infrastructure built around the country. This service provides both post-paid and prepaid telephone services. You can apply for a Residential Prepaid Fixed Line service or a Residential Post-paid service and or you can apply for a Business Post-paid service at your nearest Telikom Business Office. Once you have Fixed Line connected to your home or business premises, you can also apply for standard ADSL internet broadband connection via your copper cables so you can enjoy high speed internet up to 24mbps.

Draft Digital Government Plan 2023-2027 For Consultation (28th July 2022) (Source: https://www.ict.gov.pg/draft-digital-government-plan-2023-2027/)

The draft Digital Government Plan 2023 -2027 ('the Plan') is out for consultation. The draft Plan leads on from the ICT Roadmap 2018, the PNG Digital Transformation Policy 2020 and the Digital Government Act 2022.

The draft Plan proposes to digitize and automate all of public service and make services:

* fast, simple and clear for the people;
* transparent and efficient by government;
* increase government revenue generation through the uptake of SME and foreign direct investments; and
* grow the digital economy

The draft Plan recognizes the absence of appropriate ICT policy interventions within the Development Strategic Plan 2030 and therefore positions itself as a strategic delivery plan for the anticipated Medium Term Revenue Strategy 2023 – 2027 and to complement the delivery of the Medium-Term Development Plan 2023 – 2027.

The following documents are downloadable for reference:

* Draft Digital Government Plan 2023-2027
* Summary and Call for Feedback Paper
* Press Statement on the Release of the draft Plan for consultation.

Figure 6.
Source: https://www.nicta.gov.pg/2022/12/gpn-0-34/

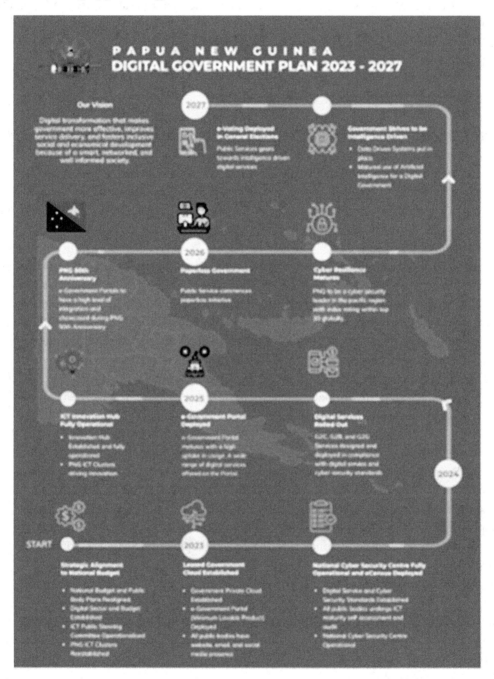

Retail Service Determination in relation to On-net and Offnet Calls-CONSULTATIVE PAPER (21 October, 2022 Consultative Papers, Public Inquiries, Public Notices)Official Notice: Public Notice - Public Inquiry Retail Service Determination (Source: nicta.gov.pg/2022/10/cp-0-25/)

Figure 7.
Source: https://www.nicta.gov.pg/2022/12/gpn-0-34/

Public Inquiry– Potential Retail Service Determination in Relation to Voice and Data Services – on-net/off-net Voice and Messaging Services. On 18 March 2022, the National Information and Communications Technology Authority (NICTA) commenced a Public Inquiry into a potential retail service determination in relation to voice and data services.

The terms of reference of the inquiry are to consider:

- whether or not a recommendation should be made to the Minister under section 159 of the National Information and Communications Technology Act 2009 (the Act) that:
  ◦ national voice services supplied by Digicel;
  ◦ mobile data services supplied by Digicel; and
  ◦ fixed data services supplied by Telikom.

should be subject to retail service determinations to control price levels, and, in the case of (a) to prohibit price discrimination between on-net and off-net calls; and, if so;

- the appropriate terms of such a retail service determination; and
- the extent to which those terms would meet the retail regulation criteria in section 158 of the Act.

Following the first phase of the Public Inquiry, and taking into account comments in submissions from operators and other interested parties, and having regard to new competitive entry into the market, NICTA decided not to proceed with any form of price capping for these services. However, the issues associated with price discrimination and differentials between on-net and offnet voice and messaging services were raised. The second phase of the Public Inquiry has now commenced into whether a draft retail service determination that

NICTA has prepared is appropriate to address the issues raised. A discussion paper for the purposes of Section 232 of the Act is available on NICTA's website (www.nicta.gov.pg) from Friday October 21, 2022. The public inquiry shall commence from that date and end in early by or before December 2022. Up to date information on the inquiry shall be available from NICTA's website. All written submissions should be submitted by email to: consultation.submission@nicta.gov.pg by close of business, Friday November 4, 2022. Copies of the submissions received will be published on NICTA's Public Register consistent with the requirements under subsection 229(3) of the Act. Any respondent that wishes to claim confidentiality over information that it submits should follow the procedures set out in the current guidelines on the submission of written comments to public consultations and public inquiries, which are also available from NICTA's Public Register at www.nicta.gov.pg

Corporate Plan 2020-2024

Papua New Guinea's Vision 2050 envisages a smart, healthy and wise society. Therefore, information and communication technology (ICT) is an enabler and a significant tool to realise this vision. Taking cue from this broad vision, the National Strategy for Responsible Sustainable Principles (STARS) and the Development Strategic Plan (2010-2030) and other succeeding plans were developed. The Corporate Plan 2020-2024 has been written to address changes and challenges posed by the rapid development in the ICT sector and its impact on our economy (Singh, 2017). It includes restrategizing and adding new dimensions to the Department's key functional areas of ICT policies and legislations, Digital Government

Technology Platforms, Digital Government Office Platform, Digital Government Transformation and challenges facing the Dissemination of Development Information to our communities. These activities will be further elaborated and expanded in the sections covering divisional and individual work plans, setting out specific output for a particular year, and providing the basis for assessment of Department's performance

Figure 8. Corporate plan

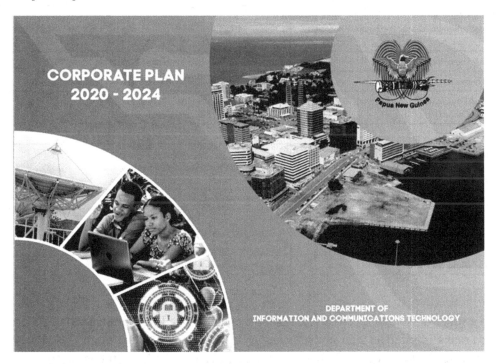

Telecommunication in Papua New Guinea (https://www.worlddata.info/oceania/papua-new-guinea/telecommunication.php#:~:text=Compared%20to%20the%20United%20States,average%20of%200.49%20per%20person.)

Compared to the United States, Papua New Guinea is massively lagging behind in the development of telecommunications. Under the country code +675, there were a total of 4.98 million connections in 2021. Among them were 4.82 million mobile phones, which corresponds to an average of 0.49 per person. In the US, this figure is 1.1 mobile phones per person. With about 5,006 webhosts, Papua New Guinea is below the world's average by population. At the end of 2019, 498 of these, or about 10 percent, were secured with SSL or comparable encryption.

Development of telephone and internet connections (https://www.worlddata.info/oceania/papua-new-guinea/telecommunication.php#:~:text=Compared%20to%20the%20United%20States,average%20of%200.49%20per%20person.)

Table 1. Quick facts of telecommunication in Papua New Guinea

Quick Facts	Papua New Guinea
Capital	Port Moresby
Land Area	462,840 sqkms
Current Weather	Maximum temperature: 88 °F Minimum temperature: 83 °F
Population (https://www.worldometers.info/world-population/papua-new-gui nea-population/)	9,379,475 as of Sunday, January 22, 2023
Languages (with %age of speakers, if available) (https://www.hcipom.gov.in/page/fact-sheet-on-papua-new-guine a/)	English (official language) Pidgin, Motu& Over 800 local languages
Religions (with %age, if available)	Christianity (Catholic, Anglicans, Baptists & Lutherans)
Currency Exchange rate with US$ & INR	Kina INR 1 = Kina 0.043 approx. US$ 1= Kina 3.52 approx.
GDP per capita (https://en.wikipedia.org/wiki/Economy_of_Papua_New_Guinea)	Decrease $2,742 (nominal, 2019 est.) Increase $3,983 (PPP, 2019 est.)
TLD	.pg
Fixed Telephone (https://knoema.com/atlas/Papua-New-Guinea/topics/Telecommuni cation/Telecomm-Services/Fixed-telephone-lines)	158,000 (2017)growing at an average annual rate of 7.38%
GSM Telephone(World bank data)	4,818,000 (2020)
Fixed Broadband (https://data.worldbank.org/indicator/IT.NET.BBND.P2?contextu al=default&locations=PG)	0.22 per 100 people (2020)
Internet Users (World bank data)	11% Population (2017)

With an average download speed of 11.11 Mbit/second for fixed-network broadband internet, Papua New Guinea ranks 143rd in an international comparison. The upload rate of only 2.8 Mbit/second was significantly lower (171st place). In mobile internet, i.e., on tablets and smartphones, Papua New Guinea comes 105th with a download speed of 17.85 Mbit/second. The upload speed of around 12 Mbit was enough for 49th place. The Speedtest Global Index published regularly by Ookla is based on several million individual measurements in October 2022 from 180 countries. The following diagrams show the development of the various telephone and internet connections as a percentage of the country's population. Values above 100 percent mean that, on average, every inhabitant has more than one connection.

Figure 9.
Source: https://www.worlddata.info/oceania/papua-new-guinea/telecommunication.php#:~:text=Compared%20to%20the%20
United%20States,average%20of%200.49%20per%20person

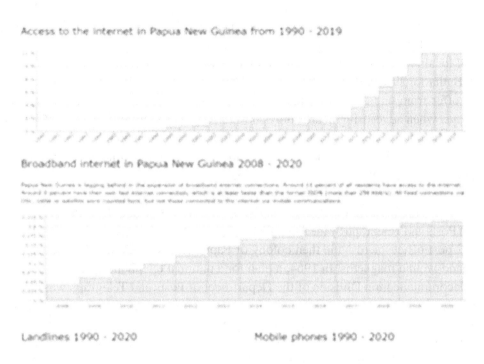

Figure 10.
Source: https://www.worlddata.info/oceania/papua-new-guinea/telecommunication.php#:~:text=Compared%20to%20the%20
United%20States,average%20of%200.49%20per%20person

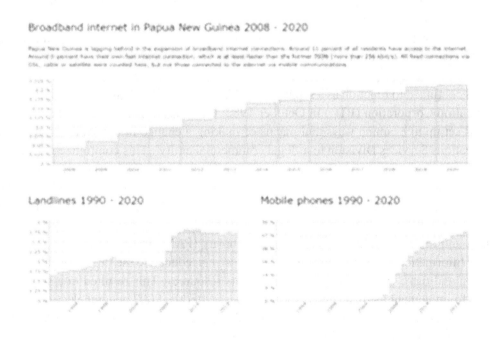

CONCLUSION

There was a time, when the only telephone service provider in Saudi Arabia was STC – Saudi Telecom Company. Those were days of costly local and international calls. The scenario suddenly changes with entry of UAE based Etisalat telecom operator through the name Mobily. International calls had become affordable and locals were also cheap. Having a mobile was easy for common man and gone were the long lines in Batha for sim card. The competition drove the call rates lower and lower and every few months there offer from one company and immediate counteroffer from the other telecom company. Those were days, when advertising boards only showed STC and Mobily. The entry of Zain was much advertised but it did not live up to its image. There was not much change in the market rates. Zain's connectivity and range still raises some questions. To know the best at any time, you can visit the website of companies and compare. We tried working on preparing a comparison for different service providers, but with everyday changing rates, it was hard to keep up to date.

The Department of Information & Communication Technology was initially established in 1955 as the Department of Posts and Telegraph by the Australian colonial administration. At this time, the Department consisted of 42 post offices across the then colony of Papua and New Guinea 17 telephone exchanges operated by hand-wound magnetos. In 1964, a plan for a national telephone system in PNG was drawn up when a Telecommunication Division of the Department of Posts and Telegraph was established and 'overseas' expert advice was sought from Australia. A telephone service was subsequently introduced. In 1973, the Department was reestablished as the Department of Information and Communication Services was established when the National Broadcasting Commission (NBC) was set up to take over the PNG branch of the Australian Broadcasting Commission. The NBC became the broadcasting arm of the department. This was a vital event in PNG's history. Given the very rugged topography and the isolation of many clans, radio played a crucial role in the dissemination of information throughout the land, using an extensive network of provincial radio stations. Radio has subsequently played a huge role in building a more cohesive society from what was then more than 1000 diverse tribes. After gaining independence from Australia in September 1975, the Department of Information and Communication Services became responsible for information services, communication policy, and research and development while the newly formed Department of Public Utilities took over the functions and the responsibilities of the Department of Posts and Telegraphs and became the Division of Postal and Telecommunication Services (DPTS). DPTS continued to function as a separate organization until it was incorporated as the Post and Telecommunication Corporation (PTC) in October 1982. On 9 September 1981 an executive steering committee was set up to examine ways and means of making a change in the status of the Postal and Telecommunications Services Division to a 'legal commercial entity'. This committee presented its report to the (then) National Executive Committee (NEC; effectively the Cabinet) on 16 December 1981 and the NEC gave approval to draft enabling legislation. The Post and Telecommunication Corporation Act 1982 was passed by the National Parliament on 15 February 1982. Due to a change in government policy in 1996, the PTC was split up and corporatized. The split saw the creation of Telikom PNG Ltd, Post PNG Ltd, and the PNG Telecommunications Authority (PANGTEL; now NICTA). In 1997, the Department of Information and Communication Services was reduced to the Office of Information and Communication and there were tighter constraints on its resources. This resulted in a situation where it was not able to implement its mandated responsibilities. After the 2002 general elections, however, a new government established the Department of Public Enterprises, Information and Development Corporation (DPEIDC). Its core functions included national information and communication policy, rural connectivity and development, and the integrated government information system. It was also required under the government's Medium Term Development Strategy (2005–10) to expand telecommunication infrastructure and services. With the re-establishment of the Ministry for Information and Communication Services in 2007, all matters relating to PANGTEL (now NICTA), NBC and the Office of Information and Communication were placed under its administration. On 13 August 2020, NEC renamed the Department to Department of Information and Communications Technology to which the Department maintains policy and service delivery oversight and coordination. The Department has come a long way since 1955. Under NEC Decision 252/2020, the Department is going through major reform and restructure with a specific focus on a Digital Government to ensure people access government services through Information & Communication Technology. (Source: https://www.ict.gov.pg/our-history/)

REFERENCES

Anand, Dinesh, Obaid, Malik, Sharma, Dumka, Singh, & Khatak. (2022). Securing e-Health application of cloud computing using hyperchaotic image encryption framework. *Computers and Electrical Engineering, 100*. doi:10.1016/j.compeleceng.2022.107860

Holzinger, A., Dehmer, M., & Jurisica, I. (2014). Knowledge discovery and interactive data mining in bioinformatics - state-of-the-art, future challenges and research direc-tions. *BMC Bioinformatics, 15*(S6), I1. doi:10.1186/1471-2105-15-S6-I1 PMID:25078282

Jordan, M. I., & Mitchell, T. M. (2015). Machine learning: Trends, perspectives, and prospects. *Science, 349*(6245), 255–260. doi:10.1126cience.aaa8415 PMID:26185243

Le Cun, Y., Bengio, Y., & Hinton, G. (2015). Deep learning. *Nature, 521*(7553), 436–444. doi:10.1038/nature14539 PMID:26017442

Naim, A., & Kautish, S. K. (Eds.). (2022). *Building a Brand Image Through Electronic Customer Relationship Management*. IGI Global., doi:10.4018/978-1-6684-5386-5

Naim & Praveen. (2022). *Competitive Trends and Technologies in Business Management*. doi:10.52305/VIXO9830

Python Machine Learning. (2020). *A Guide To Getting Started*. Built In.

Singh, A. K. (2017a). The active impact of human computer interaction (HCI) on economic, cultural and social life. *IIOAB Journal, 8*(2), 141-146. https://www.iioab.org/vol8n2

Singh, A. K. (2017b). Persona of social networking in computing and informatics era. *International Journal of Computer Science and Network Security, 17*(4), 95-101. http://search.ijcsns.org/07_book/2017_04.h

Singh, A. K. (2019). A Wireless Networks Flexible Adoptive Modulation and Coding Technique in advanced 4G LTE. *International Journal of Information Technology, 11*(1), 55-66. https://link.springer.com/article/10.1007/s41870-018-0173-5 doi:10.1007/s41870-018-0173-5

Singh, A. K. (2020). *Digital Era in the Kingdom of Saudi Arabia: Novel Strategies of the Telecom Service Providers Companies*. http://www.webology.org/issue.php?volume=1&issue=1&page=2 doi:10.14704/WEB/V17I1/a219

Singh, A. K. (2021). Machine Learning in OpenFlow Network: Comparative Analysis of DDoS Detection Techniques. *The International Arab Journal of Information Technology, 18*(2), 221-226. https://iajit.org/PDF/Vol%2018,%20No.%202/19667.pdf doi:10.34028/iajit/18/2/11

Singh, D. K., Sobti, R., Jain, A., & Malik, P. K. (2022). LoRa based intelligent soil and Irrigation Using Machine Learning", Security and Communication Networks, vol. weather condition monitoring with internet of things for precision agriculture in smart cities. *IET Communications, 16*, 604–618. doi:10.1049/cmu2.12352

Singh. (2017). Security and Management in Network: Security of Network Management versus Management of Network Security (SNM Vs MNS). *International Journal of Computer Science and Network Security, 17*(5), 166-173. http://search.ijcsns.org/07_book/2017_05.htm

Singh & Pandey. (2021). *IoT for Automation Clustering to Detect Power losses with Efficiency of Energy Consumption and survey of defense machinery against attacks.* CRC Press. https://www.routledge.com/Applied-Soft-Computing-and-Embedded-System-Applications-in-Solar-Energy/Pachauri-Pandey-Sharmu-Nautiyal-Ram/p/book/9780367625122

Singh. (2019a). An Intelligent Reallocation of Load for Cluster Cloud Environment. *International Journal of Innovative Technology and Exploring Engineering, 8*(8). https://www.ijitee.org/download/volume-8-issue-8/

Singh. (2019b). Texture-based Real-Time Character Extraction and Recognition in Natural Images. *International Journal of Innovative Technology and Exploring Engineering, 8*(8). https://www.ijitee.org/download/volume-8-issue-8/

Singh, Sobti, Malik, Shrestha, Singh, & Ghafoor. (2022). *IoT-Driven Model for Weather and Soil Conditions Based on Precision.* doi:10.1155/2022/7283975

Chapter 17
Crisis Management and Social Media Platforms:
A Review and Future Research Agenda

R. Selvakumar
https://orcid.org/0000-0003-2159-842X
SRM University, India

Vimal Babu
SRM University, India

ABSTRACT

Performing crisis management (CM) through social media platforms (SMP) is the modern way of handling crisis events. The chapter aims to identify core research on CM along SMP. By employing bibliometric network analysis, the authors aim to review published works in Scopus-indexed journals from the year 2019 to 2023. Scopus database and VOS (visualizing scientific landscapes) viewer have been combinedly used to identify the most influential journals, top-ranking countries, and institutions, most cited articles, most occurred keywords, and the pattern of authorship in CM along SMP publications. The present study undertakes a pioneering bibliometric analysis aimed at exploring scholarly publications on the field of CM facilitated through SMP. To the authors' knowledge, this work is the first study to use a bibliometric approach to research this area, thereby contributing to the nascent literature on the subject. The unique insights garnered from this analysis are expected to provide valuable guidance to researchers and scholars interested in this emerging field.

INTRODUCTION

In the era of globalization and digitalization, crises can occur anywhere and anytime, creating severe disruptions in the functioning of organizations. To mitigate the impact of crises, organizations need to have a well-planned and efficient crisis management strategy (Coombs, 2019). One of the critical components of modern crisis management is SMPs, which can act as a two-edged knife in times of crisis.

DOI: 10.4018/978-1-6684-8953-6.ch017

The major advantage of SMP is its capability in enabling the dissemination of information and offering a means for establishments to interact with their stakeholders.

Social media platforms become a vital part of disaster management strategies for most of organizations because of their capability to spread vital information faster and reach a wider audience. By utilizing the social media platforms nay organization can distribute real-time information and communicate with their stakeholder swiftly, which will help the organization to condense the misinformation and confusion during a crisis event. (Veil, Buehner, & Palenchar, 2011). However, social media can also exacerbate negative emotions and false information, leading to a deepening crisis. Recent studies have inquired into the significance of social media platforms in managing crises. As stated by Casero and Ripollés (2020), SMPs are an important element of CM, and organizations must establish competent approaches to utilize them. In addition, Hassankhani and Alidadi (2021) emphasized the significance of SMPs in emergency transmissions and recommends that organizations implement best practices for effective crisis management. Other studies, such as those by Sharifi and Azhdari (2021), Mak (2019), Song (2019), Pang (2021), Cai and Jiang (2021), and Chan (2021), have also contributed to our understanding of crisis management along SMP. However, research in this field is still fragmented thus makes it difficult to better understand the current state of the research area and to forge a path ahead in the leadership literature. The present study aims to contribute to the crisis leadership literature by providing an updated review of the latest crisis leadership articles and their findings. Thus, will advance the crisis leadership literature and offer a valuable theoretical guide for the researchers to further advance the literature.

LITERATURE REVIEW

A recent study by Stieglitz et al (2013) conducted on airline passengers found that the passengers who got updates regarding the crisis through social media platforms had more positive perceptions about the crisis management of the airline company than those who didn't receive crisis updates through the social media platforms. From this study, they found that the use of social media platforms at the time of crisis events can attract a positive perception of stakeholders about the crisis management strategy of an organization and it can increase the stakeholder's trust in the organization (Stieglitz & Dang-Xuan, 2013). Sharifi and Azhdari (2021) highlighted SMP's importance as an essential element in disaster management, while Mak (2019) identified the benefits and drawbacks of using SMPs at the time of crisis management. Song (2019) investigated how SMPs impact disaster communication and highly recommends that organizations make use of its benefits at the time of crisis management. Pang (2021) analyzed how Chinese organizations use SMPs in disaster management and identified the variables influencing their effectiveness. Cai and Jiang (2021) investigated the impact of SMPs in CM from the public point of view, while Chan (2021) evaluated SMP's role in disaster management of tourism industries.

CRISIS

The crisis is a complex phenomenon that requires an urgent response from various stakeholders. According to Coombs and Holladay (2019), Crisis is an occurrence or circumstance that poses a serious risk to people, groups, or society as a whole and necessitates rapid action to avert additional harm. Crises can take many forms, including natural disasters, economic downturns, health emergencies, and social upheavals. Crisis events, such as financial meltdowns, environmental disasters, and health epidemics, can have significant and far-reaching impacts on societies (Mishkin, 2011; Haines & Ebi, 2019; Wang et al., 2020). Understanding the underlying mechanisms and factors contributing to these crises is essential for effective crisis management and prevention. This research article reviews empirical evidence from multiple disciplines to provide a comprehensive overview of crisis phenomena, intending to hand out well grasp of the complexities of crises and their implications for society.

CRISIS MANAGEMENT

Crisis management refers to the procedures involved in recognizing, evaluating, and taking action in response to an unexpected situation or emergency that may have adverse effects on an organization's activities or reputation. This process involves creating a comprehensive plan of action, including communication strategies, to address the crisis events and to diminish its effect on the organization (Coombs, 2019).

SMPs

SMPs are online applications or resources that let people produce, distribute, engage, and communicate with content. With billions of people utilizing them every day, SMP's become commonplace in contemporary culture. Several studies have demonstrated that using SMPs have both negative and positive impact on mental soundness, social connections, and general well-being in both favorable and unfavorable ways (Lin, L. Y., et al, 2016).

CRISIS MANAGEMENT AND SMPs

Due to the increasing usage and popularity of SMPs, CM becomes much more complicated. SMPs can amplify the impact of a crisis event and disseminate misinformation rapidly, making it difficult for organizations to control the narrative and manage public perception, as indicated by Veil, Buehner, and Palenchar in 2011. Organizations must have a well-planned and coordinated response strategy that involves monitoring social media channels, engaging with stakeholders, and providing accurate and timely information to better handle crisis events (Veil et al., 2011). For example, throughout the COVID-19 crisis, organizations had to manage crisis communication on social media by providing updates on their operations, responding to customer inquiries, and sharing accurate information on the virus, as noted by Paton, Zheng, and Wang in 2020. In addition, research by Kim et al. (2018) examined how SMPs were used during the 2015 Nepal earthquake and discovered that SMPs were crucial for spreading information and organizing relief operations. The study makes the case that SMPs may act as an important instrument for crisis coordination and communication, especially in circumstances where conventional communication routes may be compromised.

BACKGROUND STUDY

Research in the field of using social media platforms in times of crisis has been increasing in recent years, by exploring the advantages and challenges of using social media platforms (Veil, Buehner, & Palenchar, 2011; Stieglitz & Dang-Xuan, 2013). However, there is still a theoretical gap exists in the literature when it comes to bibliometric studies to analyze the intellectual structure of the research area. The bibliometric analysis will help us to discover the most cited authors, articles, most influential journals, countries, and the emerging trend in the research field, this could pave new paths toward future studies and could shed light on the better grasping of the effect of social media platforms at the time of crisis situations. Bibliometric analysis has emerged as a valuable tool for assessing research productivity and detecting emerging research patterns (Leydesdorff & Rafols, 2009). Nonetheless, to our knowledge, there has been no bibliometric study initiated in the past literature to analyze the field of Crisis Management (CM) through Social Media Platforms (SMP). Given this theoretical gap, this bibliometric study focuses to analyze and identify the most influential journals (highest publications), top-ranking countries, and institutions, most cited articles, frequently occurring keywords, and authorship patterns in CM-SMP publications.

METHODOLOGY

Choosing the appropriate methodology is crucial in research as it determines the reliability and validity of the findings. A well-defined research methodology helps in collecting and analyzing data and ensures that the research is conducted ethically and efficiently. It also helps to increase the chances of producing accurate and useful results. Bibliometric analysis is a useful tool for mapping the research landscape in a given field, identifying influential authors and institutions, and tracking the impact of research over time (Shaikh & Bhutto, 2021). It is commonly used to identify influential authors, institutions, and research areas within a field, track research trends over time, and assist in decision-making related to funding, publishing, and collaborations. The findings of the current bibliometric analysis can offer valuable perspectives on the influence of research and support researchers and institutions in making knowledgeable choices about their research priorities and approaches.

Sample

The authors have followed the PRISMA (Preferred Reporting Items for Systematic Reviews and Meta-nalysis) style of literature reporting mentioned by Liberati, A., et al (2009), which is considered to be the widely accepted and hustle-free literature review technique (Bolbot, V., et al 2022) and authors utilized Scopus data to conduct a bibliometric analysis using the VOS viewer application, VOS is an open-source software for data analysis and visualization. Figure 1 presents the flow of the literature review process by using the PRISMA literature statement method. The initial search in the Scopus database with the search term ("crisis" OR "Leadership" OR "crisis leadership" OR "crisis management") AND ("social media" OR "social media platforms" OR "social networking sites" OR "social capital theory" OR "social capital") yielded 5998 search items, which were then refined to a final sample of 329 articles. The authors subjected the Scopus data to several filtering processes. The search items contained articles published from 1979 onwards. The first filtering step involved restricting the articles to those published within the past five years (2019-2023), resulting in the exclusion of 4,022 articles and the retention of 5,998 articles. The articles which had incomplete and duplicate records (793), were published in languages other than English (645), were still in press (313), belonged to document categories other than articles and review papers (1,831), were published in low-ranking journals (214), or were excluded based on title and abstract screening (1,873).

The following are the bibliometric indicators employed in this study:

1. What has been the trend in CM SMP publications over the years, and is there a notable increase or decrease in the number of publications?
2. Who is considered the leading, most influential author in the area of CM SMP publications, and what are the most frequently cited articles in this field?
3. Which countries, institutions, and journals have contributed the most to the field of CM SMP publications, and are there any notable trends or patterns in their contributions?
4. What are the most used keywords in CM SMP publications, and how do they vary across different subtopics and research areas?

Method of Analysis

To discover the emerging trends in the literature the authors used manual calculation with the help of scopus data and VOS viewer, VOS viewer is an open-source software that is widely used to visualize the bibliographic network of a research area (Van Eck et al., 2014). The authors performed 4 types of bibliographic analysis by utilizing the VOS viewer, namely: (1)Citation analysis (2)Country co-authorship analysis (3) Journal co-citation analysis (4) Keyword-co-occurrence analysis. Citation analysis helps the authors to identify the most cited authors and articles in a research domain (Hota, P. K., et al., 2020), Country co-authorship analysis helps the researcher to find the leading country in a research field (Kim and Song (2021), Journal co-citation analysis discovers the most influential journal in a research domain (Zhu, J et al, 2019) and Keyword co-occurrence analysis helps the authors to find the most co-occurred keywords in a research area (Zhao et al., 2021). As a result of these four bibliometric approaches, this study offers unique perspectives on how knowledge is positioned and created in the CM via the SMP research domain.

FINDINGS

1. Emerging trends in CM via SMP publication

The presentation of Table 1 and Figure 2 has achieved the primary goal of this bibliometric inquiry, which was to identify the dominant patterns in the field of CM via SMP publications. Which presents the distribution of research papers based on the year of publication. It is important to examine the temporal distribution of research output to identify trends, assess the impact of recent developments, and inform future research directions.

Figure 1. PRISMA model of inclusion and exclusion criteria

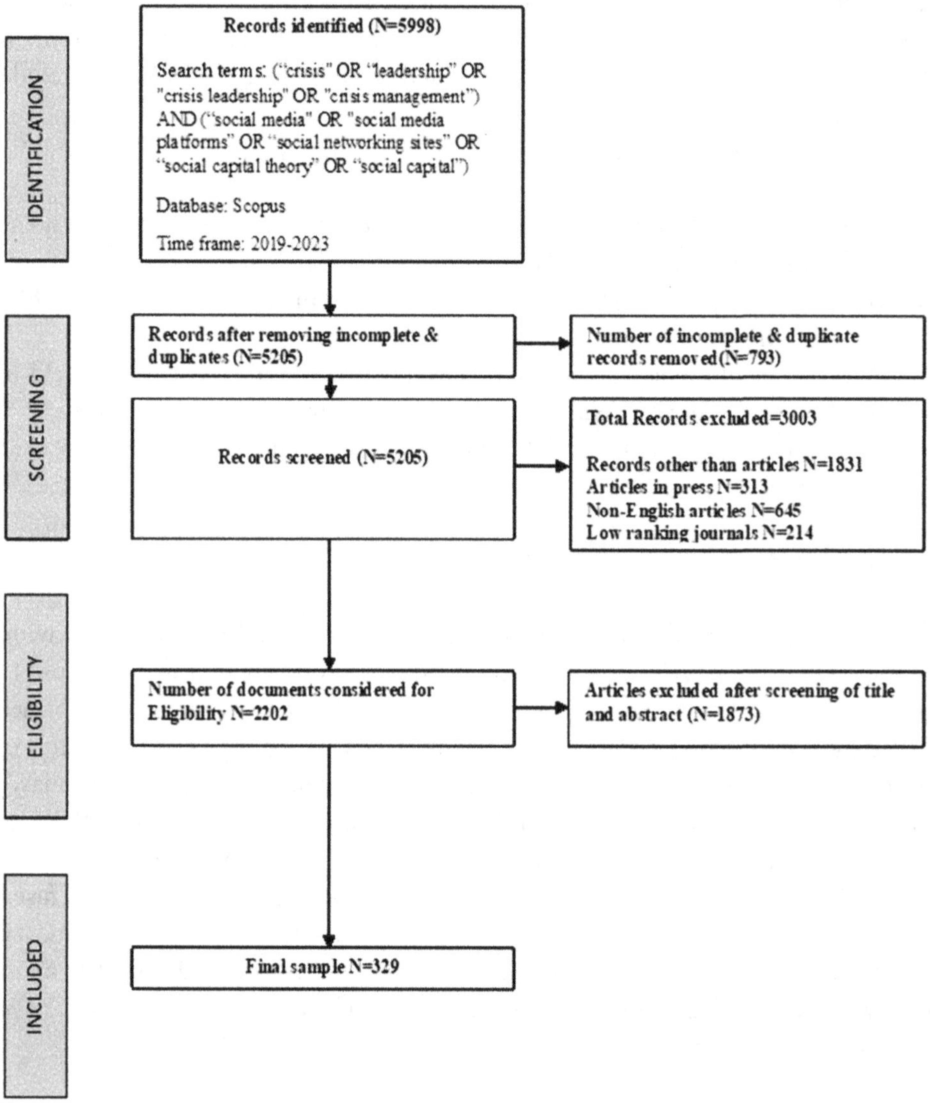

Table 1. Emerging developments in crisis management leveraging social media channels

Year of Publication	No. of Research Papers
2023	63
2022	184
2021	62
2020	5
2019	15

Source: Manual calculation by using the data from Scopus and VOS viewer

Figure 2. Emerging developments in crisis management leveraging social media channels
Source: Manual calculation of author by using Table 1

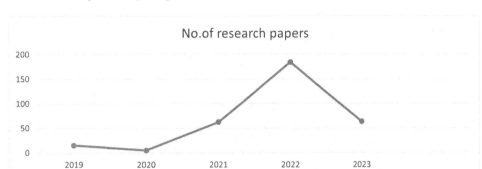

As evident from the table, A large number of research articles were published in 2022 and 2023, with 184 and 63 papers respectively. The year 2021 also witnessed substantial contributions, with 62 research papers. On the other hand, a smaller number of research papers were published in the years 2020, 2019, and prior years. The high concentration of research output in recent years reflects the growing interest and importance of the field, indicating the need for more in-depth and comprehensive investigations in this domain. These findings underscore the relevance and timeliness of our research, which contributes to the available literature in this research area.

2.   Most influential authors and articles in CM via SMP publications

Table 2 lists the top 20 research articles related to crisis communication published in recent years, ranked according to the number of citations they obtained. The articles cover a variety of disasters, including the corona pandemic, refugee disaster, and measles outbreak, and explore different aspects of crisis communication, such as social media analytics, news media coverage, and the impact of crises on public sentiment. The table provides information on the authors, title, year of publication, and number of citations for each article.

Table 2. Leading and most influential authors and most frequently cited articles in the area of CM SMP publications

S.N	Authors	Title	Year	Citations
1	Casero, Ripollés A.	Impact of covid-19 on the media system. Communicative and democratic consequences of news consumption during the outbreak	2020	222
2	Griffith, J., Marani, H., & Monkman, H.	COVID-19 vaccine hesitancy in Canada: Content analysis of tweets using the theoretical domains framework	2021	89
3	Casale, S., & Flett, G. L.	Interpersonally-based fears during the covid-19 pandemic: Reflections on the fear of missing out and the fear of not mattering constructs	2020	65
4	Park D., Kim W.G., Choi S.	Application of social media analytics in tourism crisis communication	2019	52
5	Hassankhani M., Alidadi M., Sharifi A., Azhdari A.	Smart City and crisis management: Lessons for the covid-19 pandemic	2021	38

continues on following page

Table 2. Continued

S.N	Authors	Title	Year	Citations
6	Li Y., Guan M., Hammond P., Berrey L.E.	Communicating COVID-19 information on TikTok: A content analysis of TikTok videos from official accounts featured in the COVID-19 information hub	2021	30
7	Cheng Y., Lee C.J.	Online crisis communication in a post-truth Chinese society: Evidence from an interdisciplinary literature	2019	30
8	Wang Y., Zhang M., Li S., McLeay F., Gupta S.	Corporate Responses to the Coronavirus Crisis and their Impact on Electronic-Word-of-Mouth and Trust Recovery: Evidence from Social Media	2021	26
9	Meadows C.W., Meadows C.Z., Tang L., Liu W.	Unraveling Public Health Crises Across Stages: Understanding Twitter Emotions and Message Types During the California Measles Outbreak	2019	24
10	Pasquinelli C., Trunfio M., Bellini N., Rossi S.	Sustainability in overtouristified cities? A social media insight into Italian branding responses to the covid-19 crisis	2021	23
11	Mak A.K.Y., Song A.O.	Revisiting social-mediated crisis communication model: The Lancôme regenerative crisis after the Hong Kong Umbrella Movement	2019	21
12	Chan M.K., Sharkey J.D., Lawrie S.I., Arch D.A.N., Nylund Gibson K.	Elementary School Teacher Well-Being and Supportive Measures Amid COVID-19: An Exploratory Study	2021	20
13	Nerghes A., Lee J.-S.	Narratives of the refugee crisis: A comparative study of mainstream media and Twitter	2019	20
14	Mackay M., Colangeli T., Gillis D., McWhirter J., Papadopoulos A.	Examining social media crisis communication during early covid-19 from public health and news media for quality, content, and corresponding public sentiment	2021	18
15	Pang P.C.I., Cai Q., Jiang W., Chan K.S.	Engagement of government social media on Facebook during the COVID-19 pandemic in Macao	2021	17
16	Sng K., Au T.Y., Pang A.	Social Media Influencers as a Crisis Risk in Strategic Communication: Impact of Indiscretions on Professional Endorsements	2019	17
17	Jayasekara P.K.	Role of Facebook as a disaster communication media	2019	16
18	Marin A., Hampton K.N.	Network Instability in Times of Stability	2019	16
19	Lang L.D., Behl A., Dong N.T., Thu N.H., Dewani P.P.	Social capital in agribusiness: an exploratory investigation from a supply chain perspective during the COVID-19 crisis	2022	15
20	Lwin m.o. (2Lwin M.O., Lee S.Y., Panchapakesan C., Tandoc E.023)	Mainstream News Media's Role in Public Health Communication During Crises: Assessment of Coverage and Correction of COVID-19 Misinformation	2023	14

Source: Manual calculation by the author using the data from Scopus and VOS viewer

The above table displays the 20 most highly cited articles, revealing the most influential authors in the area of CM SMP publications. Casero, Ripolles A. is the leading author with over 200 citations (222).

3. Leading countries in CM via SMP publications

Table 3 and Figure 3 display a ranking of the nations based on the volume of papers and citations in the area of CM via SMP. The figures are sourced from the Scopus database and analyzed with the help of a VOS viewer. The table includes the country rank, the name of the country, the quantity of articles published, and the overall citation count.

Table 3. Leading countries in publishing research articles in CM SMP publications.

S.N	Country	Articles	Citations
1	United States	95	360
2	Spain	15	266
3	Canada	20	208
4	Italy	20	137
5	United Kingdom	30	104
6	China	30	74
7	South Korea	6	70
8	India	22	65
9	Australia	22	60
10	Singapore	8	52
11	Iran	6	44
12	Saudi Arabia	10	37
13	Netherlands	5	36
14	Indonesia	7	30
15	Hong Kong	6	29
16	Turkey	5	28
17	Macau	5	22
18	Portugal	7	20
19	Germany	9	20
20	Taiwan	5	18

Source: Manual calculation by the author using the data from Scopus and VOS viewer

Figure 3. Leading countries in CM SMP publications

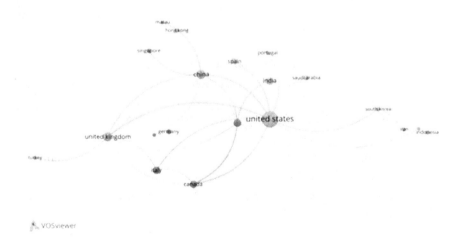

Table 3 and Figure 3 highlight the countries that are leading in publishing and advancing the field of CM in SMP publications. The United States ranks first on the list, with an overall citation count of 360 and the highest level of collaboration with other countries. This implies that the United States is playing a noteworthy part in making innovative contributions and collaborating with other countries to enhance the field of CM via SMP publications.

4.   Leading journals in CM via SMP publications

Figure 4 presents conclusive evidence demonstrating that the International Journal of Environmental Science has made the most significant contribution to the field of CM in SMP publications. This is demonstrated by the journal's citation count, which is the highest among all the journals analyzed. It is common practice for researchers to use citation counts as an indicator of a journal's impact and quality. Researchers may evaluate the importance and influence of journals in their particular disciplines using citation analysis, which is a very useful tool. Therefore, the authors conducted citation analysis to compute the influence and quality of the journals in the field of CM via SMP.

Figure 4. Leading journals in CM SMP publications

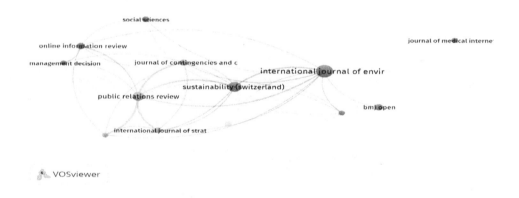

Figure 4 illustrates the highly referenced journals publishing in the domain of crisis management through SMPs, in addition to the connections between them in terms of citations.

Most Co-Occurred Keywords in CM via SMP Publications

The analysis presented in Figure 5 provides valuable insights into the most frequently discussed keywords in the area of CM and SMP. The prominence of "Social media" and "COVID-19" as the most co-occurring keywords suggest that social media portrayed a substantial part in the management of the corona pandemic. This discovery has significant ramifications for practitioners and policymakers who want to comprehend the value of SMPs in CM. The author's choice of using the VOS viewer to identify the most commonly discussed constructs in the area of CM via SMP is an important contribution to the field. It provides a roadmap for researchers to explore key concepts and themes and can guide future research directions. However, there is a sizable vacuum in the literature due to the scant number of research that has examined the connection between CM, crisis leadership, and SMPs. This emphasizes the need for more study to explore how SMPs might be used to improve CM and crisis leadership. Such research can provide valuable insights for policymakers, practitioners, and organizational leaders who need to be equipped to handle crises effectively.

Figure 5. Most co-occurred keywords

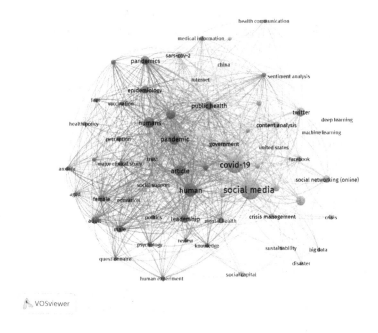

The findings presented in Figure 5 underscore the importance of SMPs in CM, particularly in the context of crisis events. The use of a VOS viewer to identify commonly discussed constructs can assist the researchers in obtaining a clearer insight into the field. However, the need for further research to investigate the connection between CM, crisis leadership, and SMP's critical to enhancing the CM of the organizations.

DISCUSSION

The role of social media platforms (SMPs) in crisis management (CM) has gained increasing attention in recent years, particularly during the COVID-19 pandemic. This bibliometric study analyzed publications associated with CM and SMPs to provide insights into trends and contributions in this field. The study found an increasing trend in publications related to CM via SMPs, which is consistent with the findings of Y. Cheng and C.-J. Lee (2019), who conducted a thematic review of 118 articles and found that increased academic attention has been given to the area of online crisis communication.

Numerous studies have reported that the use of SMPs during crisis events can improve overall crisis management effectiveness. For instance, a study by Hassankhani et al. (2021) found that the use of SMPs and other technology policies helps to improve overall crisis management and community well-being.

Li, Y., Guan, M., et al. (2021) analyzed the emerging SMP TikTok and found that videos posted in the information hub provided by the platform dedicated to the COVID-19 crisis reached millions of views and received significant attention. The authors suggested that public health agencies should be aware of and utilize such platforms during crisis events to communicate effectively with people. MacKay, M., et al. (2021) studied the crisis communication of the Canadian health sector via Facebook and suggested increasing positive statements and building trust among followers. Similarly, Pang, P. C. I., et al. (2021) analyzed the crisis management of the Macao government via Facebook and found that follower engagement was low during the COVID-19 pandemic. The authors suggested that the government should focus on mental health and provide regular updates on crisis events. Jayasekara (2019) studied different types of posts shared via Facebook at different stages of crisis events in Sri Lanka and found that people shared posts intending to share crisis information, and warnings, seek help and provide feedback. The author suggested that the government should start its official social media channel to provide necessary information to people during crisis events. All these studies suggest that governments should utilize the power of SMPs to manage crisis events effectively.

However, only a few studies have investigated the organizational context of this research domain, A recent study by Meadows et al. (2019) found that organizations can use SMPs to obtain public opinions and emotions during every stage of crisis events. Wang, Y., Zhang, M., et al. (2021) analyzed COVID-19 announcements of major food outlets in the UK on Twitter and found that using a defensive corporate strategy with emotionally framed tweets received more positive consumer E-WOM. Therefore, they suggested using emotional announcements during crisis events to gain consumer trust more efficiently. Similarly, Nerghes and Lee (2019) studied how SMPs create new complementary media space to inform the public and include them in building narratives. Griffith et al. (2021) used Twitter to assess the reasons for people's hesitancy to accept and take the COVID-19 vaccination. They screened around 3,915 tweets and found that people are hesitant about vaccination because of the lack of knowledge about the vaccine, confusing communication from top leaders, and mistrust toward the medical industry. They utilized Twitter to better understand the reason for people's hesitancy toward the COVID-19 vaccination. D. Park et al. (2018) conducted a study in the tourism sector to find out how tourists can find accurate and updated information during crises. They found that using SMP data during crises can provide more accurate and reliable information, and it can help manage crisis organizations' reputations during crisis response and recovery phases. Pasquinelli et al. (2021) utilized insights from Facebook posts to assess the sustainability of over-touristed cities during the COVID-19 pandemic.

In recent years, several studies have highlighted the negative effects of social media usage during crisis events. Casero and Ripollés (2020) conducted a study on the news consumption habits of people during the COVID-19 pandemic and found that while there was an increase in the consumption of news from social media platforms, it was considered less credible due to the high percentage of fake news and rumors. This finding is consistent with the works of Gil de Zúñiga and Diehl (2019), Lee and Xenos (2019), and Silvia Casale et al. (2020), who also found that social media platforms are not a reliable source of information during crisis events. Furthermore, Silvia Casale et al. (2020) investigated the negative effects of social media usage on people's mental health during the COVID-19 pandemic. They discovered that participants used social media excessively due to a fear of losing out and not feeling included in society, resulting in undesirable results such as sleeping issues. This study supports the findings of Scott and Woods (2018), who discovered that excessive social media use is related to unfavorable outcomes.

A recent study by Mak and Song (2019) analyzed an organizational crisis event related to Lancôme Hong Kong and found that social media influencers can use their power to create sub-crisis events by reframing messages, which can affect their followers' emotions. They suggested that organizations need to understand and analyze such emotions to improve their crisis response strategies. Similarly, Chan et al. (2021) conducted an online survey to assess the well-being of elementary school teachers during the COVID-19 pandemic and found that they struggled to adapt to teaching children via social media platforms. This finding highlights the challenges that arise from relying on social media platforms during crisis events. Likewise, K. Sng et al. (2019) found that social media influencers can attract Para crises to an organization and suggested that organizations should conduct well-structured screening of social media influencers and their followers before hiring them. Finally, Lwin et al. (2021) studied the fake news detection and correction function of mainstream news dailies in Singapore and emphasized the importance of fake news gatekeeping during public health crisis events. These studies underscore the critical need to address the negative effects of social media usage during crisis events and to develop effective strategies to mitigate their impact.

CONCLUSION

In this bibliometric study, the authors analyzed publications on Crisis Management (CM) along Social Media Platforms (SMP) to identify influential journals, top-ranking countries, and institutions, the most cited articles, the most frequently occurring keywords, and the pattern of authorship. The study revealed that social capital theory plays a crucial role in CM via SMP publications. Collaborative efforts among authors, institutions, and countries were observed, which can be considered a form of social capital that supports the growth and transfer of knowledge in this research area. The study further suggests that the high level of collaboration among authors from different countries and institutions demonstrates the utilization of social capital to create networks and partnerships that facilitate knowledge exchange and innovative solutions for managing crises via SMPs. Overall, the concept of the social capital theory is a vital component in the expansion and dissemination of knowledge in the field of CM via SMP publications and it must be further investigated in the forthcoming studies. Additionally, the findings indicate an increase in the use of social media platforms in the wake of COVID-19. As a result, most publications focused on the use of SMPs during the COVID-19 pandemic, implying the importance of using social media platforms in future crisis events while also considering and overcoming any potential disadvantages.

MANAGERIAL AND THEORETICAL IMPLICATIONS

The study presents valuable insights for academics, practitioners, and policymakers to acquire a clearer grasp of the trends, and patterns in the field of CM in SMP publications and to identify new opportunities for collaboration and knowledge exchange.

Government agencies and business organizations are suggested to better understand the importance of using social media platforms at the time of crisis events by considering utilizing the social media platform's advantages to better their crisis management effectiveness, This novel bibliometric analysis in the area of CM via SMP publications fills the theoretical gap and adds to the existing literature, also the findings of this bibliometric analysis revealed the current trend of the research domain and thus opens up the opportunities for new research directions.

FUTURE RESEARCH AREA

As the use of social media platforms (SMPs) in crisis management (CM) continues to grow, it is becoming increasingly important to identify potential future research areas in this field. The authors observed that there are only a few studies have been conducted in the business organization context, hence that could be a possible future research area in CM via SMP domain. Also, several researchers have suggested possible avenues for future research in CM via SMPs. Park D et al., (2019) suggested a future study on the tourism sector by collecting data from Twitter and also suggested conducting a study by adopting clustering network analysis measures to develop a deeper understanding of crisis communication network structures. Li Y., et al (2021) suggested conducting a study on the user's demographic and cognitive, behavioral & emotional responses to health information videos on the social media platforms like TikTok. Y Cheng et al., (2019) encourage the researchers to conduct further studies on how the different types of fake news in social media may influence crisis communication strategies and their overall effectiveness. Y wang et al., (2021) recommended that researchers investigate the effect of corporate response to public health crisis events on consumer sentiment across various social media platforms. Coombs (2017) and AK. Y mak ET AL., (2019) suggested investigating the overall effect of the response strategy to be taken at the turning point of the double crisis situation

REFERENCES

Casale, S., & Flett, G. L. (2020). Interpersonally-based fears during the COVID-19 pandemic: Reflections on the fear of missing out and the fear of not mattering constructs. *Clinical Neuropsychiatry*, *17*(2), 88. PMID:34908975

Casero-Ripollés, A. (2020). Impact of Covid-19 on the media system. Communicative and democratic consequences of news consumption during the outbreak. *El Profesional de la Información*, *29*(2), e290223. doi:10.3145/epi.2020.mar.23

Chan, M. K., Sharkey, J. D., Lawrie, S. I., Arch, D. A., & Nylund-Gibson, K. (2021). Elementary school teacher well-being and supportive measures amid COVID-19: An exploratory study. *The School Psychologist*, *36*(6), 533–545. doi:10.1037pq0000441 PMID:34292036

Cheng, Y., & Lee, C. J. (2019). Online crisis communication in a post-truth Chinese society: Evidence from interdisciplinary literature. *Public Relations Review*, *45*(4), 101826. doi:10.1016/j.pubrev.2019.101826

Coombs, W. T., & Holladay, S. J. (2019). *The Handbook of Crisis Communication* (3rd ed.). Wiley-Blackwell.

Griffith, J., Marani, H., & Monkman, H. (2021). COVID-19 vaccine hesitancy in Canada: A content analysis of tweets using the theoretical domains framework. *Journal of Medical Internet Research*, *23*(4), e26874. doi:10.2196/26874 PMID:33769946

Hassankhani, M., Alidadi, M., Sharifi, A., & Azhdari, A. (2021). Smart city and crisis management: Lessons for the COVID-19 pandemic. *International Journal of Environmental Research and Public Health*, *18*(15), 7736. doi:10.3390/ijerph18157736 PMID:34360029

Jayasekara, P. K. (2019). Role of Facebook as a disaster communication media. *International Journal of Emergency Services*, *8*(2), 191–204. doi:10.1108/IJES-04-2018-0024

Kim, Y., Chen, J., & Huang, L. (2018). Social media use during natural disasters: The case of the 2015 Nepal earthquake. *International Journal of Information Management*, *38*(1), 86–95. doi:10.1016/j.ijinfomgt.2017.08.003

Leydesdorff, L., & Rafols, I. (2009). A Global Map of Science Based on the ISI Subject Categories. *Journal of the American Society for Information Science and Technology*, *60*(2), 348–362. doi:10.1002/asi.20967

Lin, L. Y., Sidani, J. E., Shensa, A., Radovic, A., Miller, E., Colditz, J. B., Hoffman, B. L., Giles, L. M., & Primack, B. A. (2016). Association between social media use and depression among US young adults. *Depression and Anxiety*, *33*(4), 323–331. doi:10.1002/da.22466 PMID:26783723

Lwin, M. O., Lee, S. Y., Panchapakesan, C., & Tandoc, E. (2023). Mainstream news media's role in public health communication during crises: Assessment of coverage and correction of COVID-19 misinformation. *Health Communication*, *38*(1), 160–168. doi:10.1080/10410236.2021.1937842 PMID:34157919

MacKay, M., Cimino, A., Yousefinaghani, S., McWhirter, J. E., Dara, R., & Papadopoulos, A. (2022). Canadian COVID-19 crisis communication on Twitter: Mixed methods research examining tweets from government, politicians, and public health for crisis communication guiding principles and tweet engagement. *International Journal of Environmental Research and Public Health*, *19*(11), 6954. doi:10.3390/ijerph19116954 PMID:35682537

Mak, A. K., & Song, A. O. (2019). Revisiting social-mediated crisis communication model: The Lancôme regenerative crisis after the Hong Kong Umbrella Movement. *Public Relations Review*, *45*(4), 101812. doi:10.1016/j.pubrev.2019.101812

Meadows, C. W., Meadows, C. Z., Tang, L., & Liu, W. (2019). Unraveling public health crises across stages: Understanding Twitter emotions and message types during the California measles outbreak. *Communication Studies*, *70*(4), 453–469. doi:10.1080/10510974.2019.1582546

Mishkin, F. S. (2011). Over the cliff: From the Subprime to the global financial crisis. *The Journal of Economic Perspectives*, *25*(1), 49–70. doi:10.1257/jep.25.1.49

Nerghes, A., & Lee, J. S. (2019). Narratives of the refugee crisis: A comparative study of mainstream media and Twitter. *Media and Communication, 7*(2), 275-288.

Pang, P. C. I., Cai, Q., Jiang, W., & Chan, K. S. (2021). Engagement of government social media on Facebook during the COVID-19 pandemic in Macao. *International Journal of Environmental Research and Public Health*, *18*(7), 3508. doi:10.3390/ijerph18073508 PMID:33800621

Park, D., Kim, W. G., & Choi, S. (2019). Application of social media analytics in tourism crisis communication. *Current Issues in Tourism*, *22*(15), 1810–1824. doi:10.1080/13683500.2018.1504900

Pasquinelli, C., Trunfio, M., Bellini, N., & Rossi, S. (2021). Sustainability in overtouristified cities? A social media insight into Italian branding responses to the Covid-19 crisis. *Sustainability (Basel)*, *13*(4), 1848. doi:10.3390u13041848

Paton, D., Zheng, T., & Wang, L. (2020). Disaster resilience in the context of COVID-19: A framework for analyzing impacts and responses. *International Journal of Disaster Risk Reduction, 51*, 101789. doi:10.1016/j.ijdrr.2020.101789

Sng, K., Au, T. Y., & Pang, A. (2019). Social media influencers as a crisis risk in strategic communication: Impact of indiscretions on professional endorsements. *International Journal of Strategic Communication, 13*(4), 301–320. doi:10.1080/1553118X.2019.1618305

Stieglitz, S., & Dang-Xuan, L. (2013). Crisis communication in the age of social media: A network analysis of Zika virus coverage. *Journal of Risk Research, 20*(1), 1–14.

Veil, S. R., Buehner, T., & Palenchar, M. J. (2011). A work-in-progress literature review: Incorporating social media in risk and crisis communication. *Journal of Contingencies and Crisis Management, 19*(2), 110–122. doi:10.1111/j.1468-5973.2011.00639.x

Wang, C., Horby, P. W., Hayden, F. G., & Gao, G. F. (2020). A novel coronavirus outbreak of global health concern. *Lancet, 395*(10223), 470–473. doi:10.1016/S0140-6736(20)30185-9 PMID:31986257

Wang, X., Tang, L., Zhang, L., & Zheng, J. (2022). The initial stage of the COVID-19 pandemic: A perspective on health risk communications in the restaurant industry. *International Journal of Environmental Research and Public Health, 19*(19), 11961. doi:10.3390/ijerph191911961 PMID:36231263

Woods, C. L. (2022). Extinguishing a fictional fire: Responding to emotional and misinformed audiences. *Corporate Reputation Review, 25*(4), 239–252. doi:10.105741299-021-00125-5

Zhang, J., & Wang, Y. (2022). Effectiveness of corporate social responsibility activities in the COVID-19 pandemic. *Journal of Product and Brand Management, 31*(7), 1063–1076. doi:10.1108/JPBM-07-2021-3551

Zhao, Y., Zhu, S., Wan, Q., Li, T., Zou, C., Wang, H., & Deng, S. (2022). Understanding How and by Whom COVID-19 Misinformation is Spread on Social Media: Coding and Network Analyses. *Journal of Medical Internet Research, 24*(6), e37623. doi:10.2196/37623 PMID:35671411

Zheng, H., & Jiang, S. (2022). Linking the pathway from exposure to online vaccine information to cyberchondria during the COVID-19 pandemic: A moderated mediation model. *Cyberpsychology, Behavior, and Social Networking, 25*(10), 625–633. doi:10.1089/cyber.2022.0045 PMID:36037024

Compilation of References

Aaltola, P. (2018). Investing in strategic development. *Qualitative Research in Accounting & Management*, *15*(2), 206–230. doi:10.1108/QRAM-05-2017-0044

Abdul-Hakim, Russayani, & Abdul-Razak. (2010). The Relationship between Social Capital and Quality of Life Among Rural Households in Terengganu, Malaysia. *OIDA International Journal of Sustainable Development*, *1*(5), 99-106. https://ssrn.com/abstract=1671066

Aboagye, E., Yawson, J. A., & Appiah, K. N. (2021). COVID-19 and E-learning: The challenges of students in tertiary institutions. *Social Education Research*, 1–8.

Abu-Jaber, A., Alshurideh, M., & Tadros, R. (2021). The impact of social media on social capital: A systematic literature review. *Behaviour & Information Technology*, *40*(6), 593–610.

Achrol, R. S., Reve, T., & Stern, L. W. (1983). The environment of marketing channel dyads: A framework for comparative analysis. *Journal of Marketing*, *47*(4), 55–67. doi:10.1177/002224298304700407

Adams, O. K. (2016). Impact of Social Network on Society: A Case Study of Abuja. *American Scientific Research Journal for Engineering, Technology, and Sciences*, *21*(1), 1–17.

Adler, P. S., & Kwon, S. W. (2002). Social capital: Prospects for a new concept. *Academy of Management Review*, *27*(1), 17–40. doi:10.2307/4134367

Adnan, N., Bhatti, O. K., & Baykal, E. (2022). A phenomenological investigation on ethical leadership and workplace engagement from a multi-cultural perspective. *International Journal of Organizational Leadership.*, *11*(2), 206–234. doi:10.33844/ijol.2022.60327

Agarwal, S. (2019). *Are social networks good for our society?* Christ University. https://www.researchgate.net/publication/339780597

Agent. (2020). What Sells in Dark Web Markets in 2020? *AGENT*, 3.

Agrawal, A., Catalini, C., & Goldfarb, A. (2015). Crowdfunding: Geography, Social Networks, and the Timing of Investment Decisions. *Journal of Economics & Management Strategy*, *24*(2), 253–274. Advance online publication. doi:10.1111/jems.12093

Ahmad, T., Alvi, A., & Ittefaq, M. (2019). The Use of social media on Political Participation Among University Students: An Analysis of Survey Results from Rural Pakistan. *SAGE Open*, *9*(3). Advance online publication. doi:10.1177/2158244019864484

Akıncı, T., & Ekşi, H. (2017). Lise Öğretmenlerinin Yönetici Ruhsal Liderlik Algılarının Öğretmen Liderliği ve Öz-Yetkinliklerine Etkisi. *Değerler Eğitimi Dergisi, 15*(34).

Alhabash, S., & Ma, M. (2021). Social media use, network heterogeneity, and social capital. *Communication Research*, *48*(4), 573–595.

Ali, Balta, & Papadopoulos. (2023). Social media platforms and social enterprise: Bibliometric analysis and systematic review. *Int. J. Inf. Manage.*, *69*, 102510. . doi:10.1016/j.ijinfomgt.2022.102510

Ali, W. (2020). Online and remote learning in higher education institutes: a necessity in light of COVID-19 pandemic. *Higher Education Studies*, *10*(3), 16–25.

Ali, M., Usman, M., Aziz, S., & Rofcanin, Y. (2022). Undermining alienative commitment through spiritual leadership: A moderated mediation model of social capital and political skill. *Journal of Asian Business and Economic Studies*, *29*(4), 263–279. doi:10.1108/JABES-09-2021-0155

Allen, I. E., & Seaman, J. (2017). *Digital Learning Compass: Distance Education Enrollment Report 2017*. Babson Survey Research Group.

Almeida, D. J., Byrne, A. M., Smith, R. M., & Ruiz, S. (2021). How relevant is grit? The importance of social capital in first-generation college students' academic success. *Journal of College Student Retention*, *23*(4), 539–559. doi:10.1177/1521025119854688

Al-Naabi, I. (2023). Did They Transform Their Teaching Practices? A Case Study on Evaluating Professional Development Webinars Offered to Language Teachers during COVID-19. *International Journal of Higher Education*, *12*(1), 36. doi:10.5430/ijhe.v12n1p36

Alqahtani, H., & Naim, A. (2022). Critical Success Factors for Transforming CRM to SCRM for building E-CRM. In A. Naim & S. Kautish (Eds.), *Building a Brand Image Through Electronic Customer Relationship Management* (pp. 139–168). IGI Global. doi:10.4018/978-1-6684-5386-5.ch007

Alsharo, M., Gregg, D., & Ramirez, R. (2017). Virtual Team Effectiveness: The role of knowledge sharing and trust. *Information & Management*, *54*(4), 479–490. doi:10.1016/j.im.2016.10.005

Amigó, E., Deldjoo, Y., Mizzaro, S., & Bellogín, A. (2023). A unifying and general account of fairness measurement in recommender systems. *Information Processing & Management*, *60*(1), 103115. doi:10.1016/j.ipm.2022.103115

Anand, Dinesh, Obaid, Malik, Sharma, Dumka, Singh, & Khatak. (2022). Securing e-Health application of cloud computing using hyperchaotic image encryption framework. *Computers and Electrical Engineering, 100*. doi:10.1016/j.compeleceng.2022.107860

Anbalagan, G. (2017). New technological changes in Indian banking sector. *International Journal of Scientific Research and Management*. doi:10.18535/ijsrm/v5i9.11

Andriivna, O. (2021). Psychological Difficulties during the COVID Lockdown: Video in Blended Digital Teaching Language, Literature, and Culture. *Arab World English Journal*. https://ssrn.com/abstract=3851685

Anggraeni, A., Putra, S., & Suwito, B. P. (2020). Examining the Influence of Customer-To-Customer Electronic Word of Mouth on Purchase Intention in Social Networking Sites. *ACM International Conference Proceeding Series*. 10.1145/3387263.3387274

Apriliyanti, D. L. (2021). Teachers' Encounter of Online Learning: Challenges and Support System. *Journal of English Education and Teaching*, *5*(1), 110–122. doi:10.33369/jeet.5.1.110-122

Aras, Abdulkadir, & Serpil. (2017). Social Networking Sites as Communication, Interaction, and Learning Environments: Perceptions and Preferences of Distance Education Students. Anadolu University, Turkey. *Journal of Learning for Development, 4*(3), 348-365.

Arora Akhil, S. R. (2017). *Debunking the Myths of Influence Maximization: An In-Depth Benchmarking Study.* ACM.

Atmacasoy. (2018). Blended learning at pre-service teacher education in Turkey: a systematic review. *Education Information Technology, 23*(6), 2399-2422.

Bae, S. M. (2019). The relationship between smartphone use for communication, social capital, and subjective well-being in Korean adolescents: Verification using multiple latent growth modeling. *Children and Youth Services Review, 96*, 93–99. doi:10.1016/j.childyouth.2018.11.032

Baloran, E. T., Hernan, J. T., & Taoy, J. S. (2021). Course satisfaction and student engagement in online learning amid COVID-19 pandemic: A structural equation model. *Turkish Online Journal of Distance Education, 22*(4), 1–12. doi:10.17718/tojde.1002721

Banerjee, S., Jenamani, M., & Pratihar, D. K. (2020). A survey on influence maximization in a social network. *Knowledge and Information Systems, 62*(9), 3417–3455. doi:10.100710115-020-01461-4

Bao, C., Li, Y., & Zhao, X. (2023). The Influence of Social Capital and Intergenerational Mobility on University Students' Sustainable Development in China. *Sustainability (Basel), 12*(7), 2849. doi:10.3390u15076118

Bargh, J., & McKenna, K. (2004). The Internet and social life. *Annual Review of Psychology, 55*(1), 573–590. doi:10.1146/annurev.psych.55.090902.141922 PMID:14744227

Barseli, M., Sembiring, K., Ifdil, I., & Fitria, L. (2019). The Concept of Student Interpersonal Communication. *Journal of Research in Indonesian Education, 3*(2), 129–134.

Baykal, E. (2019a). Rol-İçi ve Rol-Üstü Performansın İşyeri Ruhsallığı İle Arttırılması. *Uluslararası Hukuk ve Sosyal Bilim Araştırmaları Dergisi, 1*(1), 15–25.

Baykal, E. (2019b). Human factor in change management: An example from turkish banking sector. *Balkan Sosyal Bilimler Dergisi, 8*(16), 187–198.

Baykal, E. (2019c). A Comparison About Eudaimonic Wellbeing in Authentic and Spiritual Leadership. *Uluslararası Hukuk ve Sosyal Bilim Araştırmaları Dergisi, 2*(1), 61–73.

Baykal, E. (2021). Meeting customer expectations in Islamic tourism: Effects of Islamic business ethics. In *Multidisciplinary Approaches to Ethics in the Digital Era* (pp. 276–291). IGI Global. doi:10.4018/978-1-7998-4117-3.ch015

Baykal, E. (2021). Understanding Religion As a Phenomenon in Workplace Sprituality: A Durkheimian Approach. *Spiritual Psychology and Counseling, 6*(2), 27–41. doi:10.37898pc.2021.6.2.134

Beggs, J. J., Haines, V. A., & Hurlbert, J. S. (1996). Revisiting the Rural-Urban Contrast: Personal Networks in Nonmetropolitan and Metropolitan Settings. *Rural Sociology, 61*(2), 306–325. doi:10.1111/j.1549-0831.1996.tb00622.x

Beier, M., & Wagner, K. (2015). Crowdfunding success: A perspective from social media and e-commerce. *2015 International Conference on Information Systems: Exploring the Information Frontier, ICIS 2015.*

Bello-Pintado, A., & Bianchi, C. (2020). Workforce education diversity, work organization and innovation propensity. *European Journal of Innovation Management, 24*(3), 756–776. doi:10.1108/EJIM-10-2019-0300

Bendapudi, N., & Berry, L. (1997). Customers' motivation for maintaining relationships with service providers. *Journal of Retailing, 73*(1), 15–38. doi:10.1016/S0022-4359(97)90013-0

Bennis, W. (1997). *Organizing genius: The secrets of creative collaboration.* Addison-Wesley.

Bernard, R. M., Abrami, P. C., Borokhovski, E., Wade, C. A., Tamim, R. M., Surkes, M. A., & Bethel, E. C. (2009). A meta-analysis of three types of interaction treatments in distance education. *Review of Educational Research*, *79*(3), 1243–1289. doi:10.3102/0034654309333844

Bhandari, H., & Yasunobu, K. (2009). What is Social Capital? A Comprehensive Review of the Concept. *Asian Journal of Social Science*, *37*(3), 480–510. doi:10.1163/156853109X436847

Bhowmik, N. R., Arifuzzaman, M., Mondal, M. R. H., & Islam, M. S. (2021). Bangla Text Sentiment Analysis Using Supervised Machine Learning with Extended Lexicon Dictionary. *Nat. Lang. Process. Res.*, *1*(3–4), 34. doi:10.2991/nlpr.d.210316.001

Bhuvaneswari, Jones, Thomas, & Kesavan. (2020). Embedded Bi-directional GRU and LSTM Learning Models to Predict Disasters on Twitter Data. *Procedia Computer Science, 165C*, 101-106.

Bhuvaneswari, A., & Valliyammai, C. (2019). Information entropy based event detection during disaster in cyber-social networks. *Journal of Intelligent & Fuzzy Systems*, *36*(5), 3981–3992. doi:10.3233/JIFS-169959

Biedenbach, G., Biedenbach, T., Hultén, P., & Tarnovskaya, V. (2022). Organizational resilience and internal branding: Investigating the effects triggered by self-service technology. *Journal of Brand Management*, *29*(4), 420–433. doi:10.105741262-022-00275-9

Bikhchandani, S., & Sharma, S. (2000). Herd behavior in financial markets. *IMF Staff Papers*. Advance online publication. doi:10.5539/ibr.v6n6p31

Bi, S., Liu, Z., & Usman, K. (2017). The influence of online information on investing decisions of reward-based crowdfunding. *Journal of Business Research*, *71*, 10–18. Advance online publication. doi:10.1016/j.jbusres.2016.10.001

Bizzi, L. (2015). Social Capital in Organizations. In J. D. Wright (Ed.), *International Encyclopedia of the Social & Behavioral Sciences* (2nd ed., Vol. 22, pp. 181–185). Elsevier. doi:10.1016/B978-0-08-097086-8.73108-4

Blessinger, P., Sengupta, E., & Meri-Yilan, S. (2023). *How students and faculty can build their social capital*. Retrieved from https://www.universityworldnews.com/post.php?story=20230314110328688

Block, J., Hornuf, L., & Moritz, A. (2018). Which updates during an equity crowdfunding campaign increase crowd participation? *Small Business Economics*, *50*(1), 3–27. Advance online publication. doi:10.100711187-017-9876-4

Bloomberg, L. D. & Volpe, M. (2008). *Completing Your Qualitative Dissertation: A Roadmap from Beginning to End*. Sage Publications.

Bolino, M., Turnley, W., & Bloodgood, J. (2002). Citizenship behavior and the creation of social capital in organizations. *Academy of Management Review*, *27*(4), 505–522. doi:10.2307/4134400

Bolliger, D. U. (2004). Key factors for determining student satisfaction in online courses. *International Journal on E-Learning*, *3*(1), 61–67.

Borst, I., Moser, C., & Ferguson, J. (2018). From friendfunding to crowdfunding: Relevance of relationships, social media, and platform activities to crowdfunding performance. *New Media & Society*, *20*(4), 1396–1414. Advance online publication. doi:10.1177/1461444817694599 PMID:30581357

Bourdieu, P. (1998). *Distinction. A social critique of the judgment of taste*. Harvard University Press.

Bourideu, P., & Passeron, J. C. (1990). *Reproduction in education, society, and culture*. Sage Publications.

Boyatzis, R. E. (1998). *Transforming Qualitative Information: Thematic and Code Development*. Sage Publications.

Bozbura, F. T., & Toraman, A. (2010). Türkiye'de Entelektüel Sermayenin Ölçülmesi İle İlgili Model Çalışması Ve Bir Uygulama. *İtüdergisi/D, 3*(1), 77-93.

Britannica. (n. d.). *Social capital.* https://www.britannica.com/topic/social-capital

Budhiraja, K. (2023). Infrastructures of Sociality: How Disadvantaged Students Navigate Inequity at the University. *Sociological Forum, 38*(1), 231–256. doi:10.1111ocf.12874

Burt, R. S. (1992). *Structural holes. The social structure of competition.* Harvard University Press. doi:10.4159/9780674029095

Burt, R. S. (2000). The Network Structure of Social Capital. *Research in Organizational Behavior, 22,* 345–423. doi:10.1016/S0191-3085(00)22009-1

Bushong, S., Cleveland, S., & Cox, C. (2018). Crowdfunding for Academic Libraries: Indiana Jones Meets Polka. *Journal of Academic Librarianship, 44*(2), 313–318. Advance online publication. doi:10.1016/j.acalib.2018.02.006

Butticè, V., Colombo, M. G., & Wright, M. (2017). Serial crowdfunding, social capital, and project success. *Entrepreneurship Theory and Practice, 41*(2), 183–207. doi:10.1111/etap.12271

Cao, C., & Meng, Q. (2020). Effects of online and direct contact on Chinese international students' social capital in intercultural networks: Testing moderation of direct contact and mediation of global competence. *Higher Education, 81*(4), 1131–1149. doi:10.100710734-020-00501-w

Capron, L., & Hulland, J. (1999). Redeployment of brands, sales forces, and general marketing management expertise following horizontal acquisitions: A resource-based view. *Journal of Marketing, 63*(2), 41–54. doi:10.1177/002224299906300203

Casale, S., & Flett, G. L. (2020). Interpersonally-based fears during the COVID-19 pandemic: Reflections on the fear of missing out and the fear of not mattering constructs. *Clinical Neuropsychiatry, 17*(2), 88. PMID:34908975

Casero-Ripollés, A. (2020). Impact of Covid-19 on the media system. Communicative and democratic consequences of news consumption during the outbreak. *El Profesional de la Información, 29*(2), e290223. doi:10.3145/epi.2020.mar.23

Castells, M. (2001). *The Internet Galaxy: Reflections on the Internet, Business, and Society.* Oxford University Press. doi:10.1007/978-3-322-89613-1

Castillo, C., Mendoza, M., & Poblete, B. (2013). Information credibility on Twitter. *Proceedings of the 20th International Conference on World Wide Web,* 675-684.

Cefis, E., & Marsili, O. (2018). Good times, Bad Times: Innovation and survival over the business cycle. *Proceedings - Academy of Management, 2018*(1), 17783. doi:10.5465/AMBPP.2018.17783abstract

Černe, M., Jaklič, M., & Škerlavaj, M. (2013). Decoupling management and technological innovations: Resolving the individualism–collectivism controversy. *Journal of International Management, 19*(2), 103–117. doi:10.1016/j.intman.2013.03.004

Chakrabarty, K. C. (2013). *Frauds in the Banking Sector: Causes, Concerns and Cures.* Delhi: Reserve Bank of India (RBI Bulletin).

Chamakiotis, P., Panteli, N., & Davison, R. M. (2021). Reimagining e-leadership for reconfigured virtual teams due to covid-19. *International Journal of Information Management, 60,* 102381. doi:10.1016/j.ijinfomgt.2021.102381 PMID:34934257

Chan, M. K., Sharkey, J. D., Lawrie, S. I., Arch, D. A., & Nylund-Gibson, K. (2021). Elementary school teacher well-being and supportive measures amid COVID-19: An exploratory study. *The School Psychologist*, *36*(6), 533–545. doi:10.1037pq0000441 PMID:34292036

Chaudhry, M., & Salazar, J. (2020). Trust and influence in social media: The role of gender. *Journal of Business Research*, (110), 62–70.

Chaum, D. (1981, Feb). *Untraceable electronic mail, return addresses, and digital pseudonyms.* Retrieved from Digital Library: https://dl.acm.org/doi/10.1145/358549.358563

Chekkai, N., & Kheddouci, H. (2022). TOP-Key Influential Nodes for Opinion Leaders Identification in Travel Recommender Systems. In P. Fournier-Viger, A. Hassan, L. Bellatreche, A. Awad, A. Ait Wakrime, Y. Ouhammou, & I. Ait Sadoune (Eds.), *Advances in Model and Data Engineering in the Digitalization Era* (pp. 149–161). Springer Nature Switzerland. doi:10.1007/978-3-031-23119-3_11

Cheng. (2020). Identification of influential users in social network using gray wolf optimization algorithm. *Phys. A Stat. Mech. its Appl.*, *142*(1), 112971. . doi:10.1016/j.eswa.2019.112971

Cheng, W., Chen, H., & Wang, Y. (2013). The role of trust in social media information sharing. *Computers in Human Behavior*, *2013*, 14–32.

Cheng, Y., & Lee, C. J. (2019). Online crisis communication in a post-truth Chinese society: Evidence from interdisciplinary literature. *Public Relations Review*, *45*(4), 101826. doi:10.1016/j.pubrev.2019.101826

Chen, L., & Zhu, J. (2021). Social media use and social capital among young adults in China. *Telematics and Informatics*, 101654.

Chen, W., Lakshmanan, L. V. S., & Castillo, C. (2013). Information and Influence Propagation in Social Networks. *Synthesis Lectures on Data Management*, *5*(4), 1–177. doi:10.1007/978-3-031-01850-3

Chen, W., Wang, C., & Wang, Y. (2010). Scalable Influence Maximization for Prevalent Viral. *16th ACM SIGKDD Int. Conf. Knowl. Discov. data Min.*, 1029–1038.

Chen, Y., & Liu, B. (2023). Advertising and pricing decisions for signaling crowdfunding product's quality. *Computers & Industrial Engineering*, *176*, 108947. Advance online publication. doi:10.1016/j.cie.2022.108947

Chichkanov, N., Miles, I., & Belousova, V. (2019). Drivers for innovation in KIBS: Evidence from Russia. *Service Industries Journal*, *41*(7-8), 489–511. doi:10.1080/02642069.2019.1570151

Child, J. (1972). Organizational structure, environment and performance: The role of strategic choice. *Sociology*, *6*(1), 1–22. doi:10.1177/003803857200600101

Choi, H. J., & Park, C. H. (2019). Emerging topic detection in twitter stream based on high utility pattern mining. *Expert Systems with Applications*, *115*, 27–36. doi:10.1016/j.eswa.2018.07.051

Cialdini, R. B., & Fincham, R. L. (1990). Trust and the development of interpersonal relationships. *Psychological Bulletin*.

Clark, J. L., & Barbour, K. (2021). Social media and social capital: A review of empirical research. *New Media & Society*, *23*(2), 318–338.

Coleman, J. S., & Thomas, H. (1987). *Public and private high schools: The impact of communities.* Basic Books. Retrieved at https://www.psychreg.org/social-media-education

Coleman, J. S. (1988). Social capital in the creation of human capital. *American Journal of Sociology*, *94*, S95–S120. doi:10.1086/228943

Colombo, M. G., Franzoni, C., & Rossi-Lamastra, C. (2015). Internal social capital and the attraction of early contributions in crowdfunding. *Entrepreneurship Theory and Practice*, *39*(1), 75–100. doi:10.1111/etap.12118

Coman, C., Țîru, L. G., Meseșan-Schmitz, L., Stanciu, C., & Bularca, M. C. (2020). Online teaching and learning in higher education during the coronavirus pandemic: Students' perspective. *Sustainability (Basel)*, *12*(24), 10367. doi:10.3390u122410367

Contreras, F., Baykal, E., & Abid, G. (2020). E-Leadership and Teleworking in Times of COVID-19 and Beyond: What We Know and Where Do We Go. *Frontiers in Psychology*, *11*(590271), 590271. Advance online publication. doi:10.3389/fpsyg.2020.590271 PMID:33362656

Cook, S. ((2023). *Identity theft facts & statistics: 2019-2022*. https://www.comparitech.com /identity-theft-protection/identity-theft-statistics/

Coombs, W. T., & Holladay, S. J. (2019). *The Handbook of Crisis Communication* (3rd ed.). Wiley-Blackwell.

Copeland, M. K. (2014). The emerging significance of values based leadership: A literature review. *International Journal of Leadership Studies*, *8*(2), 105.

Creswell, J. W. (2007). *Qualitative inquiry and research design: Choosing among five approaches* (2nd ed.). Sage Publications, Inc.

Creswell, J. W. (2009). *Research design: Qualitative, quantitative, and mixed methods approaches* (3rd ed.). Sage Publications, Inc.

Crosetto, P., & Regner, T. (2014). *Crowdfunding: Determinants of success and funding dynamics*. Jena Economic Research Papers.

CSO. (2018). What is the Tor Browser? How it works and how it can help you protect your identity online. *CSO*, 1-8.

Cui. (2018). DDSE: A novel evolutionary algorithm based on degree-descending search strategy for influence maximization in social networks. *J. Netw. Comput. Appl.*, *103*, 119–130. . doi:10.1016/j.jnca.2017.12.003

Customer satisfaction towards internet banking with special reference to North Chennai. (2019). *International Journal of Recent Technology and Engineering*, *8*(4S3), 284–286. doi:10.35940/ijrte.D1058.1284S319

Customers' perception towards mobile banking with reference to Chennai city. (2019). *International Journal of Recent Technology and Engineering*, *8*(4S3), 312–315. doi:10.35940/ijrte.D1066.1284S319

Dabiri, S., & Heaslip, K. (2019). Developing a Twitter-based traffic event detection model using deep learning architectures. *Expert Systems with Applications*, *118*, 425–439. doi:10.1016/j.eswa.2018.10.017

Dan, S. M., Spaid, B. I., & Noble, C. H. (2018). Exploring the sources of Design Innovations: Insights from the computer, communications and Audio Equipment Industries. *Research Policy*, *47*(8), 1495–1504. doi:10.1016/j.respol.2018.05.004

Dasgupta, B. (2020). Credit, debit card data of half a million Indians up for sale on dark web. *Hindustan Times*, 1-2.

Datta, A., Sahaym, A., & Brooks, S. (2019). Unpacking the Antecedents of Crowdfunding Campaign's Success: The Effects of Social Media and Innovation Orientation. *Journal of Small Business Management*, *57*(sup2), 462–488. Advance online publication. doi:10.1111/jsbm.12498

Dattée, B., Alexy, O., & Autio, E. (2018). Maneuvering in poor visibility: How firms play the ecosystem game when uncertainty is high. *Academy of Management Journal*, *61*(2), 466–498. doi:10.5465/amj.2015.0869

Daykin, N., Mansfield, L., & Victor, C. (2020). Singing and wellbeing across the lifecourse: Evidence from recent research. In R. Heydon, D. Fancourt, & A. Cohen (Eds.), Routledge Companion to interdisciplinary studies in singing: Volume III well-being (pp. 30–31). Routledge.

De Buysere, K., Gajda, O., Kleverlaan, R., & Marom, D. (2012). *A framework for european crowdfunding*. Crowdfunding.

Debertin & Goetz. (2013). *Social Capital Formation in Rural, Urban and Suburban Communities.* University of Kentucky Staff Paper 474.

Deshpande, B. N. (2018). Digitalization in banking sector. *International Journal of Trend in Scientific Research and Development*, 80–85. doi:10.31142/ijtsrd18677

Di Marco, M., Chong, M. N., Piciucco, A., Cresci, S., & Petrocchi, M. (2021). Covid-19 on Twitter: Analyzing misinformation in tweets with topic modeling and supervised classification. *IEEE Access : Practical Innovations, Open Solutions*, 9, 68504–68516.

Dinçer, H., Baykal, E., & Yüksel, S. (2021). Analysis of spiritual leadership and ethical climate for banking industry using an integrated IT2 fuzzy decision-making model. *Journal of Intelligent & Fuzzy Systems*, 40(1), 1443–1455. doi:10.3233/JIFS-201840

Doherty, I. (2010). Agile project management for e-learning developments. *International Journal of E-Learning & Distance Education/Revue internationale du e-learning et la formation à distance*, 24(1), 91-106.

Donath, J., & Boyd, D. (2004). Public displays of connection. *BT Technology Journal*, 22(4), 71–82. doi:10.1023/B:BTTJ.0000047585.06264.cc

Dulebohn, J. H., & Hoch, J. E. (2017). Virtual teams in organizations. *Human Resource Management Review*, 27(4), 569–574. doi:10.1016/j.hrmr.2016.12.004

Dzenopoljac, V., Yaacoub, C., Elkanj, N., & Bontis, N. (2017). Impact of intellectual capital on corporate performance: Evidence from the Arab region. *Journal of Intellectual Capital*, 18(4), 884–903. doi:10.1108/JIC-01-2017-0014

Edelman. (2022). *2022 Edelman trust barometer*. https://www.edelman.com/trust/2022-trust-barometer

Edmunds, J. A., Gicheva, D., Thrift, B., & Hull, M. (2021). High tech, high touch: The impact of an online course intervention on academic performance and persistence in higher education. *The Internet and Higher Education*, 49, 100790. doi:10.1016/j.iheduc.2020.100790

Edstro¨m, A., & Galbraith, J. (1977, June). Transfer of managers as a coordination and control strategy in multinational organizations. *Administrative Science Quarterly*, 22(2), 248–263. doi:10.2307/2391959

Edvinsson, L., & Ve Malone, M.S. (1997). *Intellectual Capital Realizing Your Company's True Value By Finding Its Hiden Brainpower*. Harperbusiness.

Elad, B. (2023). Crowdfunding Statistics – By Country, Success Rate, Region, Funding Amount, Industry. *Enterprise-AppsToday*. https://www.enterpriseappstoday.com/stats/crowdfunding-statistics.html#:~:text=Inthe respective following years,expected to reach %241.10 million

Ellison, N. B., Steinfield, C., & Lampe, C. (2007). The benefits of Facebook "friends:" Social capital and college students' use of online social network sites. *Journal of Computer-Mediated Communication*, 12(4), 1143–1168. doi:10.1111/j.1083-6101.2007.00367.x

Ellison, N. B., Vitak, J., Gray, R., & Lampe, C. (2014). Cultivating social resources on social network sites: Facebook relationship maintenance behaviors and their role in social capital processes. *Journal of Computer-Mediated Communication, 19*(4), 855–870. doi:10.1111/jcc4.12078

Ellison, N. B., Vitak, J., Gray, R., & Lampe, C. (2020). Cultivating social resources on social media: Facebook relationship maintenance behaviors and their role in social capital processes. *Journal of Computer-Mediated Communication, 25*(1), 40–56.

Entrepreneurial enactment as social value creation: An exploration of the Aberdeen entrepreneurial ecosystem. (2022). Academic Press.

Ergün, E., Taşçı, B. S., & Latifoğlu, N. (2019). *İnsan Sermayesi: Öğrenen Organizasyonlar, Kurumsal Akademiler, Şirket Üniversiteleri.* Ekin Yayınevi.

Eriksson, M., Santosa, A., Zetterberg, L., Kawachi, I., & Ng, N. (2021). Social Capital and Sustainable Social Development - How Are Changes in Neighbourhood Social Capital Associated with Neighbourhood Sociodemographic and Socioeconomic Characteristics? *Sustainability (Basel), 12*(6), 2506. doi:10.3390u132313161

Faisal, R. A., Jobe, M. C., Ahmed, O., & Sharker, T. (2021). Mental health status, anxiety, and depression levels of Bangladeshi university students during the COVID-19 pandemic. *International Journal of Mental Health and Addiction*, 1–16. doi:10.100711469-020-00458-y PMID:33424514

Fan, Z., & Zhai, X. (2023). The Performance Improvement Mechanism of Cross-Border E-Commerce Grassroots Entrepreneurship Empowered by the Internet Platform. *Sustainability (Basel), 15*(2), 1178. doi:10.3390u15021178

Faqih, K. M. (2016). Which is more important in e-learning adoption, perceived value or perceived usefulness? Examining the moderating influence of perceived compatibility. *4th global summit on education GSE.*

Fatima, S., Alqahtani, H., Naim, A., & Alma'alwi, F. (2022). E-CRM Through Social Media Marketing Activities for Brand Awareness, Brand Image, and Brand Loyalty. In A. Naim & S. Kautish (Eds.), *Building a Brand Image Through Electronic Customer Relationship Management* (pp. 109–138). IGI Global. doi:10.4018/978-1-6684-5386-5.ch006

Fischer, E., & Rebecca Reuber, A. (2014). Online entrepreneurial communication: Mitigating uncertainty and increasing differentiation via Twitter. *Journal of Business Venturing, 29*(4), 565–583. doi:10.1016/j.jbusvent.2014.02.004

Fischer, E., & Reuber, A. R. (2011). Social interaction via new social media: (How) can interactions on Twitter affect effectual thinking and behavior? *Journal of Business Venturing, 26*(1), 1–18. Advance online publication. doi:10.1016/j.jbusvent.2010.09.002

Ford, R. C., Piccolo, R. F., & Ford, L. R. (2017). Strategies for building effective virtual teams: Trust is key. *Business Horizons, 60*(1), 25–34. doi:10.1016/j.bushor.2016.08.009

Forster, A. G., & Van de Werfhorst, H. G. (2020). Navigating institutions: Parents' knowledge of the educational system and students' success in education. *European Sociological Review, 36*(1), 48–64.

Foundation, E. F. (2005). *Torproject.* Retrieved from Torproject: https://www.torproject.org/about/overview.html.en

Frank, K. A., Zhao, Y., & Borman, K. (2004). Social capital and the diffusion of innovations within organizations: The case of computer technology in schools. *Sociology of Education, 77*(2), 148–171. Advance online publication. doi:10.1177/003804070407700203

Friedman, R., & Krackhardt, D. (1997). Social capital and career mobility: A structural theory of lower returns to education for Asian employees. *The Journal of Applied Behavioral Science, 3*(3), 316–334. doi:10.1177/0021886397333004

Fry, L. W. (2003). Toward A Theory Of Spiritual Leadership. *The Leadership Quarterly*, *14*(6), 693–727. doi:10.1016/j.leaqua.2003.09.001

Fry, L. W., & Cohen, M. P. (2009). Spiritual Leadership As A Paradigm For Organizational Transformation And Recovery From Extended Work Hours Cultures. *Journal of Business Ethics*, *84*(2), 265–278. doi:10.100710551-008-9695-2

Fry, L. W., Latham, J. R., Clinebell, S. K., & Krahnke, K. (2017). Spiritual leadership as a model for performance excellence: A study of Baldrige award recipients. *Journal of Management, Spirituality & Religion*, *14*(1), 22–47. doi:10.1080/14766086.2016.1202130

Fukuyama, F. (2002). Social capital and development: The coming agenda. *SAIS Review (Paul H. Nitze School of Advanced International Studies)*, *22*(1), 23–27. doi:10.1353ais.2002.0009

Ganguly, S. (2019). India Loses $18.5 Bn Due To Illegal Business Done Over Darknet. *Inc42*, 1-2.

Gao, S., Liu, J., & Zhao, Y. (2019). Quantifying Information Propagation in Disaster Response on Social Media. *IEEE Transactions on Computational Social Systems*, *6*(2), 337–349.

Genç, A. K. (2018). *Entelektüel Sermaye ve Büyük Ölçekli İşletmelerin Katma Değerine Etkisi: Türkiye'de Bir Araştırma.* Yayınlanmamış Doktora Tezi, İstanbul Üniversitesi–Sosyal Bilimler Enstitüsü.

Gerber, E. M., & Hui, J. (2013). Crowdfunding: Motivations and deterrents for participation. *ACM Transactions on Computer-Human Interaction*, *20*(6), 1–32. Advance online publication. doi:10.1145/2530540

GhoshR.SurachawalaT.LermanK. Entropy-based Classification of 'Retweeting' Activity on Twitter. Social and Information Networks, Computers and Society,2011, arXiv:1106.0346v1.

Giudici, G., Nava, R., Rossi Lamastra, C., & Verecondo, C. (2012). Crowdfunding: The New Frontier for Financing Entrepreneurship? SSRN *Electronic Journal*. doi:10.2139/ssrn.2157429

Gkritsi, E. (2021). *Clubhouse invites for sale on Alibaba's used goods app.* Available at: https://technode.com/2021/02/02/clubhouse-invites-for-sale-on-alibabas-used-goodsapp

Gong, M., Song, C., Duan, C., Ma, L., & Shen, B. (2016). An Efficient Memetic Algorithm for Influence Maximization in Social Networks. *IEEE Computational Intelligence Magazine*, *11*(3), 22–33. doi:10.1109/MCI.2016.2572538

Goyal, A., Lu, W., & Lakshmanan, L. V. S. (2011). CELF++: Optimizing the greedy algorithm for influence maximization in social networks. *Proceedings of the 20th International Conference Companion on World Wide Web, WWW 2011*, 47–48. 10.1145/1963192.1963217

Grafton, R. Q. (2005). Social capital and fisheries governance. *Ocean and Coastal Management*, *48*(9–10), 753–766. doi:10.1016/j.ocecoaman.2005.08.003

Granovetter, M. (1983). The Strength of Weak Ties: A Network Theory Revisited. *Sociological Theory*, *1*, 201. doi:10.2307/202051

Granovetter, M. S. (1973). The strength of weak ties. *American Journal of Sociology*, *78*(6), 1360–1380. doi:10.1086/225469

Grant, R. M. (1996). Toward a knowledge-based theory of the organization [Winter special issue]. *Strategic Management Journal*, *17*(S2), 109–122. doi:10.1002mj.4250171110

Griffith, J., Marani, H., & Monkman, H. (2021). COVID-19 vaccine hesitancy in Canada: A content analysis of tweets using the theoretical domains framework. *Journal of Medical Internet Research*, *23*(4), e26874. doi:10.2196/26874 PMID:33769946

Gudup, M. S. (2016). The study of frauds and safety in e-banking. *NIL: Anveshana's International Journal of Research in Regional Studies, Law, Social Sciences.*

Gultom, J. M. P., Paat, V. B. G. D., & Harefa, O. (2022). Christian Mission, Spiritual Leadership and Personality Development of the Digital Generation. *PASCA: Jurnal Teologi dan Pendidikan Agama Kristen, 18*(1), 47-63.

Guo, L., Wang, H., Chen, H., & Zeng, D. (2013). Identifying and analyzing topical authorities in microblogs. *Proceedings of the 2013 IEEE/ACM International Conference on Advances in Social Networks Analysis and Mining*, 613-617.

Haas, P., Blohm, I., & Leimeister, J. M. (2014). An empirical taxonomy of crowdfunding intermediaries. *35th International Conference on Information Systems "Building a Better World Through Information Systems", ICIS 2014.*

Hale, T. M., O'Brien, E., & Chen, Y. (2020). A systematic review of social capital research in online health communities. *Journal of Health Communication, 25*(2), 166–181.

Hamilton, W., Duerr, D. E., Hemphill, C., & Colello, K. (2023). Techno-capital, cultural capital, and the cultivation of academic social capital: The case of adult online college students. Internet High. Educ., 56, 100891. doi:10.1016/j.iheduc.2022.100891

Hampton, K., & Wellman, B. (2003). Neighboring in Netville: How the Internet supports community and social capital in a wired suburb. *City & Community, 2*(4), 277–311. doi:10.1046/j.1535-6841.2003.00057.x

Han, C., & Gao, S. (2019). A chain multiple mediation model linking strategic, management, and technological innovations to firm competitiveness. *Revista Brasileira de Gestão de Negócios, 21*(4), 879–905. doi:10.7819/rbgn.v21i5.4030

Hand, J. R., & Lev, B. (Eds.). (2003). *Intangible Assets: Values, Measures, And Risks: Values, Measures, And Risks.* Oup Oxford.

Han, J. K., Kim, N., & Srivastava, R. K. (1998). Market orientation and organizational performance: Is innovation a missing link? *Journal of Marketing, 62*(4), 30–45. doi:10.1177/002224299806200403

Harchekar, M. J. S. (2018). Digitalization in banking sector. *International Journal of Trend in Scientific Research and Development,* 103–109. doi:10.31142/ijtsrd18681

Harvey, M., & Buckley, M. (1997). Managing inpatriates: Building a global core competency. *Journal of World Business, 32*(1), 34–45. doi:10.1016/S1090-9516(97)90024-9

Harvey, M., & Novicevic, M. (2001). Selecting expatriates for increasingly complex global assignments. *Career Development International, 6*(2), 67–78. doi:10.1108/13620430110383357

Harvey, M., & Novicevic, M. (2002). Selecting appropriate marketing managers to effectively Control global channels of distribution. *International Marketing Review, 19*(5), 74–86. doi:10.1108/02651330210445310

Hasan, M. R., Shams, S. M. R., Rahman, M., & Haque, S. E. (2020). Analysing pro-poor innovation acceptance by income segments. *Management Decision, 58*(8), 1663–1674. doi:10.1108/MD-09-2019-1301

Hasan, M., Orgun, M. A., & Schwitter, R. (2019). Real-time event detection from the Twitter data stream using the TwitterNews+ Framework. *Information Processing & Management, 56*(3), 1146–1165. doi:10.1016/j.ipm.2018.03.001

Hassankhani, M., Alidadi, M., Sharifi, A., & Azhdari, A. (2021). Smart city and crisis management: Lessons for the COVID-19 pandemic. *International Journal of Environmental Research and Public Health, 18*(15), 7736. doi:10.3390/ijerph18157736 PMID:34360029

Helliwell, J., & Putnam, R. (1995). Economic growth and social Capital in Italy. *Eastern Economic Journal, 21*, 295–307.

He, Q., Wang, X., Lei, Z., Huang, M., Cai, Y., & Ma, L. (2019). TIFIM: A Two-stage Iterative Framework for Influence Maximization in Social Networks. *Applied Mathematics and Computation, 354*, 338–352. doi:10.1016/j.amc.2019.02.056

Heredia Pérez, J. A., Geldes, C., Kunc, M. H., & Flores, A. (2019). New approach to the innovation process in emerging economies: The manufacturing sector case in Chile and Peru. *Technovation, 79*, 35–55. doi:10.1016/j.technovation.2018.02.012

Hidayat, S., Febrianto, Z., Purwohedi, U., Rachmawati, D., & Zahar, M. (2023). Proactive personality and organizational support in television industry: Their roles in creativity. *PLoS One, 18*(1), e0280003. doi:10.1371/journal.pone.0280003 PMID:36626372

Hilmersson, M., Pourmand Hilmersson, F., Chetty, S., & Schweizer, R. (2022). Pace of innovation and speed of small and medium-sized enterprise international expansion. *International Small Business Journal, 41*(2), 181–203. doi:10.1177/02662426221085193

Hoch, J. E., & Kozlowski, S. W. (2014). Leading virtual teams: Hierarchical leadership, structural supports, and shared team leadership. *The Journal of Applied Psychology, 99*(3), 390–403. doi:10.1037/a0030264 PMID:23205494

Hoda, N., Gupta, S. L., Ahmad, M., & Gupta, U. (2021). Modelling the relationship between linked-in usage and social capital formation. *European Journal of Sustainable Development, 10*(1), 624–635. doi:10.14207/ejsd.2021.v10n1p624

Holland, P., & Bardoel, A. (2016). The impact of technology on work in the twenty-first century: Exploring the smart and dark side. *International Journal of Human Resource Management, 27*(21), 2579–2581. doi:10.1080/09585192.2016.1238126

Holle, D. (2020). Student engagement and blended learning: Portraits of risk. *Computers & Education, 54*(3), 693-700.

Holzinger, A., Dehmer, M., & Jurisica, I. (2014). Knowledge discovery and interactive data mining in bioinformatics - state-of-the-art, future challenges and research direc-tions. *BMC Bioinformatics, 15*(S6), I1. doi:10.1186/1471-2105-15-S6-I1 PMID:25078282

Hommerová, D. (2020). Crowdfunding as a new model of nonprofit funding. In Financing Nonprofit Organizations. doi:10.4324/9780429265419-16

Hong, Y., Hu, Y., & Burtch, G. (2015). How does social media affect contribution to public versus private goods in crowdfunding campaigns? *2015 International Conference on Information Systems: Exploring the Information Frontier, ICIS 2015.*

Hossain, M. A., Yesmin, N., Jahan, N., & Reza, S. M. A. (2023). Effect of Social Presence on Behavioral Intention to Social Commerce Through Online Social Capital. *International Journal of e-Collaboration, 19*(1), 1–23. doi:10.4018/IJeC.315779

Huber, S. G., & Helm, C. (2020). COVID-19 and schooling: Evaluation, assessment and accountability in times of crises reacting quickly to explore key issues for policy, practice and research with the school barometer. *Educational Assessment, Evaluation and Accountability, 32*(2), 237–270. doi:10.100711092-020-09322-y PMID:32837626

Hughes & Palen. (2009). Twitter Adoption and Use in Mass Convergence and Emergency Events. *Int. J. of Emergency Management, 6*, 248–260.

Hui, J. S., Greenberg, M. D., & Gerber, E. M. (2014). Understanding the role of community in crowdfunding work. *Proceedings of the ACM Conference on Computer Supported Cooperative Work, CSCW.* 10.1145/2531602.2531715

Huppert, U. (2017). *Measurement really matters. Discussion paper 2.* What Works Centre for Wellbeing. www.whatworkswellbeing.org/product/measurement-really-matters-discussion-paper-2/

Imran, M., Castillo, C., Diaz, F., & Vieweg, S. (2015). Processing social media messages in mass emergency: A survey. *ACM Computing Surveys*, *47*(4), 67–105. doi:10.1145/2771588

Imran, M., Elbassuoni, S. M., Castillo, C., Diaz, F., & Meier, P. (2015). Practical extraction of disaster-relevant information from social media. *Proceedings of the 24th International Conference on World Wide Web*, 1023-1028.

IndiaTimes. (2020a, Dec. 9). Data of 70 lakh Indian cardholders leaked on dark web. *The Economic Times(CIO) IndiaTimes*.

IndiaTimes. (2020b, July 28). About 84,545 bank fraud cases reported during 2019-2020, says RBI, in reply. *The Economic Times(BFSI) IndiaTimes*, 1-2.

Itani, O. S., Badrinarayanan, V., & Rangarajan, D. (2023, January). The impact of business-to-business salespeople's social media use on value co-creation and cross/up-selling: The role of social capital. *European Journal of Marketing*, *57*(3), 683–717. doi:10.1108/EJM-11-2021-0916

Jain, M., & Popli, G. S. (2012). Role of information technology in the development of banking sector in India. SSRN *Electronic Journal*. doi:10.2139/ssrn.2151162

Jalayer, M., Azheian, M., & Agha Mohammad Ali Kermani, M. (2018). A hybrid algorithm based on community detection and multi attribute decision making for influence maximization. Comput. Ind. Eng., 120, 234–250. doi:10.1016/j.cie.2018.04.049

Janes, E., Livingstone, S., Lum, K., Boler, M., & Ringrose, J. (2022). Online harassment of women: The role of gender, misogyny, and victimization. *Social Media + Society*.

Jayasekara, P. K. (2019). Role of Facebook as a disaster communication media. *International Journal of Emergency Services*, *8*(2), 191–204. doi:10.1108/IJES-04-2018-0024

Jiang, Y. (2021). Problematic Social media usage and anxiety among university students during the COVID-19 pandemic: The mediating role of psychological capital and the moderating role of academic burnout. Frontiers in Psychology, 12, 612007. https://dx.doi.org/ doi:10.3389/fpsyg.2021.612007

Jiang, Q., Song, G., Cong, G., Wang, Y., Si, W., & Xie, K. (2011). Simulated annealing based influence maximization in social networks. *Proc. Natl. Conf. Artif. Intell.*, 1, 127–132. 10.1609/aaai.v25i1.7838

Johnson, B., Davis, E., & Williams, L. (2000). A Collaborative Filtering Approach for Friend Recommendation in Social Networks. *Proceedings of the International Conference on Machine Learning*, 456-467.

Jordan, M. I., & Mitchell, T. M. (2015). Machine learning: Trends, perspectives, and prospects. *Science*, *349*(6245), 255–260. doi:10.1126cience.aaa8415 PMID:26185243

Joshi, A., Vinay, M., & Bhaskar, P. (2021). Impact of coronavirus pandemic on the Indian education sector: Perspectives of teachers on online teaching and assessments. *Interactive Technology and Smart Education*, *18*(2), 205–226. doi:10.1108/ITSE-06-2020-0087

Kaartemo, V. (2017). The elements of a successful crowdfunding campaign: A systematic literature review of crowdfunding performance. *International Review of Entrepreneurship*.

Kamal, S., Naim, A., Magd, H., Khan, S. A., & Khan, F. M. (2022). The Relationship Between E-Service Quality, Ease of Use, and E-CRM Performance Referred by Brand Image. In A. Naim & S. Kautish (Eds.), *Building a Brand Image Through Electronic Customer Relationship Management* (pp. 84–108). IGI Global. doi:10.4018/978-1-6684-5386-5.ch005

Kaminski, J., Hopp, C., & Tykvová, T. (2019). New technology assessment in entrepreneurial financing – Does crowd-funding predict venture capital investments? *Technological Forecasting and Social Change*, *139*, 287–302. Advance online publication. doi:10.1016/j.techfore.2018.11.015

Kapasia, N., Paul, P., Roy, A., Saha, J., Zaveri, A., Mallick, R., & Chouhan, P. (2020). Impact of lockdown on learning status of undergraduate and postgraduate students during COVID-19 pandemic in West Bengal, India. *Children and Youth Services Review*, *116*, 105194. doi:10.1016/j.childyouth.2020.105194 PMID:32834270

Kaulio, M., Thorén, K., & Rohrbeck, R. (2017). Double ambidexterity: How a Telco incumbent used business-model and Technology Innovations to successfully respond to three major disruptions. *Creativity and Innovation Management*, *26*(4), 339–352. doi:10.1111/caim.12246

Kaur, H., & Gera, J. (2017). Effect of Social Media Connectivity on Success of Crowdfunding Campaigns. *Procedia Computer Science*, *122*, 767–774. Advance online publication. doi:10.1016/j.procs.2017.11.435

Kawachi, I., Kennedy, B. P., & Lochner, K. (1997). Long live community: Social Capital as public health. *The American Prospect*, *35*, 56–59.

Kawachi, I., Subramanian, I. V., & Kim, D. (2008). *Social capital and health*. Soc. Cap. Heal. doi:10.1007/978-0-387-71311-3

Kelly, H. (1984). The transitional descriptions of interdependence by means of transition lists. *Journal of Personality and Social Psychology*, *47*(5), 956–982. doi:10.1037/0022-3514.47.5.956

Kemp, S. (2023). *Digital 2023: The United States of America*. https://datareportal.com/ reports/digital-2023-united-states-of-america#:~:text=The%20USA%20was%20home%20to,percent%20 of %20the%20total%20population

Kempe, D., Kleinberg, J., & Tardos, É. (2003). Maximizing the spread of influence through a social network. *Proceedings of the ACM SIGKDD International Conference on Knowledge Discovery and Data Mining*, 137–146. 10.1145/956750.956769

Kempe, D., Kleinberg, J., & Tardos, É. (2015). Maximizing the spread of influence through a social network. *Theory Comput.*, *11*(1), 105–147. doi:10.4086/toc.2015.v011a004

Khan, M. A., Kamal, T., Illiyan, A., & Asif, M. (2021). School students' perception and challenges towards online classes during COVID-19 pandemic in India: An econometric analysis. *Sustainability (Basel)*, *13*(9), 4786. doi:10.3390u13094786

Kim, J., & Park, J. (2021). The impact of ease of use and feature relevance on social media use: A cross-platform study. *Information Systems Research*, *32*(2), 436–454.

Kim, M., Newth, D., & Christen, P. (2013). Modeling Dynamics of Diffusion Across Heterogeneous Social Networks: News Diffusion in Social Media. *Entropy (Basel, Switzerland)*, *15*(12), 4215–4242. doi:10.3390/e15104215

Kim, S. H., & Kim, S. (2021). Social trust as an individual characteristic or societal property? *International Review of Public Administration*, *26*(1), 1–17. doi:10.1080/12294659.2020.1834677

Kim, Y., Chen, J., & Huang, L. (2018). Social media use during natural disasters: The case of the 2015 Nepal earthquake. *International Journal of Information Management*, *38*(1), 86–95. doi:10.1016/j.ijinfomgt.2017.08.003

Kim, Y., & Sundar, S. S. (2014). Does Facebook use lead to digital inequality? Differential effects of Facebook use on social capital among young adults. *Journal of Computer-Mediated Communication*, *19*(3), 855–870.

Kıyat, G. B. D., Özgüleş, B., & Günaydın, S. C. (2018). Algılanan kurumsal itibar ve işe bağlılığın duygusal emek davranışı üzerine etkisi: Sağlık çalışanları örneği. *Hacettepe Sağlık İdaresi Dergisi*, *21*(3), 473–494.

Klessova, S., Engell, S., & Thomas, C. (2022). Assessment of the advancement of market-upstream innovations and of the performance of Research and Innovation Projects. *Technovation*, *116*, 102495. doi:10.1016/j.technovation.2022.102495

Knack, S., & Keefer, P. (1997). Does social Capital have an economic payoff? A cross-country investigation. *The Quarterly Journal of Economics*, *112*(4), 1251–1288. doi:10.1162/003355300555475

Kogut, B., & Zander, U. (1992). Knowledge of the organization, combinative capabilities, and the replication of technology. *Organization Science*, *3*(3), 383–397. doi:10.1287/orsc.3.3.383

Kohli, A. K., & Jaworski, B. J. (1990). Market orientation: The construct, research, propositions, and managerial implications. *Journal of Marketing*, *54*(2), 1–18. doi:10.1177/002224299005400201

Kolade, O., Atiase, V., Murithi, W., & Mwila, N. (2021). The business models of Tech Hubs in Africa: Implications for viability and Sustainability. *Technology Analysis and Strategic Management*, *33*(10), 1213–1225. doi:10.1080/095373 25.2021.1947492

Konovsky, M. A. (2000). Understanding procedural justice and its impact on business organizations. *Journal of Management*, *26*(3), 489–511. doi:10.1177/014920630002600306

Korsgaard, M. A., Schweiger, D. M., & Sapienza, H. J. (1995). Building commitment, attachment, and trust in strategic decision-making teams: The role of procedural justice. *Academy of Management Journal*, *38*(1), 60–84. doi:10.2307/256728

Kostadin, K., Proulx, J. D. E., & Dunn, E. W. (2017). Digitally connected, socially disconnected: The effects of relying on technology rather than other people. *Computers in Human Behavior*, *76*(November), 68–74.

Kostova, T., & Roth, K. (2003). Social capital in multinational corporations and a micro-macro model of it formulation. *Academy of Management Review*, *28*(2), 297–313. doi:10.2307/30040714

Ko, Y. Y., Cho, K. J., & Kim, S. W. (2018). Efficient and effective influence maximization in social networks: A hybrid-approach. *Information Sciences*, *465*, 144–161. doi:10.1016/j.ins.2018.07.003

Kraus, S., Richter, C., Brem, A., Cheng, C. F., & Chang, M. L. (2016). Strategies for reward-based crowdfunding campaigns. *Journal of Innovation and Knowledge*. doi:10.1016/j.jik.2016.01.010

Kraut, R., Kiesler, S., Boneva, B., Cummings, J., Helgeson, V., & Crawford, A. (2002). Internet paradox revisited. *The Journal of Social Issues*, *58*(1), 49–74. doi:10.1111/1540-4560.00248

KrebsonSecurity. (2020). U.S. Charges 4 Chinese Military Officers in 2017 Equifax Hack. *krebsonsecurity*, 1-6.

Kriger, M., & Seng, Y. (2005). Leadership with inner meaning: A contingency theory of leadership based on the worldviews of five religions. *The Leadership Quarterly*, *16*(5), 771–806. doi:10.1016/j.leaqua.2005.07.007

Kryvasheyeu, Y., Chen, H., Obradovich, N., Moro, E., Van Hentenryck, P., Fowler, J. W., & Cebrian, M. (2016). Rapid assessment of disaster damage using social media activity. *Science Advances*, *2*(3), e1500779. doi:10.1126ciadv.1500779 PMID:27034978

Kumar, Singh, Singh, & Biswas. (2020). Link prediction techniques, applications, and performance: A survey. *Phys. A Stat. Mech. its Appl.*, *553*, 124289. doi:10.1016/j.physa.2020.124289

Kumar, S., Barbier, G., & Abbasi, M. A. (2011). TweetTracker: An analysis tool for humanitarian and disaster relief. *Proceedings of the 3rd International Conference on Web Science*, 1-8.

Kurtar, Ş. (2009). *Ruhsal Liderlik Ölçeği: Türkçe Dilsel Eşdeğerlik, Geçerlik ve Güvenirlik Çalışması*. Yayımlanmamış Yüksek Lisans Tezi. Yeditepe Üniversitesi-Sosyal Bilimleri Enstitüsü.

Kvasny, L., Haddon, L., Vitak, J., Kowert, R., & Green, T. (2021). Women's perspectives on harm and Justice after online harassment. *Information Communication and Society*, *2021*(24), 878–897.

Larson, L., & DeChurch, L. A. (2020). Leading teams in the digital age: Four perspectives on technology and what they mean for leading teams. *The Leadership Quarterly*, *31*(1), 101377. doi:10.1016/j.leaqua.2019.101377 PMID:32863679

Le Cun, Y., Bengio, Y., & Hinton, G. (2015). Deep learning. *Nature*, *521*(7553), 436–444. doi:10.1038/nature14539 PMID:26017442

Leana, C. R., & Van Buren, H. J. III. (1999). Organizational social capital and employment practices. *Academy of Management Review*, *24*(3), 538–555. doi:10.2307/259141

Lechtenbörger, J., Stahl, F., Volz, V., & Vossen, G. (2015). Analysing observable success and activity indicators on crowdfunding platforms. *International Journal of Web Based Communities*, *11*(3/4), 264. Advance online publication. doi:10.1504/IJWBC.2015.072133

Lee, E., Lee, J., Moon, J.-H., & Sung, Y. (2014). How do people use Facebook features to manage social capital? *Computers in Human Behavior*, *36*, 449–455. doi:10.1016/j.chb.2014.04.007

Lei, D., Hitt, M. A., & Bettis, B. (1996). Dynamic core competencies through meta-learning and strategic context. *Journal of Management*, *22*(4), 247–267. doi:10.1177/014920639602200402

Leskovec, J., Adamic, L. A., & Huberman, B. A. (2007). The dynamics of viral marketing. *ACM Transactions on the Web*, *1*(1), 5. Advance online publication. doi:10.1145/1232722.1232727

Levy, Y. (2007). Comparing dropouts and persistence in e-learning courses. *Computers & Education*, *48*(2), 185–204. doi:10.1016/j.compedu.2004.12.004

Lewicki, J. A., McAllister, R. J., & Bies, R. H. (1998). Trust as a foundation for relationship quality. *Journal of Personality and Social Psychology*.

Lewis, K. (n.d.). *How social media networks facilitate identity theft and fraud.* https://www.eonetwork.org/octane-magazine/special-features/social-media-networks-facilitate-identity-theft-fraud#:~:text=With%20limited%20government%20oversight%2C%20industry%20standards%20or%20incentives,are%20likely%20vulnerable%20to%20outside%20%28or%20inside%29%20attack

Leydesdorff, L., & Rafols, I. (2009). A Global Map of Science Based on the ISI Subject Categories. *Journal of the American Society for Information Science and Technology*, *60*(2), 348–362. doi:10.1002/asi.20967

Liben-Nowell, D., & Kleinberg, J. M. (2007). The Link Prediction Problem for Social Networks. *Journal of the American Society for Information Science and Technology*, *58*(7), 1019–1031. doi:10.1002/asi.20591

Li, D., Wang, C., Zhang, S., Zhou, G., Chu, D., & Wu, C. (2017). Positive influence maximization in signed social networks based on simulated annealing. *Neurocomputing*, *260*, 69–78. doi:10.1016/j.neucom.2017.03.003

Li, J., & Che, W. (2022). Challenges and coping strategies of online learning for college students in the context of COVID-19: A survey of Chinese universities. *Sustainable Cities and Society*, *83*, 103958. doi:10.1016/j.scs.2022.103958 PMID:35620298

Li, L., Li, J., Li, X., & Liu, J. (2019). Real-time Geographical Location Extraction during Disasters Using Social Media. *International Journal of Geographical Information Science*, *33*(8), 1543–1561.

Lin. (2001). *Social Capital: A Theory of Social Structure and Action*. Academic Press.

Lin, L. Y., Sidani, J. E., Shensa, A., Radovic, A., Miller, E., Colditz, J. B., Hoffman, B. L., Giles, L. M., & Primack, B. A. (2016). Association between social media use and depression among US young adults. *Depression and Anxiety*, *33*(4), 323–331. doi:10.1002/da.22466 PMID:26783723

Lin, N. (2001). *Social Capital: A Theory of Social Structure and Action*. Cambridge University Press. doi:10.1017/CBO9780511815447

Lin, W. Y., Zhang, X., & Song, Y. (2020). Online social capital and civic engagement: A systematic review and meta-analysis. *Information Communication and Society*, *23*(10), 1403–1423.

Lin, Y., Xu, C., Zhu, Y., & Chen, Z. (2020). Quantifying Information Propagation on Twitter during Hurricane Harvey. *Natural Hazards*, *104*(3), 2073–2092.

Li, Q., Cheng, L., Wang, W., Li, X., Li, S., & Zhu, P. (2023). Influence maximization through exploring structural information. *Applied Mathematics and Computation*, *442*, 127721. Advance online publication. doi:10.1016/j.amc.2022.127721

Liu, S. B., Chen, H., & Zhu, X. (2012). Mining social media data for public health surveillance and monitoring. *Health Information Science and Systems*, *2*(1), 1–11.

Liu, S., Tang, J., & Yang, M. (2018). Deep learning for link prediction in social networks. *IEEE Intelligent Systems*, *33*(5), 38–46.

Liu, S., Yamada, M., Collier, N., & Sugiyama, M. (2013). Change-point detection in time-series data by relative density-ratio estimation. *Neural Networks*, *43*, 72–83. doi:10.1016/j.neunet.2013.01.012 PMID:23500502

Liu, X., & Wang, Z. (2022). The impact of personal values on social media use: A cross-cultural study. *Computers in Human Behavior*, *2022*(125), 106748.

Li, W., Gillies, R., He, M., Wu, C., Liu, S., Gong, Z., & Sun, H. (2021). Barriers and facilitators to online medical and nursing education during the COVID-19 pandemic: Perspectives from international students from low-and middle-income countries and their teaching staff. *Human Resources for Health*, *19*(1), 1–14. doi:10.118612960-021-00609-9 PMID:33980228

Li, X., Cheng, X., Su, S., & Sun, C. (2018). Community-based seeds selection algorithm for location aware influence maximization. *Neurocomputing*, *275*, 1601–1613. doi:10.1016/j.neucom.2017.10.007

Li, Y., Fabbre, V. D., & Gaveras, E. (2023). Authenticated social capital: Conceptualising power, resistance and well-being in the lives of transgender older adults. *Culture, Health & Sexuality*, *25*(3), 352–367. doi:10.1080/13691058.2022.2044519 PMID:35235503

Li, Y., & Li, J. (2021). A deep learning based framework for real-time disaster event detection from social media. *International Journal of Disaster Risk Reduction*, *65*, 102402.

Li, Z., & Jarvenpaa, S. L. (2015). Motivating IT-mediated crowds: The effect of goal setting on project performance in online crowdfunding. *2015 International Conference on Information Systems: Exploring the Information Frontier, ICIS 2015*. 10.2139srn.2672056

Li, Z., Ren, T., Ma, X., Liu, S., Zhang, Y., & Zhou, T. (2019). Identifying influential spreaders by gravity model. *Scientific Reports*, *9*(1), 1–7. doi:10.103841598-019-44930-9 PMID:31182773

Lu, C., Xie, S., Kong, X., & Yu, P. S. (2014). Inferring the Impacts of Social Media on Crowdfunding Categories and Subject Descriptors. *Proceeding WSDM '14 Proceedings of the 7th ACM International Conference on Web Search and Data Mining*.

Luetz, J. M., Nichols, E., du Plessis, K., & Nunn, P. D. (2023). Spirituality and Sustainable Development: A Systematic Word Frequency Analysis and an Agenda for Research in Pacific Island Countries. *Sustainability (Basel)*, *15*(3), 2201. doi:10.3390u15032201

Lü, L., & Zhou, T. (2011). Link Prediction in Complex Networks: A Survey. *Physica A*, *390*(6), 1150–1170. doi:10.1016/j.physa.2010.11.027

Luo, T., Zhou, C., & Zhao, Y. (2021). Uncovering flood-related topics in social media using topic modeling and clustering analysis. *International Journal of Disaster Risk Reduction*, *64*, 102464.

Luo, Y. (1997). Guanxi and performance of foreign-invested enterprises in China: An empirical inquiry. *Management International Review*, *37*(1), 51–70.

Lwin, M. O., Lee, S. Y., Panchapakesan, C., & Tandoc, E. (2023). Mainstream news media's role in public health communication during crises: Assessment of coverage and correction of COVID-19 misinformation. *Health Communication*, *38*(1), 160–168. doi:10.1080/10410236.2021.1937842 PMID:34157919

Maatuk, A. M., Elberkawi, E. K., Aljawarneh, S., Rashaideh, H., & Alharbi, H. (2022). The COVID-19 pandemic and E-learning: Challenges and opportunities from the perspective of students and instructors. *Journal of Computing in Higher Education*, *34*(1), 21–38. doi:10.100712528-021-09274-2 PMID:33967563

Macinko, J., & Starfield, B. (2001). The utility of social Capital in research on health determinants. *The Milbank Quarterly*, *79*(3), 387–427. doi:10.1111/1468-0009.00213 PMID:11565162

MacKay, M., Cimino, A., Yousefinaghani, S., McWhirter, J. E., Dara, R., & Papadopoulos, A. (2022). Canadian COVID-19 crisis communication on Twitter: Mixed methods research examining tweets from government, politicians, and public health for crisis communication guiding principles and tweet engagement. *International Journal of Environmental Research and Public Health*, *19*(11), 6954. doi:10.3390/ijerph19116954 PMID:35682537

Mak, A. K., & Song, A. O. (2019). Revisiting social-mediated crisis communication model: The Lancôme regenerative crisis after the Hong Kong Umbrella Movement. *Public Relations Review*, *45*(4), 101812. doi:10.1016/j.pubrev.2019.101812

Mallios & Moustakis. (2023). *Social Media Impact on Startup Entrepreneurial Intention : Evidence from Greece*. Academic Press.

Maniates, H., & Sakalli, E. (2020). Gender differences in trust and distrust: An examination of trust dynamics in online and offline contexts. *Journal of Applied Social Psychology*, *50*(1), 20-35.

Manning, R. A. (2020). *Emerging Technologies. New Challenges to Global Stability*. Atlantic Council. Available at: https://www.jstor.org/stable/resrep26000

Marhaini, M. N. (2018). Rural Community Digital Technology Connectedness: Does Ict In Rural Areas Contributes To Rural Development In Malaysia? *Social Sciences*.

Marlow, S. L., Lacerenza, C. N., & Salas, E. (2017). Communication in virtual teams: A conceptual framework and research agenda. *Human Resource Management Review*, *27*(4), 575–589. doi:10.1016/j.hrmr.2016.12.005

Martinez, R. A., Bosch, M. M., Herrero, M. H., & Nunoz, A. S. (2007). Psychopedagogical components and processes in e-learning. Lessons from an unsuccessful on-line course. *Computers in Human Behavior*, *23*(1), 146–161. doi:10.1016/j.chb.2004.04.002

Matthew, Sadiku, Adedamola, Omotoso, & Musa. (2019). Social Networking. Roy G. Perry College of Engineering, Prairie View A&M University, Prairie View. *International Journal of Trend in Scientific Research and Development*, *3*(3). www.ijtsrd.com

Mayer, R. D., Davis, J. H., & Schoorman, F. D. (1995). Trust in business relationships: A meta-analysis. *Journal of Business Ethics*.

McKenny, A. F., Allison, T. H., Ketchen, D. J., Short, J. C., & Ireland, R. D. (2017). How Should Crowdfunding Research Evolve? A Survey of the Entrepreneurship Theory and Practice Editorial Board. In Entrepreneurship: Theory and Practice. doi:10.1111/etap.12269

Meadows, C. W., Meadows, C. Z., Tang, L., & Liu, W. (2019). Unraveling public health crises across stages: Understanding Twitter emotions and message types during the California measles outbreak. *Communication Studies*, *70*(4), 453–469. doi:10.1080/10510974.2019.1582546

Means, B., Toyama, Y., Murphy, R., & Baki, M. (2013). The effectiveness of online and blended learning: A meta-analysis of the empirical literature. *Teachers College Record*, *115*(3), 1–47. doi:10.1177/016146811311500307

Merriam, S. B. (2009). *Qualitative Research: A Guide to Design and Implementation* (2nd ed.). John Wiley & Sons.

Merriam, S. B. (2009). *Qualitative research: A guide to design and implementation*. Jossey-Bass.

Merriam, S. B., & Tisdell, E. J. (2016). *Qualitative Research A Guide to Design and Implementation* (4th ed.). Jossey Bass.

Mesgari, I., Kermani, M. A. M. A., Hanneman, R., & Aliahmadi, A. (2015). Identifying Key Nodes in Social Networks Using Multi-Criteria Decision-Making Tools. In D. Mugnolo (Ed.), *Mathematical Technology of Networks* (pp. 137–150). Springer International Publishing. doi:10.1007/978-3-319-16619-3_10

Mikiewicz, P. (2021). Social capital and education – An attempt to synthesize conceptualization arising from various theoretical origins. *Cogent Education, 8*(1), 1907956. . doi:10.1080/2331186X.2021.1907956

Miles, M. B., & Huberman, A. M. (1994). *An Expanded Sourcebook: Qualitative Data Analysis* (2nd ed.). Sage Publications.

Mishkin, F. S. (2011). Over the cliff: From the Subprime to the global financial crisis. *The Journal of Economic Perspectives*, *25*(1), 49–70. doi:10.1257/jep.25.1.49

Mishra, A., Padhi, S. S., Kumar, S., & Swain, S. (2022). An efficient deep learning-based approach for disaster event detection using Twitter data. *Information Processing & Management*, *59*(1), 102737.

Mollick, E. (2014). The dynamics of crowdfunding: An exploratory study. *Journal of Business Venturing*, *29*(1), 1–16. Advance online publication. doi:10.1016/j.jbusvent.2013.06.005

Mont'Alerne, C., Arguedas, A. R., Toff, B., Fletcher, R., & Nielsen, R. K. (2022). *The trust gap: how and why news on digital platforms is viewed more skeptically versus news in general*. https://reutersinstitute.politics.ox.ac.uk/trust-gap-how-and-why-news-digital-platforms-viewed-more-sceptically-versus-news-general#header--0

Moore, M. G., & Kearsley, G. (2012). *Distance education: A systems view of online learning*. Cengage Learning.

Moritz, A., & Block, J. H. (2015). Crowdfunding: A Literature Review and Research Directions. SSRN *Electronic Journal*. doi:10.2139/ssrn.2554444

Morrison-Smith, S., & Ruiz, J. (2020). Challenges and barriers in virtual teams: A literature review. *SN Applied Sciences*, *2*(6), 1096. Advance online publication. doi:10.100742452-020-2801-5

Mozer, P. (2006). Social network analysis and social capital. *International Relations and Security Network*. https://www.files.ethz.ch/isn/130867/ISN_Special_Issues_Jun.2006.pdf

Mutakinati, L. (2020). The Impact of Covid-19 to Indonesian Education and Its Relation to the Philosophy of Merdeka Belajar. *Studies in Philosophy of Science and Education*, *1*(1), 38–49. doi:10.46627ipose.v1i1.9

Naim & Praveen. (2022). *Competitive Trends and Technologies in Business Management.* doi:10.52305/VIXO9830

Naim, A., & Alahmari, F. (2020). Reference model of e-learning and quality to establish interoperability in higher education systems. *International Journal of Emerging Technologies in Learning, 15*(2), 15–28. doi:10.3991/ijet.v15i02.11605

Naim, A., Alahmari, F., & Rahim, A. (2021). Role of Artificial Intelligence in Market Development and Vehicular Communication. Smart Antennas. *Recent Trends in Design and Applications, 2,* 28–39. doi:10.2174/9781681088594121020006

Naim, A., Alqahtani, H., Muniasamy, A., Bilfaqih, S. M., Mahveen, R., & Mahjabeen, R. (2023). Applications of Information Systems and Data Security in Marketing Management. In A. Naim, P. Malik, & F. Zaidi (Eds.), *Fraud Prevention, Confidentiality, and Data Security for Modern Businesses* (pp. 57–83). IGI Global. doi:10.4018/978-1-6684-6581-3.ch003

Naim, A., Hussain, M. R., Naveed, Q. N., Ahmad, N., Qamar, S., Khan, N., & Hweij, T. A. (2019, April). Ensuring interoperability of e-learning and quality development in education. In *2019 IEEE Jordan International Joint Conference on Electrical Engineering and Information Technology (JEEIT)* (pp. 736-741). IEEE. 10.1109/JEEIT.2019.8717431

Naim, A., & Kautish, S. K. (Eds.). (2022). *Building a Brand Image Through Electronic Customer Relationship Management.* IGI Global. doi:10.4018/978-1-6684-5386-5

Naim, A., Malik, P. K., & Zaidi, F. A. (Eds.). (2023). *Fraud Prevention, Confidentiality, and Data Security for Modern Businesses.* IGI Global. doi:10.4018/978-1-6684-6581-3

Nair, A. R. (2019). ndian Banks Review Leak After Details Of 1.3 Million Cards Surface On Dark Web . *Bloomberg (bqprime),* 1-2.

Najmul, H., & Mahmoud, F. (2022). Social Networking Site Usage, Social Capital and Entrepreneurial Intention: An Empirical Study from Saudi Arabia. *Journal of Asian Finance, 9*(5), 421–0429. doi:10.13106/jafeb.2022.vol9.no5.0421

Narayan, D., & Pritchett, L. (1997). Cents and Sociability: Household Income and Social Capital in RuralTanzania. *World Bank Policy Research Working Paper, 1796*(July).

Narcıkara, E. (2017). *Spiritüel Liderlik Davranışının Algılanan Performans Üzerine Etkisi. (Yayınlanmış Doktora Tezi).* Yıldız Teknik Üniversitesi Sosyal Bilimler Enstitüsü.

Narcıkara, E. B., & Zehir, C. (2016). Effect Of Organizational Support İn The Relationship Between Spiritual Leadership And Performance. *International Journal of Humanities and Social Science, 6*(12), 29–42.

Nerghes, A., & Lee, J. S. (2019). Narratives of the refugee crisis: A comparative study of mainstream media and Twitter. *Media and Communication, 7*(2), 275-288.

Newman, M. E. J. (2010). *Networks: An Introduction.* Oxford University Press. doi:10.1093/acprof:oso/9780199206650.001.0001

Newman, N., Fletcher, R., Robertson, C. T., Eddy, K., & Nielsen, R. K. (2022). *Digital news report 2022.* Reuters Institute for the Study of Journalism.

News, B. (2021). 10 crore Indians' card data selling on Dark Web. *BFSI.com(from The Economic Times),* 1-3.

News, C. (2020). Data of 70 lakh Indian cardholders leaked on dark web. *CIO.Com(From Economic Times),* 1-2.

NewsClick. (2020). 84,545 Bank Fraud Cases Worth Rs 1.85 Lakh Cr Reported During 2019-20. *NewsClick,* 1-2.

Nguyen, D. T., & Jung, J. E. (2017). Real-time event detection for online behavioral analysis of big social data. *Future Generation Computer Systems, 66,* 137–145. doi:10.1016/j.future.2016.04.012

Nguyen, H. T., Thai, M. T., & Dinh, T. N. (2016). Stop-and-Stare: Optimal sampling algorithms for viral marketing in billion-scale networks. *Proc. ACM SIGMOD Int. Conf. Manag. Data*, *26*(20), 695–710. 10.1145/2882903.2915207

Nieman, A. (2006). Social Capital and Social Development. *Social Work/Maatskaplike Werk, 42*(2). https://socialwork.journals.ac.za/

Nouri, J. (2020). Covid-19 and Crisis-Prompted Distance Education in Sweden. Technology, Knowledge and Learning, 26, 443-459. doi:10.100710758-020-09470-6

O'Brien, L., & Jones, C. (1995). Do rewards really create loyalty? *Harvard Business Review, 70*(3), 75–82.

Oduma, C. A., Onyema, L. N., & Akiti, N. (2019). E-learning platforms in business education for skill acquisition. *Nigerian Journal of Business Education, 6*(2), 104–112.

Oliver, R. L. (1999). Whence consumer loyalty. *Journal of Marketing, 63*(4_suppl1), 33–44. doi:10.1177/00222429990634s105

Olteanu, A., Vieweg, S., & Castillo, C. (2015). What to expect when the unexpected happens: Social media communications across crises. *Proceedings of the 18th ACM Conference on Computer Supported Cooperative Work & Social Computing*, 994-1009. 10.1145/2675133.2675242

Özdemir, S., & Karakoç, M. (2018). *Bilgi Ekonomisi Özelinde Üniversitelerde Entelektüel Sermayenin Ölçülmesi ve Raporlanması*. Academic Press.

Ozuem, W., Howell, K. E., & Lancaster, G. (2019). Consumption and communication perspectives of it in a developing economy. *Technology Analysis and Strategic Management, 31*(8), 929–942. doi:10.1080/09537325.2019.1574971

Pang, P. C. I., Cai, Q., Jiang, W., & Chan, K. S. (2021). Engagement of government social media on Facebook during the COVID-19 pandemic in Macao. *International Journal of Environmental Research and Public Health, 18*(7), 3508. doi:10.3390/ijerph18073508 PMID:33800621

Pantano, E. (2016). Benefits and risks associated with time choice of innovating in retail settings. *International Journal of Retail & Distribution Management, 44*(1), 58–70. doi:10.1108/IJRDM-03-2015-0047

Park, D., Kim, W. G., & Choi, S. (2019). Application of social media analytics in tourism crisis communication. *Current Issues in Tourism, 22*(15), 1810–1824. doi:10.1080/13683500.2018.1504900

Park, S. H., & Luo, Y. (2001). Guanxi and organizational dynamics: Organizational networking in Chinese organizations. *Strategic Management Journal, 22*(5), 455–477. doi:10.1002mj.167

Parmelee, M. (2021). *Twelve innovators that are transforming the future of education*. Retrieved from https://www.weforum.org/agenda/2021/09/education-innovation-uplink-skills-work-edtech

Pasquinelli, C., Trunfio, M., Bellini, N., & Rossi, S. (2021). Sustainability in overtouristified cities? A social media insight into Italian branding responses to the Covid-19 crisis. *Sustainability (Basel), 13*(4), 1848. doi:10.3390u13041848

Paton, D., Zheng, T., & Wang, L. (2020). Disaster resilience in the context of COVID-19: A framework for analyzing impacts and responses. *International Journal of Disaster Risk Reduction, 51*, 101789. doi:10.1016/j.ijdrr.2020.101789

Paul, L. (2011). The Use of Social Networking in Community Development. Academic Press.

Paul, K. C., Hamzah, A., Samah, B. A., Ismail, I. A., & D'Silva, J. L. (2014). Value of Social Network for Development of Rural Malay Herbal Entrepreneurship in Malaysia. *Procedia: Social and Behavioral Sciences, 130*, 59–64. doi:10.1016/j.sbspro.2014.04.008

Peng, M. W., & Luo, Y. (2000). Managerial ties and organization performance in a transition economy: The nature of a micro- macro link. *Academy of Management Journal*, *43*(3), 486–501. doi:10.2307/1556406

Perez, S. (2021). *Social audio app Clubhouse has topped 8 million global downloads*. Available at: https://techcrunch.com/2021/02/18/report-social-audio-app-clubhouse-has-topped-8-million-global-downloads

Peter, M. (2016, July). Social media, community development and social capital. *Community Development Journal: An International Forum*, *51*(3), 419–435. doi:10.1093/cdj/bsv040

Pew Research Center. (2022). *Public trust in government: 1958-2022*. https://www.pewresearch.org/ politics/2022/06/06/public-trust-in-government-1958-2022/

Picciano, A. G. (2017). Theories and frameworks for online education: Seeking an integrated model. *Online Learning : the Official Journal of the Online Learning Consortium*, *21*(3), 166–190. doi:10.24059/olj.v21i3.1225

Podgorskaya, S., & Schitov, S. (2021). The role and importance of social capital in rural development. *E3S Web Conf.*, *273*, 08072. doi:10.1051/e3sconf/202127308072

Portes, A. (1998). Social capital: Its origins and applications in modern sociology. *Annual Review of Sociology*, *24*(1), 1–24. doi:10.1146/annurev.soc.24.1.1

Porup, J. (2019). What is the Tor Browser? And how it can help protect your identity. *CSO INDIA*, 2-7.

Punch, K. F. (2005). *Introduction to Social Research: Quantitative and Qualitative Approach* (2nd ed.). SAGE Publications.

Putnam, R. D. (1993). Making democracy work: civic tradition in modern Italy. Princeton University Press.

Putnam, R. D. (2000). Bowling Alone: The Collapse and Revival of American Community. New York: Simon & Schuster.

Putnam, R. D. (2017). *Social Capital Primer. Bowling alone*. Professor Putnam's Harvard webpage.

Putnam. (2000). *Bowling Alone: The Collapse and Revival of American Community*. Academic Press.

Putnam, R. (1993). The prosperous community: Social capital in public life. *The American Prospect*, *13*, 35–42.

Putnam, R. D. (1993). *Making democracy work*. University Press.

Putnam, R. D. (2000). *Bowling alone: The collapse and revival of American community*. Simon & Schuster.

Python Machine Learning. (2020). *A Guide To Getting Started*. Built In.

Qi, X., Duval, R. D., Christensen, K., Fuller, E., Spahiu, A., Wu, Q., Wu, Y., Tang, W., & Zhang, C. (2013). Terrorist Networks, Network Energy and Node Removal: A New Measure of Centrality Based on Laplacian Energy. *Social Networking*, *02*(01), 19–31. doi:10.4236n.2013.21003

Raffaella, Putnam, & Leonardi. (1994). *Making Democracy Work: Civic Traditions in Modern Italy*. Academic Press.

Raghuram, S., Hill, N. S., Gibbs, J. L., & Maruping, L. M. (2019). Virtual work: Bridging research clusters. *The Academy of Management Annals*, *13*(1), 308–341. doi:10.5465/annals.2017.0020

Rameshkumar, K., Suresh, R. K., & Mohanasundaram, K. M. (2005). Discrete particle swarm optimization (DPSO) algorithm for permutation flowshop scheduling to minimize makespan. Lect. Notes Comput. Sci., 3612(3), 572–581. doi:10.1007/11539902_70

Raza, S. A., Qazi, W., & Umer, A. (2016). Facebook is a source of social capital-building among university students. *Journal of Educational Computing Research*. Advance online publication. doi:10.1177/0735633116667357

Reichheld, F. F., & Teal, T. (1996). *The loyalty effect: The hidden force behind growth, profits, and lasting value.* Harvard Business School Press.

Resnick, P. (2001). Beyond bowling together: Sociotechnical capital. In J. Carroll (Ed.), *HCI in the New Millennium* (pp. 247–272). Addison-Wesley.

Roca, J. C., & Gagné, M. (2008). Understanding e-learning continuance intention in the workplace: A self-determination theory perspective. *Computers in Human Behavior*, *24*(4), 1585–1604. doi:10.1016/j.chb.2007.06.001

Rogers, E. M. (2010). *Diffusion of innovations* (4th ed.). Free Press.

Rönnerstrand, B. (2013). Social capital and immunisation against the (2009). A (H1N1) pandemic in Sweden. *Scandinavian Journal of Public Health*, *41*(8), 853–859. doi:10.1177/1403494813494975 PMID:23843025

Rossman, M. H., & Rossman, M. E. (1995). Facilitating Distance Education. Jossey-Bass Inc., Publishers.

Roth, K., & Nigh, D. (1992). The effectiveness of headquarters- subsidiary relationships: The role of coordination, control, and conflict. *Journal of Business Research*, *25*(4), 277–301. doi:10.1016/0148-2963(92)90025-7

Ruef. (2010). *The Social Capital of Entrepreneurial Newcomers: Bridging.* Status-power, and Cognition.

Russon, A.-M. (2021). *Clubhouse confirms data spillage of its audio streams.* Available at: https://www.bbc.com/news/business-56163623

Saeed, I., Khan, J., Zada, M., Ullah, R., Vega-Muñoz, A., & Contreras-Barraza, N. (2022). Towards examining the link between workplace spirituality and workforce agility: Exploring higher educational institutions. *Psychology Research and Behavior Management*, *15*, 31–49. doi:10.2147/PRBM.S344651 PMID:35027852

Saenz, C. (2023). Corporate social responsibility strategies beyond the sphere of influence: Cases from the Peruvian mining industry. Resour. Policy, 80, 103187. doi:10.1016/j.resourpol.2022.103187

Saha, S., Mondal, S., & Saha, S. (2021). Quantifying Information Propagation Rate in Disaster-affected Areas through Social Media Analysis. *International Journal of Disaster Risk Reduction*, *55*, 102027.

Sahaym, A., Datta, A., & Brooks, S. (2021). Crowdfunding success through social media: Going beyond entrepreneurial orientation in the context of small and medium-sized enterprises. *Journal of Business Research*. Advance online publication. doi:10.1016/j.jbusres.2019.09.026

Sakaki, T., Okazaki, M., & Matsuo, Y. (2010). Earthquake shakes Twitter users: real-time event detection by social sensors. *Proceedings of the 19th International Conference on World Wide Web*, 851-860. 10.1145/1772690.1772777

Salil Panchal, P. S. (2019). *Seven recent banking frauds that have rocked India.* Retrieved from Forbes India: https://www.forbesindia.com/article/leaderboard/seven-recent-banking-frauds-that-have-rocked-india/55613/1

Salimi, G., Heidari, E., Mehrvarz, M., & Safavi, A. A. (2022). Impact of online social capital on academic performance: Exploring the mediating role of online knowledge sharing. *Education and Information Technologies*, *27*(5), 6599–6620. doi:10.100710639-021-10881-w PMID:35075344

Salloum, S. A., Alhamad, A. Q. M., Al-Emran, M., Monem, A. A., & Shaalan, K. (2019). Exploring students' acceptance of e-learning through the development of a comprehensive technology acceptance model. *IEEE Access : Practical Innovations, Open Solutions*, *7*, 128445–128462. doi:10.1109/ACCESS.2019.2939467

Samul, J. (2019). Spiritual Leadership: Meaning in The Sustainable Workplace. *Sustainability (Basel)*, *12*(1), 267. doi:10.3390u12010267

Saxton, G. D., & Wang, L. (2014). The Social Network Effect: The Determinants of Giving Through Social Media. *Nonprofit and Voluntary Sector Quarterly, 43*(5), 850–868. Advance online publication. doi:10.1177/0899764013485159

Schwarzmüller, T., Brosi, P., Duman, D., & Welpe, I. M. (2018). How does the digital transformation affect organizations? key themes of change in work design and leadership. *Management Review, 29*(2), 114–138. doi:10.5771/0935-9915-2018-2-114

Schwienbacher, A., & Benjamin, L. (2010). Crowdfunding of Small Entrepreneurial Venturs. In Handbook of Entrepreneurial Finance. Academic Press.

Seclen-Luna, J. P., Fernandez, P. M., Güenaga, J. B., & Ferrucci, L. (2022). Innovation in micro firms builders of machine tool? effects of T-KIBS on technological and non-technological innovations. *Revista Brasileira de Gestão de Negócios, 24*(1), 144–158. doi:10.7819/rbgn.v24i1.4163

Secur. (2020). Understanding How To Use Tor. *Secur,* 2-6.

Selvan, A., Ramesh, V., & Natarajan, S. (2021). A novel hybrid approach for effective disaster response using social media and machine learning. *Sustainable Cities and Society, 72,* 103110.

Selvaraj, A., Radhin, V., Nithin, K. A., Benson, N., & Mathew, A. J. (2021). Effect of pandemic-based online education on teaching and learning system. *International Journal of Educational Development, 85,* 102444. doi:10.1016/j.ijedudev.2021.102444 PMID:34518732

Shang, R., Luo, S., Li, Y., Jiao, L., & Stolkin, R. (2015). Large-scale community detection based on node membership grade and sub-communities integration. Phys. A Stat. Mech. its Appl., 428, 279–294. doi:10.1016/j.physa.2015.02.004

Shirky, C. (2008). *Here Comes Everybody: The Power of Organizing Without Organizations.* Penguin Books.

Simonson, M., Smaldino, S., Albright, M., & Zvacek, S. (2019). *Teaching and learning at a distance: Foundations of distance education.* Information Age Publishing.

Singh & Pandey. (2021). *IoT for Automation Clustering to Detect Power losses with Efficiency of Energy Consumption and survey of defense machinery against attacks.* CRC Press. https://www.routledge.com/Applied-Soft-Computing-and-Embedded-System-Applications-in-Solar-Energy/Pachauri-Pandey-Sharmu-Nautiyal-Ram/p/book/9780367625122

Singh, A. K. (2017a). The active impact of human computer interaction (HCI) on economic, cultural and social life. *IIOAB Journal, 8*(2), 141-146. https://www.iioab.org/vol8n2

Singh, A. K. (2017b). Persona of social networking in computing and informatics era. *International Journal of Computer Science and Network Security, 17*(4), 95-101. http://search.ijcsns.org/07_book/2017_04.h

Singh, A. K. (2019). A Wireless Networks Flexible Adoptive Modulation and Coding Technique in advanced 4G LTE. *International Journal of Information Technology, 11*(1), 55-66. https://link.springer.com/article/10.1007/s41870-018-0173-5 doi:10.1007/s41870-018-0173-5

Singh, A. K. (2020). *Digital Era in the Kingdom of Saudi Arabia: Novel Strategies of the Telecom Service Providers Companies.* http://www.webology.org/issue.php?volume=1&issue=1&page=2 doi:10.14704/WEB/V17I1/a219

Singh, A. K. (2021). Machine Learning in OpenFlow Network: Comparative Analysis of DDoS Detection Techniques. *The International Arab Journal of Information Technology, 18*(2), 221-226. https://iajit.org/PDF/Vol%2018,%20No.%202/19667.pdf doi:10.34028/iajit/18/2/11

Singh, Sobti, Malik, Shrestha, Singh, & Ghafoor. (2022). *IoT-Driven Model for Weather and Soil Conditions Based on Precision.* doi:10.1155/2022/7283975

Singh. (2017). Security and Management in Network: Security of Network Management versus Management of Network Security (SNM Vs MNS). *International Journal of Computer Science and Network Security, 17*(5), 166-173. http://search.ijcsns.org/07_book/2017_05.htm

Singh. (2019a). An Intelligent Reallocation of Load for Cluster Cloud Environment. *International Journal of Innovative Technology and Exploring Engineering, 8*(8). https://www.ijitee.org/download/volume-8-issue-8/

Singh. (2019b). Texture-based Real-Time Character Extraction and Recognition in Natural Images. *International Journal of Innovative Technology and Exploring Engineering, 8*(8). https://www.ijitee.org/download/volume-8-issue-8/

Singh, D. K., Sobti, R., Jain, A., & Malik, P. K. (2022). LoRa based intelligent soil and Irrigation Using Machine Learning", Security and Communication Networks, vol. weather condition monitoring with internet of things for precision agriculture in smart cities. *IET Communications, 16*, 604–618. doi:10.1049/cmu2.12352

Singh, S. S., Kumar, A., Singh, K., & Biswas, B. (2019). LAPSO-IM: A learning-based influence maximization approach for social networks. *Applied Soft Computing, 82*, 105554. doi:10.1016/j.asoc.2019.105554

Singh, S. S., Singh, K., Kumar, A., & Biswas, B. (2020). ACO-IM: Maximizing influence in social networks using ant colony optimization. *Soft Computing, 24*(13), 10181–10203. doi:10.100700500-019-04533-y

Singh, S. S., Srivastva, D., Verma, M., & Singh, J. (2022). "Influence maximization frameworks, performance, challenges and directions on social network: A theoretical study," *J. King Saud Univ. -. Comput. Inf. Sci., 34*(9), 7570–7603. doi:10.1016/j.jksuci.2021.08.009

Sitzmann, T., Kraiger, K., Stewart, D., & Wisher, R. (2006). The comparative effectiveness of Web-based and classroom instruction: A meta-analysis. *Personnel Psychology, 59*(3), 623–664. doi:10.1111/j.1744-6570.2006.00049.x

Skirnevskiy, V., Bendig, D., & Brettel, M. (2017). The Influence of Internal Social Capital on Serial Creators' Success in Crowdfunding. *Entrepreneurship Theory and Practice, 41*(2), 209–236. Advance online publication. doi:10.1111/etap.12272

Slater, S. F., & Narver, J. C. (1999). Market-oriented is more than being customer-led. *Strategic Management Journal, 20*(12), 1165–1168. doi:10.1002/(SICI)1097-0266(199912)20:12<1165::AID-SMJ73>3.0.CO;2-#

Smedley, J. (2012). Implementing e-learning in the Jordanian Higher Education System: Factors Affecting Impact. *International Journal of Education and Development using ICT, 8*(1). https://www.learntechlib.org/p/188017/

Smith, A., Johnson, B., & Brown, C. (2000). Friend Recommendations using Neural Networks. *Journal of Artificial Intelligence, 10*(2), 123-140.

Smith, D. (2015). Comparing social isolation effects on learner's attrition in online versus face-to face courses in computer literacy. *Issues in Informing Science and Information Technology, 12*, 11–20. Retrieved from http://iisit.org/Vol12/IISITv12p011-020Ali1784.pdf

Smith, J. A., Spears, A. L., & Ellefsen, A. M. (2018). The impact of social media on youth: A review of the literature. *Developmental Review.*

Sng, K., Au, T. Y., & Pang, A. (2019). Social media influencers as a crisis risk in strategic communication: Impact of indiscretions on professional endorsements. *International Journal of Strategic Communication, 13*(4), 301–320. doi:10.1080/1553118X.2019.1618305

SOCRadar. (2021). Under the Spotlight: Most Popular Dark Web Marketplaces (DWMs). *SOCRadar(Your Eyes Beyond)*, 2.

Song, L., Singleton, E. S., Hill, J. R., & Koh, M. H. (2004). Improving online learning: Student perceptions of useful and challenging characteristics. *The Internet and Higher Education*, *7*(1), 59–70. doi:10.1016/j.iheduc.2003.11.003

Spottswood, E. L., & Wohn, D. Y. (2020). Online social capital: Recent trends in research. *Current Opinion in Psychology*, *36*, 147–152. doi:10.1016/j.copsyc.2020.07.031 PMID:32950953

Srivastava, S., Mendiratta, A., Pankaj, P., Misra, R., & Mendiratta, R. (2022). Happiness at work through spiritual leadership: A self-determination perspective. *Employee Relations: The International Journal*.

Starbird, K., Palen, L., Hughes, A. L., & Vieweg, S. (2010). Chatter on the Red: What hazards threat reveals about the social life of microblogged information. *Proceedings of the ACM 2010 Conference on Computer Supported Cooperative Work*, 241-250. 10.1145/1718918.1718965

Statista. (2022). *Statista Digital Market Outlook @ Statista 2022*. https://www.statista.com/outlook/digital-markets

Stieglitz, S., & Dang-Xuan, L. (2013). Crisis communication in the age of social media: A network analysis of Zika virus coverage. *Journal of Risk Research*, *20*(1), 1–14.

Suh, A., Kim, S., Kim, Y., & Kim, S. (2021). Monitoring and prediction of wildfire using social media and deep learning models. *Information Processing & Management*, *58*(5), 102566.

Summers, J. D., Chidambaram, L., & Young, A. G. (2016). Venture signals and social media buzz in crowdfunding: Are "buzzworthy" projects worth the hype? *Proceedings of the Annual Hawaii International Conference on System Sciences*. 10.1109/HICSS.2016.440

Tabrizi, B., Lam, E., Girard, K., & Irvin, V. (2019). Digital transformation is not about technology. *Harvard Business Review*, *13*(March), 1–6.

Tandi, M. (2021). *Arming youth with a sense of purpose to navigate this rapidly evolving world of education - Today in Bermuda*. https://todayinbermuda.com/mukesh-tandi-arming-youth-with-a-sense-of-purpose-to-navigate-this-rapidly-evolving-world-of-education

Tang, J. (2019). Identification of top-k influential nodes based on enhanced discrete particle swarm optimization for influence maximization. Phys. A Stat. Mech. its Appl., 513, 477–496. doi:10.1016/j.physa.2018.09.040

Tang, J., Zhang, R., Wang, P., Zhao, Z., Fan, L., & Liu, X. (2020). A discrete shuffled frog-leaping algorithm to identify influential nodes for influence maximization in social networks. *Knowledge-Based Systems*, *187*, 104833. doi:10.1016/j.knosys.2019.07.004

Tan, J. J., & Litschert, R. J. (1994). Environment-strategy relationship and its performance implications: An empirical study of the Chinese electronics industry. *Strategic Management Journal*, *15*(1), 1–20. doi:10.1002mj.4250150102

Taylor, C. (2020). Tor Browser. *CyberHoot*, 1-2.

Thies, F., Wessel, M., & Benlian, A. (2018). Network effects on crowdfunding platforms: Exploring the implications of relaxing input control. *Information Systems Journal*, *28*(6), 1239–1262. Advance online publication. doi:10.1111/isj.12194

Tian, S., Mo, S., Wang, L., & Peng, Z. (2020). Deep Reinforcement Learning-Based Approach to Tackle Topic-Aware Influence Maximization. *Data Science and Engineering*, *5*(1), 1–11. doi:10.100741019-020-00117-1

Torres, P., & Augusto, M. (2019). Understanding complementarities among different forms of innovation. *European Journal of Innovation Management*, *23*(5), 813–834. doi:10.1108/EJIM-01-2019-0012

Trabucchi, D., Pellizzoni, E., Buganza, T., & Verganti, R. (2017). Interplay between technology and meaning: How music majors reacted? *Creativity and Innovation Management*, *26*(4), 327–338. doi:10.1111/caim.12234

Trepte, S., & Reinecke, L. (2021). The social capital of news use: How online news reading and commenting contribute to online and offline social ties. *New Media & Society*, *23*(3), 706–725.

Trepte, S., & Reinecke, L. (2022). The Internet and social capital: A meta-analysis. *New Media & Society*, *24*(2), 622–643.

Tristan, C. (2020). *Trust and trustworthiness: An aspect of the relational dimension of social capital.* Social Capital Research. https://www.socialcapitalresearch.com/trust-and-trustworthiness/#comment-25209

Trusov, M., Bucklin, R. E., & Pauwels, K. (2009). Effects of word-of-mouth versus traditional marketing: Findings from an internet social networking site. *Journal of Marketing*, *73*(5), 90–102. Advance online publication. doi:10.1509/jmkg.73.5.90

Twingate. (2020). *Privacy for a premium.* https://www.twingate.com/research/privacy-for-a-premium-exploring-peoples-sentiments-on-paying-for-social-media

U.S. Department of Education, Office of Planning, Evaluation, and Policy Development. (2010). *Evaluation of Evidence-Based Practices in Online Learning: A Meta-Analysis and Review of Online Learning Studies.* Author.

Valentine. (2016). Tor Explained-ish. *Anonymity*, 1-2.

Valenzuela, S., Park, N., & Kee, K. F. (2009). Is there social capital in a social network site? Facebook use and college students' life satisfaction, trust, and participation. *Journal of Computer-Mediated Communication*, *14*(4), 875–901. doi:10.1111/j.1083-6101.2009.01474.x

Vallo Hult, H., & Byström, K. (2021). Challenges to learning and leading the Digital workplace. *Studies in Continuing Education*, *44*(3), 460–474. doi:10.1080/0158037X.2021.1879038

Van de Ven, A., Delbecq, A., & Koenig, R. (1976). Determinants of coordination modes within organizations. *American Sociological Review*, *41*(2), 322–338. doi:10.2307/2094477

Veil, S. R., Buehner, T., & Palenchar, M. J. (2011). A work-in-progress literature review: Incorporating social media in risk and crisis communication. *Journal of Contingencies and Crisis Management*, *19*(2), 110–122. doi:10.1111/j.1468-5973.2011.00639.x

Venunath, M., Sujatha, P., & Koti, P. (2023). Identifying Top-N Influential Nodes in Large Complex Networks Using Network Structure. In R. Buyya, S. M. Hernandez, R. M. R. Kovvur, & T. H. Sarma (Eds.), *Computational Intelligence and Data Analytics* (pp. 597–607). Springer Nature Singapore. doi:10.1007/978-981-19-3391-2_45

Victor, C., Mansfield, L., Kay, T., Daykin, N., Lane, J., Grigsby Duffy, L., Tomlinson, A., & Meads, C. (2018). *An overview of reviews: The effectiveness of interventions to address loneliness at all stages of the life-course.* What Works Centre for Wellbeing. https://whatworkswellbeing.org/product/tackling-loneliness-full-review/

VillaD. (2020). Secondary Teachers' Preparation, Challenges, and Coping Mechanism in the Pre-Implementation of Distance Learning in the New Normal. *IOER International Multidisciplinary Research Journal*, *2*(3), 144 – 154. https://ssrn.com/abstract=3717608

Vitak, J., Ellison, N. B., & Steinfield, C. (2011). The ties that bond: Re-examining the relationship between Facebook use and bonding social capital. In *Proceedings of the fourth international conference on Communities and technologies* (pp. 417-426). 10.1109/HICSS.2011.435

von Delft, S., & Zhao, Y. (2021). Business models in Process Industries: Emerging Trends and Future Research. *Technovation*, *105*, 102195. doi:10.1016/j.technovation.2020.102195

Wagner, N., Hassanein, K., & Head, M. (2008). Who Is Responsible for E-Learning Success in Higher Education? A Stakeholders' Analysis. *Journal of Educational Technology & Society*, *11*(3), 26–36. Retrieved January 14, 2023, from https://www.learntechlib.org/p/75266/

Walder, A. G. (1995). Local governments as industrial organizations: An organizational analysis of China's transitional economy. *American Journal of Sociology*, *101*(2), 263–301. doi:10.1086/230725

Waldkirch, M., Bucher, E., Schou, P., & Grünwald, E. (2021). Controlled by the algorithm, coached by the crowd – how HRM activities take shape on digital work platforms in the gig economy. *International Journal of Human Resource Management*, *32*(12), 2643–2682. doi:10.1080/09585192.2021.1914129

Walker, R. M., Chen, J., & Aravind, D. (2015). Management innovation and firm performance: An integration of research findings. *European Management Journal*, *33*(5), 407–422. doi:10.1016/j.emj.2015.07.001

Wallet, B. (2021). We are donating to Tor! *blockwallet.medium*, 1-3.

Wang, Chen, & Yu. (2012). The impact of trust on information sharing in social media. *Journal of Computer-Mediated Communication*, 10–16.

Wang, C., Horby, P. W., Hayden, F. G., & Gao, G. F. (2020). A novel coronavirus outbreak of global health concern. *Lancet*, *395*(10223), 470–473. doi:10.1016/S0140-6736(20)30185-9 PMID:31986257

Wang, J., & Zhang, J. (2020). The impact of perceived credibility and trustworthiness on social media use: A cross-platform study. *Journal of Business Research*, *2022*(112), 186–195.

Wang, X., Tang, L., Zhang, L., & Zheng, J. (2022). The initial stage of the COVID-19 pandemic: A perspective on health risk communications in the restaurant industry. *International Journal of Environmental Research and Public Health*, *19*(19), 11961. doi:10.3390/ijerph191911961 PMID:36231263

Wang, Y. S., Wang, H. Y., & Shee, D. Y. (2007). Measuring e-learning systems success in an organizational context: Scale development and validation. *Computers in Human Behavior*, *23*(4), 1792–1808. doi:10.1016/j.chb.2005.10.006

Wang, Y., & Wellman, B. (2020). Social connectivity in America: Changes in adult friendship network size from 2002 to 2017. *The American Behavioral Scientist*, *64*(6), 693–707.

Wardle, C, & Derakhshan, H. (2017). *The role of social media in the spread of misinformation.* Center for Internet & Society at Harvard University.

Watts, D. J. (2004). The "New" Science of Networks. *Annual Review of Sociology*, *30*(1), 243–270. doi:10.1146/annurev.soc.30.020404.104342

Wellman, B., & Haythornthwaite, C. (2002). The Internet in Everyday Life: An Introduction. In The Internet in Everyday Life (pp. 3-41). Wiley Online Library.

Wellman, B., Boase, J., & Chen, W. (2003). The Social Affordances of the Internet for Networked Individualism. *Journal of Computer-Mediated Communication*, *8*(3), 1–28. doi:10.1111/j.1083-6101.2003.tb00216.x

Wellman, B., Haase, A. Q., Witte, J., & Hampton, K. (2001). Does the Internet increase, decrease, or supplement social capital? Social networks, participation, and community commitment. *The American Behavioral Scientist*, *45*(3), 436–455. doi:10.1177/00027640121957286

Wenlin, L., Anupreet, S., Amanda, M. B., & Thomas, V. (2017) Social Network Theory. University of Southern California. doi:10.1002/9781118783764.wbieme0092

West, C. (2021). *Twelve ways to use social media for education.* Retrieved from https://sproutsocial.com/insights/social-media-for-education

Wewege, L. (2017). *The Digital Banking Revolution: How financial technology companies are rapidly transforming the traditional retail banking industry through disruptive innovation.* Scribl. https://economictimes.indiatimes.com/nation-world/heres-the-story-of-atms-over-the-years/worldwide-launch/slideshow/55511212.cms

Wibawa, I. (2014). *Peranan Budaya Organisasi terhadap Kepemimpinan Spiritual, Modal Insani, dan Loyalitas Karyawan (Studi pada Rumah Sakit Swasta di Kota Denpasar Bali)* [Doctoral dissertation]. Universitas Brawijaya.

Wicks, A., Berman, S., & Jones, T. (1999). The structure of optimal trust: Moral and strategic implications. *Academy of Management Review*, *24*(1), 99–116. doi:10.2307/259039

Widipedia. (n.d.). *Pragmatism.* https://en.wikipedia.org/wiki/Pragmatism

Widodo, S., & Suryosukmono, G. (2021). Spiritual leadership, workplace spirituality and their effects on meaningful work: Self-transcendence as mediator role. *Management Science Letters*, *11*(7), 2115–2126. doi:10.5267/j.msl.2021.2.016

Williamson, O. (1993). Calculativeness, trust and economic organization. *The Journal of Law & Economics*, *36*(1, Part 2), 453–486. doi:10.1086/467284

Woods, C. L. (2022). Extinguishing a fictional fire: Responding to emotional and misinformed audiences. *Corporate Reputation Review*, *25*(4), 239–252. doi:10.105741299-021-00125-5

Wu, Y., Song, Y., & Kafai, M. (2020). Identifying Geographical Locations and Quantifying Information Propagation during Disaster Events on Social Media. *Journal of Contingencies and Crisis Management*, *28*(1), 58–69.

Xiang, T., Li, Q., Li, W., & Xiao, Y. (2023). A rumor heat prediction model based on rumor and anti-rumor multiple messages and knowledge representation. *Information Processing & Management*, *60*(3), 103337. Advance online publication. doi:10.1016/j.ipm.2023.103337

Yang, S., & Sun, M. (2020). Family Background, Major Choice and Economic Returns: An Empirical Study Based on Chinese General Social Survey. *Northwest Population Journal*, *41*, 52–66.

Yang, Y., Lichtenwalter, R. N., & Chawla, N. V. (2015). Evaluating link prediction methods. *Knowledge and Information Systems*, *45*(3), 751–782. doi:10.100710115-014-0789-0

Ye, S., Jiang, H., & Guo, H. (2021). Quantifying Information Propagation and Opinion Evolution in Social Media during Natural Disasters. *Journal of Disaster Research*, *16*(4), 602–614.

Yin, J., Lampert, A., Cameron, M., Robinson, B., & Power, R. (2012). Using social media to enhance emergency situation awareness. *IEEE Intelligent Systems*, *27*(6), 52–59. doi:10.1109/MIS.2012.6

Zald, M. N. (1970). Political economy: A framework for comparative analysis. In M. N. Zald (Ed.), *Power in organizations* (pp. 221–261). Vanderbilt University Press.

Zander, U., & Kogut, B. (1995). Knowledge and the speed of the transfer and initiation of organizational capabilities: An empirical test. *Organization Science*, *6*(1), 76–92. doi:10.1287/orsc.6.1.76

Zareie, A., Sheikhahmadi, A., & Khamforoosh, K. (2018). Influence maximization in social networks based on TOPSIS. *Expert Systems with Applications*, *108*, 96–107. doi:10.1016/j.eswa.2018.05.001

Zhang, K., Du, H., & Feldman, M. W. (2017). Maximizing influence in a social network: Improved results using a genetic algorithm. Phys. A Stat. Mech. its Appl., 478, 20–30. doi:10.1016/j.physa.2017.02.067

Zhang, A., Li, Y., & Li, L. (2020). A Novel Method for Extracting Geographical Locations from Social Media during Disasters. *Journal of Cleaner Production*, *247*, 11926–11938.

Zhang, D., & Nunamaker, J. F. (2003). Powering e-learning in the new millennium: An overview of eLearning and enabling technology. *Information Systems Frontiers*, *5*(2), 207–218. doi:10.1023/A:1022609809036

Zhang, J., & Wang, Y. (2022). Effectiveness of corporate social responsibility activities in the COVID-19 pandemic. *Journal of Product and Brand Management*, *31*(7), 1063–1076. doi:10.1108/JPBM-07-2021-3551

Zhang, Q., Shuai, B., & Lü, M. (2022). A novel method to identify influential nodes in complex networks based on gravity centrality. *Information Sciences*, *618*, 98–117. doi:10.1016/j.ins.2022.10.070

Zhang, X., Zhao, X., & Sun, Y. (2015). A hybrid link prediction algorithm for friend recommendation. *Knowledge-Based Systems*, *82*, 159–167.

Zhang, Y., & Ma, Z. F. (2020). Impact of the COVID-19 Pandemic on Mental Health and Quality of Life among Local Residents in Liaoning Province, China: A Cross-Sectional Study. *International Journal of Environmental Research and Public Health*, *17*(7), 2381. doi:10.3390/ijerph17072381 PMID:32244498

Zhao, J., Wen, T., Jahanshahi, H., & Cheong, K. H. (2022). The random walk-based gravity model to identify influential nodes in complex networks. *Information Sciences*, *609*, 1706–1720. doi:10.1016/j.ins.2022.07.084

Zhao, Y., Zhu, S., Wan, Q., Li, T., Zou, C., Wang, H., & Deng, S. (2022). Understanding How and by Whom COVID-19 Misinformation is Spread on Social Media: Coding and Network Analyses. *Journal of Medical Internet Research*, *24*(6), e37623. doi:10.2196/37623 PMID:35671411

Zheng, H., & Jiang, S. (2022). Linking the pathway from exposure to online vaccine information to cyberchondria during the COVID-19 pandemic: A moderated mediation model. *Cyberpsychology, Behavior, and Social Networking*, *25*(10), 625–633. doi:10.1089/cyber.2022.0045 PMID:36037024

Zheng, H., Li, D., Wu, J., & Xu, Y. (2014). The role of multidimensional social capital in crowdfunding: A comparative study in China and US. *Information & Management*, *51*(4), 488–496. doi:10.1016/j.im.2014.03.003

Zheng, Z., & Chen, H. (2020). Age sequences of the elderly' social network and its efficacies on well-being: An urban-rural comparison in China. *BMC Geriatrics*, *20*(1), 372. doi:10.118612877-020-01773-8 PMID:32993525

Zhu, L. L. (2019). *An Empirical Study on the Influence of Family Capital on University Students' Interpersonal Skills* [Ph.D. Thesis]. Zhejiang Normal University, Jinhua, China.

Zousuls, K. M., Miller, C. F., Ruble, D. N., Martin, C. L., & Fabes, R. A. (2011). Gender development research in sex roles: Historical trends and future directions. *Sex Roles*, *64*(11-12), 826–842. doi:10.100711199-010-9902-3 PMID:21747580

Zvilichovsky, D., Inbar, Y., & Barzilay, O. (2013). Playing both sides of the market: Success and reciprocity on crowdfunding platforms. *International Conference on Information Systems (ICIS 2013): Reshaping Society Through Information Systems Design*. 10.2139srn.2304101

About the Contributors

Najmul Hoda is an Assistant Professor in Department of Business Administration at the College of Business, Umm Al-Qura University. He was awarded PhD in Management from Birla Institute of Technology, India in 2015. His dissertation focused on faith-based microfinance institutions. His main research interests are social banking, sustainable finance, entrepreneurial finance, and pedagogy in higher education. He also served as Assistant Manager in Federal Bank and as Director – Research and Training in a microfinance institution based in New Delhi. He has published research papers in journals indexed in SSCI/ESCI/Scopus, as well as contributed book chapters. He is associated with several WoS/Scopus indexed journals as reviewer/advisor. He is also the founding member of International Social Capital Association, New Zealand.

Arshi Naim is an Associate Professor and Quality Programme head in Business Management, KSA She has completed her PHD in business management Singhania University Rajasthan, MBA in marketing management from HNB University and economics honours from AMU, Aligarh, India. Also, she has accomplished some certificates like QM peer reviewer and E-Learning expert from quality matters, US, ICDL from Australia and certificate on digital skills and digital marketing from UK. She is expert in curriculum and programme development, quality and accreditation process, E-learning and Quality Matters Peer Reviewer. She has research publications in Web of Sceince, IEEE, ACM, and Scopus Indexed Journals. She has also published books with Taylor and Francis, Nova Science Publications, IGI, and Springer. She is also closely associated with international and national universities for supervising PHD students.

* * *

Blessing F. Adeoye is a Professor of Educational Technology and a U.S Ambassador Distinguished Scholar at Dilla University, Ethiopia. He mentored Doctorate students in Educational Technology at Walden University, USA (2015-2022). He loves helping students achieve their academic goals by completing their theses/dissertations and publishing their work with top-quality publishers. His current research interests focus primarily on the relationship between culture and technology and the use of research to improve the quality of teaching and learning in schools. He has presented at numerous conferences. Prof. Adeoye has published over 40 peer-reviewed articles and ten books on Educational Technology. At Dilla University, he teaches the doctoral capstone and mentors Ph.D. and EDD candidates. He has also chaired numerous doctoral student dissertation committees.

Mohammad Zubair Ahmad is an expert in entrepreneurship and skill development. He completed his PhD in agripreneurship and is actively engaged in consulting, teaching, and training activities.

Nor Aziah Alias is an honorary professor of Teaching and Learning at of Universiti Teknologi MARA (UiTM). She was formerly the UiTM Director of Academic Development (2014-2021). She has a Masters and Bachelor degree in Physics from Indiana University, Bloomington. She earned a Graduate Certificate in ODL from USQ, Australia and a doctoral degree in the field of instructional technology from IIUM Malaysia. Dr Nor Aziah's fields of interest include Instructional Design and Technology (IDT) and ICT for Development (ICT4D). Dr Nor Aziah once won the Amy Mahan Research Fellowship from IDRC, Canada that allowed her to study the use of ICT for rural empowerment. She is also involved in digital education projects and researching technology for the needs of learners with disabilities. She conceptualized the Virtual Centre for Innovative Delivery and Learning Development @UiTM and spearheaded Education 5.0@UiTM, a strategic initiative to develop a holistic values-based and technology rich academic ecosystem. Dr. Nor Aziah has published in journals and books published by MIT Press, Springer, Sage, Information Age Publishing, Copenhagen Business School Press, Libri Press (UK) and IGI Global (USA). She is currently active in various Malaysian higher education ministry funded projects.

Vimal Babu is Associate Professor of HR/OB area in Management, Paari School of Business, SRM University, Amaravati, AP, India. He is a negotiation coach and works in the interdisciplinary area of Organizational Behviour and Entrepreneurship. He holds about two decades of rich experience in training, teaching and research in negotiation, leadership and behavioural aspects of employees. His publications are with ABDC-indexed and Scopus listed international journals. He earned his Ph.D. in Management, concentration in transformational leadership, Faculty for Management Studies, Jamia Millia Islamia, New Delhi, India.

Elif Baykal is Head of Business Administration Department at İstanbul Medipol University.

Komal Bhardwaj has done Ph.D., MBA in Finance, currently working as Assistant Professor at MMIM, Maharishi Markandeshwar (Deemed to be University), NAAC Accredited Grade 'A++' University, Mullana, Ambala (Haryana). She has more than 7 years of experience in academics and 5 Years of experience in research. She has written 15+ research papers for various Scopus and UGC listed referred National & International Journals. .She has research experience in the areas of Assets Pricing, Derivatives, Option Pricing, study on stock volatility, Social Media Marketing.

A. Bhuvaneswari is working as Assistant Professor (Senior Grade) in School of Computer Science Engineering, VIT University, Chennai, India. She is an active Researcher and Mentoring students/research scholars in specific research domains including Social Network Analysis, Big Data Analytics, Machine Learning, Network Graphs, Web Mining, Recommendation Engines. She has published several International Journals, Book Chapters and presented her research findings in Reputed International Conferences apart from several papers at national level. She has 10+ years of teaching & research experience. She is been a reviewer for reputed journals indexed in SCOPUS, Web of Science and SCI/SCI-E.

Youmei Liu earned her doctoral degree in Curriculum and Instruction focusing on instructional technology in 2003 from the University of Houston. She worked as an instructional designer and educational production specialist. Currently she is the Director of Assessment and Accreditation Services at the University of Houston. She also served as Vice President and Conference Chairs for the Society of International Chinese Educational Technology and Chinese American Educational Research & Development Association. Dr. Liu has rich research experiences and has numerous publications in the area of quality course design, innovative use of educational technology, distance education, mobile learning and student learning assessment. She has extensive accomplishments in collaborative research with faculty, in development of evaluation programs to assess teaching and learning quality, in conducting major innovative research projects on instructional technology, and in presenting research projects at important national and international conferences. She has also served as an evaluator for several NSF grants in higher educational institutions.

Ibtissem Missaoui is a lecturer in the Finance and Accounting Department at the Higher Institute of Management of Sousse (Tunisia). She obtained her PhD in Finance from the Institute of Advanced Studies of Sousse and the Higher Institute of Management of Sousse (Tunisia). Her doctoral thesis focused on the impact of stock market development and institutional factors on the cost of capital. Her main research interests include sustainable development, renewable energy, and the stock market. She has published several research papers in journals and has also conducted exchanges and research in French laboratories such as the Laboratoire d'Économie Dionysien (LED) at the University of Paris 8 and the Laboratoire Magtech in Lille. Additionally, she is a member of the Laboratory of Innovation and sustainable development management research (LAMIDED) at the University of Sousse.

Nor Hafizah Mohamed Harith is an Associate Professor in Universiti Teknologi MARA (UiTM), Malaysia. She holds a PhD in Sociology and Anthropology from International Islamic University Malaysia, Master's degree in Social Science Education & Bachelor of Arts (Honours) from Flinders University of South Australia, Adelaide. Her research interests are Urban Sociology, Social Policy, Qualitative Research, Policy Analysis and Community Development. Currently, she holds several research grants as principal investigator and team member mainly in socio-economic developmental policies. She has more than 20 years of teaching experiences of undergraduate and postgraduate Studies. Her teaching courses taught include Research Methods and Data Analysis, Urban Sociology, Public Policy Analysis and Organizational Behavior. She is actively supervising PhD, Master by Research and Coursework students and journal reviewers and writers. Her administrative experiences in University Teknologi MARA include Deputy Dean of Academic Affairs & Coordinator and Liaison Officer for International Affairs.

Anandhavalli Muniasamy, MCA, MPhil, Ph.D., is currently working as an Associate Professor, at the College of Computer Science, King Khalid University, Saudi Arabia. Her areas of interest are data mining, machine learning, and soft computing. She has published more than 30 research publications in highly reputed international journals and book chapters. She has attended and presented at more than 25 national & international conferences. She served as a principal investigator for the funded project from the All India Council for Technical Education (AICTE). She served as a manuscript reviewer for renowned international journals for the past 15 years, and Ph.D. thesis reviewer for several universities. She has been invited to give guest lectures and as an editorial board member for a few journals and conferences. She is a member of the International Association of Engineers, IEEE - Western Saudi Arabic Section, Computer Society of India, and the International Association of Computer Science and Information Technology.

Marhaini Mohd Noor is a senior lecturer in policy studies; her aim is to employ knowledge and skills in policy and development studies through research, expert consultation and community partnership. Her key areas are rural development and regional development policy, ICT for development (ICT4D), community informatics, cyber security and maritime studies. She has published her publications in journals, monographs and book chapters published by UMT Publishers, UiTM Publishers, and MIT. The latest publication is "Assessing Rural Telecentres in Malaysia Using Program Logic Framework". She has evaluated the conference paper for the Interdisciplinary ICT Practice 2017 (IIPC), Australian Journal of Information Systems, Reviewer, 2015, International Conference Proceeding: ICoPS, Reviewer, 2015 and writing a journal article titled "Building social capital through community informatics: Strong local community participation and engagement at RICs." She had won the Best Paper Award at IPID Postgraduate Strand at Royal Holloway University of London, UK, through her thesis entitled 'Evaluating the Contribution of Community Informatics to Rural Development: The Case of Malaysia's Rural Internet Centers'. She has received an Excellent Service Award, FSPPP, UiTM, 2007 and Bronze Award from University Research Innovation Symposium Exposition 2015 (RISE 2015), MOSTI. She is currently involved in Ministry of Education grant (FRGS 2019-2022), researching a study on cyber security and coastal community. Thus, managed to supervise a PhD and Master students in the area. The research grant title: "Developing a scale-up social capital framework of cyber security initiative for rural community wellbeing in East Coast Peninsular Malaysia".

Gayathri R. is currently an Assistant Professor at School of Management, SASTRA Deemed University in India. An excellent orator with a Doctorate in Economics (2013) from Bharathidasan University, India. Her areas of interest include International Business, Marketing and Business Ethics. She handles courses such as Economics and Marketing. She has a rich academic experience of 19 years in teaching and 7 years in Research. Her focus is on contemporary social research and she is a co-investigator in the funded project funded by the Ministry of Rural Development, Government of India. She has presented papers at international and national level conferences and seminars. She has published a number of research articles and case studies in referred Scopus indexed journals.

Selvakumar R. is a research scholar in the Dept. of Management, Paari School of Business (PSB), SRM University, Amaravati, AP, India. He is interested in the research area of HRM, Organisational Behaviour, and Crisis Leadership.

Deepa Sharma has done Ph.D., MBA in Human Resource Management, currently working as Assistant Professor at MMIM, Maharishi Markandeshwar (Deemed to be University), NAAC Accredited Grade 'A++' University, Mullana, Ambala (Haryana). She has more than 7 years of experience in academics. She has written 45+ research papers for various Scopus and UGC listed referred National & International Journals.

Arun Kumar Singh is working as an Asso. Professor in the Department of Mathematics and Computer Science (PNG University of Technology, PNG). He received Ph.D. in CS/IT under the guidance of Dr. Neelam Srivastava (IET Lucknow) and Dr. R. P. Agarwal (IIT Roorkee), M.Tech. (IT-WCC) degree in 2005 from IIIT-Allahabad under the guidance of Prof. M. Radha Krishnan and B.E. (ECE) degree in 2002 from Dr. B. R. Ambedkar University, Agra, India. His research interests are IoT, Machine Learning, Big Data, Network Management, Wireless networking, Social Networking and Mobile computing.

Devendra Singh, B.Com. (Hons.), M.Com, LL.B. (Hons.), MBA (FIN), and Ph.D., is Professor & Head of Finance, Accounting & Law at Amity University, noida. He did his Ph.D. in Management & possesses around twenty years of experience in teaching and academic administration, industry, consultancy, and research; Handling academics & academic administration & working as a resource person in various capabilities. Before joining the Amity University he was associated with Galgotias Business School & Accurate institute of management & technology, Greater noida as Professor & Head PGP (DEAN). He was one of the Founder faculty members of GBS, Where his primary area of functionality is Finance, Accounts, e-banking analysis and corporate finance & laws, investment banking and research work in area of finance, accounts & law, management.

Sumitra Singh is Associate Professor at Amity University.

Azizan Zainuddin is an Associate Professor. She has 17 years of teaching and research experience in Universiti Teknologi MARA under the Faculty of Administrative Science & Policy Studies, Shah Alam. She has served private sector for 10 years in the field of human resource. She obtained her PhD in Ethnic Studies from Universiti Kebangsaan Malaysia (UKM-2015), Master of Science in Human Resource Development from Universiti Putra Malaysia (UPM-2000), Bachelor of Public Administration (Hons) from Universiti Utara Malaysia (UUM-1995) and Diploma in Public Administration from Institut Teknologi MARA (ITM-1991), Shah Alam, Selangor. She teaches the course of Public Service and Quality Management and Public Policy Analysis. Her research and publications focus on public policy and public administration revolving around the area of gender, women in politics, entrepreneurship and human development.

Index

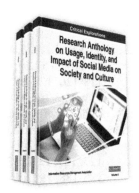

   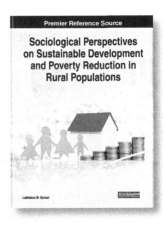

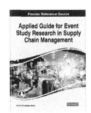
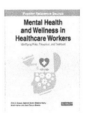

Printed in the United States
by Baker & Taylor Publisher Services